Abruzzo

the Bradt Travel Guide

Luciano Di Gregorio

edition
2

www.bradtguides.com

Bradt Travel Guides Ltd, UK
The Globe Pequot Press Inc, USA

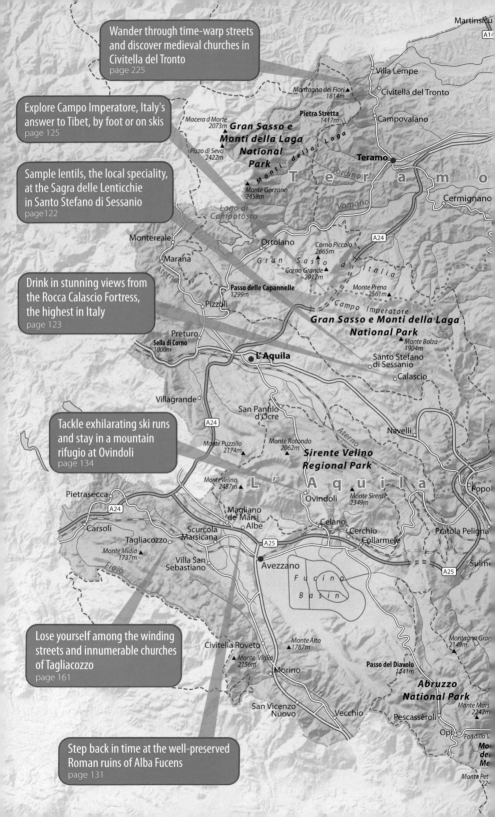

Wander through time-warp streets and discover medieval churches in Civitella del Tronto
page 225

Explore Campo Imperatore, Italy's answer to Tibet, by foot or on skis
page 125

Sample lentils, the local speciality, at the Sagra delle Lenticchie in Santo Stefano di Sessanio
page122

Drink in stunning views from the Rocca Calascio Fortress, the highest in Italy
page 123

Tackle exhilarating ski runs and stay in a mountain rifugio at Ovindoli
page 134

Lose yourself among the winding streets and innumerable churches of Tagliacozzo
page 161

Step back in time at the well-preserved Roman ruins of Alba Fucens
page 131

Martinsicu

A14

Villa Lempe

Montagna dei Fiori
1814m

Civitella del Tronto

Pietra Stretta
1417m

Campovalano

Macera d Morte
2073m

Gran Sasso e
Monti della Laga
National
Park

Teramo

Pizzo di Sevo
2422m

Monte Gorzano
2458m

Cermignano

Lago di
Campotosto

Vomano

Montereale

Ortolano

A24

Corno Piccolo
2665m

Marana

Gran Sasso d'Italia

Corno Grande
2912m

Aterno

Passo delle Capannelle
1299m

Monte Prena
2561m

Pizzoli

Campo Imperatore

Gran Sasso e Monti della Laga
National Park

Preturo

Sella di Corno
1000m

Monte Bolza
1904m

L'Aquila

Santo Stefano
di Sessanio

Calascio

Villagrande

San Panfilo
d'Ocre

Navelli

A24

Monte Puzzillo
2174m

Monte Rotondo
2062m

Aterno

Sirente Velino
Regional Park

Popo

Pietrasecca

MonteVelino
2487m

L' A q u i l a

Monte Sirente
2349m

Carsoli

A24

Ovindoli

Magliano
de' Marsi
Albe

Celano

Cerchio

Pratola Peligna

Tagliacozzo

Monte Midia
1737m

Scurcola
Marsicana

Collarmele

Sulm

Fliolo

Villa San
Sebastiano

A25

Avezzano

A25

Fucino

Basin

Civitella Roveto

Monte Alto
1787m

Montagna Gran
2149m

Monte Viglio
2156m

Passo del Diavolo
1441m

Morino

Abruzzo
National Park

San Vicenzo
Nuovo

Vecchio

Pescasseroli

Monte Mars
2242m

Opi

Fondillo

Mo
de
Me

Monte Pet
22

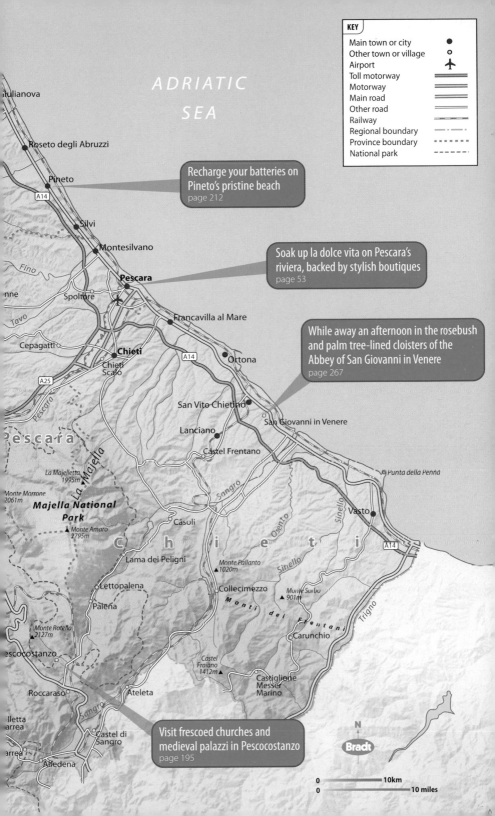

ADRIATIC

SEA

KEY

● Main town or city
○ Other town or village
✈ Airport
Toll motorway
Motorway
Main road
Other road
Railway
Regional boundary
Province boundary
National park

Giulianova

Roseto degli Abruzzi

Pineto

Recharge your batteries on Pineto's pristine beach
page 212

A14

Silvi

Montesilvano

Pescara

Soak up la dolce vita on Pescara's riviera, backed by stylish boutiques
page 53

Spoltore

Fino

nne

Tavo

Cepagatti

Chieti

Chieti
Scalo

A25

Pescara

Francavilla al Mare

A14

Ortona

While away an afternoon in the rosebush and palm tree-lined cloisters of the Abbey of San Giovanni in Venere
page 267

San Vito Chietino

San Giovanni in Venere

Lanciano

Castel Frentano

Punta della Penna

P e s c a r a

La Majelletta
1995m

La Majella

Monte Morrone
2061m

Majella National Park

▲ Monte Amaro
2795m

Sangro

Càsoli

C   h   i   e   t   i

Vasto

A14

Sinello

Oventa

Lama dei Peligni

Monte Pallanto
▲1020m

Sinello

Lettopalena

Collecimezzo

Monte Sorbo
▲ 901m

Palena

M o n t i   d e i   F r e n t a n i

Trigno

Monte Rotella
▲ 2127m

Carunchio

scocostanzo

Roccaraso

Ateleta

Castel
Fraiano
1412m▲

Castiglione
Messer
Marino

lletta
arrea

Sangro

Visit frescoed churches and medieval palazzi in Pescocostanzo
page 195

Castel di
Sangro

N

arrea

Alfedena

Bradt

0   10km
0   10 miles

Abruzzo
Don't
miss...

Beaches
Abruzzo has a wealth of pristine beaches, many of which have been awarded Blue Flag status
(TS/A) page 46

Pescara
The capital of Abruzzo is an unassuming, laidback city with a working port and buzzing beach culture
(LDG) page 53

Roman heritage
The layout of the 1st-century amphitheatre at Alba Fucens has been completely preserved
(LDG) page 131

Castles and forts
Celano's imposing Piccolomini Castle dates from 1392 and has survived a number of earthquakes
(CB/D) page 129

Medieval towns
The imposing walls and mighty fortress of Civitella del Tronto have allowed it to withstand a number of lengthy sieges over the centuries
(LDG) page 225

Abruzzo in colour

above The town of Loreto Aprutino is surrounded by olive groves, and olive oil forms the mainstay of the local economy (CD/D) page 79

left The formidable defences of L'Aquila's castle, or Forte Spagnolo, is testament to the onetime Spanish dominance of this area (W) page 115

below The main draw in Francavilla al Mare is the town's attractive beachfront (J/D) page 263

above left   In the heart of Abruzzo National Park, Pescassèroli makes an ideal base for forays into the surrounding wildlife-rich countryside (DM/D) page 167

above right   Ortona is home to one of the largest ports on the Adriatic (SS) page 264

right   The wall-enclosed town of Civitella del Tronto has some of the most atmospheric medieval streets in the region (LDG) page 225

below   Ovindoli is Abruzzo's skiing and snowboarding Mecca, and has been drawing in winter sports enthusiasts from Rome and beyond since the 1890s (CI/A) page 134

above left The church of Santa Maria in Piano, Loreto Aprutino, contains a number of majestic frescoes which have been painstakingly restored (SS) page 80

above right The octagonal church of Santa Maria della Pietà lies within the massive Rocca Calascio fortress complex (LDG) page 123

below The Abbey of San Giovanni in Venere, dating from 1165, is thought to have been built on the site of a Roman temple dedicated to Venus (TS/A) page 267

AUTHOR

Born and raised in Pescara, **Luciano Di Gregorio** spent his teen years in Melbourne, Australia, before spending much time back in the mother country during his 20s. After extensive travel, he became a secondary-school English and foreign language teacher. Now based in Melbourne, he works as a teacher, while continuing to edit and write for various magazines and newspapers. He is fluent in three languages – Italian, English and Spanish – and dabbles in French and Japanese.

CONTRIBUTING EDITOR

Maria Lord is a London-based writer and editor specialising in travel and the arts. Her areas of interest cover music, India, Greece, Italy and central Europe. Recent books she has worked on include a history of Western classical music and travel guides to Prague, Florence, Salzburg and Delhi.

AUTHOR'S STORY

In 2003, I began research on my family tree. I drove my uncle's 1971 Fiat 500 from my family's house in the medieval town of Abbateggio on a quest for documentation about my great-grandfather's great-grandfather, born in 1773. Pia, an elderly woman with all the clichés and contradictions of a traditional dress with a mobile phone tied to her belt, directed me to Don Francesco's door, where I was greeted by a bespectacled man with a welcoming smile. He told me of the church attic, in which I would find records from the 1400s to 1780.

The first inklings of this book were born in that attic, overlooking Abruzzo's rolling hills, medieval towns and Roman ruins. As I searched the records, I heard church bells tolling across the hills, and the sound went straight to my core. I realised people needed to know about Abruzzo – a region long overshadowed by its more 'touristy' neighbours. I had grown up in a typical Abruzzese family who fostered a love for the region of my birth. Now I wanted to be the first to write a full, English-language guide to this beautiful place.

I spent many months researching the region, travelling through mountains, national parks and beaches, and charming ancient towns in the depths of Abruzzo. I already knew the place like the back of my hand, yet it was a daunting task. And then there was the shocking earthquake of April 2009. I was in Australia at the time, but I knew I had to return to see the ramifications for myself. Unfortunately, researching the second edition of this book revealed just how extensive the damage was: the outlook may have been somewhat optimistic following the earthquake, but it is clear now more than ever that rebuilding will take the better part of a decade.

Writing a travel guide is great fun, but it is also a mammoth undertaking. One hot day, I was exploring L'Aquila Province. The path seemed unending, and I felt I would never make it to my destination. I decided to take my mind off the distance by watching my feet instead. When I arrived, I realised I should tackle the book in the same way – step by step. And here it is, in its second edition.

PUBLISHER'S FOREWORD   *Adrian Phillips, Publishing Director*

In 2009, as Luciano wrote up his research for the first edition of the Bradt guide to Abruzzo, L'Aquila was hit by a devastating earthquake that made headlines around the world. In the aftermath, Luciano was adamant that publication should go ahead, both to honour L'Aquila's former beauty and to showcase the countless highlights to be enjoyed in the rest of the region. We agreed. It seemed incredible that this area – with its pretty coastline, mountain hiking trails, hilltop towns and cobbled streets – had been largely overlooked by tourists. As L'Aquila continues to rebuild, Luciano continues to offer visitors the information and encouragement to explore a glorious area of Europe in this thoroughly updated second edition.

Second edition February 2013   First published January 2010

Bradt Travel Guides Ltd
IDC House, The Vale, Chalfont St Peter, Bucks SL9 9RZ, England
www.bradtguides.com

Print edition published in the USA by The Globe Pequot Press Inc, PO Box 480, Guilford, Connecticut 06437-0480

Text copyright © 2013 Luciano Di Gregorio
Maps copyright © 2013 Bradt Travel Guides Ltd
Photographs copyright © 2013 Individual photographers (see below)

ISBN: 978 1 84162 446 4 (print)
e-ISBN: 978 1 84162 752 6 (e-pub)
e-ISBN: 978 1 84162 654 3 (mobi)

British Library Cataloguing in Publication Data
A catalogue record for this book is available from the British Library

Photographs Alamy: Vito Arcomano (VA/A), Bon Appetit (BA/A), Cuboimages srl (CI/A), Saverio Maria Gallotti (SMG/A), imagebroker (I/A), Realy Easy Star/Toni Spagnone (TS/A); CuboImages: Alfio Giannotti (AG/CI); Dreamstime: Andreavagnoni (A/D), Claudio Balducelli (CB/D), Bitsuicide (B/D), Cristina Deidda (CD/D), Jojobob (J/DT), Lcampane (LC/D), Lianem (L/D), Mightymogwai (M/D), Mirka101 (M101/D), Danilo Mongiello (DM/D), Konstantinos Papaioannou (KP/D), Antonio Veraldi (AV/D); FLPA: Emanuele Biggi (EB/FLPA), Michael Breuer/Biosphoto (MB/B/FLPA), Fabien Bruggmann/Biosphoto (FB/B/FLPA), Gianpiero Ferrari (GF/FLPA); Luciano Di Gregorio (LDG); Shutterstock: Fotografiche (F/S), Armando Iozzi (AI/S); SuperStock (SS); Wikimedia Commons (W)
Front cover Pacentro (AG/CI)
Front cover picture research Pepi Bluck, Perfect Picture
Back cover Church in the hills above Villetta Barrea (SS)
Title page Cellino Attanasio, Teramo province (LDG); the belltower of Teramo Cathedral (M/D); confetti (sugared almonds) on sale in Sulmona (M101/D)

Maps David McCutcheon FBCart.S. Regional and colour maps compiled from Philip's 1:1,000,000 European mapping (*www.philips-maps.co.uk*).
Colour map Relief base map by Nick Rowland FRGS

Typeset from the author's disc by Wakewing, High Wycombe
Production managed by Jellyfish Print Solutions; printed in India
Digital conversion by Firsty

Acknowledgements

Listing all the people I want to mention is not realistic, so I'll keep this as short as possible. I'd like to thank everyone at Bradt for their help and advice.

Infinite thanks are due to my family and friends. Though I would really need pages for that, some cannot be omitted. In Australia: Mum, Dad, Marco, Julia, Nonno and the rest of my family. My good friend Peter for listening to me rant, rave and complain, as well as for writing the photography section. In Abruzzo: I must thank zia Silvana who put up with me coming and going at all hours for months as I researched this book; zio Silvio, zia Tiziana and my cousins Ilenia and Andrea for their support; a special mention to my cousin Sonia, who was instrumental in helping me carry out ground research and negotiate the post-earthquake bureaucracy in and around L'Aquila – a very difficult feat even for two locals presenting a united front; my cousin Gianna, her husband Vincenzo and their family; my godparents Lella and Antonio and their family; my very close friend and soul-bro Davide Silvestri for his support during a particularly difficult period as I researched this book, and for his help with the admin side of my ground research; the lovely Annamaria Rapani for giving up her time to help me out in Chieti.

Last but most certainly not least, thank you, Andrew: for all your help, support and suggestions, for putting up with my highs and lows during the research and writing of this book, and for your invaluable contribution on the natural history and environment sections. I couldn't have done it without you.

Oh – and a big *grazie* to the people of Abruzzo, but most especially for the Pescaresi: *nu sèm nu!*

DEDICATION

Per i miei genitori e i miei nonni
To my parents and grandparents

Contents

OCCHIO!

Few readers will be unaware of the earthquake that devastated L'Aquila and
the surrounding area on 7 April 2009. It is likely to take the better part of a
decade to rebuild. While places affected are described in this guide as if they
had been restored to their former glory, information about damage or special
warnings regarding access have been highlighted. *Occhio:* watch out!

LIST OF MAPS

FEEDBACK REQUEST

Abruzzo is slowly seeing an influx of international tourists and is therefore constantly changing. While researching this book, I spent much time in the various nooks and crannies of the region taking notes on everything imaginable. However, things change and Abruzzo will continue to evolve long after the writing and publication of this book – particularly, and poignantly, following the rebuilding after the 2009 earthquake, which is still taking place some years later. Given this, I would very much appreciate your feedback, information, tips and experiences for the next edition of the book! You can reach me by email at e info@bradtguides.com or by snail mail to Luciano Di Gregorio, c/o Bradt Travel Guides Ltd, IDC House, The Vale, Chalfont St Peter, Bucks SL9 9RZ, UK. I may post 'one-off updates' on the Bradt website at www. bradtguides.com/guidebook-updates. Alternatively you can add a review of the book to www.bradtguides.com or Amazon.

Introduction

As I sit on my sun-drenched balcony overlooking Pescara and the Adriatic, I reflect on my connection to Abruzzo, a connection born out of two distinct and mutually exclusive parts of my being. The first, my Italian side, born and raised as a child in the very streets of this city and the hills of the surrounding countryside, possesses an indisputable natural connection to this land, its people, its culture. The second, the Australian part of me, raised as a teenager and flourishing as an adult in '90s Melbourne, has gained a natural traveller's curiosity and fascination for this place, one which is more often than not missing in the indifferent and complacent attitudes of locals to their own land. Whilst these two sides are distinct, they mesh to create a love for Abruzzo which can be viewed through two lenses: the subjectivity of my perception and pride as a local and, relative to the purposes of this book, the objectivity of an inquisitive traveller.

We've all read the stories of wine-tasting tours of Tuscany, the food experience in Rome or the romance of Venice. However, intrepid travellers are often surprised – though thrilled – to discover that there is an area of this popular country that has not been trodden and devoured by the travelling masses. From breathtaking, ancient hilltop towns, a little ragged around the edges, to Neolithic caves, Roman ruins, and the best beaches in the country, Abruzzo is as surprising and rare a find as an Egyptian tomb in a scoured desert.

While the earthquake of April 2009 took its toll on the areas in and around the city of L'Aquila, the rest of the region remains, for the most part, unscathed. It is a testament to the company's pioneering spirit that Bradt allowed me to retain the original descriptions of the many sights and landmarks that were destroyed in L'Aquila as a tribute to their former glory, alongside up-to-date information detailing the rebuilding process and the current state of individual sites. Part of the decision in taking this approach was the recognition that tourists visiting elsewhere in the region will be able to enjoy the charms of Abruzzo while contributing to the local economy, thereby helping the reconstruction efforts in L'Aquila.

There's simply so much to do in Abruzzo. We owe part of the diversity of this region to the Gran Sasso d'Italia and the Majella, the two tallest mountain ranges in mainland Italy south of the Alps. In fact, almost two-thirds of the region is mountainous and provides for a stunning contrast with the rolling plains and 130km of pristine, Adriatic coastline. Yesterday, I floated, arms spread and ears below water on the Adriatic Sea with endless views of blue sky and coastline. Today, I took a short drive inland and hiked a trail on the slopes of the Majella mountain range. Tomorrow? Wine tasting along olive-strewn roads that disappear into the labyrinths of ancient towns? Shopping until I drop through the sunny, pastel streets of Pescara? Skiing on the highest peaks of the central Apennines? I think I will decide in the morning. *Piano, piano… con calma*. That's the way of it in Abruzzo.

Part One

GENERAL INFORMATION

ABRUZZO AT A GLANCE

Country name Italy (Italia), the Republic of Italy (Repubblica Italiana)
Region name Abruzzo, often referred to in English as the Abruzzi
Location In Italy's geographical centre, on the Adriatic Sea. Bordered by Le Marche to the north, Lazio to the west and Molise to the south.
Size 10,974 km^2
Climate Mediterranean
Population 1,342,366 (2011)
Life expectancy 82 years
Regional capital L'Aquila
Provinces Pescara (pop 323,184), L'Aquila (pop 309,820), Teramo (pop 312,239), Chieti (pop 397,124)
Largest city Pescara (pop 123,077)
Main airport Pescara (Aeroporto d'Abruzzo)
Language Italian, many native dialects
Religion Roman Catholic
GDP €23.59 billion
Currency Euro (€)
Exchange rate £1 = €1.24, US$1 = €0.77, AU$1 = €0.80 (December 2012)
International telephone code +39
Time GMT +1
Electrical voltage 220V/50Hz, two-pin plugs
National flag Three equal-length, vertical bands: green, white, red
Regional flag Three diagonal bands: white, green, blue
Tourist board www.regione.abruzzo.it
Public holidays 1 January, 6 January, Easter Monday, 25 April, 1 May, 2 June, 15 August, 1 November, 8 December, 25–26 December (see *Public holidays and festivals*, page 43)

Background Information

GEOGRAPHY

The region of Abruzzo is in the centre of the Italian peninsula, surrounded by Lazio to the west, Le Marche to the north, Molise to the south, and the waters of the Adriatic to the east. In the northeast, the region is less than 15km from the borders of Umbria. Occupying an area of around 10,975km² (just over 3.5% of Italy), it is the 13th-largest region in the country. Its western border is approximately 80km from the Italian capital city, Rome, and is closer to the metropolis than to the coastal city of Pescara, the largest in Abruzzo.

The region has four provinces, which are named after their largest cities. The main city, L'Aquila, is situated in a strategic position in the west of Abruzzo at 714m above sea level. Pescara, an important port and economic hub, is situated at the centre of Abruzzo's east-facing coastline, while the region's two other provincial capitals are Chieti, around 10km from Pescara, and Teramo, nestled between the Gran Sasso mountain range and the Adriatic coast.

Because of its position in the central Apennines, over two-thirds of Abruzzo's terrain comprises rugged mountains, with some of the most dramatic scenery in Italy. It is home to the two tallest peaks in the Apennines (Corno Grande in the Gran Sasso National Park at 2,912m and Monte Amaro in the Majella National Park at 2,793m), and, indeed, in all of mainland Italy outside of the Alps. No fewer

Background Information GEOGRAPHY

MOUNTAIN PEAKS

The peaks of Abruzzo over 2,000m are, in descending order of height:

Corno Grande	2,912m	La Meta	2,241m
Monte Amaro	2,795m	Monte Tartaro	2,191m
Corno Piccolo	2,665m	Monte Genzana	2,176m
Monte Corvo	2,623m	Monte Altare	2,174m
Monte Camicia	2,570m	Monte Puzzillo	2,174m
Monte Prena	2,561m	Montagna Grande	2,149m
Monte Velino	2,487m	Monte Rotella	2,127m
Monte Gorzano	2,458m	Monte Jamiccio	2,074m
Pizzo di Sevo	2,422m	Macera di Morte	2,073m
Monte Sirente	2,349m	Monte Rotondo	2,062m
Monte Greco	2,283m	Monte Morrone	2,061m
Monte Petroso	2,247m	Monte Cavallo	2,039m
Monte Marsicano	2,242m	Monte Palombo	2,013m

3

than 24 other mountains reach a height of over 2,000m above sea level. Most of these lie within the boundaries of the region's three national parks (Gran Sasso and Monti della Laga, Majella, and the National Park of Abruzzo) and the Sirente Velino Regional Park, which have a combined total area of over 300,000ha. The mountains form a spectacular backdrop to the gently rolling hills and plains along Abruzzo's 130km-long Adriatic coast.

The region is crossed by several rivers, the two longest being the Aterno-Pescara and the Sangro. The 150km-long Aterno-Pescara, which has one of the largest Adriatic drainage basins, originates in the Monti della Laga, a mountain range in the northeast bordering Le Marche and Lazio. In the south of Abruzzo the Sangro River runs for 122km, its passage roughly marked by the SS652. Lakes abound in the region and can be found dotted throughout the mountains and hills.

GEOLOGY *Andrew Burns (e abruzzoguide@gmail.com)*

The topography of Abruzzo clearly shows the violent geological forces that have shaped the region for millions of years. Central Italy lies on two fault lines and at the edge of the Eurasian and African continental plates. These plates meet in the middle of the Mediterranean Sea. The result has been a constant process of tectonic upheaval as the earth adjusts to release the pressures, which build up over millions of years as the plates collide. Earthquakes have been a constant reminder of the geological battle being waged below Abruzzo. The most recent example was the earthquake that devastated L'Aquila and the surrounding area in April 2009, though there have been many others, such as the equally terrible quakes of 1703 in L'Aquila and 1915 in Avezzano. The region's mountains, hills and valleys are also largely the result of this tectonic activity.

In the west the mountains of Abruzzo are primarily composed of marine deposited limestone. This was laid down during the Pliocene and early Pleistocene periods under the sea within the Peri-Adriatic basin. Over time, through a combination of sea level change, natural sediment deposition and the rupturing, buckling and folding of the Earth's crust, mountains such as Gran Sasso and Majella were pushed upwards. The gradual erosion of the rock over countless years by wind, water and ice has created the spectacular mountain peaks, domes, valleys and caves visible today.

In the east the land gently slopes down to sea level. Here it is comprised of clays and limestone laid down during the Cenozoic period, which have been severely eroded. The combination of the erosion of the limestones and the wave action of the Adriatic has blessed much of the coast with extensive sandy beaches, punctuated in places by the mouths of the region's rivers such as the Pescara and the Sangro.

CLIMATE

Abruzzo has a typically Mediterranean climate, characterised by hot, dry summers, with coastal areas enjoying an average temperature of over 23°C during the warmest month, July, and maximums above 35°C. That said, the exceptionally hot summer of 2003 took its toll on the region, with weeks of maximum temperatures above an unrelenting 40°C. However, the summer of 2007 saw this trumped, with thermometers soaring to over 45°C, particularly in Pescara, which, for a period of about two weeks, was the hottest city in Italy, if not in all of Europe. The fact that the weather is relatively stable rather than changeable means that summer can often feel uncomfortably hot for long periods of time.

EARTHQUAKES THAT HAVE SHAKEN THE REGION

1349 Major earthquake devastates L'Aquila.
1461 Just over 100 years later, L'Aquila suffers again.
1703 L'Aquila partly destroyed and thousands killed.
1915 Earthquake rocks the city of Avezzano and surrounding area.
2009 L'Aquila and surrounding area devastated by an earthquake measuring 6.3 on the Richter scale. Reverberations were felt throughout Abruzzo and hundreds of aftershocks rocked the region.

Winters are cool to mild in coastal areas but can be rather cold in the mountain regions, where snow can linger until early May. The coolest month is January, with temperatures averaging around 6°C. Inland and at over 700m, L'Aquila's lowest and highest average temperatures are 0° and 18°C respectively. Rainfall patterns are greatly influenced by the mountainous terrain, making the distribution and timing of downpours hard to predict, though generally the wettest month is November, with the driest period being summer.

NATURAL HISTORY AND CONSERVATION   *Andrew Burns*

Abruzzo offers some of the most accessible, diverse and visually stunning natural landscapes anywhere in Europe. As one of Italy's 'wildest' regions, its natural features have captured the imagination since the Romans discovered them during their attempts to cross the Apennines. In modern times the region has been at the forefront of efforts to protect the country's natural heritage and pioneered the idea of conservation in Italy. As a consequence it is home to Italy's oldest national park, Parco Nazionale d'Abruzzo.

FLORA AND FAUNA Species such as the beautiful yellow-and-black orchid, Apennine edelweiss, Marsican bear, Apennine wolf and the enigmatic Apennine chamois headline an impressive list of unique flora and fauna found in the Abruzzo region. The Abruzzese have lived alongside this diversity of plant and animal life for thousands of years, developing a keen understanding of some of these species and

THE TRANSHUMANCE TRAILS

In Abruzzo transhumance, the movement of shepherds and their sheep from the central Appenines down to the plains of Puglia, has a heritage going back hundreds of years. The shepherds followed three main trails. One, perhaps the longest and most important, stretched some 350km from the capital, L'Aquila, to the Apulian city of Foggia, via Lanciano. Another went from the town of Pescassèroli (see page 167) to the town of Candela. The shortest trail led from Castel di Sangro to the Apulian town of Lucera. The trails saw some interesting traffic jams – sheep in Abruzzo numbered around a million in the 14th century, around three million in the late 16th century and some 5.5 million in the early 17th century.

The trails were often wide roads that were furnished with churches so the shepherds could worship, and lodgings so they could rest.

the need to preserve them for future generations. Other species owe their survival to the landscape of Abruzzo itself. Many parts of the region are inhospitable to a permanent human population, which has in turn reduced human contact with many of the species that make these corners of the region their home.

Flora Abruzzo's Mediterranean climate has had a direct impact on the floral diversity of the region. Prehistorically, the region's flora was influenced by Alpine, Balkan, Mediterreanean, central European and even Arctic species. The retreat of the Adriatic Sea during periods of glaciation, combined with fluctuations in temperature, has enabled the migration of species between areas which are now geographically and climatically isolated. As the climate warmed, some species found refuge high in the mountains while others flourished at lower latitudes. Common species such as holly oak (*Quercus ilex*), flowering ash (*Fraxinus ornus*) and hornbeam (*Carpinus betulus*) are present and are well adapted to the Mediterranean climate which dominates much of the region. However, woven into this natural tapestry are a number of unexpected surprises. The mountainous nature of the region's interior has protected many traditional alpine species such as the Swiss mountain pine (*Pinus mugo*), beech (*Fagus sylvatica*), alpine poppy (*Papaver alpinum*) and the endemic Apennine edelweiss (*Leontopodium nivale*). These species are perfectly adapted to the colder, wetter and rocky environment found high in the region's interior and have thrived in a seemingly unsuitable position so far south and removed from the European Alps.

For a list of common flowers, shrubs and trees of the region, see *Appendix 2, Glossary of flora and fauna*, page 275.

Yellow-and-black orchid (Cypripedium calceolus) Also known as Venus' little shoe and Our Lady's slipper, this beautiful little orchid was once common throughout Europe and parts of Asia. The spread of human settlement and agriculture means that it is now rare. Standing at 80cm tall, it is Abruzzo's largest orchid and its rarest. It is found on the edge of woods and riparian environments at latitudes between 1,100m and 1,500m. In the Abruzzo National Park it can be seen at Camosciara and the Val Fundillo, and in the Majella National Park in the Valle di Fara San Martino. It has striking, irregular-shaped yellow-and-black flower heads, which appear between June and July.

Apennine edelweiss (Leontopodium nivale) An endemic regional variation of the more widely known European edelweiss of the Alps, this small alpine flower is found high on rocky plateaux and crevices above the treeline, over 2,000m, in Majella and Gran Sasso national parks. This flower is quite distinct, with both leaves and flowers being covered in fine woolly hairs, giving it a silver appearance. This is an evolutionary adaptation to the harsh and cold climate high in the mountains. Flowers stalks can vary in length from 3cm to 20cm and terminate with five yellow flower heads clustered together and surrounded by white petal-like leaflets arranged in a star formation. Flowers appear from midsummer to early autumn.

Marsican iris (Iris marsica) Endemic to the central Apennines, this striking iris has only recently been described by science as a separate species and was previously thought to be a variant of the German iris (*Iris germanica*). It stands approximately 60cm tall and has large royal purple flower heads, characterised by a curling deep blue-violet standard and a white beard, which appear in May and June. This annual species is found in arid pastures at an altitude of 1,000–1,700m above sea level.

Superficially it has a similar appearance to the German iris, which is the most common species grown in gardens. It is found in the Marsica region of western Abruzzo, and is best viewed in the wild in the Sirente Velino Regional Park on Mount Velino in the Valle di Sevice.

Beech (Fagus sylvatica) The European beech is a large deciduous tree species found across the continent. In the wilds of Abruzzo it carpets mountainsides and valleys in extensive forests. This species covers up to 60% of the Abruzzo, Majella and Gran Sasso national parks and grows at altitudes of between 900m and 1,800m in relatively homogenous stands. An individual tree can grow up to 50m high, but average heights generally range between 25m and 35m. These trees have a distinctive smooth grey trunk. Leaves are ovoid, with crenate margins and distinct straight veins arranged diagonally from the edge down to the central vein. The leaves are glossy and smooth with a dark green colour that changes to yellow and then a deep copper orange before falling in autumn. One of the most spectacular sights to be seen in the region is this change of autumn colours in the beech forests.

Fauna Abruzzo is a refuge for a wide variety of animal species. The region's extensive national parks and nature reserves create the ideal network of habitats to ensure the survival of self-sustaining ecosystems. In recent decades, species which have been in decline within the region and Italy, such as the Apennine chamois, have been the subject of successful breeding and re-introduction programmes, thereby increasing the region's biodiversity.

Most visitors to the region in search of a close encounter with the region's fauna hope to see one of the 'big three' species: the Marsican bear (*Ursus arctos marsicanus*), the Apennine wolf (*Canis lupo italicus*) and the Apennine chamois (*Rupicapra rupicapra ornata*). However, there are also a number of other rare, endangered, endemic and interesting species to see in Abruzzo. Venturing out into one of the region's nature reserves or parks may give you the chance to catch a glimpse of the extremely rare lynx (*Lynx lynx*), otter (*Lutra lutra*), Apennine golden eagle (*Aquila chrysaetos chrusaetos*) or any number of deer, bats, birds, amphibians and reptiles. A selection of species found in the region is listed in *Appendix 2, Glossary of flora and fauna*, page 275.

Marsican bear (Ursus arctos marsicanus) The Marsican is a subspecies of the European brown bear. Critically endangered, the 30–50 surviving individuals of these large mammals are found within the National Park of Abruzzo. While it is speculated that some other individuals may roam in other national parks and reserves in Abruzzo and even Trentino in northern Italy, this remains unconfirmed.

Not much is known about this species, a situation that is compounded by its nocturnal habits, though it is hoped that recent efforts to study its lifestyle and biology will reveal some much-needed scientific information. At up to 220kg and with a height of 1.8m–1.9m when standing on its hind legs, it is the largest animal native to Abruzzo. With a varied omnivorous diet highly dependent on seasonal availability, a bear can feed on fish, mammals, roots, nuts, berries and other plant matter as need dictates, though up to 60–70% of its diet can consist of vegetable matter.

One or two cubs (rarely three) are born between December and January, each weighing around 500g. For the next three years the cubs will remain with their mother as she devotes all her energy to them, ignoring the attention of courting males, as they slowly develop their independence. Individuals have a large natural range of up to 12km², but are not fiercely territorially. The typical habitat for these bears is in beech woods between 800m and 1,700m above sea level. They have suffered at the hands of man for many centuries, and hunting and habitat destruction have reduced the population to unsustainable levels. While the plight of this magnificent mammal is now becoming widely known, its survival is still under threat, primarily from increasing tourism development and illegal hunting.

Apennine wolf (Canis lupus italicus) This rare subspecies of the grey wolf (*Canis lupus*) is found throughout the Apennine mountain range of central Italy. In recent decades its population has grown from a historical low of around 100 individuals in the 1970s to the present estimated 600 individuals. The Apennine wolf can be found in woods within Abruzzo's national parks, though as it is shy and nocturnally active, it is rarely spotted by humans. It is not as large as the grey wolf, and reaches a weight of 30–40kg with a body length around 100–140cm. Its coat can vary greatly in appearance from grey, beige to grey-brown; some completely black individuals have even been reported. Scientific studies show that this subspecies is genetically purer than its grey wolf cousin, which hybridises commonly with wild dogs. The wolf lives in packs consisting of an alpha male and female with their immature offspring, numbering around six to seven individuals in total. Mating occurs typically once a year between February and March with a litter of between two to eight cubs (dependent on the age of the mother) being born after a two-month gestation. Individuals tend to live for eight to ten years.

Apennine chamois (Rupicapra rupicapra ornata) There is still some debate as to whether the Apennine chamois is a subspecies of the more populous European chamois (*Rupicapra rupicapra*), which is found in the mountains of central and eastern Europe, or whether it constitutes a separate species altogether. However, since it is estimated that there are fewer than 800 of these shy mountain goat-antelope left, it is not disputed that it is in danger of extinction.

The majority of the remaining Apennine chamois are found in the National Park of Abruzzo, where a concerted conservation programme seeks to stabilise and increase numbers. An adult can weigh up to 50kg and stand 75cm tall. A set of small horns, slightly longer and straighter than those of its European cousin, protrudes straight up from the head and tapers backwards slightly at the tip. Individual chamois have a thick, rich, brown fur with a distinct black line down the spine from head to tail and with dark patches on the flanks. A black strip runs down both sides of the head from the base of the horns through the eye and to the tip of the snout. In winter, the animal's coat is usually lighter in colour than its grey European counterpart. Females live in herds with juveniles, while males live a solitary life. The only time this solitude is broken is during the rut in November. During this time the males return to the herds and conduct violent battles between themselves for the right to mate with the females. A single kid is born in spring after a 20–23-week gestation. Males will stay with their mothers until two years of age.

Apennine golden eagle (Aquila chrysaetos chrysaetos) A majestic bird of prey and the largest bird found in western Abruzzo, this subspecies of the more widely spread golden eagle, was once common throughout the Apennines. Adults vary considerably in size, depending on the location; some females can reach a wingspan over 2m, a body length of up to 1m and an overall weight of 6kg. The bird's plumage ranges in colour from a dark brown to a lighter brown, with a golden speckled crown and neck, which gives the species its common name. The tail is typically quite large, up to half an individual's length, and features a white band.

Juveniles often have lighter patches spread over their bodies and lose the white tail band during an annual moult until they are two years of age. Individuals can live up to 15 or 20 years, with mating couples pairing for life. They construct a number of nests on ledges in rocky ravines and crevices overlooking alpine grasslands where they hunt for food. They feed on a mixture of small mammals, birds and carrion. The adults hunt co-operatively in pairs, with one of the pair driving the prey towards the other. With highly efficient long-range eyesight an eagle can spot its prey from up to a kilometre away. Females lay two eggs between January and September. After an incubation period of 45 days, pure white downy chicks hatch and remain in the nest for 50 days until they fledge.

Eurasian lynx (Lynx lynx) The Eurasian lynx, or *gattopardo* (spotted cat), as it has been known to the Abruzzesi for generations, is one of the success stories of Italy's conservation programmes. It is the largest of the world's lynx species at 80 to 130cm in length and 70cm high, and is also the largest feline in Europe. It is a beautiful and enigmatic creature that once roamed extensively throughout the countries of Europe. However, through hunting pressures on its prey and conflict with humans its natural range has been greatly reduced. In fact, by the early 20th century it was thought to be extinct throughout Italy, although many unconfirmed reports of sightings persisted for over 100 years in Abruzzo and other parts of Italy. In the last five years confirmed sightings have been recorded in the Italian Alps and Abruzzo. It is uncertain whether these are the result of re-introduction programmes or natural growth, but these cats can now infrequently be sighted in the Abruzzo National Park and the Majella National Park. A list of distinctive characteristics will help you distinguish it from other cat species, specifically the long and powerful legs which it uses to climb trees and to help navigate rocky terrain. Long tufts of coarse black hair stand up from the tips of its large ears, like little antennae. These tufts match the colour of its small stumped tail, which resembles that of the domestic Manx cat. It also has a thick tan coat covered in black spots, which in the Italian variety has a distinctive reddish tinge. Capable of bringing down prey four times its size, the Southern Eurasian lynx is one of the largest predators in the areas in which it is found. It breeds in a small period between February and March and females have two to three kittens after a 68-day gestation period.

Griffon vulture (Gyps fulvus) This distinctive and noble bird has dark brown plumage covering its body, tipped with a black trim. At the base of the neck this plumage gives way to a ruffle of soft white down. From here a thin covering of this down covers the remains of the neck and head, giving it the appearance of a typical vulture. In Europe its natural range traditionally fringed the warmer lands surrounding the Mediterranean. However, in Italy it only survived on the island of Sardinia until 2006 when a re-introduction programme tried to re-establish it within peninsular Italy. Since then individuals have been frequently sighted in areas of the Gran Sasso d'Italia National Park. With a wingspan just shy of 3m and weighing up 10kg, along with the golden eagle it is one of the largest birds in Abruzzo. A long-living scavenger that reaches up to 40 years of age, it survives by feeding on carrion spotted by soaring over open areas. It is also a sociable bird, frequently moving in flocks.

NATIONAL AND REGIONAL PARKS Hidden within the landscape of Abruzzo is a large variety of landforms, such as the Caldarone, Europe's southernmost glacier. There is also a staggering array of caves (grottoes) and rock formations to explore, many easily accessible. This geodiversity is equally matched by the region's biodiversity, much of it found within the jewels of Abruzzo: its four largest nature reserves, known as the Gran Sasso e Monti della Laga National Park, Majella National Park, the National Park of Abruzzo and the Sirente Velino Regional Park.

Parco Nazionale d'Abruzzo/National Park of Abruzzo Founded in 1922, making it Italy's oldest national park, the Parco Nazionale d'Abruzzo straddles the regions of Abruzzo, Molise and Lazio, covering an area of 40,000ha. It is located in the southwest corner of Abruzzo and is geographically the remotest of the region's parks. This explains the diverse range of flora and fauna found within its borders. It harbours some of the region's most spectacular and pristine terrain as well as the 'big three' mammals (Apennine chamois, Marsican bear and Apennine wolf) and numerous other species. The highest points within the park are Monte Petrosa (2,247m) and Mount Marsicano (2,242m). Two-thirds of the park is covered in extensive beech forest and it also protects 2,000 other significant plant species such as the yellow-and-black orchid, the Swiss mountain pine and the Italian black pine. The River Sangro originates within the park near Devil's Pass and runs southeast to Lago di Barrea, a wetland that is protected under the Ramsar Covention. It is definitely the most precious of Abruzzo's parks and reserves and despite its remoteness is easily accessible from other parts of the region and from further afield.

Parco Nazionale della Majella/Majella National Park This park is centred around the Majella massif, one of the highest ranges within the Apennine mountain chain. Along with the Gran Sasso massif, the Majella visually dominates the region with its highest point being the calcareous dome of La Majella (2,793m). The park protects 74,000ha of alpine plateaux and woodland and is classified in scientific terms as falling between the biogeographical regions of the Mid-European and Mediterranean. Additionally, in prehistoric times it had a paleogeographical connection with the Balkan Peninsula. All this means that the park is home to an extensive range of flora, last estimated at 2,100 individual species. These species are found on large alpine plains at high altitudes. On the edges of the massif, steep valleys sharply fall away and harbour additional species which benefit from the shelter found there. Additionally, the park is home to numerous mammal species including the Apennine chamois, Apennine wolf, Italian fox and European otter.

The park is popular all year round as it is easily accessible from places such as Pescara and Chieti. It has extensive hiking trails for the summer months and winter snowfields which attract snowsports enthusiasts. It is also the location of the Grotta del Cavallone, one of the largest and deepest caves in Europe. At Sant'Eufemia a Majella are the Daniele Brescia Botanic Gardens, which offer a convenient way to get up close to many of the region's unique flora species.

Parco Nazionale del Gran Sasso d'Italia e Monti della Laga/Gran Sasso and Laga Mountains National Park This national park was created only in 1993 and covers 203,000ha of alpine terrain centred around the dramatic Gran Sasso d'Italia (Great Stone of Italy). The Gran Sasso is a group of high alpine peaks, with the tallest being Corno Grande (2,912m), which is also the highest point of the Apennines. It is at the base of Corno Grande that you will find the Calderone Glacier. Unlike the rounded massif of the neighbouring Majella, Gran Sasso is characterised by jagged limestone peaks jutting up above a number of alpine plateaux, such as the Campo Imperatore (see page 125), which is home to Italy's oldest continuously operating ski field.

The dramatic geology and landforms of this park make it popular with hikers and climbers. Additionally, the forests, alpine meadows and valleys are home to a wide variety of alpine grasses and wild flowers such as the Apennine edelweiss and fauna such as the Marsican bear, Apennine wildcat, Apennine chamois, Italian fox, wild boar, grass snakes, golden eagle and Apennine wolf. There are also the Alpine Botanic Gardens founded in 1952, displaying some 300 species of alpine flora, at Campo Imperatore. The park is close to the region's largest cities: L'Aquila, Pescara, Teramo and Avezzano.

Parco Naturale Regionale Sirente Velino/Sirente Velino Regional Park This 50,250ha park was founded in July 1989 and is centred around the massifs of Sirente (2,348m) and Velino (2,456m). It is located in the far west of the region, almost on the border with Lazio overlooking the Avezzano plain, and just north of the A26, which is the main *autostrada* between Abruzzo and Rome. The park protects some 1,926 species of flora, 216 vertebrates, 149 species of bird (one-third of all breeding bird species found in Italy), 43 mammals (46% of Italian mammal species), 13 reptiles and 11 amphibians. Amongst these fauna are the Marsican bear, Apennine wolf, Apennine wildcat, Orsini's viper, Eurasian (or common) kingfisher, salamander, pine and beech martens, dormouse and various deer species. Plans are also being developed for the re-introduction of the Apennine chamois. The park's flora includes the glacial-era saxifrage (*Saxifraga marginata*), rare peonies and violets, and various orchids. This diversity is due to geological and climatic factors such as the varying altitudes which allow a variety of bioregions to be found in such a small area. The park is of particular interest to geologists as the mountains are characterised by Mesozoic formations and cretaceous limestone, with some limestones reaching as far back as the Jurassic period. The park is also home to the Sirente Crater and a variety of karst formations. Extensive beech, birch, hornbeam and oak forests and woods can be found at lower elevations. Winter skiing is available on the peaks of Monte Magnola and on the Campo Felice.

HISTORY

The history of Abruzzo is as long as it is complex. The region's name is said to derive from the earlier Latin Aprutium, though the geographical area known today as Abruzzo has been given various titles throughout history, including, by the Romans, Samnium and Picenum. It wasn't until the Middle Ages that the present name came into use to describe an area that also included Molise. Right up until the 1960s, Abruzzo and Molise were one region, known as the Abruzzi.

There is evidence of human activity in the region dating back 300,000 years, attested to by archaeological discoveries such as those from Caramanico Terme (see page 93). However, we know very little of Abruzzo before around 1500BC, and even then, details are sketchy at best. It is thought that during the Bronze Age, the climate was largely maritime, with rich soil and abundant growth of vegetation, creating excellent conditions for sheep farming. Because of this, until the 20th century Abruzzo was largely a sheep farming region (see box, *The transhumance trails*, page 5).

PRE-ROMAN: THE ITALIC TRIBES By the Iron Age (around the turn of the first millennium BC), around nine Italic tribes were present in and around Abruzzo: the Paeligni, Aequi, Marrucini, Vestini, Marsi, Frentani and Sabine and, to a lesser extent, the Picene and Preatutii. All have left marks on a land later conquered numerous times, and all have in some way shaped the fabric of Abruzzo's history and identity.

11

It is often difficult to clearly define the areas of Abruzzo that the Italic tribes occupied. However, the following breakdown is generally accepted to be correct:

Tribe	Modern-day area
Paeligni	In and around the Sulmona Valley
Vestini	A large portion of the Pescara Province
Marruccini	Northern Chieti Province
Frentani	Coastal Chieti Province
Marsi	Area south of the ancient Fucino Lake
Aequi	Southwest Abruzzo north of Fucino Lake
Sabine	Northwest Abruzzo into Umbria and Marche
Picene	Northern coastal Abruzzo
Preatutii	Northern coastal Abruzzo, particularly around Teramo

Until the middle of the Iron Age, these tribes were quite independent and separate, and hostility led to many inter-tribal squabbles. However, during the middle of the first millennium BC, the tribes began to intermingle and trade. Then, faced with a common enemy, they formed a united front against the invading Romans.

The Italic tribes were responsible for the founding of many towns and cities in the region. The modern-day city of Teramo was founded by the Praetutii tribe, who called it Pretut (it was later renamed Interamnia by the Romans and Teramo in the Middle Ages). Some 50km away, Pinna (modern-day Penne) was the capital of the Vestini tribe, and similarly Chieti and Sulmona were the principal cities for the Marruccini and Paeligni tribes respectively.

ROMAN COLONISATION Abruzzo presented something of a problem for the Romans. For one thing, the land was mountainous, impenetrable and inhospitable. For another, the people of the region soon became known to the Romans – with some justification – as 'wild mountain people'. However, the Romans were formidable colonisers, and in the second half of the first millennium BC they began to show a great interest in the lands of their Italic neighbours.

Due to their geographical position, occupying modern-day Lazio, the Aequi were one of the first Italic tribes to come into direct contact with the Romans, most notably at the fierce Battle of Mons Algidus (458BC), which left the Aequi defeated and humiliated. Some two decades later, in 435BC, Rome enjoyed its second victory over the tribes of the region with its capture of Anxanum (modern-day Lanciano), which later became a municipality of Rome.

However, it wasn't until the 4th century BC that the Romans began to make greater headway in their penetration into the Abruzzo region, though still with some difficulty. The Samnite tribes of modern-day Molise and Campania urged the Italic tribes of Abruzzo to overcome their differences and stand united against Rome. Over the course of the three Samnite Wars, which spanned half a century from 343BC to 290BC, most of the Italic tribes across the Italian peninsula would become involved in resisting Roman colonisation. However, during the final war, in which an attempt was made to overthrow Rome completely, the Samnites and Italic tribes of Abruzzo were defeated. Following this, Roman expansion in the region was again challenged during the Social Wars (91–88BC). The Italic tribes mustered up an army of more than 100,000 soldiers to oppose continued Roman occupation and expansion. The tribes' headquarters were in modern-day Corfinio in Abruzzo, which was symbolically renamed from Corfinium to Italica. With casualty figures for the war running into the tens of thousands, the Roman army, eager to be finished with what they saw as an assault on their just occupation, made several concessions to the Italic tribes, including a law (the *Lex Julia*) conceding full citizenship to Italic communities.

Once peace had been imposed the Italic and Roman populations began to assimilate and the region began to prosper. The Romans took over several existing towns and cities as well as founding new ones. A number of these were made into municipalities (important centres for the Roman Empire), including Teate (Chieti), Pinna (Penne), Anxanum (Lanciano), Histonium (Vasto), Interamnia (Teramo) and Sulmo (Sulmona).

MIDDLE AGES–20TH CENTURY: FROM FRAGMENTS TO THE KINGDOM OF ITALY

Following the fall of the Roman Empire during the 5th century AD, the Gothic War of the 6th century BC, and the subsequent spread of Christianity, the region underwent many changes of ruler due to its strategic position in central Italy. In AD570 it came under the rule of the Lombards who established the Duchy of Spoleto, which included parts of modern-day Abruzzo, Umbria and Lazio. The duchy was later given to the Church by Charlemagne, who insisted on remaining in control of delegating important appointments within the duchy. During the following centuries, monasticism became a powerful force in the region and a number of great religious houses and churches were founded, such as the Abbey of San Clemente a Casauria (see page 87).

The history of Abruzzo becomes more confusing from the 11th century onwards. The Normans extended their reach to southern Italy and thus the region came under their control, with the Norman king of Sicily invested as its feudal overlord in the 12th century. Abruzzo continued as an important part of the Kingdom of Sicily, which changed hands at various times throughout the Middle Ages, from the Normans to the Swabians in the late 12th century, until the Battle of Tagliacozzo (see box, *A battle to end all battles*, page 162) in 1268. This ended Swabian rule in southern Italy and saw the beginning of Angevin rule in the region. During the rule of the House of Anjou, the region became part of the Kingdom of Naples. It wasn't until Spanish occupation in the 16th century that it became part of the larger Kingdom of the Two Sicilies. It continued as part of this kingdom throughout the following period of Bourbon rule, up until the unification of Italy in 1861.

Brief chronology

603	Most of the region comes under the control of the Lombards and their Duchy of Spoleto.
843	The region is renamed Marsia.
12th C	Swabian control of the region. Frederick II of Swabia creates Justitieratus Aprutii, a separate administrative area that takes in almost the entire region, with Sulmona as its capital.
1254	L'Aquila is founded (see *History*, page 100).
1266	Charles of Anjou arrives in the region.
1268	Battle of Tagliacozzo ends Swabian control (see box, page 162).
1294	Pietro da Marrone is named Pope Celestine V (see page 101).
1458	University of L'Aquila is founded.
1503	The region (part of the Kingdom of Naples) comes under Spanish control.
1647	Beginnings of revolt against Spanish rule.
1684	Three provinces formed: Abruzzo Ulteriore I (L'Aquila), Abruzzo Ulteriore II (Teramo) and Abruzzo Citeriore (Chieti). This provincial structure lasted until 1927, when the Province of Pescara was added.

17th C	Castelli ceramics become important to the prosperity and development of the region.
1703	A major earthquake destroys part of L'Aquila.
1790s	The cities of Teramo and Pescara resist French troops.
1854	The beginnings of an ambitious project to drain Lake Fucino.
1861	The final Bourbon town, Civitella del Tronto, falls to the Kingdom of Italy (see page 225).
1915	May: Italy enters World War I
1940	June: Italy enters World War II

WORLD WAR II Like the rest of Italy, Abruzzo fell on hard times during the 1930s and World War II had an enormous impact on its residents. The effects of economic hardship, and the widespread destruction that followed, can still be seen in the region through the large number of émigrés who left Abruzzo.

The region was to see some of the bloodiest fighting in all of peninsular Italy, especially at the Battle of Ortona. From September 1943 onwards, the town of Ortona had become a crucial escape route for the Italian monarchy, who boarded ships for Brindisi in southern Italy, an area already liberated by the Allied forces. However, the months that followed would be some of the saddest in Ortona's history. A decisive moment in World War II, the battle that was fought in the city opened the way for Allied forces to reach the Italian capital.

During the summer of 1943, the Allies had progressed through the peninsula, liberating the south of Italy quite easily. Hitler, however, had set up several command centres in central Italy and was adamant that they be defended. On 2 October, Hitler gave orders for the area around Ortona to be protected at all costs. Thus the Gustav Line was founded and Abruzzo became the backdrop for a battle between the two armies. As the Allied forces advanced, the Germans did everything in their power to attempt to halt their progress, destroying towns along the way and killing thousands.

Events came to a head in December 1943, with some of the worst fighting taking place after Christmas. Ortona became a battlefield as fighting raged in the streets. There are many accounts of people hiding throughout the city, hearing the agonising screams of other townsfolk but unable to rescue them lest they be cut down by artillery fire. When, on the morning of 28 December, locals realised that the Germans had fled, they came out of hiding to join the Allied forces.

MODERN ABRUZZO Post-war emigration from Abruzzo took its toll on the economy of the region. As with many other parts of Mediterranean Europe, it wasn't until the 1970s that Abruzzo began flourishing again. The building of *autostradas* connecting parts of Abruzzo to Rome was at least in part responsible for this. However, the mid- to late 1980s was a time of economic hardship that saw a second wave of emigration: many headed off in search of work in Rome or Milan, as well as America, Australia and Britain.

As with other Italian regions, Abruzzo has suffered from the constant change of government at a national level. However, local government during the 1990s and early 2000s did make an effort to develop the region. Left-wing city governments (such as that of Pescara) in the early 2000s undertook renovation and beautification works: Pescara's main shopping street was pedestrianised and lined with trees, piazzas were cleaned up and a number of historic buildings reconstructed. Despite this, little help came from the right-wing, Berlusconi-led national government in Rome.

In 2009, a major earthquake (of 6.3 on the Richter scale) hit the city of L'Aquila, killing hundreds of people and injuring and displacing thousands of others. In the following weeks and months aftershocks were felt, some as strong as 4.8 on the Richter scale. Berlusconi made L'Aquila the centre of attention when he decided to move the 2009 G8 summit to the ruined city rather than hold it at a resort on the island of Sardinia. Some say this is the least he could have done in the interests of the people, though most Abruzzesi (and Aquilani in particular) saw it as a major hassle that did little to benefit the residents.

In June 2009, Pescara became the focus of Mediterranean Europe when it hosted the Mediterranean Games (see page 54). This two-week event featuring 23 countries saw the host city inundated with visitors from all over Italy and further afield.

Over recent years, Abruzzo has seen harsh summers followed by some bitter winters. The 2011/2012 winter season saw perhaps some of the most significant snowfalls in the region; even coastal cities were buried under feet of snow. On the other hand, at the time of writing in summer 2012, the region has suffered through countless days of 40°C+ temperatures.

GOVERNMENT AND POLITICS

The Italian political system is that of a parliamentary, democratic republic. There is a multi-party structure led by the President of the Council, or prime minister. Regional politics are based on a similar system. The Italian regions have a presidential representative democracy, with power being exercised by the President of the Regional Government. The President of the Region is elected by popular ballot and may preside for a term of no longer than five years. He is assisted by a vice-president and ten ministers (or assessors). Together, they wield the region's executive power. The current President of the Region is Gianni Chiodi from the right-wing People of Freedom Party, re-elected in 2009. Legislative power is shared with the Regional Council of 40 members. The majority of these members, who may serve for a total of five years, are elected through proportional representation.

ECONOMY

Prices have risen above the official rate of inflation in Italy ever since the introduction of the euro in 2002, and salaries have failed to keep pace with this rise, making life tough for the average earner. However, Abruzzo's economy is generally much healthier than those of its southern neighbours, and Pescara has one of the higher standards of living, with low unemployment, reasonable salaries and a relatively low cost of living. Despite this, Abruzzo took a fair battering in the global financial crisis of 2008 and the years that followed. If there seemed to be a brief reprieve in 2010, it was nothing but a false alarm. The Abruzzesi continue to struggle under the weight of unemployment and, along with the rest of Italy, it does not look likely that the region will recover in the foreseeable future. Consequently, the price of food, goods and services has had to remain at all-time lows.

In terms of exports, the region does well out of its pasta, oil and wine. In fact, two of the nation's most popular and trusted pasta brands, De Cecco and Delverde, are from Abruzzo, as is Cocco, which makes pasta for the Pope.

PEOPLE

It is no easy task to collectively define the Abruzzesi. Their strength of, and conviction in, local identification means that even their closest neighbours inhabit a world somewhat foreign to their own. Indeed, geography – both the region's place in Italy and its own mountainous terrain – plays a large part in perceptions of local identity.

The Abruzzesi, like many Italians, are not terribly patriotic or nationalistic when it comes to the Italian state as a whole. Unlike in some other countries, if, say, an international swimming race featured an Italian, the Abruzzese would certainly support the Italian, but faster than you could say 'on your marks', the inevitable question would arise, 'which part of Italy are they from?' This would be deemed to be important and it would certainly have a bearing on how they perceived the participant, whether positively, negatively or even indifferently. When Italy beat France in the FIFA World Cup final in 2006, Abruzzo was fiercely proud; on that warm summer evening I witnessed the region's main towns in gridlock after hundreds of thousands took to the streets waving flags and tooting their horns. However, while the achievements of the entire team as a whole were praised, the Abruzzesi could not help but put emphasis on their regional hero (who isn't even Abruzzese-born but spent a long time playing for regional teams), Fabio Grosso.

Although the concept of an 'Italian' geographical area goes back a few thousand years, this strong identification with a region rather than the nation is not entirely unusual for a country unified from a collection of disparate states only a century

THREE TYPICAL ABRUZZESI FAMILIES

MARGHERITA Margherita was born in Pescara and is 22 years old. She attended a high school and gained a secondary-school qualification. Since leaving school, she's been unsure of what to do. Going to university was not really an option for her: the course she was interested in was only offered in Rome and she knew her parents could never afford to support her while she studied, let alone pay the fees. Consequently, for the last few years she has flitted from job to job, never quite satisfied, never quite sure what to do.

During the summer, Margherita spends virtually every afternoon at the beach. She couldn't imagine living more than 5km from Abruzzo's coast, which, while taken for granted most of the time, is at the centre of her world. There isn't much to do in winter, so she takes herself window shopping down Corso Vittorio Emanuele several times a week.

Margherita has a few very close friends and is dedicated to her family. She has one grandparent left, her mother's father. He lives with the family and dotes on and fusses over Margherita. Occasionally, he slips her €50, which is enough for some socialising, but mostly it's eaten up by her self-professed bad habit, smoking. Her father doesn't know this, which is just as well.

While her parents are at work and her younger sister is at school, Margherita dreams of travelling, though secretly she knows she probably wouldn't bother even if it were cheaper: it's all too far away and she knows she could not handle being on a plane for more than two hours. Her cousin lives in London and she has visited him twice, thanks to the cheap flights from Pescara.

MARCO Marco is 35 years old and lives in a rural town near L'Aquila. He didn't finish high school and had a series of manual labouring jobs before being employed by a company dealing in truck and van sales. He earns a decent wage as a salesman and, recently married, is expecting a baby (whom they will call Sonia) with his wife, Ilenia. Marco and Ilenia, who recently gave up her part-time job as a receptionist, live in a house he inherited from his father's family. The absence of a mortgage is a and a half ago. Indeed, it is often perpetuated and encouraged, especially in popular culture. *Affari Tuoi*, the Italian equivalent of television game show *Deal or No Deal*, for instance, not only sees the contestants' boxes numbered, but also identifies clearly which region they are from.

It is thus not surprising to see this way of thinking, played out at a more local level, forming a significant element of the Abruzzese character. Within the region itself, the majority of Abruzzesi are fiercely loyal to their immediate surroundings. To the cosmopolitan Romans, the Italic tribes of Abruzzo were seen as wild mountain people. This was in part because of the region's topography: towns developed, thrived and functioned largely in isolation and independence from each other, even developing their own local dialect. The people developed an affinity with their surroundings because they depended on them far more than on trade with people from other towns, and their land was crucial to their survival. Before they had access to paved roads and shiny Alfa Romeos, the Abruzzesi travelled on donkeys, or horses if they could afford them. While trade was important to the functioning of the region, travelling to the next town could take a full day of uncomfortable riding through harsh, untamed mountainous territory. Even today, my grandfather tells of the hassle of reaching a town not terribly far away, and that was only 60 years ago.

godsend and means that they were free to take out a small loan to put their own stamp on the house.

Marco and Ilenia love to travel, though only within Europe as the rest of the world is, apparently, unreachable. They have visited Barcelona, London and Munich, and have travelled extensively in Italy. Marco loves the countryside, especially the wilderness of the mountains in Abruzzo where he spends much of his time.

Both their families live within a five-minute drive and regularly eat together in the evenings. The grandmothers to-be have already bought all the clothing and accoutrements their firstborn grandson could ever need.

RAFFAELE AND DONATA Raffaele and Donata are in their 70s and live in a large coastal town in the province of Teramo. They are both retired, having left their family business to their three children, Raffaele, Gianna and Giampiero.

They both grew up in Abbateggio, a town in the province of Pescara. Donata had a minimal education and Raffaele left middle school to help his father on the family farm. Like many others in Abruzzo, World War II took its toll on both their families, who made do on meagre food rations in a hostile environment. They both remember vividly the smell of smoke that wafted through the town as they were forced into cellars by parents fearful for the lives of their children. The couple have known each other since childhood, and Raffaele began to court Donata at the age of 14. They have been together ever since, and happily married since the late 1940s.

Their business was a successful provider of house fixtures for over three decades and Raffaele and Donata are enjoying a very comfortable retirement, spending their time between their primary residence and their two holiday homes, one in Positano on the Amalfi coast and the other deep in the countryside of Abruzzo in Chieti Province.

Despite all their wealth, what really matters to them is the happiness of their children and eight grandchildren.

The implications for modern Abruzzo are clear: generations of relative isolation have created a general 'rivalry' between the towns and cities of the region. Mostly these rivalries are harmless and are played out through humour. An Abruzzese won't treat a person differently because he or she is from three towns thataway, which, especially to the older generations, might be considered the back of beyond. At its most evident, the strong rivalry between, for instance, residents of Pescara and those from Chieti, a mere 15km away, amounts to nothing more than a few sniggered words over, for instance, driving ability or taste in clothing.

Generally, to the Abruzzese, everything is far away. While the average Australian and American might think nothing of a 30km commute to work, travelling 10km to the next town seems like a chore to the Abruzzese, let alone what lies beyond the Apennine range.

The Abruzzesi are exceptionally family-oriented. Immediate and (very) extended families tend to be no more than a ten-minute drive away, and it is not unusual for at least three generations to live under the same roof, which is why many Abruzzesi children develop close bonds with their grandparents. *Nonna* and *nonno* are an endless fountain of love and kisses, not to mention toys, food and pocket money. The whole family eating together might consist of parents, grandparents, brothers, sisters, uncles, cousins and cousins of cousins. Should you be asked to eat with an Abruzzese family it will be one of the most fascinating and rewarding experiences of your travels in the region.

The Abruzzese tend to have an intense love affair with the region's gastronomy, convinced that theirs is the best food not only in all of Italy but in the entire world. Indeed, some Abruzzesi can often be hesitant to expand their culinary horizons whilst abroad. Cousins and friends staying with me in London or Melbourne run a mile at the thought of eating a traditional English breakfast, or raise their eyebrows in scepticism as I enthuse about the food in Hong Kong or Marrakesh.

Demographically, the overwhelming majority of Abruzzo's 1.3 million residents are Italian. As of January 2011, ISTAT, the Italian Institute of Statistics, puts Abruzzo's foreign population at just over 80,000 (around 6%), a massive increase of 40,000 since 2005, mainly due to the entrance of Romania and Bulgaria into the European Union. There is a decent-sized Roma population in Abruzzo, but despite many of them being Italian citizens, they face considerable discrimination, as well as an increasingly shrill campaign by Italy's growing far-right to blame them for many of the country's problems. The treatment of the Roma, which has included violent attacks, demolition of their settlements and plans to fingerprint Roma children, has led to Italy being warned by the EU about its infringement of human rights.

EMIGRATION Abruzzo's history of emigration is complex and spans two centuries, although most emigration from the region took place in the 20th century. Post-war emigration was all the rage in the 1950s, as World War II left many towns and cities in the region (as well as the economy) bruised and tattered. Many left their homes in search of a better life elsewhere, some with hopes of returning, having made their small fortunes. It is thought that about 15% of Abruzzesi live abroad, although this figure includes second-generation immigrants born to Abruzzesi parents.

Abruzzesi in the United States of America and Canada Over the last century, the USA has welcomed hundreds of thousands of Abruzzesi. It is hard to pinpoint exactly how many emigrants arrived as many had their surnames changed by immigration officials or felt it was best to change their names themselves in order to avoid discrimination.

Some 15 million Americans claim Italian descent, and it is likely that the true figure is higher; the Census Bureau estimates that one in ten Americans have Italian ancestors and puts the number of Italian descendants, including many from Abruzzo, at about 26 million.

However, the Canadian city of Toronto claims to be the second-largest Abruzzese city in the world, after Pescara, with a population of around 80,000 Abruzzesi among the half-million people of Italian descent that call the city home.

Abruzzesi in South America There are many people descended from Abruzzese émigrés in South America, with around 14 associations for Abruzzesi in the country of Argentina alone. Italian immigration to Argentina began as early as the 1850s, and around 10–30% of these immigrants are thought to have been from the region of Abruzzo. Recent estimates put the population of first-, second- and third-generation Abruzzesi at no fewer than a million. Elsewhere in South America, Brazilian residents of Italian origin alone number around 22 million, with many from the region of Abruzzo, and Venezuela also has a sizeable Abruzzese population.

Abruzzesi in Australia Italian immigration to Australia dates back to the 1920s. Early immigrants faced discrimination from white, Anglo-Saxon Australians, being called names such as 'darkie' and 'wog'. Many Abruzzesi first docked in the port of Fremantle, from where they would catch another ship bound for Melbourne or Sydney, or travel up the Swan River and move into the interior. While some arrived from the mid-1920s onwards, the main period of immigration dates from the end of World War II to the 1970s. In 1945, a programme to bring immigrants into the country saw the entry of around 33,000 Abruzzesi. The later Italy/Australia Agreement of 1951 proved beneficial to both countries: many Italians were looking to move because of the dire post-war economic crisis and Australia needed workers. Having had their fare and accommodation paid, the immigrants had to accept any work that was given to them and stay in Australia for at least two years.

There are now about 170,000 Abruzzesi in Australia, largely concentrated in Victoria (40%). There are large communities also in New South Wales (27%), South Australia and Western Australia (13% respectively), and Queensland (7%). Italian is said to be the second most spoken language on the island-continent.

Abruzzesi in Europe Italian immigration to the rest of Europe also took place on a large scale, especially to Belgium, Luxembourg, Germany, France and Switzerland. In the first decade and a half of the 1900s, around half a million Abruzzesi left for other European countries in search of work. A further wave of immigration took place after World War II.

LANGUAGE

While most readers will assume, quite rightly, that the language of Abruzzo is Italian, the reality is rather more complex. Abruzzo is home to a wealth of dialects that verge on being different languages. The language spoken in Abruzzo falls within a set of languages known as Italo-Dalmatian, which also includes standard, official Italian. Within this group of languages, Abruzzesi dialects are broken into two main classes. A small part of Abruzzo around its capital, L'Aquila, falls into the Central Italian group, whose languages are closely related to Tuscan and standard Italian. However, most of the region falls within a class simply known as 'Neapolitan'. This

A general characteristic of Abruzzese dialects is that words in standard Italian often have their endings chopped off, especially names. The verb 'to go' below is used as an example to highlight just how much dialect can differ from standard Italian. Please note that 'j' is pronounced like the 'y' in *yell*, and the accent denotes a stress on that letter (for pronunciation of other letters of the alphabet, see the *Language* appendix, page 271).

VERB: *ANDARE*, TO GO

Dialect	Standard Italian	English
Vàje	*Vado*	I go
Vi	*Vai*	You go
Va	*Va*	He/she/it goes
Jèm	*Andiamo*	Let's go
Jèt	*Andate*	You (pl) go
Vànn	*Vanno*	They go
Jàmmè	*Andiamo*	Let's go (hurry up)
Me ne ting'a'ji	*Me ne devo andare*	I have to go
Se n'ha jìt	*Se n'è andato*	He left (around Pescara)
Se n'ha jòt	*Se n'è andato*	He left (around Teramo)

label is deceptive, as the dialect of Naples is often unintelligible to Abruzzesi; the link is historical rather than strictly linguistic, with the region having formed part of the Kingdom of Naples and the Two Sicilies. This group of languages, as with many other in Italy, stems from Vulgar Latin.

Furthermore, due to Abruzzo's mountainous terrain, the general Abruzzese dialect developed its own form from town to town. Within a matter of a few kilometres, the vocabulary and accent can change quite remarkably. For example, a person speaking in true Pescarese fashion will be clearly distinguishable from a resident of Teramo.

Unfortunately, it is now unfashionable, and seen as uncouth, to be heard speaking dialect in public, so Abruzzo's dialects, with their rich vocabularies, proverbs and sounds, are in danger of dying out.

Aside from their dialects most regions of Italy also have a distinct accent and cadence in spoken standard Italian, and Abruzzo is no exception. Not long ago, chatting to an Italian waiter in a central London café, I was stopped mid-sentence and asked if I was from Pescara. It turns out my waiter was from the hills of L'Aquila Province and immediately recognised my accent, despite the fact that we spoke standard Italian. A demonstration of how an Italian's origin can often be easily identified by their accent and where they place the stress in a sentence.

RELIGION

Abruzzo's fierce loyalty to its culture and traditions goes hand in hand with the importance of religion, and overwhelmingly that religion is Roman Catholic. The region's festivals and events might be divided into two groups, the largest group being those of a religious nature, and many of Abruzzo's traditions are inextricably linked to its saints and churches. The rest are generally devoted to food, another of the region's passions.

There is an enormous number of churches in the region, forming some of Abruzzo's greatest attractions with their relics and paintings. During the Middle Ages, a town's church was one of its most important buildings and life tended to centre around it and its activities. Centuries later, this hasn't changed much, especially in the smaller settlements.

CULTURE

ART AND ARCHITECTURE Abruzzo is dotted with thousands of medieval abbeys, churches, monasteries and civic buildings. For a taste of the wealth of paintings, sculptures and statues that decorate the region's important religious and residential buildings it is best to start with a visit to Chieti's National Archaeological Museum of Abruzzo (see page 244).

It is worth remembering that the heritage of Abruzzo is inextricably linked to that of the rest of Italy. While there are a number of revered Abruzzese painters and sculptors, such as Nicola da Guardiagrele (see box, page 255), many of the artistic works that enliven Abruzzo's churches and buildings are the work of masters from around the country.

One of the greatest art treasures from the region is the statue known as the 'Warrior of Capestrano' (see box, page 22), now housed in Chieti's National Archaeological Museum. Because of the size and sheer domination of this statue, said to reflect the attitude of the native Italic tribes of Abruzzo, it has come to symbolise the strength of Abruzzese identity and the region's complex history.

LITERATURE Over the centuries, Abruzzo has also been the place of birth of a number of renowned writers: Ovid, Gabriele D'Annunzio and Ignazio Silone.

Ovid Born Publius Ovidius Naso in Sulmona in 43BC, Ovid was a Roman poet. Though it was his family's wish that he take up a career in the law, Ovid's talent for writing soon became clear. He travelled throughout Italy, Greece and parts of Asia, returning to Italy to become a writer, particularly of poetry, which focuses largely on emotional rhetoric. He was a prolific author, inspiring later writers and artists such as Chaucer, Botticelli and Shakespeare. His most famous works include: *Amores* ('The Loves', 16BC), *Ars Amatoria* ('The Art of Love', 1BC) and *Tristia* ('Sorrows', AD10). He died in the town of Tomis, modern-day Constanţa in Romania.

Ignazio Silone Silone was born as Secondo Tranquilli on 1 May 1900, later adopting the pseudonym by which he is better known, and died on 22 August 1978. He had a particularly difficult childhood: his father died when Ignazio was aged 11 and he later lost his mother in the earthquake of 1915. In his 20s, Ignazio was one of the founders of the Italian Communist Party and his brother, Romolo, was imprisoned and killed in 1931 for his involvement with the party. Ignazio settled in Switzerland in the 1930s where he was diagnosed with depression and spent time recovering. It was there that he wrote one of the works for which he is best known, *Fontamara*. This was published in 1933 and became the first part of his *Abruzzo Trilogy* that also includes *Pane e Vino* ('Bread and Wine') and *Il Seme Sotto la Neve* ('The Seed Beneath the Snow'). The trilogy became popular because of its accurate depiction of peasant culture in Abruzzo. It has been translated into English and French.

Silone did not return to central Italy until 1944, having fought in the resistance against Nazi Germany in northern Italy during World War II. In 1969 he was

Discovered by a labourer working in a vineyard in 1934, the famed *Guerriero di Capestrano* ('Warrior of Capestrano') is a pre-Roman, native Italian work of art depicting a soldier from around the 6th century BC. Standing underneath the statue instils a feeling of unease: clad in his fighting gear, including amongst other things an axe and sword, and standing at around 2.09m or 6.85ft, the warrior is larger than life. Later investigations revealed that the vineyard in which it was found was situated above a cemetery, with no fewer than 21 graves dating from the 6th and 7th centuries BC. The statue, carved out of soft limestone from the area, is thought to have no link to the gravesite and archaeologists have argued as to whether or not the imposing work of art actually stood above a tomb.

awarded the Jerusalem Prize, given to authors who deal with issues of freedom and the individual. He died at the age of 78 in Geneva, Switzerland.

Gabriele D'Annunzio Born in 1863 as Gaetano Rapagnetta, Gabriele D'Annunzio was to become one of the most famous of all Italian writers. He was born in Pescara to relatively wealthy parents who recognised his talent from a young age. He was sent to study in Tuscany and later attended the University of Rome (La Sapienza) and began publishing newspaper articles. He soon attracted attention, mainly as a result of his dubious political leanings; he was said to be a great source of inspiration to, and influence on, the fascist Benito Mussolini.

Around the turn of the century, D'Annunzio published some of his finest works, including *Il Poema Paradisiaco* ('The Paradise Poem', 1893) and *Le Novelle della Pescara* ('The Novels of Pescara', 1902). Falling into debt at the beginning of the 1910s, he escaped to France. It was here that he met and worked with the composer Claude Debussy on the play *Le Martyre de Saint Sébastien*, a text that saw D'Annunzio's work placed on the Vatican's *Index Librorum Prohibitorum* ('List of Forbidden Books'). Returning to Italy, D'Annunzio spoke in favour of Italy's involvement on the side of the Allies in World War I, and then retired to his home in northern Italy to concentrate on his writing.

D'Annunzio is seen as one of the ideological founders of Italian fascism although his direct political involvement was minimal. In 1924, he was given the title of Prince of Montenevoso by the fascist-sympathising Italian king, Vittorio Emanuele III. He died of a stroke in 1938, aged 75. His place of birth and residence in Pescara is now a museum (see page 69).

MUSIC Abruzzo's claim to fame in the music world is as a result of the Pescara International Jazz Festival, held in July. It first took place in 1969 and has been an annual event since 1981; the 2013 festival will be the 41st. Over the years, the festival has drawn some of the biggest and best names in jazz history: Ella Fitzgerald, Duke Ellington and Woody Herman, to name a few. Recently, the producers of the festival have tried to expand the repertoire by including such artists as Bob Dylan, Gary Burton and James Taylor.

FILM A number of Italian films have either been partly or entirely filmed on location in Abruzzo. These include classics such as Fellini's *La Strada* (1985) and Lizzani's *Fontamara* (1977) as well as a score of other lesser-known films. In 2010,

George Clooney's *The American* was shot entirely on location in Abruzzo; this garnered the region a fair amount of attention on the world stage. Less known to some is the shooting of part of Sean Connery's *The Name of the Rose* (1986), an adaptation of Umberto Eco's classic novel *Il Nome della Rosa* (1980).

2

Practical Information

WHEN TO VISIT

Abruzzo is, to coin an old travel cliché, a truly 'all-year-round destination', with ancient villages, castles, lakes and rivers nestling between soaring mountains offering some of the best skiing in the country, a mere 30km from a pristine coastline.

Abruzzo's climate is Mediterranean, with hot, dry summers and cold winters (especially in the region's interior); for details, see *Climate*, page 4. However, each season has its own charm, not to mention a plethora of seasonal activities and sightseeing, no matter what the month. The spring and summer period bring pastel-coloured fields with red and purple flowers, an endless calendar of events in charming medieval towns with warm terracotta roofs and, of course, packed beaches. The months of July and August can often be relentlessly hot and dry for long periods, with days of 38–40°C. While travellers from places such as Australia will not find the sun as intense as back home, it is still powerful and protection is a must. Some years, it can be warm to hot as early as April and well into October. ✦

During the colder periods, the region opens up to lovers of winter sports, especially during the months of December to February. Snow can fall as early as October and as late as April, and during midwinter it is bitterly cold in the higher mountains. Sunny winter days can be magical in the mountains and the snow gives the towns and villages a fairy-tale appearance.

HIGHLIGHTS AND ITINERARIES

THE BEST OF ABRUZZO The following lists are intended to give an idea of the best attractions in each category – in no particular order. However, keep in mind that beauty is in the eye of the beholder.

THE MOST BEAUTIFUL VILLAGES IN ITALY

In March 2001, the Consulta del Turismo dell'Associazione dei Comuni Italiani (an alliance of Italian towns which loosely oversees matters of tourism) began the programme known as Borghi Più Belli d'Italia: the Most Beautiful Villages in Italy. The initiative ranked and categorised villages (and towns) according to aesthetic beauty but also for the likes of historical importance, art, culture and liveability. Currently, 21 of Abruzzo's towns and villages have won the right to call themselves the most beautiful villages in Italy. Interestingly, the region ranks second for the number of villages that have made the cut, preceded only by Umbria with 22 villages.

Top five medieval towns and villages, L'Aquila Province
- Santo Stefano di Sessanio, page 122
- Castelvecchio Calvisio, page 124
- Pacentro, page 195
- Scanno, page 182
- Pescocostanzo, page 195

Top five medieval towns and villages, Pescara Province
- Loreto Aprutino, page 79
- Città Sant'Angelo, page 75
- San Valentino in Abruzzo Citeriore, page 90
- Penne, page 82
- Spoltore, page 77

Top five medieval towns and villages, Teramo Province
- Atri, page 210
- Civitella del Tronto, page 225
- Campli, page 228
- Castelli, page 231
- Pietracamela, page 232

Top five medieval towns and villages, Chieti Province
- Guardiagrele, page 251
- Lanciano, page 247
- Atessa, page 254
- Carunchio, page 256
- Rocca San Giovanni, page 266

Top five churches
- Abbey of San Clemente a Casauria, page 87
- Abbey of San Giovanni in Venere, page 267
- Basilica di Santa Maria di Collemaggio, page 110
- Collegiate of Santa Maria del Colle, page 196
- Church of San Pietro ad Alba Fucense, page 133

Top five castles
- Rocca Calascio, page 123
- Ocre, page 143
- Celano, page 129
- Pacentro, page 195
- L'Aquila, page 115

Top five beaches
- Fossacesia, page 267
- Scerne di Pineto, page 214
- Pescara, page 70
- Francavilla, page 263
- Vasto, page 268

Top skiing hotspots
- Ovindoli, page 134

- Roccaraso, page 197
- Prati di Tivo, page 234

Best deserted villages
- Faraone Antico, page 225
- Albavecchio, page 133

Best war cemeteries
- Sangro River War Cemetery, page 269
- Moro River War Cemetery, page 269

SUGGESTED ITINERARIES

Spring and summer The countryside of Abruzzo comes into full bloom and forms the perfect backdrop to visits to the region's ancient towns. The rivers come into spate as the snows melt and hiking and wildlife-watching opportunities open up through the three national parks and the many natural reserves. Head for the buzzing coastal areas and enjoy sun-drenched days on the beach followed by evening strolls along the promenade.

Long weekend: around Pescara In Pescara, enjoy a Saturday-morning breakfast at La Bresciana, in the city centre. Head across the river to the old town and take in the Museum of the People of Abruzzo for a look into the history of the Abruzzesi and their culture. A five-minute walk away is the house of Gabriele D'Annunzio, one of Italy's most famous writers and a personal friend of Mussolini. Spend the afternoon shopping in the city centre before having dinner at around 20.00; it is very rare for locals to eat earlier than this. Food is important in Pescara and there are many decent restaurants. During the summer, try the fish at one of the *stabilimenti* (see page 46) that line the beaches, then stroll along the promenade and tuck into one of the city's revered *gelati* at either Chicco d'Oro (in neighbouring Montesilvano) or Bontà. If you're feeling up to it, head for the nightlife around Corso Manthonè in the old town. Spend the next day at the beach or head for the hills, visiting the historic centres of Chieti, Spoltore or Città Sant'Angelo.

Long weekend: the capitals Take a wander through the four provincial capitals: Pescara, Teramo, L'Aquila and Chieti. Spend one day in Pescara's centre and on its coast, then head to Chieti and meander through the old town centre for a few hours. From Chieti, drive the stunning SS153 then SS17 to L'Aquila and check out its imposing castle. Spend the night before moving onto Teramo to soak up the atmosphere in Piazza della Libertà.

Long weekend: around the Majella From Pescara's international airport, hire a car and head for the lower areas of the Majella National Park, taking in wonderful towns such as Abbateggio, San Valentino, Caramanico Terme and Tocco. Stay in a family-run *agriturismo*.

Long weekend: western Abruzzo By car, take the A25 from Rome International Airport. Base yourself in the fortified town of Tagliacozzo, or a town in the Sirente Velino Regional Park such as Ovindoli or Celano. Visit the ruins of the Roman towns of Alba Fucens near Avezzano and Amiternum near L'Aquila. If you have time, also take in the Grottoes of Stiffe.

One week Start in Pescara and spend a few days lazing around and soaking up the sun on the city's 16km of coastline. With a car explore the towns of one of the three national parks, taking in some wildlife spotting on the way. Alternatively, drive from Pescara through to the province of L'Aquila (steering clear of the A25 motorway) through the hills. Unfortunately, following the earthquake of April 2009, and the subsequent rebuilding efforts, visits to L'Aquila are heavily restricted to the few streets that have since reopened.

Two weeks Again, start in Pescara and then head out into the national parks, exploring the Chieti and Teramo provinces in greater depth and perhaps climbing a mountain or two (such as La Majelletta) for the excellent views. Wildlife lovers should head to the protected areas in the Majella and the National Park of Abruzzo. Explore Roman sites such as Iuvanum or the Italic sites at Schiavi d'Abruzzo. Don't forget to spend some time relaxing on Abruzzo's 130km-long coastline.

Three weeks Start in Pescara and drive the coast-hugging A14 motorway south to Vasto, perhaps stopping at Ortona, San Vito Chietino and Lanciano along the way. Head inland to the Italic temple of Schiavi d'Abruzzo and then through the National Park of Abruzzo. Base yourself at Pescassèroli and hike through the marked trails around the park. Swap the National Park of Abruzzo for the Majella National Park (about half an hour's drive) and take in some inspiring sunsets. Drive northwest to the Gran Sasso and stay at a quiet *agriturismo* on Lake Campotosto while exploring medieval villages. Return to Pescara via the Teramo coast, stopping at seaside resort towns such as Giulianova, Roseto and Pineto.

Autumn and winter A whole different perspective on the region becomes apparent during the colder months. The towns are illuminated with fairy lights, there are Christmas markets and, usually, there is plenty of snow.

Long weekend If you like skiing then this is the time to head for the hills. Land in either Pescara or Rome and travel up to the mountains of the national parks. Alternatively, for shopping and excellent food, stick around in Pescara, taking in the Christmas market and a walk on the (hopefully) sunny beach.

One or two weeks Explore the Pescara region and go skiing with some winter hiking thrown in before heading off to tour the smaller towns of the region, transformed by a blanket of thick snow.

TOURIST INFORMATION

The tourist organisation of Abruzzo, Abruzzo Promozione Turismo (APTR) (*www.abruzzoturismo.it*), provides a wealth of information on local sightseeing, accommodation, dining and tours. Their provincial head offices are as follows:

APTR Pescara Corso Vittorio Emanuele II 301; 085 4290 0212; e presidio.pescara@abruzzoturismo.it

APTR L'Aquila Piazza S Maria di Paganica 5; 0862 410808; e presidio.laquila@abruzzoturismo.it

APTR Teramo Via Guglielmo Oberdan 16; 0861 244222; e presidio.teramo@abruzzoturismo.it

APTR Chieti Via B Spaventa 47; 0871 63640; e presidio.chieti@abruzzoturismo.it

APTR Pescasseroli Via Principe di Napoli; 0864 69351; e presidio.pescasseroli@abruzzoturismo.it

TOUR OPERATORS

There are various operators running tours of Abruzzo. However, most are relatively small and many are affiliated with local tourist offices. Tourist information offices can often provide guides upon request, especially for the national and regional parks.

Absolutely Abruzzo Tours +61 7 3399 4384; e info@absolutelyabruzzo.com; www. absolutelyabruzzo.com. Luciana Masci & Michael Howard, the company's directors & well-informed guides, organise tours of Abruzzo departing at various times throughout the year. For dates & times keep an eye on the website. There are currently 2 8-day tours, 'Along the Shepherds' Tracks' & 'The Medieval Magic of Abruzzo', taking in many towns, castles & parks. There is also a 3-day 'Gourmet Getaway' tour. Prices for the 8-day tours start at around £3,000 (US$4,800/AU$4,700) pp, including meals, accommodation, drinks &

transport, but not flights to/from Rome or Pescara. The company is based in Queensland, Australia.
Abruzzo Cibus m 329 9854121; e info@ abruzzocibus.com; www.abruzzocibus.com. Based in the town of Carunchio, in the province of Chieti, Abruzzo Cibus runs 3- & 7-day cooking classes & culinary tours of the region, as well as short general tours. The itineraries are varied, informative & fun.
Luciano Di Gregorio www.lucianodigregorio. com. The author of this guide runs various guided tours of Abruzzo, for individuals, couples or groups, which can be tailored to specific needs. See website for details on current tours.

RED TAPE

VISAS Abruzzo is a region of the Italian Republic and therefore bound by all internal entry regulations as well as those governed or required by the European Union and the Schengen Agreement. In addition to citizens of European Union member states, holders of passports from the following areas do not need a visa for stays of 90 days or less: Andorra, Argentina, Australia, Brazil, Brunei, Canada, Chile, Costa Rica, El Salvador, Guatemala, Honduras, Hong Kong, Israel, Japan, Malaysia, Macao, Mexico, Monaco, New Zealand, Nicaragua, Panama, Paraguay, South Korea, Singapore, Switzerland, United States, Uruguay and Venezuela.

Theoretically, all foreigners are required to register their presence with the police within eight days of their arrival in the country, but in practice few people bother; in any case, your hotel should take your passport and residence details for this exact purpose.

For citizens of non-EU countries, remaining legally in Italy for longer than 90 days can be rather difficult. Italy currently offers around 21 types of entry visas, few of which are entirely clear in their regulations and limitations, let alone in their explanation of what's required in order to secure one. The most common types of foreign visa are those based on study, work and elective residence.

Study visas A study visa requires you to have proof of the following:

- Intended accommodation
- Financial support of no less than around €350 per calendar month
- Ability to cover medical expenses (such as private health insurance)
- Funds to be able to return to your own country
- An intended place of study

Work visas Work visas are not easy to procure. You must already have secured a position from an Italian employer, who is then required to file the required paperwork. Although many people work in bars and restaurants without valid

2

visas, this is not advisable, particularly given the government's recent crackdown on illegal immigration and employment.

Employment It is now harder than ever to secure employment in Abruzzo, particularly if you need sponsorship for a work visa. Though Abruzzo's rate of unemployment is lower than the national average, the job market is extremely competitive and is coping with locals trying to make a living as well as those coming up in search of work from the southern regions of Italy.

Elective residence visas Ever wondered how it works when someone ups and moves to the supposed idyll of rural Italy? Well, if you've ever asked yourself how they legally remain in the country, it is the elective residence visa that does the trick. It sounds easy but it's not: you must have substantial proof of private income from the likes of properties and a pension.

EMBASSIES AND CONSULATES There are no foreign embassies or consulates in the region of Abruzzo.

Overseas

❸ Australia 12 Grey St, Deakin, Canberra, ACT 2600; ☎+61 2 6273 3333; e ambasciata. canberra@esteri.it; www.ambcanberra.esteri.it; ☉ Mon–Fri 09.00–12.00

❸ Canada 275 Slater St, 21st Floor, Ottawa, Ontario K1P 5H9; ☎+1 613 232 2401; e ambasciata.ottawa@esteri.it; www.ambottawa. esteri.it; ☉ Mon–Tue & Thu–Fri 09.00–12.00, Wed 09.00–12.00 & 14.00–16.00

❸ Ireland 63/65 Northumberland Rd, Dublin 4; ☎+353 1 660 1744; e ambasciata.dublino@

esteri.it; www.ambdublino.esteri.it; ☉ Mon–Wed & Fri 10.00–12.00, Thu 13.30–15.30

❸ UK Consulate 14 Three Kings Yd, London W1K 4EH; ☎+44 20 7312 2200; e ambasciata.londra@ esteri.it; www.amblondra.esteri.it; ☉ Mon–Fri 09.00–12.00

❸ USA Consulate 690 Park Av, NY 10065; ☎+1 202 612 4400; e info.newyork@esteri.it; www.ambwashingtondc.esteri.it; ☉ Mon–Fri 09.00–17.00

GETTING THERE AND AWAY

BY AIR

To Pescara Abruzzo airport (*Via Tiburtina Km 229,100, 65131 Pescara;* ☎*895 898 9512; www.abruzzoairport.com*), ten minutes by bus from the centre of Pescara, is the main gateway to the region. Passenger numbers have risen over 400% over the last decade and an increasing number of international airlines are now using this small though often busy airport.

From UK and Ireland
✈ **Ryanair** www.ryanair.com. Flights to & from London Stansted. During off-peak times, flights are reduced to 2–4 a week, depending on the time of year. From May to Oct, flights operate daily. Prices from £0.01 (excluding taxes).

From continental Europe
✈ **Alitalia** ☎06 65649, call centre from Italy ☎892010; www.alitalia.com. Daily direct flights to & from Milan.

✈ **FlyOnAir** www.flyonair.it. Flights from Pescara to Sicily, Sardinia, Crete & Croatia. Prices from €29.99 (excluding taxes).
✈ **Ryanair** www.ryanair.com. Flights to & from 'Frankfurt' Hahn, Girona (for Barcelona), Eindhoven (for Amsterdam), Düsseldorf, Oslo, Beauvais (for Paris) & Charleroi (for Brussels). Prices from £0.01 (excluding taxes).

Domestic flights

✈ **Air Vallee** ☏ 01 6530 3303; www.airvallee. com. Flights from Turin. Frequency varies according to season.

✈ **Ryanair** www.ryanair.com. Flights to & from Bergamo (for Milan), & Cagliari in Sardinia. Prices can be as low as €2.50 including taxes.

To Rome

Many will find it more convenient to fly to Rome and travel from there to Abruzzo. Rome's **Fiumicino Airport** (*www.adr.it*) is a 2½-hour drive from the centre of Pescara and only 45 minutes from the border between Abruzzo and Lazio. Numerous international airlines from the UK, USA and elsewhere service the airport.

If you do not have your own transport, there are various options for getting to Abruzzo from Rome. The quickest is via the airport train terminal to Rome's Tiburtina station. From there, buses are available to the larger cities such as Pescara. To travel on by train you must head for Rome's Termini station. Be aware that while the bus journey takes around 2½ hours, the train can often take four hours. See below and page 32 for details.

Alternatively, Rome **Ciampino airport** is approximately 15km southeast of the centre of Rome. It is a major hub for both Ryanair and easyJet, so you may well find yourself arriving here. From the UK, there are flights from numerous regional airports as well as from London. To get to Abruzzo from here by public transport, it is necessary to make your way into the centre of Rome and out again by either train or bus from Tiburtina station. Should you wish to hire a car, you will find all of the major hire firms situated south of the departure hall.

From the USA

Flights leave most major American cities on a daily basis bound for Rome. Airlines include Continental, American, United and Delta. Flight times vary depending on the city of departure. However, expect an eight-hour flight from New York and 13 hours from the likes of Los Angeles and San Francisco.

From Australia and New Zealand

Flights leaving from Melbourne, Sydney, Brisbane, Adelaide, Perth and Auckland all connect with flights direct to Rome from Asian cities such as Singapore, Bangkok, Kuala Lumpur and Hong Kong. Airlines include Qantas, Singapore, Thai, Cathay and Air New Zealand. Expect a total of around 24 hours in transit from Melbourne and Sydney, and around 27 hours from Auckland.

BY COACH

A number of coach companies operate services from various European countries to Abruzzo. Check out www.busweb.it for information on services including times, prices and booking options.

International services

Below is a list of countries from which there are coach services to Pescara, together with the relevant operator and website. Note that long-distance coach tickets are unlikely to be any cheaper than a low-cost flight from a budget airline. Not to mention a likely sore bum after hours on a bus.

From	Company
Albania	Baltour (*www.baltour.it*)
Bulgaria	Atlassib (*www.atlassib.ro*)
	Eurolines (*www.eurolines.co.uk*)
Czech Republic	Eurolines (*www.eurolines.co.uk*)
Germany	SAPS (*www.sapsbusline.it*)

Latvia	Eurolines (*www.eurolines.co.uk*)
Lithuania	Eurolines (*www.eurolines.co.uk*)
Luxembourg	FNM (*www.fnmautoservizi.it*)
Moldavia	Atlassib (*www.atlassib.ro*)
Poland	Eurobus Trans Service (*www.eurobus.pl*)
	Superpol (*www.superpol.com.pl*)
	Bispol (*www.bispol.com*)
	Eurolines (*www.eurolines.co.uk*)
Romania	Atlassib (*atlassib.ro*)
	Ognivia (*www.ognivia.ro*)
Switzerland	Baltour (*www.baltour.it*)
Ukraine	Trans Eurolines (*www.eurolines.com*)

National services Autolinee Regionali Pubbliche Abruzzesi (✆ *800 762622; www.arpaonline.it*), commonly known as ARPA, **Di Febo Capuani** (✆ *085 946 2119; www.difebocapuani.com*) and **Di Fonzo** (✆ *087 336 4536; www.difonzobus. com*) operate alternating regular services from Rome to Pescara. One-way from Rome costs €15 at the ticket office and €16 on board. There are nine scheduled departures per day. ARPA also connects Pescara with Naples, and nearby Salerno, which will set you back around €20.

Gruppo La Panoramica (✆ *085 421 0733; www.gruppolapanoramica.it*) has services from the northern Italian cities of Sanremo (€42), Genova (€34) and Bologna (€24). These are not straight-through services but stop along the way in places such as Ancona, Rimini and Parma.

BY TRAIN Travelling through Europe by train is an immensely rewarding way of reaching Abruzzo, and if you are coming from the UK it also means you can make stops along the way. Take the Eurostar (*www.eurostar.com*) across the Channel and connect with services to Italy.

Ferrovie dello Stato (✆ *06 44101; www.ferroviedellostato.it*), otherwise known as Trenitalia, operates the country's rail network. Pescara is a key stop along the Adriatic train route linking Milan with the southern city of Lecce, via Bologna, Ancona and Bari. The four hours 20 minute trip on the Eurostar (high-speed) train to Milan will set you back around €70, while the 6½-hour trip on the regional train costs only €40.

European rail passes are a great way to get around the continent and there are many different types. **EURail** (*www.eurail.com*) provides a wealth of information on the various types of passes available. In London, you can also visit the **Rail Europe Travel Centre** (*193 Piccadilly, London W1J 9EU;* ✆ *0844 848 4064;* e *reservations@ raileurope.co.uk; www.raileurope.co.uk;* ⊕ *Mon–Fri 10.00–18.00, Sat 10.00–17.00*).

The train from Rome to Pescara can take anything up to five hours, due to the number and location of the stops. A ticket to Pescara is €11.70 for second class. Expect to pay €10.50 for a connecting service to L'Aquila. As trains will go via Pescara or even Ancona in some instances, taking a train from Rome to Teramo is inconvenient.

BY FERRY Ferry services to Pescara from Hvar (Stari Grad) and Split in Croatia are run by **SNAV** (*www.snav.it*). Journey times from Split are approximately five hours and 45 minutes, travelling via Hvar (three hours and 45 minutes). Tickets can be bought through the **Sanmar** agency (*www.sanmar.it*) at Pescara's port, from where the ferries depart. Passage for an adult during high season costs €89, and bringing your own vehicle will cost a further €95 or so. All passengers are subject to a €2 tax, not included in the ticket price.

DINING ON THE MOTORWAY

Autogrill (*www.autogrill.it*), with its instantly recognisable logo of a white 'A' on a red background, is an Italian institution, with outlets dotted all along the nation's motorway network. Starting with one restaurant in 1946, the chain has grown to over 900 restaurants. Dining options vary according to the size of the restaurant: some of the bigger establishment offer full buffet-style sit-down meals, whilst most display an assortment of *focaccias* and sandwiches with a myriad different meats and cheeses. Not to mention salad bars, fruit baskets, biscuits and an array of cakes, tarts and pastries to put a French *boulangerie* to shame. You will also find maps, reading material, CDs and other road-trip essentials. Most importantly, no trip on an Italian *autostrada* is complete without an Autogrill espresso. However, be aware that as many travellers use Autogrill, their car parks are, from time to time, targeted by thiefs looking to steal your belongings. Unfortunately, locking your car does not help. Make sure you do not leave any valuables unattended.

BY CAR Italy's extensive network of motorways (*autostrade*) is well kept and equipped. It's run by **Autostrade per L'Italia** (*www.autostrade.it*) who seem to put the money they rake in from the toll system to good use. It's rare for Italians to fly domestically although the increasing number of low-cost carriers is slowly changing this. Abruzzo is well serviced by autostrade. The A14, running straight through coastal Abruzzo, is the major Adriatic artery linking the southern city of Taranto with Bologna, from where it changes into the A1 to Milan and beyond. The A24 links Rome with the provincial capitals of L'Aquila and Teramo, while the A25 crosses the peninsula from Rome to Pescara. Use of the autostrade is tolled on a distance basis. A one-way journey from Rome to Pescara costs around €16, to L'Aquila around €8 and to Teramo approximately €11. From Pescara to Milan, expect to pay upwards of €35. The website includes a journey planner.

Car rental For international car-hire firms, see page 55. Companies include Hertz, Avis, Europcar, Sixt and the Italian Maggiore. Most have offices in all the major cities and towns.

HEALTH AND SAFETY

HEALTH Aside from the risks posed by exposure to the sun (both in summer and winter), and the nuisance of mosquitoes, health issues in Abruzzo are no different from those in other Westernised countries.

Travellers with any form of **mobility problems**, though, will find the cobbled streets of medieval towns a considerable challenge, and few of the provincial towns have any form of access facilities for the disabled. That said, one of the organisations that offer services to travellers with disabilities is Accessible Italy (\ *+378 941111; www.accessibleitaly.com*). More information can also be found through Able Travel Accessible Adventures (*www.able-travel.com*).

SAFETY Whilst Abruzzo, as with most of Italy, is generally a safe place to travel, a sensible level of awareness is advised. This is particularly true in Pescara, where you should keep an eye on your belongings, especially in and around the station.

2

Women travelling alone Women travelling alone or in small groups should not encounter any particular problems in Abruzzo, especially in the countryside. If possible, try to avoid arriving or leaving the stations of Pescara, Chieti, Teramo and L'Aquila too late at night. There have been problems and complaints in the past of things such as bag snatching, harassment, etc, though no more or less than in any other cities of their size throughout Europe.

The beaches of coastal Abruzzo are generally a safe place for lone women to be. This is also true of the nightlife in and around the *stabilimenti*, which are often patrolled.

GLBT travellers Attitudes towards gay, lesbian, bisexual and transgender people are consistent with those of the rest of Italy outside the bigger cities. A normal amount of discretion is advised. You are unlikely to be harassed in the provincial capitals, though the residents of country towns are likely to display a mixture of confusion and animosity, especially teenagers and the elderly. However, hotel workers are unlikely to question a gay or lesbian couple requesting a double room.

Pescara has its own gay nightclub, bar and sauna, Phoenix (see page 63), though it has recently been subjected to a spate of homophobic attacks on cars parked around the venue. There is a section of beach in the area of Scerne di Pineto which is frequented by many gays and lesbians, especially on Sundays.

PHOTOGRAPHY   *Peter Franc (www.peterfranc.com)*

Abruzzo's landscapes are incredible but often when you get back home your holiday photographs don't do the destination justice. This need not be the case and a small amount of preparation can improve your pictures no end. A creative eye, good timing and patience are often what's needed. But if you want to make your photos even better consider taking along a few extra items.

RECOMMENDED GEAR

Tripods A tripod allows shooting in low light and allows the use of camera settings that enhance the quality of your photos. Essentially, it may be the difference between having a photo and having a blurry mess. When shooting landscapes with a tripod, consider putting your camera into manual mode and using an aperture of f11 or higher. Your shutter speed will likely be a few seconds long, but the higher aperture will result in a crisper image. When doing this, it is important to keep your ISO low, preferably on 100, so as to keep 'noise' (that grainy look) to a minimum. If you're shooting in automatic, use the 'landscape' camera setting that's on most cameras, even professional DSLR ones, as it will boost colours and optimise image settings. If a tripod is too cumbersome for your trip, consider propping your camera on a high wall, windowsill or even your backpack. Just make sure you keep hold of the strap!

Wide-angle lens These are perfect for travel and landscape photography. A lens that starts at a focal length of around 18mm on a full-frame camera (or 12mm on a crop sensor camera, such as most entry-level DSLRs) is probably the single most important piece of equipment to bring to Abruzzo, particularly if you're heading into the mountains or to those medieval towns.

When shooting 'wide', much more of the scene will be captured than you would expect. It is important to choose and compose your scenes carefully. Due to the extreme perspective being captured, shooting 'wide' often results in things looking

Despite some recent concerns, attitudes are slowly relaxing with growing awareness of the issue of discrimination towards GLBT men and women in Italy, and is being discussed in media and politics. However, drastic change is unlikely to take place, given the pressures and influences of the Vatican City, a short distance (physically and metaphorically) from the central government in Rome.

WHAT TO TAKE

Although the days are gone when even travelling from one town to the next meant a day on the road, this does not mean that you will find everything you could possibly need in Abruzzo. It is advisable to visit a travel or electronics shop in your country of origin and purchase a plug adapter or power converter, so as to not be stranded without a working shaver, hairdryer or mobile phone charger.

Definitely worth a place in your suitcase are your favourite pair of trunks, bikini or swimming costume, a good beach towel and a pair of sunglasses. Especially if you come from the UK or northern America, much of the year will be warm enough for a dip or a walk down the beach. The region has very few pebble beaches, but the ones that are tend to be less crowded and therefore have cleaner water, so you might like to pack a pair of beach flip-flops.

very small. When shooting a large space, get close to an object in the foreground; it will not only give context to the picture, but also create a comparison to show just how grand your scene is. Another good tip is to get up high; it will add depth and perspective to your scene. Where you can, it is also a good idea to include a person in your landscape, to give an idea of scale and add a human element to your scene.

Polarising filter Although they can be pricy, polarising filters can be a sound investment as they eliminate reflection in water resulting in deeper colours with more contrast. This works not only for lakes, but also for the moisture in the atmosphere; clouds appear whiter, and the sky a much deeper blue.

Shooting conditions Amazing photos can be taken from any kind of camera (or even your phone): it's essentially about capturing a mood or a special moment. Take for example one of the many sunsets you're likely to want to record, particularly in the countryside. To allow for some variety between your sunset photos, consider capturing people's impressions of the sunset. It could be your friends, a local villager, other tourists, a tree silhouette or a cat lazing on the ground. Remember to look around and consider what the fading sunlight is highlighting behind you as well. Look up, look down, and – whenever you leave an area – look behind you on the way out.

Warm Mediterranean hues are unsurpassed in Abruzzo and those who rise early to take advantage of the first hour after sunrise will be richly rewarded with not only golden light for excellent photographs, but opportunities for scenes that are unlikely to be as interesting during the middle of the day. The same can be said for the hour or two before sunset: as the light fades, it becomes softer and brings out richer colours. Due to the high mountain ranges, the skies of Abruzzo present some striking cloud formations. Consider shooting a lot of sky with a small amount of land for some variety in the photos you bring home.

Given the region's mountainous terrain it is likely that you will be doing a lot of exploring on foot, so do bring some comfortable shoes. If you intend to do some heavy-duty hiking, a good pair of boots is recommended, especially in the colder, wetter months; otherwise a sturdy pair of trainers or shoes will suffice. The taller mountain ranges can be a little fresh during summer as well, so you might consider packing a pullover or long-sleeve cotton top. If you intend to do some camping, the usual gadgets like penknives, bottle and can openers will come in handy.

Cash cards and Visa are accepted in most of the more populous corners of the region, though do carry cash if you plan to go off the beaten track (see *Money and banking*, below, for details on using cards in Abruzzo).

ELECTRICITY In common with the rest of mainland Europe, Italy uses electricity at a current of 220 volts at 50 cycles per second (50Hz). Plug adapters and power converters can be purchased from electronic stores. You may see wall sockets with extended or bigger holes. These are known as Schuko grounded sockets and can be used with larger appliances for extra safety.

MAPS

Maps of Abruzzo can be found at bookshops such as Librerie Universitarie (in cities such as Chieti and L'Aquila) and the larger chain La Feltrinelli (which has a branch in Pescara, see page 67) as well as at tourist information points.

De Agostini (℅ *199 120120; www.deagostini.it*) publishes excellent maps of the region including province maps and town plans. Many of these are prepared on behalf of Abruzzo Promozione Turismo (see page 28), and are available free at tourist information points (though these are usually the less detailed town plans). The company issues a 1:250,000 regional map of Abruzzo as well as a smaller one at 1:200,000 (versions of which are available through tourist offices). Touring Club Italiano (℅ *02 575473; www.touringclub.com*) also publishes a good road map of Abruzzo which is available at bookshops.

Walking maps of Abruzzo are available from the relevant tourist offices. For instance, if you are walking in the Val Fondillo (see page 175), an excellent walking map is available from Abruzzo Promozione Turismo in Pescasseroli and at the entrance to the valley for €5. Similarly, skiing maps are available free at tourist offices in the relevant towns. These are usually not very detailed, but you should be able to use the information listed in the skiing areas in this guide in conjunction with the tourist-office maps in order to make informed choices about your skiing.

MONEY AND BANKING

Italy's national currency is the euro (€). There are banks all over the region, though it is important to note that, at times, Italy's ATM connections with the rest of the world are unreliable. These issues are slowly being rectified, though you may find that you are unable to withdraw money for hours at a time from non-Italian bank accounts. This is especially true of connections with English banks, but, oddly, less so with smaller Australian banks, building societies and credit unions. Strangely enough, this problem does not present itself when paying by credit or debit card at a store or restaurant.

Credit cards are accepted at most major points of sale as well as restaurants and hotels. However, to avoid any embarrassing situations, it is advised that you ring ahead and confirm this, particularly with restaurants.

BANKS AND BANKING Amenities in Abruzzo can be very few and far between. If there is a bank with an ATM in a town or village, then this has been listed in the following chapters. However, you should not expect just to turn up and find such amenities everywhere. Abruzzo is very different from the more touristy parts of central Italy such as Tuscany and Umbria and still has the feel of travelling off the beaten track, which is, after all, part of its charm.

Banks open Monday to Friday at 08.30 and close for lunch at 13.00. Afternoon hours are 14.45–16.00.

BUDGETING Abruzzo is not a particularly expensive region compared with its more visited counterparts such as Tuscany and Umbria, or cities like Rome and Milan. This is particularly true in the current economic climate, where shops and food outlets need to remain competitive. On a shoestring, excluding accommodation, you could probably get by on around €15–20 (£10–15) a day for food, drink and the occasional bus to the beach or the next town. I have made do with a €2 breakfast (a cappuccino and jam croissant), €5 lunch (two slices of pizza and a bottle of water at the beach), a €10 dinner (a plate of pasta and a glass of wine) and €2 of bus fares. If your budget is mid-priced, then you can expect to do well on around €30, again, not including accommodation. This will allow for better meals at a good restaurant. At the extreme end of the spectrum, you can treat yourself as you would in a world-class metropolis, and maybe even a whole lot better for a whole lot less. Around €60 a day will get you excellent meals and even a taxi here and there. For accommodation budgeting, see page 38.

GETTING AROUND

BY CAR Some parts of Abruzzo have sparse public transport connections so, unless you are only visiting Pescara, this is the quickest and most convenient way of getting around. See page 55 for details on car hire.

BY BUS ARPA (see page 32) is Abruzzo's main bus and coach company and the method of public transport generally preferred by the Abruzzesi. Services are particularly good, especially to and from the four major cities, but also amongst the smaller provincial towns.

BY TRAIN Whilst getting to and from the region by train can be time-consuming, train travel within the region can often be worthwhile – but only if you intend to move up and down the coast or in a westerly direction from Pescara. As Abruzzo is on the main railway line connecting the southern Adriatic coast to the northern cities, travelling by train can be a particularly convenient way if you are moving between the coastal hubs. The other line connects Pescara to Rome, east to west, and cutting straight through the region.

BY BICYCLE Getting around by bicycle in the provincial capitals can be ideal – distances are relatively short. In Pescara, there is the added benefit of the *strada parco* (road through the park), which runs the length of the whole city between the Via Nazionale (the main thoroughfare through the city) and the Riviera. A disused railway line, the *strada parco* has been paved and is lined with trees and residential buildings.

Getting around the rest of the region by bicycle should not present a problem, although you should be aware that many country roads are in poor condition and will leave you wishing you had caught a bus instead. So, too, might the constant rolling hills right up to the coastline; you'll need a certain level of fitness for longer bike trips.

ACCOMMODATION

There is certainly no shortage of accommodation in Abruzzo. The domestic tourist market as well as the slow stream of international tourists has awakened many Abruzzesi to the need for accommodation, and hotels, bed and breakfasts and *pensioni* are popping up quicker than you can say 'vacancy'. In fact, even just ten years ago the situation was entirely different, particularly in the countryside, where finding a night's rest could be a chore unless you had your own transport. Now, while you won't be spoilt for choice in some of the smaller rural villages, this is no longer the case, especially in the developed coastal areas.

Due to the popularity of said coastal areas during the months of July and August, it pays to book well in advance. This is a must for the entire month of August, when the whole country shuts down and grinds to a halt, Italians all over the peninsula stop pretending to work and the beaches fill up quickly. The mountain areas can also be a popular place to spend the holidays and whilst not jam-packed, may present problems to those who have not pre-booked. June can often be just as hot as July but then, as with the rest of the year, accommodation is readily available.

The star-rating system seems to mean very little in Abruzzo; I often wondered how the most luxurious hotels along the coast could manage to rake up only three to four stars. However, the rating system does give an idea of what type of accommodation you might expect, especially at the lower end of the scale. A one-star hotel in the cities may be an indication of very simple, sometimes shabby rooms with a bathroom that's shared, at times, amongst multiple rooms. However, you will find many one-star establishments in the villages and countryside are often cleaner, friendlier and better equipped than two- or three-star hotels in the cities. While there are very few five-star establishments, expect an excellent level of service whenever you encounter four stars, particularly along the coast. Many three-star hotels offer the same level of service and amenities that you would expect from a four-star establishment but at more attractive prices. In conjunction with the reviews in this guide, it's worth looking at one of the accommodation review sites on the internet, such as www.tripadvisor.com, before you part with your money. That said, because the region has not yet opened up to mass tourism, it is likely that you will only find reviews of the bigger establishments along the coast.

Most organisations, with the exception of the smaller, cheaper hotels and guesthouses (particularly away from the coast), have a website, booking system and email. Although a great many are in Italian, English is fairly well spoken and you should not have any problems with basic things such as bookings. Prices and packages are usually clearly explained, though keep in mind that some websites list prices on a per person basis, particularly for coastal hotels. Taxes are almost always included in the price, though some things, such as the use of beach facilities, may require an extra fee to be paid. Hotel listings in this guide reflect the price of a double room during high season. Where half- and full-board options are available, these are generally indicated by 'HB' and 'FB'.

HOTELS A great many hotels in Abruzzo offer three types of accommodation: full board, half board and bed and breakfast. Unless an establishment's website clearly specifies different prices for the accommodation options it offers, assume

$$$$$	£100+	US$160+	€120+
$$$$	£75–100	US$120–160	€90–120
$$$	£50–75	US$80–120	€60–90
$$	£25–50	US$40–80	€30–60
$	<£25	<US$40	<€30

it is a standard case of room and breakfast. **Full-board** packages include your accommodation and three meals (breakfast, lunch and dinner), while **half-board** includes only two meals (breakfast and either lunch or dinner). These options are usually very reasonably priced and a good way to avoid eating all your meals out, which can become expensive.

A decent three-star double room (including breakfast) in a city location will set you back around €50–80, depending on location and season.

In rural areas, you might come across 'diffused hotels', such as the one in Santo Stefano. Such establishments usually have a central administration office/reception area, with rooms 'diffused', as the name suggests, across a particular town. They essentially function as hotels though there is the added benefit of more privacy and, usually, larger rooms or apartments.

PENSIONS *Pensioni*, as they are known in Italian, are essentially guesthouses (usually run by a family) offering room, shared bathroom and breakfast. A no-frills option, these can be a great alternative to the more pricy hotels and often present the chance to meet local people. A room in a pension can be as cheap as €30 for two people.

BED AND BREAKFAST Traditional bed and breakfasts are not common in Abruzzo. There are a few scattered around, particularly in the countryside, and these usually offer friendly accommodation and a great, hearty breakfast. A room plus breakfast in a rural location is often good value for money and will set you back around €50 – more expensive than a pension, but usually rather nicer too.

HOSTELS I've yet to encounter an Abruzzese who understands the concept of a hostel and does not screw up their nose in distaste. Hostels are scarce in this part of the world and are generally only found in the larger cities and towns beyond the region, although there is one in Chieti Province on the edge of Majella National Park.

APARTMENTS Away from the coast, there are not many opportunities to rent apartments unless you know someone who has an empty place. Along the coast, there are a variety of private apartments for hire and some of the larger hotels offer apartments and suites at a fixed weekly price. As they are self-contained, these usually don't include breakfast. In places like Montesilvano, which has become increasingly popular with French and German tourists, such apartments can cost around €300 per week for two bedrooms/four people.

AGRITURISMI *Agriturismi* (singular *agriturismo*) are essentially farmstays, and you will find these dotted all over regional Abruzzo. They can be quite varied in their accommodation options, which can range from hostel style to bed and breakfast style. Some are very rustic country establishments; others are quite sophisticated with swimming pools and all mod cons. Be aware that owners are unlikely to speak English: as a generalisation, these establishments are run by older locals.

RIFUGIOS In mountainous areas, you'll sometimes come across isolated *rifugios*, which are ideal for walkers. These vary from the simplest of mountain huts, offering dormitory accommodation and basic meals, to purpose-built places with plenty of mod cons – and higher-than-expected prices that reflect the high costs of access.

CAMPING Given Abruzzo's popularity with trekkers and hikers, not to mention the three national parks, there is an abundance of campsites and, to a lesser extent, caravan parks all over the region. Most have good facilities. If you're hiking, you can expect to pay around €5–10 for a small tent for two people.

FOOD AND DRINK

Many visitors to Abruzzo, both Italian and foreign, claim that the food is one of the highlights of their stay. Indeed, many of the region's fairs and festivals revolve around food, and eating is at the core of Abruzzo's culture.

Eating out in Abruzzo is quite a simple and hassle-free affair: the quality of food and drink will be good to excellent anywhere you go. This is especially true of smaller towns. Furthermore, Abruzzo has a fine culture of casual eating alongside proper dining. The food that you encounter at street kiosks and bars is almost always of great quality. In fact, when visiting a town or village, don't hesitate to walk into a restaurant that looks more like someone's kitchen or living room than a posh restaurant; your meal is likely to be even more memorable.

So it's a lazy Sunday in Pescara, and you're keen to make the most of the region's gastronomic delights. Here's how:

BREAKFAST Get up early and head to your local bar. There is one at every street corner, so you probably needn't go very far. Order a *bomba* and a cappuccino, sit and do some people watching.

LUNCH Head to a restaurant, or, better yet, get invited to the home of a local. Here, enjoy a filling plate of *sagne e fagioli*. After your hearty meal, sip a *genziana* liqueur.

AFTERNOON SNACK At about 17.00, take yourself to a *pasticceria* (patisserie) for an espresso accompanied by two *pizzelle* filled with a mixture of jam and chocolate spread such as Nutella, a snack favoured by the Pescaresi.

DINNER Find a trattoria for the best *arrosticini* in the region. It is very common to eat at least 20 of these, accompanied by toasted bread with a dash of oil. Follow your meal with a saffron liqueur.

A TASTE OF ABRUZZO Below is a selection of pasta, meat and sweet dishes that you might expect to encounter on your trip to Abruzzo.

Maccheroni alla chitarra Traditional *maccheroni* is not like the short tubes of pasta found outside of Italy. When made 'alla chitarra' (*chitarra* means 'guitar'), it is a dish of square, spaghetti-like strands of pasta made from water, flour and eggs. The dough is kneaded into long strips about 10cm wide and then rolled over

Pasta is close to the heart of every Abruzzese: not only because it is a daily staple but also because Abruzzo is home to one of the largest pasta-making industries in the country, competing with the southern region of Campania. The region boasts no fewer than 13 pasta producers, the largest concentration of which are found in the province of Chieti.

The small town of Fara San Martino (see page 259) is home to Di Cecco and Delverde, two of the nation's largest pasta producers, as well as Pasta Cocco, which makes pasta for the Vatican City.

Generally when pasta is produced on an industrial scale, it is dried at high temperatures to make the pasta rigid and allow it to keep well in packets. In Abruzzo, the most common process is to use bronze drawing blocks that dry the pasta slowly and gently at lower temperatures for as long as 50–60 hours. This helps the pasta develop a slightly rough surface that will hold the accompanying sauce better.

a 'guitar' (hence the name), to give it its square look. The most common sauce with *maccheroni alla chitarra* is a simple *napoletana* (Neapolitan): tomato, a hint of garlic and perhaps some basil. However, many restaurants in Abruzzo also make the dish with a mushroom and truffle sauce.

Sagne e fagioli   There is hardly a single Abruzzese (including me) who did not grow up to the delights of *nonna*'s homemade *sagne e fagioli*. It is a simple pasta made from egg, flour and water. The dough is rolled flat and cut into strips about 8–10cm wide. Multiple strips (about five or six) are then placed on top of each other and the pasta is cut to make many smaller strips about 0.5cm wide and about 5cm in length. The pasta is then cooked and placed in a large saucepan with a fairly thin tomato sauce (almost half way between a soup and a thick pasta sauce) and the key ingredients, beans – white beans or kidney beans.

Scrippelle   *Scrippelle* are omelette-like crêpes made from egg, flour and water. There are many versions of *scrippelle* throughout Abruzzo, although the following two are the most popular. The first is the *scrippelle 'mbusse* which traditionally comes from Teramo Province. *'Mbusse* is a dialect phrase implying that the *scrippelle* are 'wet'. They are made in a frying pan, rolled into a long roll and served in a hot chicken broth-style sauce. The other common way to have *scrippelle* is to simply pour a tomato-based sauce over them and then to add some grated parmesan.

Ravioli dolci di ricotta   Sweet ravioli are a speciality of Abruzzo, mostly enjoyed during festivities. They are larger than normal ravioli and the ricotta filling has an interesting twist: mixed with egg yolk, sugar, lemon and cinnamon. The most common sauce to accompany sweet ravioli is a simple tomato sauce with no meat. However, they can also be served with a thin layer of sugar and a hint of cinnamon on top.

Timballo   What English speakers know as lasagna is actually called *timballo* in Abruzzo. Whilst not a traditional preparation of the region, it is one of the most common dishes to be served at large family get-togethers such as Easter and Christmas.

Arrosticini Of all the dishes covered here, *arrosticini* is no doubt the most popular. Essentially, *arrosticini* are mutton kebabs, although the meat on the skewers is much smaller than a traditional kebab. The meat, which is a dark red colour (depending on the age at which the animal has been slaughtered), is cut into cubes using a special container with blades. It is then threaded onto skewers; one skewer complete with meat will weigh about 40g and always includes around 20% fat for flavour. The meat is then grilled on what, in its domestic version, is essentially a large, long tray with four legs (it comes to about waist height) and filled with lit charcoal. They are usually generously salted to taste and eaten immediately for the tenderness and flavour of the hot meat.

Pizze fritte If arrosticini are the most popular of the foods covered here, then the much loved pizze fritte are not far behind. Usually about the size of a small dinner plate, they are made of normal pizza dough and are shallow fried rather than oven baked. Depending on which part of Abruzzo you are in, they can either be as thick as two fingers together and therefore fluffly or thinner and much crunchier. And yes: you will have a preference. They are the perfect accompaniment to *arrosticini*.

Porchetta abruzzese The making of roast pork in Abruzzo is a long-standing tradition, mentioned as far back as the 15th century. It is hard work, made from the entire carcass of the animal usually weighing around 100kg. The pig is boned though the head remains completely intact. The meat is cooked slowly and, importantly, flavoured with salt and spices. The most essential of these are rosemary, some pepper and garlic; the last is boiled in water and then evenly spread over the meat. The entire carcass is roasted in the oven for around four to six hours.

Parrozzo cake Parrozzo, which is actually a registered brand name and only produced in the province of Pescara, is one of Abruzzo's most popular cakes. The dough is beaten and kneaded, then ground peach and apricot kernels are added before it is baked in the oven and coated in a thin layer of dark chocolate. It is always made in a shape that resembles a church dome.

Pizzelle Pizzelle, essentially sweet wafers, go by different names in various parts of Abruzzo (*neole*, *nevole*, *ferratelle*, *cancellate*). Whatever they're called, they are the most traditional of Abruzzese sweets. The soft dough is made from eggs, flour, water and sugar and is spooned onto a patterned waffle iron then squashed between the two hot plates. The resulting *pizzelle* is then left to cool and can be served plain or with jam or Nutella.

Bombe Bombe (singular *bomba*) are fried doughnuts filled with *crema*, like a custard. (As an aside, the Italian for 'cream' is *panna*.) The dough is made from egg, flour and water and is fried before squeezing the custard into the doughnut. *Bombe* are an extremely popular breakfast food, usually served with a cappuccino, and as such are offered in most bars in Abruzzo. They are particularly popular on a Sunday morning, so you will need to get there early.

Ciambella Another popular breakfast cake is the simple *ciambella*. The dough is made from eggs, flour, water, sugar and, often, grated lemon peel, and is poured into a round cake tray with a large hole in the middle (like a *Kugelhupf*). It is oven baked and left to cool before being served with coffee or a glass of hot milk.

RESTAURANT PRICE CODES

Based on average price of a main course

$$$$$	£20+	US$30+	€25+
$$$$	£12–20	US$19–30	€15–25
$$$	£9–12	US$14–19	€10–15
$$	£5–9	US$7–14	€6–10
$	<£5	<US$7	<€6

DRINKS Alongside Abruzzo's food specialities are a few drinks that are peculiar to the region.

Montepulciano d'Abruzzo Montepulciano d'Abruzzo is a wine known across Italy and – increasingly – overseas. It is made from Montepulciano grapes which are grown throughout the region but particularly in the provinces of Pescara and Chieti. It is a soft and fruity wine which is not usually left to age for long periods of time.

Genziana **liqueur** *Genziana* is a bitter liqueur made from the roots of the *Genziana lutea* plant, native to this part of Italy. The *genziana* root, which is usually found at over 1,000m above sea level, is harvested around October from plants that are about five years old. They are cleaned and dried before being infused in ethyl-alcohol for about a month and a half. The liquid is then diluted with sweetened water and can be drunk without particular regard to ageing (though most will recommend you wait at least a few weeks). The average alcohol content is around 30%.

Saffron liqueur The province of L'Aquila is known for its production of saffron (see box, *A precious commodity: the saffron of the Navelli Plains*, page 149). Saffron liqueur is made by infusing L'Aquila saffron with a mixture of herbs in raw alcohol. Sweet water is added and the mixture is subsequently aged in casks of steel for many months. The end result is a silky, yellow liqueur with an alcohol content of around 40%.

Ratafia liqueur The Ratafia liqueur is a drink of medieval origins whose name means to 'ratify'; it was drunk by nobility whenever an agreement over something was reached. It is made from cherries, Montepulciano wine and sugar, and is not very strong, the alcohol content being around 20%.

PUBLIC HOLIDAYS AND FESTIVALS

Abruzzo observes all of Italy's official public holidays. The only variable date for a public holiday is Easter Monday. Note that Good Friday is *not* a public holiday.

1 January	New Year's Day
6 January	Epiphany
March/April	Easter Monday (variable)
25 April	Liberation Day
1 May	Labour Day
2 June	Anniversary of the Republic

15 August	Assumption
1 November	All Saints' Day
8 December	The Immaculate Conception
25 December	Christmas Day
26 December	St Stephen's Day

RELIGIOUS EVENTS Celebrations in Abruzzo tend to be individual to each town and city, national holiday or no. During Easter and Christmas, most towns put on a religious procession that usually consists of marching through town from the principal church to the largest piazza, usually headed by the priests and a religious relic of some sort, or a statue of Jesus or the Madonna. This is often also the case for towns that celebrate days in honour of specific saints or traditions that go back hundreds of years (for an example, see box, *La Perdonanza*, page 109).

The most important of the religious Christmas revelries takes place on Christmas Eve. Midnight Mass is extremely popular, especially with families. This is usually preceded by a Christmas Eve dinner and followed by Christmas Day lunch with extended family.

La Sagra Translating the *sagra* into English is a little troublesome; it roughly means a festival, fair or a feast. However, it is a little more than that. A *sagra* (plural *sagre*) can be dedicated to almost anything, though it mostly denotes a fair, fête or festival with a focus on a particular food. For instance, many towns have a *sagra degli arrosticini* (fair of the *arrosticini*), where the streets will come alive with stalls cooking *arrosticini* (see page 42), probably accompanied by fried pizza. Other examples are the *sagra del formaggio* (cheese), *sagra della pizza*, *sagra del vino* (wine) and *sagra dell'uva* (grapes).

The *sagre* of Abruzzo are manifold and it is well worth contacting **Borghi and Sagre** (*Piazza Garibaldi 40, Pescara;* ✆ *085 451 6136;* e *borghiesagre@quotazioni. it; www.borghiandsagre.com*), who publish a fantastic yearly guide to the *sagre* and other festivals. This is particularly handy due to the erratic nature of their timing: towns often change the dates of their *sagre*, and at times even decide not to run them at all during the year.

OPENING TIMES

For visitors, Abruzzo's attitudes to opening and closing times might be more than a little frustrating. The erratic nature of these is closely linked to the Abruzzese's attitude to work and employment in general, and as such, most complain when they are on the receiving end but shrug unperturbed when they perpetuate the unpredictability themselves.

HOTELS Unless otherwise stated, hotels are open all year round.

RESTAURANTS Abruzzesi do not like to be tied down to schedules in general, and nowhere is this more evident than with opening times for restaurants. Where times are not listed in this guide, assume that they are open daily for lunch and dinner (although it often pays to check as restaurants frequently add or alter closing days, especially during holiday periods). Usual lunchtime hours are anywhere between 12.30 and 14.30, whereas dinner can range from 19.30 to 23.00. You would be hard pressed to find a restaurant serving dinner before 19.30 unless it's in a hotel.

CAFFÈS AND BARS Caffès and bars in Abruzzo are not quite as unreliable as restaurants. They are usually open from very early in the morning (around 06.00–07.00) and close late at night, particularly during summer.

SHOPS Shops are usually open Monday to Saturday 09.00–13.00 and 16.00–20.00. In winter, this often (and without notice, depending on the shop) changes to 10.00–13.00 and 15.30–19.30. In Pescara, L'Aquila and Teramo, shops can choose to close on Thursday afternoons. However, during the sales periods (January to February and July to August) all shops remain open.

CHEMISTS Pharmacies are generally open Monday to Friday 09.00–13.00 and 15.30–19.30 (16.00–20.00 in summer). In reality, though, pharmacies usually work on a roster basis, where the times change frequently but are usually displayed clearly at the entrance. This is especially true of the four main cities, particularly in regards to weekend opening hours. To avoid any confusion, you are advised to call ahead and check.

BANKS Banks in Abruzzo open Monday to Friday at 08.30 and close for lunch around 13.00–13.30. Afternoon hours are 14.45–16.00.

POST OFFICES 'Poste Italiane' runs all the post offices in Abruzzo. The normal opening hours are Monday to Friday 08.30–13.30 and Saturday 08.30–12.30. Some post offices have longer hours, and where this is the case I have listed them explicitly.

TOURIST INFORMATION POINTS Abruzzo's IAT points are the official tourist information points. Unless otherwise stated, their operating hours are usually Monday to Saturday 09.00–13.00 and 15.00–18.00 – although you can sometimes take Saturday opening with a pinch of salt. Information points run by town and village councils also generally adhere to these hours.

CHURCHES The churches of Abruzzo are some of the most spectacular sights in the region but it can be very frustrating to hear about a marvellous, must-see church only to arrive and find its door bolted with no sign of life anywhere in the vicinity. This is a common occurrence in a region that has been largely ignored for so long.

Because opening and closing times for churches are so erratic, they have been omitted from this guide unless they are clearly advertised. Many of the larger or more important churches are generally open during the day for visitors, with some closing for the lunchtime break. Frustratingly, some display opening and closing times only to follow their 'schedule' sporadically.

If you are really determined to visit a particular church but constantly find it closed, you might contact the (rather long-named) **Soprintendenza per i Beni Ambientali, Architettonici, Artistici e Storici per L'Abruzzo** (*Via B Croce, L'Aquila;* ✆ *0862 6331;* f *0862 493096*) – although they may not always be able to help, especially if your query is relating to a church in a small village or remote location.

SHOPPING

From high-street designer clothes and accessories to fake goods and market trinkets, Abruzzo is a good place to squander some money. By far the best city for shopping is Pescara (see page 64). L'Aquila, Chieti and Teramo have an average selection of shopping outlets but many of the residents of these cities make the journey to Pescara, especially when it comes to clothes and fashion accessories. The only shopping malls worth visiting are in and around Pescara (see box, *The shopping centre craze*, page 68).

ARTS AND ENTERTAINMENT

Abruzzo has a few large **cinema** complexes, such as those found in Montesilvano or Chieti Scalo's Megalò shopping centre (see page 68). These are often quite packed during winter weekends so it's best to get your tickets early. Unfortunately, it's very rare to find a screening in original language such as English. There are also a handful of **theatres** for live performances (such as in L'Aquila, see page 108), though theatre isn't a very popular pastime in Abruzzo. Once a year, Pescara is home to the **Pescara Jazz Festival** (see page 64), the region's most famous claim to fame in the music industry.

For a region of such a relatively small size, Abruzzo has a fair number of **museums** and **galleries**, more often than not found in beautiful medieval buildings and castles. A handful of museums are also quite important on a national level, such as those in L'Aquila (see page 115) and Chieti (see page 244).

ACTIVITIES

BEACHES AND *STABILIMENTI* Beaches in Abruzzo, as with the rest of Italy, are equipped with beach umbrellas and a whole wealth of other paraphernalia. For some visitors this might seem a little odd at first: why clutter up a beautiful coastline? Well, in short, the Abruzzesi like to be comfortable at the beach. This means sunbeds without excessive amounts of sand, beach towels and drinks bottles and, without question, the chance to buy food and drinks without carting around a coolbox. Creature comforts are definitely the order of the day.

As a result, on the more developed beaches along the coastline private *stabilimenti* (singular *stabilimento*), or beach clubs for lack of a better phrase, lease sections of beach during spring and summer and sprinkle them with rows of beach umbrellas and faux palms, each with varying configurations of sunbeds (*lettini*), deckchairs (*sdraie*) or chairs (*sedie*). They lease this equipment to the public on a seasonal basis, allowing a person, family or group of friends to use it for the whole summer. Each *stabilimento* has umbrellas and beach equipment of the same design, clearly marked to avoid any confusion, and a *stabilimento* building, essentially a glorified kiosk (although taking a walk down the Pescara beachfront will show you just how chic and elegant they can be). All *stabilimenti* serve a variety of take-away food such as pizza, sandwiches and drinks, with some operating as full sit-down lunch and dinner restaurants during the warmer months. In fact, it is these *stabilimenti* restaurants that become the most popular eateries in spring and summer. There are hundreds of them spread along the coastline of Abruzzo.

Blue Flag Programme Set up in 1985, the Blue Flag Programme (*www.blueflag. org*) sets standards for the sustainable development of beaches and marinas all over the world. The programme's juries have awarded 13 Blue Flags to the region of Abruzzo, only marginally behind the regions of Tuscany (15 flags) and Liguria (14 flags). Abruzzo's 2008 Blue Flags were awarded for the beaches and marinas of Martinsicuro, Alba Adriatica, Tortoreto, Giulianova, Roseto degli Abruzzi, Scerne di Pineto, Silvi, Francavilla al Mare, San Vito Chietino, Rocca San Giovanni, Fossacesia, Vasto and San Salvo.

It is generally considered rude to use beach equipment that is not leased to you without permission. If you are coming for a day or weekend, approach a *stabilimento* and ask if you can lease equipment for the length of your stay. Many *stabilimenti* reserve a certain number of places for walk-ins.

The *stabilimenti* owners are also within their rights to stop you from lying on the sand within the boundaries of their land. However, this doesn't happen too frequently and generally only if someone decides to bring it to their attention. So if you feel you don't need those luxuries then find a place well away from the umbrellas (and keep a look out for the wagging finger of disapproval). There are also sections of beach along the coast that are not equipped or privatised and that anyone is free to use.

At dusk the *stabilimenti* close their beach umbrellas and tidy their equipment. It is not permissible to make use of any *stabilimento*'s gear at night, and, in built-up areas, coastal guards operate to ensure this doesn't happen.

SOME USEFUL BEACH VOCABULARY

acqua	water
sabbia	sand
asciugamano	towel
Vorrei affittare …	I would like to hire …
… un ombrellone/una palma …	… a beach umbrella/a beach palm …
con…	with …
… un lettino	… a bed
… una sedia a sdraio	… a deckchair
… una sedia	… a chair

Practical Information ACTIVITIES

2

Do bear in mind that just because a beach doesn't have a Blue Flag it can still be a great place to spend some time. The beaches in Pescara are still enjoyable and a great place to relax and socialise with friends and locals, and there are also sections of the Chieti Province that have not been rated by the Blue Flag Programme but which abound in white sand and turquoise waters, not to mention the culturally important *trabocchi* (fishing platforms).

WINTER SPORTS Abruzzo is a fantastic destination for skiers and snowboarders. The region's mountainous landscape, with undulating plateaux and the tallest peaks in the Apennines, is perfect for winter sports.

The ski resorts are usually open from December to April, depending on the conditions, though many resorts use 'programmed' (artificial) snow to ensure snow cover even when the weather has been too warm. The main provincial tourist offices in Pescara, Chieti, L'Aquila and Teramo can be contacted for detailed maps and advice on each ski resort. The best skiing areas are as follows:

- Prati di Tivo, page 233
- Campo Felice, page 142
- Ovindoli and Monte Magnola, page 136
- Campo Imperatore, page 125
- Scanno and Monte Rotondo, page 97

- Pescocostanzo/Roccaraso/Rivisondoli, page 195
- Pescassèroli, page 167
- Opi, page 172
- Passo Lanciano, page 258
- La Majelletta, page 258

It is worth noting that there is a ski pass which allows access to three of the best skiing points, Campo Felice, Campo Imperatore and Monte Magnola. For more information, contact the Gruppo Park Hotel (*Piazzale Magnola 69;* ✆ *0863 705058*) or visit the official website (*www.ovindolimagnola.it*).

MEDIA AND COMMUNICATIONS

PRINT Abruzzo has a number of local newspapers, many of which are regional branches of national newspapers such as *Il Tempo*. Other newspapers include the popular *Il Centro, Il Messaggero* and the widely read national newspaper *La Repubblica*. However, please note that English-language newspapers are rarely available, except at the railway station in Pescara.

Both newspapers and magazines are available from any *edicola* (something akin to a newspaper kiosk) on any street corner: there is a plethora of them and they are something of an Italian institution. You can smell the ink and fresh paper from a mile away. If you are after something to read (which will inevitably have to be in Italian), you will find the *edicole* open in the mornings until lunchtime, then in the late afternoon until dinner time.

TELEVISION AND RADIO Abruzzo's free-to-air television stations are those shared by the rest of the nation. The main ones are Rai 1, Rai 2, Rai 3, Rete 4, Canale 5 and Italia 1. However, Rete 8 is a local station focusing on all things Abruzzo. During the earthquake of 2009 (see page 99), Rete 8's coverage of the event was constant and an excellent place for up-to-date information. For local weather forecasts, though, try the Rai channels which throughout the day air TGR (Telegiornale Regione), a local news programme specific to each region.

Abruzzo's radio stations and broadcasts follow the patterns of the rest of the country: a radio station such as Radio Deejay will have different frequencies in different regions of the country as well as local news specific to that region. There are myriad radio stations and finding an unused frequency on a car stereo to plug in your iPod is definitely a challenge. Radio broadcasts are not particularly popular in Abruzzo outside the car and, nowadays, the internet. A number of local radio stations such as Radio Ciao (*www.radiociao.com*), Radio Ketchup (*www.radioketchup.com*) and Radio L'Aquila (*www.rl1.it*) are now broadcasting live radio on the net. For an interesting musical experience, check out Abruzzo FM (*www.abruzzo.fm),* an internet radio station broadcasting very old songs in various Abruzzesi dialects.

TELEPHONE Telephone numbers in Abruzzo consist of an area code followed by between four and nine digits. A few years ago, Telecom Italia introduced the obligatory dialling of area codes before the actual number. This means you will not get through to your desired number if you do not dial the area code first. Keep in mind that the telephone is not the Abruzzese's best friend, by any stretch of the imagination. In fact, it is often hard to get someone on the phone when it comes to the likes of public services such as councils and post offices, not to mention banks.

INTERNET It is my opinion that Abruzzo caught up with the internet revolution far later than most other areas in Italy. As such, you will probably be more likely to use the internet in a hotel than elsewhere. Most hotels have WiFi available, some for free and others with a small fee to pay.

POST The cost of postage is not particularly high in Italy, and contrary to popular opinion, the postal system is reliable. Whenever I have posted packages to Australia from Abruzzo, they tend to take no more than about ten days, and that's for normal air mail. Stamps to the UK (for normal letters and postcards) are about €0.65; to America, around €0.85; and to Australia about €1. Red postboxes can be found outside post offices and scattered throughout towns and cities.

For post office opening times, see page 45.

BUYING A PROPERTY

Buying a property in Abruzzo is not as cheap as it was, say, five years ago. The reason for this is the slow trickle of international tourists who are discovering beauty to rival or, indeed, surpass the Tuscan and Umbrian countryside with property at a fraction of the price. In addition, Abruzzo can be far more diverse in its offerings than its more famous neighbours and as such people feel they get far more for their money.

If you want to purchase a property, it is certainly far easier to know a local or to have at least an intermediate understanding of the Italian language. It is, though, worth bearing in mind that, as a foreigner buying property here, you will most likely pay a different price from a local who wishes to purchase the same property. I think it's important to acknowledge that this is a reality that is encountered elsewhere in Europe – it's just a matter of either accepting it (and bargaining as much as possible) or moving on.

By far the best way for a foreigner to buy a property in Abruzzo is going through an agency such House Around Italy (✆ 085 943 0256; e info@housearounditaly.com; www.housearounditaly.com), which is also able to provide information on legal documentation, opening bank accounts, insurance, building services and even investments.

GIVING SOMETHING BACK

During my research for this book, I remember encountering a small, lovely family-owned bed and breakfast overshadowed by a hotel set up by an American organisation and staffed by English speakers. Shortly after, the beautiful bed and breakfast began to struggle to keep its customers – mostly due to the fact that the elderly lady and her husband spoke little English.

As such, I feel it my duty to advise the traveller to Abruzzo of one small thing. The Abruzzo economy, whilst certainly amongst the most stable in Italy, still needs a helping hand from the traveller. Employment is definitely an issue and there is a way you might help. Though there are not that many, avoiding the large hotel chains (especially the ones owned by the English-speaking nations of the world) means that your money will go towards helping the local economy.

Practical Information GIVING SOMETHING BACK

2

Bradt Travel Guides

**Claim 20% discount on your next Bradt book when you order from
www.bradtguides.com quoting the code BRADT20**

Africa

Africa Overland	£16.99
Algeria	£15.99
Angola	£18.99
Botswana	£16.99
Burkina Faso	£17.99
Cameroon	£15.99
Cape Verde	£15.99
Congo	£16.99
Eritrea	£15.99
Ethiopia	£17.99
Ethiopia Highlights	£15.99
Ghana	£15.99
Kenya Highlights	£15.99
Madagascar	£16.99
Madagascar Highlights	£15.99
Malawi	£15.99
Mali	£14.99
Mauritius, Rodrigues & Réunion	£16.99
Mozambique	£15.99
Namibia	£15.99
Nigeria	£17.99
North Africa: Roman Coast	£15.99
Rwanda	£16.99
São Tomé & Príncipe	£14.99
Seychelles	£16.99
Sierra Leone	£16.99
Somaliland	£15.99
South Africa Highlights	£15.99
Sudan	£16.99
Swaziland	£15.99
Tanzania Safari Guide	£17.99
Tanzania, Northern	£14.99
Uganda	£16.99
Zambia	£18.99
Zanzibar	£15.99
Zimbabwe	£15.99

The Americas and the Caribbean

Alaska	£15.99
Amazon Highlights	£15.99
Argentina	£16.99
Bahia	£14.99
Cayman Islands	£14.99
Chile Highlights	£15.99
Colombia	£17.99
Dominica	£15.99
Grenada, Carriacou & Petite Martinique	£15.99
Guyana	£15.99
Haiti	£16.99
Nova Scotia	£15.99
Panama	£14.99
Paraguay	£15.99
Peru Highlights	£15.99
Turks & Caicos Islands	£14.99
Uruguay	£15.99
USA by Rail	£15.99
Venezuela	£16.99
Yukon	£14.99

British Isles

Britain from the Rails	£14.99
Bus-Pass Britain	£15.99
Eccentric Britain	£16.99
Eccentric Cambridge	£9.99
Eccentric London	£14.99
Eccentric Oxford	£9.99
Sacred Britain	£16.99
Slow: Cornwall	£14.99
Slow: Cotswolds	£14.99
Slow: Devon & Exmoor	£14.99
Slow: Dorset	£14.99
Slow: New Forest	£9.99
Slow: Norfolk & Suffolk	£14.99
Slow: North Yorkshire	£14.99
Slow: Northumberland	£14.99
Slow: Sussex & South Downs National Park	£14.99

Europe

Abruzzo	£16.99
Albania	£16.99
Armenia	£15.99
Azores	£14.99
Belarus	£15.99
Bosnia & Herzegovina	£15.99
Bratislava	£9.99
Budapest	£9.99
Croatia	£15.99
Cross-Channel France: Nord-Pas de Calais	£13.99
Cyprus see North Cyprus	
Estonia	£14.99
Faroe Islands	£16.99
Flanders	£15.99
Georgia	£15.99
Greece: The Peloponnese	£14.99
Hungary	£15.99
Iceland	£15.99
Istria	£13.99
Kosovo	£15.99
Lapland	£15.99
Liguria	£15.99
Lille	£9.99
Lithuania	£14.99
Luxembourg	£14.99
Macedonia	£16.99
Malta & Gozo	£14.99
Montenegro	£14.99
North Cyprus	£13.99
Serbia	£15.99
Slovakia	£14.99
Slovenia	£13.99
Svalbard: Spitsbergen, Jan Mayen, Franz Jozef Land	£17.99
Switzerland Without a Car	£15.99
Transylvania	£15.99
Ukraine	£16.99

Middle East, Asia and Australasia

Bangladesh	£17.99
Borneo	£17.99
Eastern Turkey	£16.99
Iran	£15.99
Israel	£15.99
Jordan	£16.99
Kazakhstan	£16.99
Kyrgyzstan	£16.99
Lake Baikal	£15.99
Lebanon	£15.99
Maldives	£15.99
Mongolia	£16.99
North Korea	£14.99
Oman	£15.99
Palestine	£15.99
Shangri-La: A Travel Guide to the Himalayan Dream	£14.99
Sri Lanka	£15.99
Syria	£15.99
Taiwan	£16.99
Tajikistan	£15.99
Tibet	£17.99
Yemen	£14.99

Wildlife

Antarctica: A Guide to the Wildlife	£15.99
Arctic: A Guide to Coastal Wildlife	£16.99
Australian Wildlife	£14.99
East African Wildlife	£19.99
Galápagos Wildlife	£16.99
Madagascar Wildlife	£16.99
Pantanal Wildlife	£16.99
Southern African Wildlife	£19.99
Sri Lankan Wildlife	£15.99

Pictorials and other guides

100 Alien Invaders	£16.99
100 Animals to See Before They Die	£16.99
100 Bizarre Animals	£16.99
Eccentric Australia	£12.99
Northern Lights	£6.99
Swimming with Dolphins, Tracking Gorillas	£15.99
The Northwest Passage	£14.99
Tips on Tipping	£6.99
Total Solar Eclipse 2012 & 2013	£6.99
Wildlife & Conservation Volunteering: The Complete Guide	£13.99

Travel literature

A Glimpse of Eternal Snows	£11.99
A Tourist in the Arab Spring	£9.99
Connemara Mollie	£9.99
Fakirs, Feluccas and Femmes Fatales	£9.99
Madagascar: The Eighth Continent	£11.99
The Marsh Lions	£9.99
The Two-Year Mountain	£9.99
The Urban Circus	£9.99
Up the Creek	£9.9

Part Two

THE GUIDE

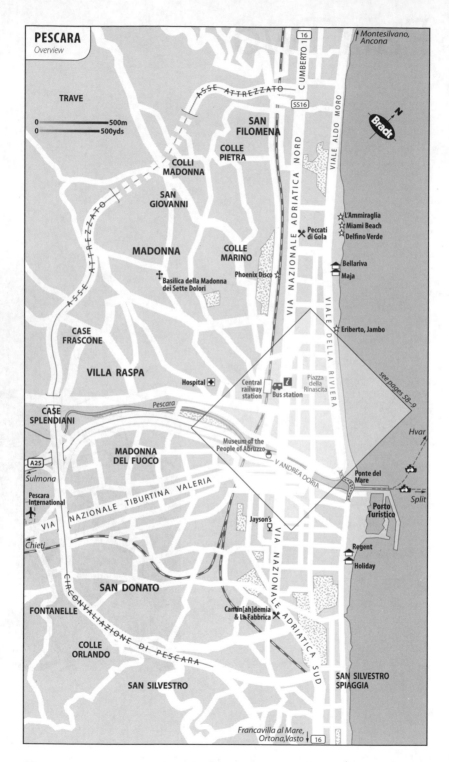

PESCARA
Overview

TRAVE

0 ———— 500m
0 ———— 500yds

COLLI
MADONNA

COLLE
PIETRA

SAN
FILOMENA

16

SS16

V UMBERTO 1

ASSE ATTREZZATO

VIALE ALDO MORO

↑ Montesilvano,
Ancona

Bradt

N

SAN
GIOVANNI

MADONNA

COLLE
MARINO

☓ Peccati
di Gola

☆ L'Ammiraglia
☆ Miami Beach
☆ Delfino Verde

✠ Basilica della Madonna
dei Sette Dolori

Phoenix Disco ☆

⌂ Bellariva
⌂ Maja

VIA NAZIONALE ADRIATICA NORD

CASE
FRASCONE

VILLA RASPA

Hospital ✚

Central
railway
station

ℹ Bus station

Piazza
della
Rinascita

☆ Eriberto, Jambo

VIALE DELLA RIVIERA

see pages 58–9

CASE
SPLENDIANI

A25

↓ Sulmona

Pescara

MADONNA
DEL FUOCO

Museum of the
People of Abruzzo

V ANDREA DORIA

Ponte del
Mare

→ Hvar

Porto
Turistico

→ Split

Pescara
International
✈

VIA

NAZIONALE TIBURTINA VALERIA

↓ Chieti

Jayson's

Regent

⌂ Holiday

CIRCONVALLAZIONE DI PESCARA

SAN DONATO

FONTANELLE

Cantin[ah]demia
& La Fabbrica ☓

VIA NAZIONALE ADRIATICA SUD

COLLE
ORLANDO

SAN SILVESTRO

SAN SILVESTRO
SPIAGGIA

*Francavilla al Mare,
Ortona, Vasto* ↓ 16

3

Pescara

The town of Pescara appeared at the end of the road, drenched in the sun, sending its sounds on the wind …

Gabriele D'Annunzio, *Le Novelle della Pescara*, 1902

Despite the obvious lack of evident history or historical landmarks, Pescara is a microcosm of some of the best things Italy has to offer: a dining culture to cherish, a summer atmosphere to knock your socks off, the best shopping in the region and a vibrant beach culture. As the economic powerhouse of Abruzzo, the city has been buffed and shined, and is ready to welcome the intrepid traveller with open arms.

During summer, Pescara has a knack for changing your outlook on what constitutes *la dolce vita*. The streets are awash with sunshine and are buzzing in the mornings and late afternoons, only to be found deserted and peacefully silent over the lunchtime and siesta hours. Nothing could be so important as to warrant shortening lunch, the most important meal of the day. Or, God forbid, missing out on those precious forty winks before heading back to work for the afternoon.

Whilst Pescara's charms are not of the slap-in-the-face variety that is so common amongst the historical cities of Italy, it is a place well worth exploring, especially in the warmer months when it really comes into its own. That said, it takes more than a moment or two to see past the concrete façades of the countless post-war apartment buildings to a vibrant, pastel-coloured coastal city that oozes rest and relaxation.

HISTORY

Many people make the mistake of giving Pescara the label of a 'modern city'. Whilst this is certainly true in appearance (particularly when compared with the history evident in the rest of Abruzzo), it is, in fact, an ancient city.

The settlement of Pescara pre-dates the Roman conquest of Abruzzo, and its history goes back so far that its origins are almost completely unknown. Very little is recorded prior to it becoming the Roman city of Aternum during the early Roman Empire, named after the river on which it was founded (with some historians referring to it as Ostia Aterni). The city was eventually connected to Rome via the Via Claudia Valeria and the Via Tiburtina sometime during the 4th century BC, the latter now being the only other vaguely direct route to Rome aside from the A25 motorway.

Aternum acquired its significance and wealth under the Romans as a crucial port city. Whilst historians have long since harboured suspicions that it also had military status, the city's ideal geographical position allowed it to become a very important centre for trade with the eastern provinces of the Roman Empire, encouraging growth and prosperity. The town itself was abundant in official and public buildings. Perhaps the most important of these was a temple dedicated to the god Jovius Aternium, of which traces have been found. For years there have been reports of the existence of an enormous bridge built by the Emperor Tiberius.

The city was almost levelled by Lombard attacks in the 6th century AD. Interestingly, the Lombards also accused its bishop, Cetteus (now the city's patron saint), of being loyal to the Greek Christians who carried out skirmishes and attacks along the Adriatic coast. Whether this is true or not remains unknown, though many historians think it unlikely due to his apparent love for the city. Despite problems with the Lombards, Aternum's hearty citizens brushed themselves down and continued work and construction. By the end of the 11th century, the city boasted many buildings of religious importance and a maze of medieval streets always bustling with the activity befitting port cities.

It wasn't until the 12th century that it acquired a name resembling its modern one: Piscaria, which means 'abundant in fish'. The next few centuries brought with them the hardships of skirmishes and raids by various leaders, with the Venetian attacks of the mid 15th century bruising the city physically and emotionally. With Spanish rule of the area, the city was very strongly fortified and it was able to withstand a siege by more than a hundred Turkish galleys in 1566.

Over time, another settlement known as Castellamare Adriatico developed north of the river, and by the early 1700s the greater area numbered a few thousand. However, after Pescara came under the control of Joseph Bonaparte in 1800, the city split and Pescara and Castellamare became separate towns. Following the unification of Italy in 1860, and having withstood so many powerful attacks across the centuries, the fortress of Pescara (including its thick, almost impenetrable walls) was disassembled. In the 20th century, the two towns united again and Pescara became the capital of a newly formed province of the same name.

As a significant Adriatic port city, Pescara was basically obliterated by the Allied forces during World War II and whatever survived of its Roman and medieval heritage was completely destroyed. The bombing during the war provided a blank canvas on which to build and develop, and this explains the city's wealth of post-war apartment buildings and its modern appearance. During the last 50 years, Pescara has become one of the economic powerhouses of central Italy and is now the largest city from Perugia to Foggia (with the exception of Rome) and the sixth-largest city on the Italian Adriatic coast. In 2009, Pescara was host city to the 16th annual Mediterranean Games. The city was spruced up and garnered attention from all over Europe. A total of 23 nations attended the games: Albania, Algeria, Andorra, Bosnia and Herzegovina, Croatia, Cyprus, Egypt, France, Greece, Italy, Lebanon, Libya, Malta, Monaco, Montenegro, Morocco, San Marino, Serbia, Slovenia, Spain, Syria, Tunisia and Turkey.

GETTING THERE

Pescara is slowly but surely opening its doors to international tourism and is now well serviced by all major public transport systems, so getting here should not present any problems.

BY AIR There are scheduled international and domestic flights to and from Pescara; for details, see page 30.

Airport transfers Bus 38 departs from outside the terminal building of Pescara's Aeroporto Internazionale d'Abruzzo and makes various stops in the centre of the city, a journey taking approximately 10–15 minutes. It operates every 20 minutes

PESCARA CENTRALE

Pescara's central train station, Pescara Centrale, can't be missed: its imposing building faces a large car park and coach station on the fringes of the centre of town. Though plans to move and modernise the station from a 19th-century palace nearby were drawn up as early as 1962, the station was not opened until 1987. The Pescaresi beamed with pride: the black, gleaming glass panels of the new building were not only a sign of Pescara's economic status in central Italy, but also of the city's boundless leaps towards the new millennium. Pescara Centrale now serves around 3.5 million passengers per year, heading south to the 'heel' of Italy, westwards to Sulmona and Rome, and north towards Milan, Switzerland and beyond.

during the day and every half-hour early in the morning and later at night. Tickets can be purchased from the newsagent in the airport.

Car rental There are seven car-hire firms at Pescara airport. With the exception of Locauto and Auto Europa, all have one or more offices in the city as well. Whilst it is certainly possible to turn up and hire a car, it is more advisable to book, especially during the summer months.

🚗 **Auto Europa** 085 431 8089; www.autoeuropa.it; daily 08.00–22.00
🚗 **Avis** 085 54116; www.avisautonoleggio.it; Mon–Fri 08.30–23.30, Sat 08.30–13.30 & 16.00–23.45, Sun 10.00–23.15
🚗 **Europcar** 085 52120; www.europcar.it; Mon–Fri 07.45–23.15, Sat 09.00-23.45, Sun 09.00–23.15
🚗 **Hertz** 085 431 5769; www.hertz.it;

Mon–Fri 08.30–19.30, Sat/Sun 08.30–13.00 & 15.30–17.30. If you fly with Ryanair, discounts are available on the Ryanair website.
🚗 **Maggiore** 085 431 1803; www.maggiore.it; Mon–Sat 08.30–13.00 & 15.00–21.30, Sun 08.00–13.00 & 15.30–22.30
🚗 **Sixt** 085 431 3690; www.e-sixt.it; Mon–Fri 08.30–12.30 & 15.30–22.00, Sat 09.00–13.00, Sun 10.30–11.30

TAXI There are taxis available outside the airport terminal. A one-way trip into the centre of town will set you back around €15

BY TRAIN For details of train services into the city, see page 32.
See box above for details of Pescara's central train station. Twelve of Pescara's 17 bus lines stop at the bus and coach station in front of the railway station, and of the remaining five, all but one have stops on parallel Corso Vittorio Emanuele. The Ferrovie dello Stato website (*www.ferroviedellostato.it*) gives information on services to and from the city. A train trip from Rome to Pescara will cost you around €12 and takes upwards of four hours. Take the bus instead.

BY BUS See page 32 for details of national services to and from Pescara. International services are also available from the likes of Eurolines (*www.eurolines.com*) and others.
The bus and coach station is situated in the square in front of the train station. ARPA, Di Febo Capuani, Di Fonzo and Gruppo La Panoramica all operate services that connect Pescara with the rest of Abruzzo and Italy. A bus trip to Teramo takes around an hour and will set you back approximately €7. To neighbouring Chieti, the trip is 20 minutes and costs about €2.

Pescara GETTING THERE 3

55

Buses for Rome depart around eight times per day. The journey by bus is much quicker than by train, though it costs €15 for a one-way ticket.

GETTING AROUND

ON PUBLIC TRANSPORT The only way around the city on public transport is by bus. Pescara's network of local **buses** is run by Gestione Trasporti Metropolitani (*www.gtm.pe.it*). There are 17 lines that cover the city's larger urban area, including Montesilvano, Spoltore and Francavilla. GTM's website has an interactive map which displays the bus lines and their corresponding routes. A 90-minute ticket costs €0.90 and a daily ticket €2.50; monthly tickets are available from €23.00. Tickets can be bought from *tabacchini* shops (distinguished by the large 'T' signs above the entrance). Buses can be somewhat unreliable.

Although Pescara has three **train stations** – Pescara Centrale, Pescara Porta Nuova and Pescara San Marco – these are not used for getting around within the city, but for onward travel along the coast.

BY CAR Driving in Pescara can be a nightmare to the untrained; the driving habits of the locals can raise the hairs on the back of your neck. While the city may be grid-like and fairly straightforward to navigate by road, the traffic can be hideous and you need to be on your constant guard. Don't be surprised at drivers who attempt to pull out of intersecting roads by edging forward and blocking the city's entire traffic flow until they are let through. Honking your horn in Pescara is considered quite rude.

ON FOOT Pescara's centre is relatively compact and can easily be seen on foot. This is the best option, as buses can often be unreliable.

TOURIST INFORMATION

 Abruzzo Promozione Turismo (APTR) Corso Vittorio Emanuele II, 301; 085 4290 0212; e iat. sede@abruzzotourismo.it; www.abruzzoturismo.it

WHERE TO STAY

Pescara is not a big city but there is certainly no dearth of accommodation, most of it to be found in the city centre and along Pescara's coastline. There are no hostels as such, but a few budget options are available out of the centre. Everything is more or less within walking distance of the central shopping areas and the beaches. The hotels below are organised into coastal and city-centre locations, and the listings are arranged from most to least expensive.

The **city centre** accommodation options are well located in the thick of the main commercial district, within easy walking distance of both the station and the beach.

Hotels located on the **central riviera** are a good option due to their proximity to, well, almost everything you could need. They're also within easy walking distance of the bus station, which is particularly handy if you decide to catch a bus from the airport. Note that during the height of summer it can get pretty crowded around here; some will enjoy being in the thick of it, while others will wish they had stayed on Pescara's north or south coasts.

During summer, the **northern riviera** is particularly popular with the younger crowd, though it is reasonably mixed, and is still quieter than the central beach.

The **southern riviera** is more popular with the area's locals because it is separated from the centre and north coasts by the port. It is a largely residential area and amenities can be a little scarce. The walk into the centre can take up to 25 minutes, although this does mean that, with the exception of the month of August, you're guaranteed peace and quiet.

CITY CENTRE

⌂ **Best Western Hotel Plaza** (68 rooms) Piazza Sacro Cuore 55; ☎085 421 4625; e piazza. pe@bestwestern.it; www.hotelplazapescara. com. Conveniently located about halfway between Pescara station & the beach. Rooms have a pleasant marble décor & the beds are comfortable. Front rooms offer views on to the piazza below. The hotel has conference rooms & a reasonably priced restaurant, & you can even book a private session with a physiotherapist/masseur. **$$$$$**

⌂ **Best Western Hotel Duca d'Aosta** (72 rooms) Piazza Duca d'Aosta 4; ☎085 374241; e duca.pe@bestwestern.it; www. ducadaostapescara.it. Popular with the business crowds, this hotel may appear run-down on the outside, but the interior is well kept & pleasantly decorated. Rooms & bathrooms are fairly large & the hotel has a bar in the lobby. Good city-centre location & about a 15-min walk from the beach. **$$$$**

⌂ **Hotel Victoria** (22 rooms) Via Piave 142; ☎085 374132; e hotel@victoriapescara.com; www.victoriapescara.com. A relative newcomer to the Pescara hospitality scene, this is an excellent choice for those who don't want all the activity associated with beachfront hotels. The only downside is that the hotel doesn't have a pool, though this is a bit of a non-issue with the beach only a 5-min walk away. There is a world-class health & spa centre as well as a very chic lounge bar. Rooms are spacious & decorated with modern fittings. Check website for some great-value packages. **$$$$**

⌂ **Pescara B&B** (1 apt) Piazza Muzii 38; m 3925 058 482; e info@pescarabb.eu; www. pescarabb.com. Situated just off one of Pescara's lively shopping strips, Pescara B&B is a family-run establishment where privacy rules. The B&B comprises a large, self-catering 90m² apartment with no staff on site. The accommodation on offer is impeccably clean, well decorated and benefits from all mod cons and the convenience of a kitchenette. A lively market is held in the piazza and the beach is a short 5-min walk away. The

owners also offer 4 further rooms at the **New York B&B**, 10 mins away. Rooms are of a similar quality though the area is considerably quieter. **$$$$**

⌂ **Hotel Alba** (60 rooms) Via M Forti 14; ☎085 389145; e info@hotelalba.pescara.it; www. hotelalba.pescara.it. The Alba is centrally located with small but clean rooms. The 1980s'-style decoration may not be to everyone's taste (it's a little rough around the edges & the fittings are very dated), but the accommodation is comfortable & within easy reach of the beach & shopping areas. **$$$**

⌂ **Hotel Ambra Palace** (61 rooms) Via Quarto dei Mille 28; ☎085 422 5795; e info@ hotelambrapalace.it; www.hotelambrapalace. it. Situated a stone's throw from the station, the Ambra Palace's rooms are comfortable & simply decorated (if a little dated), with free WiFi internet access available. Some rooms have balcony. The restaurant is decent, with some fine pasta dishes & – unlike many hotels in Pescara – room service is available 24hrs. **$$$**

CENTRAL RIVIERA

⌂ **Hotel Carlton** (64 rooms) Viale della Riviera 35; ☎085 373125; e info@carltonpescara.it; www. carltonpescara.it. Don't be fooled by the somewhat weathered exterior of this centrally located hotel. Inside, its well-proportioned rooms are tastefully decorated with pastel-coloured fittings & the service is impeccable. As with most hotels on the coast, you might consider paying the extra €15 for a room with a sea view. It does not have a pool but the beach is just across the road. There's a €20 shuttle service to & from Pescara airport. **$$$$$**

⌂ **Hotel Esplanade** (150 rooms) Piazza I Maggio 46; ☎085 292141; e reservations@ esplanade.net; www.esplanade.net. Occupying an excellent spot in the city centre across the road from a piazza & the beach, Hotel Esplanade offers pleasant rooms with a refined finish & comfortable beds; it is worth paying an extra €10 for a sea view. Parking & private beach facilities are available. The rooftop restaurant has excellent views of the Adriatic Sea & the hills behind Pescara. **$$$$**

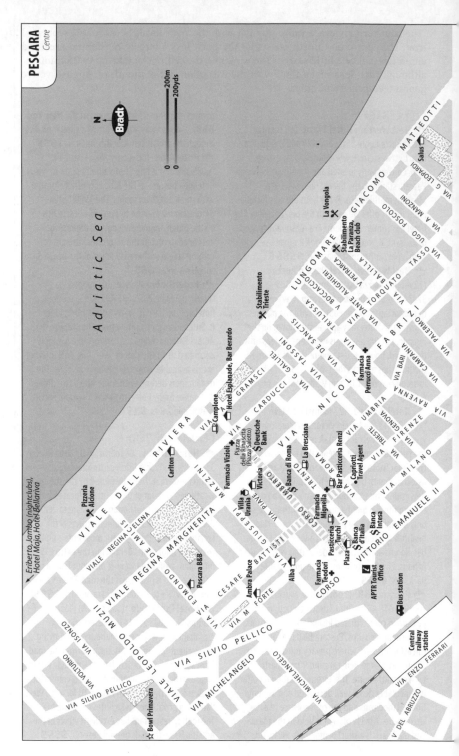

PESCARA
Centre

N

Brodt

0 ——— 200m
0 ——— 200yds

Adriatic Sea

Eriberto, Jambo (nightclubs),
Hotel Maja, Hotel Bellariva

Stabilimento
Trieste

La Vongola
Stabilimento
La Paranza,
Beach club

Salus

VIA G LEOPARDI
VIA A MANZONI
VIA UGO FOSCOLO
GIACOMO
MATTEOTTI
VIA TORQUATO TASSO
VIA PALERMO
VIA DANTE ALIGHIERI
V BOCCACCIO
V PETRARCA
VIA DELLA BAILLA
FABRIZI
VIA BARI
VIA RAVENNA
LUNGOMARE
NICOLA
VIA TRILUSSA
VIA DE SANCTIS
VIA TASSONI
VIA G GALILEI
VIA CAMPANIA
VIA UMBRIA
VIA GENOVA
VIA FIRENZE
VIA MILANO
VIA TRIESTE

Farmacia
Perrucci Anna

GRAMSCI
VIA G CARDUCCI

Pizzeria
Alcione

Campione

Hotel Esplanade, Bar Berardo

Carlton

Farmacia Vizioli
Piazza
della Rinascita
(Piazza Salotto)
Deutsche
Bank

VIA DELLA RIVIERA
VIALE REGINA ELENA
VIALE REGINA MARGHERITA
VIALE GIUSEPPE MAZZINI
VIA EDMONDO DE AMICIS
VIA CESARE BATTISTI
VIA M FORTE

Villa
Urania
Victoria
Banca di Roma
La Bresciana
Bar Pasticceria Renzi
Capriotti
Travel Agent

Farmacia
Mignella
Pasticceria
Turchi
Banca
d'Italia
Banca
Intesa

VIA PIAVE
CORSO UMBERTO
VIA TRENTO
VIA ROMA

Pescara B&B
Ambra Palace
Alba
Farmacia
Teodori
Plaza

CORSO VITTORIO EMANUELE II

APTR Tourist
Office
Bus station

VIA ISONZO
VIA VOLTURNO
VIA SILVIO PELLICO
VIALE LEOPOLDO MUZII
VIA MICHELANGELO

Bowl Primavera

Central
railway
station

VIA ENZO FERRARI
V DEL ABRUZZO

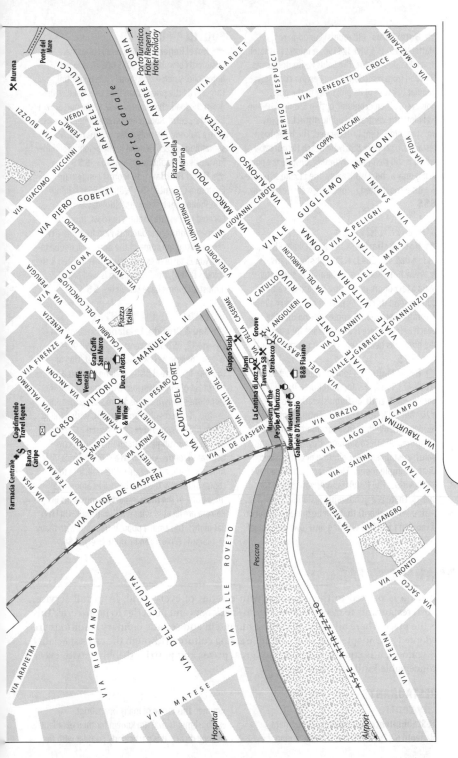

⌂ Hotel Salus (30 rooms) Lungomare
Matteotti 13/1; ✆ 085 374196; e info@salushotel.
it; www.salushotel.it. The Salus is situated across
the road from a section of the Pescara coast less
popular because of its proximity to the port.
However, it is an economic option & only a 10-min
walk into the central shopping district. Rooms
are standard & simply decorated. The hotel has a
restaurant, car park & private beach for guests –
which is still clean for swimming, despite the port
being only a short walk away. The pricing structure
is a little convoluted – check the website carefully.
$$$

NORTHERN RIVIERA
⌂ Hotel Bellariva (33 rooms) Viale Riviera
213; ✆ 085 471 2641; e info@hotelbellariva.
it; www.hotelbellariva.it. Similar to the Hotel
Maja a few doors down, the Bellariva is a little
quieter than its counterpart. It offers very simple
& comfortable rooms, some overlooking the
beach below. There is a restaurant for guests, &
the hotel has beach services & equipment for
hire. **$$$**
⌂ Hotel Maja (50 rooms) Viale Riviera 201;
✆ 085 471 1545; e info@hotelmaja.it; www.
hotelmaja.it. Little distinguishes this hotel,
a 20-min walk from the city centre, from the
residential buildings that surround it except its
1980s neo-Art Deco signage. However, it is an
unfussy establishment offering decently sized,
clean & simple rooms. Those facing the sea have
lovely views. The hotel has a private beach for
guests. There is a good-value restaurant (the
seafood is excellent) that can be quite convenient
if you don't feel like walking into town for a meal.
$$$

SOUTHERN RIVIERA
⌂ Hotel Regent (130 rooms) Lungomare
Cristoforo Colombo 64; ✆ 085 60641; e info@
hotelholiday.net; www.rhotels.it/regent.html.
Larger & a little pricier than the Hotel Holiday just
down the road, this hotel is close to the port & 2km
from the centre. Rooms are simple though spacious,
with a balcony, but only newer rooms have AC,
something to keep in mind in the height of summer.
Private beach facilities are available. **$$$**
⌂ Hotel Holiday (50 rooms) Lungomare
Cristoforo Colombo 102; ✆ 085 65563; e info@
hotelholiday.net; www.hotelholiday.net.
Located on Pescara's southern coast, this hotel
offers straightforward rooms 2km from the city
centre. Although some of the décor will not be to
everyone's taste (it is rather weather-beaten & the
colours faded), the B&B option is well priced &
almost all rooms have sea views. **$$**

OUTSIDE THE CITY CENTRE
⌂ Bed & Breakfast Flaiano (5 rooms) Via
Flaiano 12, 65127 Pescara; m 329 098 0024;
e info@flaiano.net; www.flaiano.net. One of
the very few actual B&Bs, Flaiano is located in
the heart of the oldest surviving area of Pescara,
sometimes known as the *centro storico* (historic
centre). It is accessible only on foot, with parking
some 200m away. There are 2 shared bathrooms
for the interestingly (though this is subjective)
decorated rooms, each with a theme: Africa, Asia,
America, Europa & Oceania. The walk into the
centre of town & the beaches takes around 15
mins but 2 of the most important museums in
Pescara are located within a 5-min walk. On Fri &
Sat nights, the area, a popular hangout with many
restaurants & bars, can be quite lively. **$$**

✖ WHERE TO EAT

Pescara is packed to the gunwales with eateries of every kind: from full service,
posh restaurants to casual eateries, from snack bars and pizzerias to *pasticcerie*. This
is the place where all the region's best mountain and seaside culinary traditions are
adopted and adapted to create a unique eating culture. Although the city's speciality
is seafood, it is equally renowned for great pizzas and pastries dribbling with every
conceivable kind of cream.

RESTAURANTS
City centre
✖ Stabilimento La Paranza Lungomare
Matteotti 62; ✆ 085 27914; ⊕ daily during
summer. This is one of many beachfront
establishments that are known for their excellent
seafood dishes. It is particularly popular with the

suited-up business crowd & the prices certainly match. Its signature dishes, such as the *linguine vongole*, are simple but tasty, using only the freshest of fish. Also try the freshly grilled fish, humble but extremely satisfying. **$$$**

✗ **Ristorante Murena** Lungomare Matteotti 1/3; ✆085 378246; ⊕ Mon–Sat. Come lunchtime, the unmistakable odour of seafood wafts from this restaurant & lures you in like a fish to a net. Set across the road from the beach, this is a no-nonsense eatery giving its customers top-quality food at even better prices. Aside from the excellent-value mains & seconds, desserts are delicious & cheap. **$$**

✗ **Ristorante La Vongola** Lungomare Matteotti 54; ✆085 374236; ⊕ daily lunch & dinner except Wed; www.ristorantelavongola.com. Stylish & intimate, La Vongola is one of many excellent seafood restaurants in a city that thrives on fish. The Porrini brothers have created a cosy boutique restaurant with an extensive seafood menu that satisfies & impresses at both lunch & dinner. Try the *tagliata di tonno* with *radicchio* marinated in a Montepulciano wine sauce. **$$**

Porta Nuova

✗ **La Cantina di Jozz** Via delle Caserme 61; ✆085 690383; www.jozz.it. The Jozz opened its doors in 1976 & is still something of an institution almost 40 years later. The owner's attention to detail is evident from its no-nonsense but rustic décor & clean lines. Try a mixed cheese platter followed by the thick antipasto soup (made from a variety of vegetables & chickpeas, lentils & beans), followed by the delicious pork. Otherwise

PIZZERIAS
City centre

✗ **Ristorante Pizzeria Alcione** Viale Riviera 24; ✆085 421 6830; ⊕ summer, every day until late; winter closed. Something of an old favourite, Alcione is known for making the kind of wood-fired pizza that you will talk about long after the meal is over. Pizzas are all delicious, particularly the margherita & anything with a white base (ie: without tomato). **$$$**

✗ **Stabilimento Trieste** Lungomare Matteotti 102; ✆085 421 4038; ⊕ summer daily till late, winter closed. No matter where you are along the coast of Pescara, it is worth having lunch at Trieste, where I consider the little pizzas to be the best

give yourself completely over to your waiter & let him serve up a 3-course feast of his own expert choosing. The Jozz also has an extensive list of excellent Montepulciani. **$$**

✗ **Giappo Sushi** Corso Manthonè 25; ✆085 692 2205; ⊕ daily for dinner except Mon. There are not many Japanese restaurants in the region and this relative newcomer has caused a stir. The Pescaresi are, admittedly, not particularly fond of cuisine of the non-Italian variety, although you wouldn't think so from the crowds here. The minimalist Japanese-style décor & extensive sushi menu make for an excellent dining experience. Try the scrumptious Sashimi or the sweet prawns. **$$**

✗ **Taverna 58** Corso Manthonè 46; ✆085 690724; ⊕ daily lunch & dinner except Sun; www.taverna58.it. This place is packed to the rafters on Sat nights, particularly during summer, & with good reason. The food is fantastic & there are many signature dishes from around the region. Try the massive antipasto platters followed by any of their meat dishes, such as the braised mutton. **$$**

Outside the city centre

✗ **Cantin[ah]demia** Viale Pindaro 14; ✆085 455 4250; e info@cantinahdemia.it; www. cantinahdemia.com; ⊕ summer, Wed–Sun; winter, daily. Although this place is also a nightclub, its menu is varied, the service is friendly & the décor is very Pescara chic. The pasta dishes are excellent, rivalled only by delicious pizzas. It's worth staying around after dinner & having a drink at the nightclub, particularly on Sat nights. The nightclub runs various themed evenings – check the website for details. **$$**

along the entire coast. People come from many *stabilimenti* to eat tasty tomato-based pizzas, but the white ones (no tomato or toppings, with a splash of oil & salt) are also excellent, particularly those with melted mozzarella. At about €1.50 a pop, they're quite expensive by Pescara standards though you don't really hear anyone complaining. **$**

Outside the centre

✗ **Peccati di Gola** Via Nazionale Adriatica Nord 34; ✆085 471 0461; www. pizzeriapeccatidigolape.com; ⊕ daily until late. 'Sins of the throat', in English, is one of the best places for pizza slices outside the city centre, if not in the whole of Pescara. The variation in toppings is huge, although you will have plenty of time to decide as you wait out the queues. Try the *wurstel e salame* (a pizza with sliced Frankfurt-style sausages & shavings of salami), or the potato & mayonnaise. It gets extremely busy on a Fri night so it's well worth calling ahead. The pizzeria's motto is 'the real sin is not sinning.' $

CAFÉS, *PASTICCERIE* AND ICE CREAM

La Bresciana Via Trento 96–98; 085 421 2302; www.cremeriabresciana.it; Mon-Sat. No writer, journalist or poet could really do this place justice given its warranted popularity as the best *pasticceria* for miles. Something of an institution in Pescara, it was established in 1948 & is still everybody's favourite. You must try a *bomba*, a local speciality 'doughnut', for want of a more stylish word, filled with cream & sprinkled with sugar. Eateries come & go but it is still 'in' to have a Sat morning breakfast at La Bresciana – & if you do decide to join the weekend crowd, you will have to eat standing at the bar. $

Caffè Venezia Via Venezia 27; 085 296171; www.caffevenezia.it; summer 24hrs, winter early morning to late. Often crowded, Caffè Venezia is a popular hangout for young people. On a Sun morning, for instance, they are open into the wee hours to catch the Sat night post-clubbing crowd. It's certainly amusing that your chances of finding a table at 05.00 on a Sun morning are tantamount to zero. The caffè can be a little expensive though it has the décor & presentation to match, not to mention excellent coffee & cakes. The owners have recently opened another caffè with the same name in Piazza della Rinascita, in the city centre, where it's popular for a pre- or post-dinner drink, particularly at the weekend. $$$

Camplone Corso Umberto I 125–133; 085 389148; daily until late. This stylish looking café & snack bar not only serves an abundant variety of sweets & pastries, but you can also choose from no fewer than 50 flavours of ice cream. If you're swayed by fruit, try the peach or watermelon. But if it's the creams that take your fancy, then the chocolate & hazelnut are delicious. $

Bar Pasticceria Renzi Via Roma 52; 085 421 6164. A near-rival to nearby La Bresciana, this *pasticceria* offers a large variety of pastries & cakes. Try an afternoon snack of *crostata* (fruit/jam tart) & espresso. $

Gran Caffè San Marco Via Venezia 4; 085 421 9804. This is a café-cum-snack bar with a casual look & feel but with a scrumptious variety of 'Neapolitan' pastries to tempt you at the bar. $

Pasticceria Turchi Via Trento 33; 085 810275; www.pasticceriabarturchi.it; Mon–Sat. The history of the Turchi establishments is long & complex & began in the Chieti Province in 1955. After a few relocations, the family set up shop in Pescara & the new & improved Turchi is a boutique-style *pasticceria* with so many delectable treats that your eyes won't know where to rest & your mouth won't stop watering. Try the *cornetto con crema* or the chocolate *crostata*. $

ENTERTAINMENT, NIGHTLIFE AND DRINKING

Pescara's nightlife has two very distinct seasons: summer and winter. During the winter months, the action is almost exclusively in the old town at Porta Nuova and in the few nightclubs. In summer, however, the action largely shifts to the coast (with the exception of Corso Manthonè in Porta Nuova) where the *stabilimenti* (see page 46) become beach nightclubs.

BEACH NIGHTCLUBS Interestingly, while almost all of the *stabilimenti* become discos and dance haunts at night, the popular ones vary almost from year to year. Some of the classics are:

☆ **Delfino Verde** Viale della Riviera 112; 085 471 2710

☆ **Eriberto** Viale della Riviera 42; 085 375158

☆ **Jambo** Viale della Riviera 38; 085 27949

☆ **Miami Beach** Viale della Riviera 74; 085 471 0112

☆ **L'Ammiraglia** Viale della Riviera 140; 085 471 0108

BARS, CLUBS AND OTHER PLACES TO CHILL OUT

☆ **Discoteca Cantin[ah]demia** Viale Pindaro, 14; ✆085 455 4250; e info@cantinahdemia.it; www.cantinahdemia.it; ⊕ Wed–Sun. As well as being an excellent restaurant, Cantina (as it is known) puts on one of the best parties in town during summer weekends. It is a chic place, with modern décor that recalls the boutique-style dance haunts of Manhattan. Events change regularly, so check the website for details. **$$$**

☆ **Discoteca La Fabbrica** Viale Pindaro 14; ✆085 65800; ⊕ Wed & Sat–Sun. La Fabbrica is an old favourite, especially with the young crowd. It's the most popular nightclub during the winter months & closes during summer (it couldn't possibly compete with the beachside clubs). **$$$**

♀ **Bar Berardo** Corso Umberto I 120; ✆085 294204; ⊕ daily till late. Something of a Pescara institution, Berardo is a household name & continues to reinvent itself, with its most recent fitout & overhaul in 2010. Some say it's the place to be seen; others say it's long past its heyday & is too expensive. Whichever way you look at it, Berardo continues to draw the crowds. There are comfortable couchettes & seating, not to mention outdoor heaters for the winter months. Try the coffee mousse, more like a thick espresso. **$$**

♀ **Groove** Via dei Bastioni 6; m 3283 881 436; ⊕ daily till late. Not far from the main thoroughfare of Porta Nuova, Corso Manthonè, the Groove is a big place with friendly staff & a relaxed atmosphere. It is, by all accounts, a pub, & its beer collection is extensive. However, the cocktails are also excellent, as is the finger food. It's worth going for happy hour, 21.30–23.00 on weeknights & all day Sun. **$$**

♀ **Marni** Via delle Caserme 44; ✆085 454 9081; ⊕ Wed & Fri–Sun evening only. This place has a warm, friendly & intimate feel that is conducive to a few cocktails with a small group of friends. It is very popular during summer & getting a table can be difficult, especially on a Sat night. Wed night is jazz night, when the place is far less crowded & a lot of fun. **$$**

☆ **Phoenix** Via Caravaggio 109; ✆085 73689; www.phoenixclub.it; ⊕ Thu–Sun. The fact that Pescara has a gay & lesbian nightclub is a testament to how much the city has developed over the last 10 years. This is the only exclusively gay venue in all of Abruzzo, & consequently, people come from all over the region & beyond. Recently refurbished, Phoenix offers everything from drag acts to karaoke to strip shows. It is tucked away in a side street behind the railway line & there isn't much to indicate its presence. Do not leave any belongings in your car if you are driving, as there have been a handful of instances of homophobia-related vandalism & thefts. **$$**

♀ **Strabacco** Corso Manthonè 49; m 338 9724024; ⊕ Wed–Mon evening only. This is one of the most sophisticated bars in Pescara & is quite popular with 20-something professionals. The soft lighting & comfortable seating mean you won't want to get up for hours. The wine is excellent & there is a particularly extensive selection of rums & cocktails. **$$**

♀ **Wine & Wine** Via Chieti 14; ✆085 422 3180; ⊕ daily 24hrs except Sun. This small & underrated wine bar & restaurant is a must-visit. The owners take great pride in their little enterprise & love what they do, & this comes through both in their commitment & in the service they offer. The wines are excellent, as is the selection of spirits & snacks. This is an easy place to while away a few hours before dinner, eating, drinking & chatting to the friendly staff. **$$**

♀ **Jayson's** Via Marconi 283; ✆085 496 3071; ⊕ daily 07.00–14.00. No Italian city would be complete without at least 1 very popular Irish pub, & in Pescara it is Jayson's. While it's almost a moot point to mention that Guinness is the beer of choice, it's also worth noting that there are some excellent Irish & Scottish whiskies on offer. Cheap beer 19.00–21.30. **$**

☆ **Bowl Primavera** Via Aurelio Saffi 8; ✆085 35202; ⊕ daily till late. Bowling was huge in Pescara during the 1980s & although this place has seen better days, it is still arguably the most popular place to knock down a few pins. It can become quite crowded on Sat nights so it is best to book in advance. **$**

CINEMA The Pescaresi tend to head to Montesilvano's large Warner Movie complex to catch a flick or two, though if you don't feel like making the journey, the following two cinemas will do the job:

≣ Pescara Cityplex Cinema Massimo Via Caduta del Forte; ☎085 421 2225; www. pescaracityplex.it

≣ Circus Cinema Via Lanciano 9; ☎085 442 9109

EVENTS AND FESTIVALS

For a yearly schedule of events in Pescara, visit www.comune.pescara.it or www. abruzzoturismo.it. Three major events take place during July.

PESCARA JAZZ FESTIVAL Since its birth in 1969, Pescara's International Jazz Festival (see *Music*, page 23), held in July, has become one of the most renowned in Europe. The programme changes considerably each year, as do the venues. Check out the official website at www.pescarajazz.com.

TROFEO MATTEOTTI The Pescaresi don't pay much attention to any sport that doesn't involve either a ball or a car, though the entire city stops (literally) for the Trofeo Matteotti, a one-day bicycle race usually held in July. Many of the city's major roads are blocked off for the event, which is now organised by the UCI Europe Tour, and a lot of people flock to their balconies to see the riders whizz past.

FESTA DI SANT'ANDREA Although its popularity has decreased since its heyday in the 1980s and '90s, this street fair held at the end of July since 1867 is still a big event. The southern end of the Lungomare Matteotti is completely blocked and lined with all manner of stalls selling food of all sorts, drinks, clothing and toys. There are numerous rides along the river. The fair usually lasts about three days and is concluded by a fantastic display of fireworks. Few are the Pescaresi who don't make at least one appearance, and the fair is particularly popular with families.

SHOPPING

Pescara, to use an old but, in this case, appropriate cliché, is a shopper's dream. The focal point of the city's main shopping areas is the streets around Corso Umberto I, Via Nicola Fabrizi and Corso Vittorio Emanuele II. However, boutiques and quirky shops are to be found in all corners of the city centre, including the residential areas. If shopping is one of your *raisons d'être* then it pays to set aside some time for venturing into the quieter streets – you never know what you will find.

With little exception, shops throughout the city close for the lunchtime siesta. Most establishments roughly follow opening times of 09.00–13.00 and 16.00–20.00. Some shops open and close later during summer and some choose to close on Thursday afternoons, often without notice.

CLOTHING AND FOOTWEAR From Armani to Prada, and from Benetton to Replay, it's all here in central Pescara. With the exception of Rome, Pescara is arguably the fashion capital of the central Italian regions of Lazio, Abruzzo, Molise and Le Marche. In fact, for a city of its size, this is one place that is well decked out. The Pescaresi, whose love for all fashion signed and labelled is known throughout the region, are not in the business of rejecting a spot of Saturday afternoon retail therapy. And with so many options, the escapades may spill over well into the rest of the weekend. Below is a selection of stores, but it is only the tip of the iceberg. They are arranged geographically into areas around and between Corso Umberto I, Corso Vittorio Emanuele II and Via Nicola Fabrizi.

THE 'MARROCCHINI' MARKETS

This is something of a misnomer, since very few, if any, actual Moroccans run the 'Moroccan' market stalls. In fact, depending on where you are in Italy, the word *marrocchini* can be quite derogatory. It is a general term to describe the sub-Saharan immigrants who you'll encounter doing business here. They are, more often than not, illegal immigrants, and their stalls, to the right as you exit Pescara's train station, are against the law. However, that doesn't put the locals off, and if you decide to take a peek, you'll find imitation high-street labels on sale here: everything from designer bags and accessories to shoes, trousers and jackets. You'll marvel at the quality as well as wondering how they get away with producing goods that use fashion-house logos and look almost indistinguishable from those on display in shop windows along the posher streets of Rome or Milan. If you wish to buy something, do so at your own risk and be aware that the police, fully aware of their existence, are known to attempt half-hearted crackdowns from time to time. Be aware that if you are caught buying here, you will also be fined.

Bargaining here is the order of the day; *never* accept the price that is being offered. A typical exchange should occur thus:

- Display interest in the item and wait to be approached. This will show you are keen, but not too eager.
- Ask about the price. Most of the workers here make it their business to speak a good level of English though be aware that the price tends to be higher for non-locals.
- When you have been told the price, smile and say it is far too much. Make a more reasonable offer; half the asking price is not unreasonable here.
- You will be told that this is an unfair price, that it is high-quality merchandise, that he would not make any profit, that you are his friend and he will make you an offer you simply can't refuse, so on and so forth.
- Stick to your guns. You may be willing to go up by a couple of euros or more depending on how much you want the item and what price you deem to be reasonable. Remember that a euro or two probably means more to them than to you, but also that the person offering you the item is probably very keen to make a sale.

If the seller won't bargain down to your budget, be prepared to walk away. This can be disappointing if you really want the item but chances are you will find the same thing a few stalls down. Usually you will be called back and offered something closer to your price; in this case either accept the new price or reiterate your offer. More often than not you will end up paying something very close to your first offer.

SHOPPING ON THE BEACH? Yes, the Pescaresi are so dedicated to their shopping that they'll even do it whilst reclining on a beach-bed sizzling under the heat of the summer sun. In the warmer months, you will find the *marrocchini* walking along the coast selling trinkets of all shapes and sizes to beach-goers. If you encounter one and are not interested, simply smile and refuse; they will always move on to a more receptive customer. If, on the other hand, something interests you, the above bargaining principles can also be applied.

Santomo   Corso Umberto I 82, 100 & 106; 085 28077; e santomo@santomo.it; www.santomo.it. A 3-store institution in Pescara's city centre (there are stores for men's, women's & vintage goods). A retailer for high street fashion labels such as Gucci, Prada & Armani, this place exudes elegance & begs to empty out your wallet.

MaxMara   Corso Umberto I 4; 085 422 1403; www.maxmara.it. A world-renowned Italian fashion house. Originally specialising in men's formal wear, MaxMara has for the past few decades been a specialist in luxury women's wear.

Stefanel   Corso Umberto I 74; 085 422 7020; e negozio640271@gruppo.stefanel.it; www. stefanel.it. With a store in just about every Italian city, Stefanel specialises in both men's & women's clothing.

Elena Miro   Corso Umberto I 8/10; 085 422 5507; www.elenamiro.it. Offers colourful but no-fuss women's clothing.

Luisa Spagnoli   Corso Umberto I 69; 085 422 7148. Caters for women who are looking for a splash of colour on stylish designs.

United Colors of Benetton Megastore   Corso Vittorio Emanuele II, 212; 085 205 8132; www. benetton.com. An Italian institution that is famous the world over for its 'multi-cultural' ads, socio-cultural magazine & casual wear for men & women, this store is set over 2 floors & also houses a **Sisley** collection.

Te Piace   Corso Vittorio Emanuele II 175; 085 294487. A favourite for trendy clothing with an alternative edge.

Terranova   Corso Vittorio Emanuele II 220; 085 442 9160; www.terranova-on-line.com. Casual, trendy clothing with very attractive price tags.

Corazzini   Via Nicola Fabrizi 256; 085 27146; e corazzinijeans@hotmail,com. An authorised vendor for Diesel.

Le Gabrielli   Via Nicola Fabrizi 274; 085 36153; e info@legabrielli.it; www.legabrielli.it. Features clothing, shoes & bags by the likes of DKNY & Armani.

Adriana Boutique   Via Nicola Fabrizi 250; 085 421 1615. An authorised women's clothes & accessories vendor for labels such as Fendi & Armani. The Fendi collection is arguably the largest in Pescara.

Albanese   Via Nicola Fabrizi 152 & 182; 085 27606; www.spazioalbanese.it. Albanese has perhaps seen better days but remains one of the largest vendors of the funky side of labels from the likes of Dolce & Gabbana, Galliano, & Roberto Cavalli.

Energie   Via Nicola Fabrizi 37; 085 422 7475. Energie has a store in just about every Italian city & caters to a younger crowd. Their streetwear has a funky edge. This store also sells **Miss Sixty** clothing, which is produced locally.

Carla G   Via Piave 35; 085 422 1339; e info@ carlag.it; www.carlag.it. A popular label whose stylishly expensive women's clothing is reputed to be an Italian trendsetter.

Victor Shoes   Via Cesare Battisti, 27/29; 085 421 2678; e victorshoes@tin.it. Offers a large collection of designer shoes from the likes of Prada, Gucci & other high-end fashion houses.

Replay   Via Trento 92/94; 085 421 7929; e info@replay.it; www.replay.it. Replay has established itself as a popular vendor of casual streetwear for both men & women.

Murphy & NYE   Via Trento 52/54; 085 205 8227; e pescara@store.murphynye.com; www. murphynye.com. Features casual streetwear for men & women.

SPORTS STORES   Two outlets near to each other are amongst the city's favourites when it comes to sporting goods and all things related. Conveniently, they stock a comprehensive range of beachwear to suit everyone.

EDICOLE

You will find these little news stands sprinkled all over the city of Pescara. Lovers of books and magazines will inevitably slow to cruising speeds when they encounter one, as the plethora of newspapers, books and colourful periodicals, coupled with that distinct smell of paper, draws them in. Even though there is rarely English-language material, it is worth stopping and taking a look at the sheer variety of magazines, particularly those dedicated to travel.

THE SUMMER AND WINTER SALES

No country does sales quite like Italy and no small Italian city with more fervour than Pescara. Come January and July, the Pescaresi hit the centre's pavements heavily weighed down by bags full of jaw-dropping bargains. And these are not the *faux* sales that you might be used to: prices are literally slashed and slashed until shelves are empty and shops look like they have been subjected to apocalypse-style looting. The sales follow the main fashion seasons (summer/winter) when clothing is cleared away to make room for the new collections. For those in the know, perusing the sales follows a number of rules and it pays to be aware:

The best bargains are not necessarily to be had as soon as the 'sale' signs adorn shop windows. If you have your eyes on a particular item and you have time, it may be worth coming back a few days later to check whether the price has been slashed even further. There are various 'waves' of price slashing, with shops almost giving away stock towards the end of the sale seasons. However, there's usually a reason why said stock hasn't flown out the door before the final days.

Not all merchandise is put on sale immediately, and some not at all. *Merce non a saldo* means that a particular item or range of items is not on sale.

Be ruthless. You may find yourself playing tug-o-war for that sweater you just have to have. Don't let go! You may get a dubious look that says all foreigners have no shame, but then again you got your €90 item for €15.

Dolci Sport Via Roma 52; ☎ 085 422 2898; e info@dolcisport.it; www.dolcisport.it

Zulli Sport Via Firenze 239–241; ☎ 085 421 1623

JEWELLERY AND ACCESSORIES Most of the clothing stores listed above feature a range of accessories. However, Pescara's streets are full of stores that specialise in specific markets such as watches and leather bags.

Elvira Seta Preziosi Via Venezia 74/76; ☎ 085 27824. A jewellery specialist with a varied collection. The friendly owner, Elvira, has been working in the industry for many years & can advise on the best options to suit your needs. It is also an excellent place to buy 'La Presentosa', a typical Abruzzese star-shaped piece of jewellery that is often given as a present to a lover.
La Gardenia Italia Corso Vittorio Emanuele II 241/243; ☎ 085 205 8343; www.lagardenia.com.

This & the establishment below offer a cornucopia of perfumes & related products of almost every conceivable label.
Profumeria Limoni Corso Vittorio Emanuele II 20; ☎ 085 205 8265; www.limoni.it. See above.
Voyage Via Nicola Fabrizi 278; ☎ 085 27184; e info@voyage-eclair.com; www.voyage-eclair. com. Specialises in leather bags & shoes. Labels include the ever-popular Guess.

BOOKS AND NEWSPAPERS You'll encounter a small selection of English-language books in most bookstores in Pescara, though the largest collection is to be found at La Feltrinelli (*Via Trento 5;* ☎ *085 292389;* e *pescara@lafeltrinelli.it; www.lafeltrinelli. it*) and inside the railway station, where you can also pick up English-language newspapers and maps.

GASTRONOMY Cheeses, hams, jams and biscuits are stacked floor-to-ceiling at **Salumer** (*Via Ravenna 59;* ☎ *085 442 9154*), and the friendly staff are willing to

This is one phenomenon that, unlike in the rest of the world, did not take to Abruzzo like a village rumour. While the biggest and best shopping centres were being built elsewhere as far back as the 1950s, the concept was alien to a people whose remote areas at that time were still making do with the transport power of the donkey. However, the last decade has seen a number of these malls pop up in the urban areas around Pescara.

The largest is the **Megalò** centre (*Loc Santa Filomena, 66013 Chieti Scalo;* ℡ *087 154 0010;* e *info@megaloweb.it; www.megaloweb.it*), situated just outside Chieti Scalo, Chieti's lower town. From Pescara, take the Asse Attrezzato (E80) and exit at Villareia; there is plenty of free car parking. Stores here include Zara, United Colors of Benetton, Pull & Bear, CK Jeans and many others. The centre also has a cinema complex, various restaurants and a large Iperstanda supermarket.

Before the Megalò complex cast a shadow over it, the **Ipercoop Centro d'Abruzzo** (*Sambuceto;* ℡ *085 446 4886;* e *info@centrodabruzzo.it; www. centrodabruzzo.it*) was all the rage, and is, frankly, the only other shopping centre worth your time to visit. It can be easily reached from both Pescara and Chieti. Take the Asse Attrezzato and exit at Sambuceto, and follow the signs to the shopping centre. Alternatively, you can take Via Tiburtina, behind the Porta Nuova quarter of Pescara, turn immediately after the airport and follow the signs. Here, you will also encounter the small centre of **Auchan** (*Via Tiburtina Valeria, 386;* ℡ *085 444701;* e *segdir.pescara@auchan.it; www.auchan. it*), a large supermarket surrounded by a few shops.

The most recent addition to the region is the charming **Città Sant'Angelo Village Outlet** (*Via Moscarola, Città Sant'Angelo;* ℡ *085 950302; www. cittasantangelovillage.com*), with around 100 outdoor shops layed out to resemble a pastel-coloured medieval village. Many top brands, including the likes of Calvin Klein, Valentino and Botticelli, have opened their doors here.

make suggestions to cater to your every taste. This charismatic little delicatessen chain also has two other stores in Pescara, at Via Tirino 380 and Via Cavour 41/43.

OTHER PRACTICALITIES

There are banks and post offices on almost every street corner in Pescara; those listed below are the most convenient for visitors. Be aware that the connections between **banks** in Pescara and those outside Italy are sometimes down, so you may need to try two or three different ATMs before your transaction is successful. This only happens in Pescara, and the reason for it is a mystery. Interestingly, the same issue does not present itself when paying by card at shops or restaurants.

Whilst most local travel agents can organise trips out of town and suggest accommodation and itineraries, it is worth bearing in mind that, given that Abruzzo remains largely undiscovered by international tourism, they cater mostly for outbound tourists.

BANKS
$ **Banca Caripe** Corso Vittorio Emanuele II 102
$ **Banca d'Italia** Corso Vittorio Emanuele II 65

$ **Banca di Roma** Corso Umberto I 58
$ **Banca Intesa** Corso Vittorio Emanuele II 254 & 370

$ Deutsche Bank Via Tibullo 5
$ Banca San Paolo Corso Vittorio Emanuele II 272

CHEMISTS
✚ Farmacia Centrale Corso Vittorio Emanuele II 116; ☎ 085 421 1895
✚ Farmacia Teodori Corso Vittorio Emanuele II 280; ☎ 085 421 1729
✚ Farmacia Mignella Via Firenze 189; ☎ 085 421 4177
✚ Farmacia Perrucci Anna Via Nicola Fabrizi 138; ☎ 085 295382
✚ Farmacia Vizioli Corso Umberto I 109; ☎ 085 422 7928

POST OFFICE
✉ Corso Vittorio Emanuele II 106; ☎ 085 427 9616. ⊕ Mon–Fri 08.00–18.30, Sat 08.00–12.30.

HOSPITAL
✚ Via Renato Paolini 45/47; ☎ 085 4251. (Note that the emergency medical number is ☎ 118.)

LOCAL TRAVEL AGENTS
Cagidemetrio Via Ravenna 3; ☎ 085 421 3022; e info@cagidemetrio.it; www.cagidemetrio.it. A well-known travel agent, Cagidemetrio can help with a range of services, including hotels, & train & ferry tickets from Abruzzo.
Capriotti Viaggi Via Firenze 229; ☎ 085 205 6145; e info@capriottiviaggi.com; www. capriottiviaggi.com. Pop in & ask the friendly staff if you're in need of accommodation, tours or various other things.
Ventur Viaggi Via De Sanctis 5; ☎ 085 28903; e ventur@pec.ventur.it; www.ventur.it. Excellent packages on offer.

WHAT TO SEE

Pescara's attraction is certainly not in the traditional selection of sights. It's more about the atmosphere, the relaxation, and the opportunity to witness Italian family life at its most conventional. However, there is a handful of interesting museums.

MUSEO CASA NATALE DI GABRIELE D'ANNUNZIO/HOUSE MUSEUM OF GABRIELE D'ANNUNZIO (*Corso Manthonè 100;* ☎ *085 450 3590; www.casadannunzio. beniculturali.it;* ⊕ *daily 09.00–13.30; admission adult €2, children €1*) The birthplace and childhood home of one of the greatest Italian poets, Gabriele D'Annunzio (see page 22), is now a museum and a national monument decreed in 1927. Set in the most historic street in Pescara in the so-called 'Old Town', the House Museum, restored in the 1930s, spans several rooms and is set around a charming courtyard. The house displays living rooms, valuable furniture, paintings and excerpts from some of his works.

MUSEO DELLE GENTI D'ABRUZZO/MUSEUM OF THE PEOPLE OF ABRUZZO (*Via delle Caserme 22;* ☎ *085 451 0026; e museo@gentidabruzzo.it; www.gentidabruzzo. it; admission adult/child €6/€3, free Sun;* ⊕ *Sep–Jun, Mon–Sat 09.00–14.00, Sun 10.00–14.00; Jun–Sep, Mon–Thu 10.00–14.00, Fri 10.00–14.00 & 18.30–21.30*) An interesting museum covering 15 rooms, this museum hosts displays relating to the everyday lives of people in Abruzzo over the centuries. There are recreations of natural habitats, displays of uncovered remains, exhibitions of wheat farming in Abruzzo and a long explanation of the history of the region. The museum is extremely well organised and often hosts events. Check the website for details.

MUSEO VILLA URANIA/MUSEUM OF VILLA URANIA (*Via Piave, 139;* ☎ *085 422 3426; admission adult/child €2;* ⊕ *Tue–Sat 16.30–19.30*) This museum, set in a stunning 19th-century brown-façade villa, contains the largest display of pieces from the Castelli ceramic works (see page 231) outside of Castelli itself. Works on display include those of Francesco Grue and the Cappelletti family.

Aside from these museums, there are a few other sights worth visiting.

BASILICA DELLA MADONNA DEI SETTE DOLORI Constructed in the residential area on the hills behind the coast, the Basilica della Madonna dei Sette Dolori is the oldest surviving church in Pescara. It was founded in 1757 after a supposed sighting of the Madonna on this hill. Though the façade is typical of the era, there is nothing particularly outstanding about its interior.

PIAZZA DELLA RINASCITA Known colloquially as Piazza Salotto (due to its popularity with people just 'lounging' around – *salotto* means 'lounge room'), this is the city's largest and most important square. The piazza, located at the eastern end of Corso Umberto I, hosts music events and celebrations as well as concerts, and this is where large screens are erected for watching football matches (for example, during a World Cup).

PONTE DEL MARE Rising over the mouth of the Pescara River and creating a direct path between the north and south coasts, this bridge is perhaps Pescara's most significant construction since World War II. Built over a period of almost two years from 2008 to 2009, the bridge is 466m long and rises approximately 50m above the river. It offers inspiring views of Pescara and its coastline, and is popular for an evening walk or cycle during the summer months. Until its completion in late 2009, it was a long and complicated affair to walk from the centre of Pescara or its northern coast to the south of the city, but the days of taking the long and inconvenient way around are long gone.

PORTO TURISTICO MARINA DI PESCARA (*www.marinape.com*) The port of Pescara is not only a functional port but also a tourist attraction. It is one of the largest harbours along the Adriatic coast and boasts a Blue Flag beach (see page 46). The harbour is lined with galleries and shops and hosts regular events, including rides and concerts.

4

Pescara Province

No matter what you are looking for in your visit to Abruzzo, there is a good chance you will find it in the province of Pescara. Church belltowers are framed by the tall peaks of the national parks, narrow alleyways buzz with the sounds of town fairs and beachside cities beckon you onto silky white sand.

Although all this has developed around the city of Pescara over scores of generations, the province itself is relatively young as a separate political entity. It was carved out of the Teramo and Chieti provinces at the same time as Pescara itself was created from two separate Adriatic towns in 1927. Nowadays, it is the region's smallest province in size but comes second only to Chieti Province in terms of population, with more than half of the people living close to its 20km of coastline.

SUGGESTED ITINERARY

Spend some time in Pescara, before making your way to the old town of Spoltore, then inland to Penne and Loreto Aprutino. From here, head over to the Majella National Park and its surrounding areas, exploring towns such as San Valentino, Caramanico and Popoli.

MONTESILVANO

Montesilvano is overshadowed by the larger, adjacent city of Pescara. They are actually right next to one another and the whole area is more akin to a conurbation, also taking in the towns of Spoltore, Sambuceto and Francavilla (in Chieti Province). The two cities are so interconnected that even residents of Montesilvano mean the centre of Pescara when they say they are 'going into town'. However, Montesilvano's coastal hotels tend to be more popular with tourists

> ### THE TESSERA CLUB
>
> The 'Tessera Club' is actually a membership fee that may be payable to a hotel for the use of amenities such as swimming pools, spas and gyms, and for activities like aerobics, cabaret shows and dance lessons; the list depends on the hotel. The price varies according to the establishment, but is usually around €20–35 per person. Some hotels charge this fee only once and in some instances only in summer, but others may charge weekly. Make sure you check this with your hotel when you book as some may forget to mention the extra fee.

4

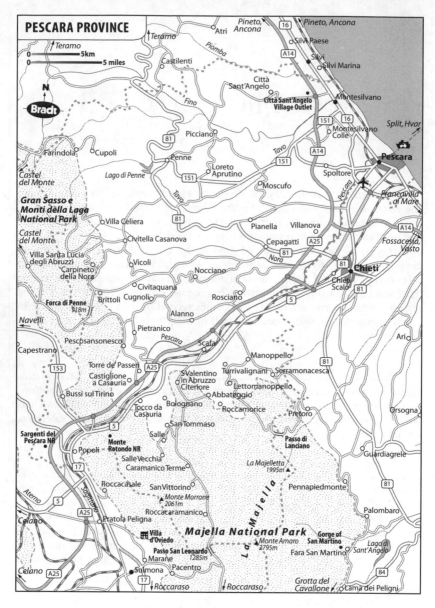

than those of Pescara. This is largely due to the more relaxed pace here, away from the bustle of the larger city.

For amenities such as banks, you are certainly better off making the short journey to the centre of Pescara (see *Chapter 3, Pescara*). There is nothing in the way of sightseeing in Montesilvano.

TOURIST INFORMATION

🛈 IAT Montesilvano Viale Europa 73/4; 📞 085 445 8859

WHERE TO STAY

In town Given Montesilvano's size and layout, most hotels in town are found within easy walking distance of the beach. They can be a good alternative to their more expensive seaside counterparts.

⌂ **Hotel Antagos** (54 rooms) Via Lago Trasimeno 8; ☎085 73870; e info@hotelantagos. com; www.hotelantagos.com. Look past the bland exterior & the (questionable) colour of some of the interior walls & you'll find a no-fuss 3-star hotel not far from the beach. Accommodation is clean & there's an excellent view of the sea from the rooftop restaurant. The hotel has a private beach for guests. **$$$**

⌂ **Hotel City** (36 rooms) Viale Europa 77; ☎085 445 3227; e htlcity@tiscali.it; www. hotelcityabruzzo.it. Situated only 50m from the beach, this modern hotel features a swimming pool, & access to a private beach is included in the price. For all its rather grand entrance the rooms & decoration are simple & it is an economic option considering its proximity to the beach. **$$$**

⌂ **Hotel Excelsior** (43 rooms) Via Bradano 5; ☎085 835510; e info@hotelexcelsiormontesilvano. it; www.hotelexcelsiormontesilvano.it. The Excelsior is only minutes from the beach. Even though some of its rooms are not as spacious as they could be, they are well decorated in a modern style. There are also some lovely 'residences' or apartments, with the added benefit of fully equipped kitchens & lounge areas, which are great for longer family stays. **$$$**

⌂ **Hotel Prestige** (43 rooms) Via Marinelli 102; ☎085 449 2630; e info@hotel-prestige.it; www. hotel-prestige.it. The lively & brightly decorated Prestige is a relatively new arrival to the area. Its owner & staff are extremely friendly & offer good-sized rooms with simple but modern furnishings. There is also a bar & restaurant dishing up some excellent seafood. HB & FB. **$$$**

⌂ **Hotel Piccolo Mondo** (19 rooms) Via Marinelli, 86; ☎085 445 2647; e reserve@ hotelpiccolomondo.com; www.hotelpiccolomondo. com. As its name ('small world') suggests, this is a somewhat small though welcoming hotel about 100m from the beach. Carrying on the theme, the rooms are on the small side but nicely done with modern decoration & all spotlessly clean. There is also a charming roof garden for a spot of relaxation after a day of sightseeing & sunbathing. HB & FB. **$$**

The 'Grand Hotels' Locally known as the Zona Grandi Hotel, this section of Montesilvano's northernmost beaches has seen considerable development over the last decade. It now comprises a handful of hotels, the majority of which (unless otherwise stated below) are conveniently situated directly on the beach. Please note that most of these hotels list their tariffs on a per person basis – but the codes in this guide indicate the cost of a double room.

⌂ **Grand Hotel Adriatico** (140 rooms) Via Carlo Maresca 10; ☎085 445 2695; e info@grandhoteladriatico.com; www. grandhoteladriatico.com. The popular & busy Grand Hotel Adriatico is set in a modern block & has a private beach as well as indoor & outdoor swimming pools. Although it's a little flash, the rooms are decorated in modern style & are decently sized. The hotel's restaurant is a great place for large functions. A 'Tessera Club' fee applies. **$$$$**

⌂ **Grand Hotel Montesilvano** (150 rooms) Piazzale Kennedy 28; ☎085 835 887; e info@ ghmeurhotels.com; www.ghmeurhotels.com. This large seafront hotel has a private beach for its guests, although a 'Tessera Club' fee is charged. There are good-sized rooms that are fairly simple but tastefully decorated as well as being bright & airy. The hotel has a restaurant & bar. The owners also operate the neighbouring **Residence Eurhotel**, which offers apartments at €225–1,310 a week, depending on the configuration & season. **$$$$**

⌂ **Hotel Duca degli Abruzzi** (57 rooms) Via Carlo Maresca 15; ☎085 445 0700; e info@ hotelducadegliabruzzi.it; www. hotelducadegliabruzzi.it. The Duca degli Abruzzi is set in 2 adjacent buildings less than 100m from the beach. It offers simple but modern rooms decorated in various shades of green. There is a bar, pool & gym, & a good restaurant serving some lovely seafood dishes. **$$$$**

⌂ **Hotel Promenade** (92 rooms) Via Aldo Moro 63; 📞085 445 2221; e info@ hotelpromenadeonline.com; www. promenadehotel.org. This is a lovely hotel offering various types of accommodation, including a number of apartments & suites. The standard rooms are bright, airy & reasonably tasteful. The friendly staff keep the building & grounds in immaculate condition. The restaurant is decently priced, & a private beach, just the other side of the fence from the hotel's pool, is available to guests for an extra fee. Prices of rooms facing the beach vary. **$$$$**

⌂ **Hotel Sea Lion** (74 rooms) Via Aldo Moro 65; 📞085 449 2736; e info@ sealionhotel.com; www.hotelsealion.com. The Clarion Hotel is one of the best known of the 'grand hotels'. The rooms, all with sea views, are clean, comfortable & spacious (some decked out in bright blue carpet). The hotel also has a good restaurant (try the excellent seafood) as well as a large pool, a health & well-being centre & a private beach for the use of guests. **$$$$**

⌂ **Nyce Club Grand Hotel Mediterraneo** (175 rooms) Via Carlo Maresca 34; 📞085 449

2771; www.nyceclub.it. This is a very pleasant 4-star establishment set directly on the beach. It has an attractive reception & public areas as well as recently renovated & spotlessly clean rooms. The hotel has a large swimming pool & a private section of beach for guests. **$$$$**

⌂ **Serena Majestic** (200 rooms, 270 apartments) Via Carlo Maresca 12; 📞085 836 9777; e info@ bluserenahotels.it; www.bluserenahotels. it. This resort is probably the biggest in the area. Set in no fewer than 5 buildings, all connected by passageways, it features 2 good restaurants (both with great seafood), 2 pools, tennis courts & a private beach for guests. The rooms & apartments are comfortable & functionally decorated. A 'Tessera Club' fee applies. **$$$$**

⌂ **Hotel Ariminum Felicioni** (29 rooms) Via Carlo Maresca 3; 📞085 445 0022; e info@ ariminum.com; www.ariminum.com. Situated about 50m from the beach, this hotel, catering to both the leisure and business traveller, may not offer the uninterrupted sea views of its neighbours but it does have simple accommodation at reasonable prices. The room decoration is pretty standard but the rooms are of a decent size. A 'Tessera Club' fee applies. **$$$**

✖ **WHERE TO EAT AND DRINK** As with most other things in Montesilvano, most people tend to head for Pescara or beyond for dinner. All the same, it does have a couple of good restaurants and an excellent gelateria.

✖ **Sapò Ristorante Marinaro** Via Irma Bandiera 3; 📞085 468 6080; ⊕ Mon–Sat; e info@ ristorantesapo.it, www.ristorantesapo.it. Tucked away in its very private corner of Montesilvano on a road heading inland, the Sapò's friendly staff serve up a feast of diverse & unique seafood dishes. Chef Sandro Pomante is passionate about seafood & presents every dish immaculately. The staff is friendly & go the extra mile to make sure your dining experience is nothing short of superb. Try the wonderful raw fish broth & the seafood salad. **$$$**

✖ **Café Pineta** Via Aldo Moro 100; 📞085 445 2657. The old café Pineta was a simple bar but has now become quite a popular eatery. The place has been spruced up, as has the menu, to offer a rewarding dining experience. It is an excellent place for *arrosticini* & their pizzas are also very good. You will need to book ahead for Fri & Sat

nights during the colder months & every night during summer. **$$**

✖ **Pizzeria Arrosticini da Luciano** Via Verrotti 50; 📞085 445 1030; ⊕ Mon–Sat. One of the best restaurants in Montesilvano & an excellent place to eat *arrosticini* if you don't have the time or means to wander further afield. The pizzas & pasta here are also good & there is an excellent local house red. The restaurant is very simply furnished in rustic brown & yellow hues, as befitting a typical trattoria. **$$**

✖ **La Polena** Via Aldo Moro 3; 📞085 66007; ⊕ Mon–Sat; www.lapolena.it. La Polena shifted its operation from Pescara to Montesilvano in 2010 & completely reinvented itself. The new premises offer a considerably better dining experience with clean lines & chic décor. At Polena, you are in for a real seafood treat. A great way to start is with the raw fish platter, a collection of over 10 different

Montesilvano's **Il Chicco d'Oro** (*Via Marinelli, 85;* ✆ *085 445 5030; www. chiccodorofamily.com;* ⊕ *daily until late, reduced opening hours in winter*) is still said to be the best place in Abruzzo for a *gelato*. *Gelato* is such big business in Abruzzo and the most frequented haunts tend to change regularly, but most agree that Il Chicco d'Oro could maintain this position for a while to come. Their flavours are many, though the fruit ones are something special. Try the yoghurt *gelato*: it is fabulous.

fish, including prawns & lobster; you could almost make an entire meal of this alone. Their pasta dishes (with fish of course) are also excellent. **$$** ✗ **Birreria Batch** Via Verrotti 176; ✆ 085 915 1688; ⊕ all evenings. Upon opening its doors a few years ago, the Batch quickly became one

of Montesilvano's coolest drinking haunts. The pub has an extensive array of beers & a warm, friendly atmosphere. It is particularly popular in the summer evenings & getting a table can be a challenge. **$**

AROUND MONTESILVANO

Montesilvano Colle Montesilvano's old fortified village is a ten-minute drive from coastal Montesilvano. There isn't a whole lot to do other than wander the streets and visit the **Church of Madonna della Neve** (Madonna of the Snow). Dating in the main from the 15th century, this church houses some interesting frescoes from the same era and an older, more significant fresco of a saint holding a cross, probably from the 12th century. There are excellent views from the church out to the surrounding hills and Gran Sasso. I spent quite a few hours in the attic here, searching baptismal records from as far back as the 16th century for an extensive family tree I compiled in 2003. I can still remember looking out of a small window to the sun-drenched hills while the church bells tolled midday, surrounded by dusty old books.

CITTÀ SANT'ANGELO

This little gem of a town sits at just over 300m above sea level, overlooking the plains of Pescara and miles of coastline. It traces its origins back more than two thousand years, with early documents mentioning it as the Vestini city of Angelus (see page 11 for Italic tribes). Its current layout dates from the 1239 reconstruction after it was destroyed by Frederick II of the Hohenstaufens for being too loyal to the Catholic Church. Its narrow streets and terracotta rooftops are beautiful and definitely worth a visit.

The suburbs of the town – of little interest to visitors – actually begin on the coast at Città Sant'Angelo Marina just north of Montesilvano.

GETTING THERE By car, follow the signs from Pescara and Montesilvano. The town is off the SS16 and has its own exit on the A14 motorway. If you're coming by bus, there are about 15 ARPA services a day from nearby Pescara. The journey takes about 45 minutes and makes various stops along the way.

TOURIST INFORMATION

ℤ **Ufficio Turismo e Cultura** Comune di Città Sant'Angelo, Piazza IV Novembre 1; ✆ 085 969

6252. This office can provide information on sightseeing & tours in the area.

WHERE TO STAY AND EAT Hotels in Città Sant'Angelo are located in the lower town, Città Sant'Angelo Marina.

⌂ **Villa Nacalua** (34 rooms) Via dell'Autostrada 5; ☎ 085 799 3019; e info@nacalua.com; www. nacalua.com. This hotel, located in the lower town near the motorway exit, was the first 5-star property to open in Abruzzo and has been recently refurbished. It offers good-quality & comfortable accommodation with basic but very clean rooms sporting simple décor. **$$$$$**

⌂ **Agriturismo Torre Mannella** (4 apts) Via F. De Blasis 15, Località Piano Della Cona; ☎ 085 960579; e info@torremannella.com; www. torremannella.com. The Rupi family have created a bucolic haven at a short distance from the throngs of beach-goers below. The *agriturismo* consists of 4 self-contained apartments in the rustic countryside of Città Sant'Angelo, around 8km from the A14 motorway exit. As is customary, the *agriturismo* produce products for the local market, and the Rupi family's fruit and Montepulciano are sold in various towns nearby. **$$$**

⌂ **Hotel Giardino dei Principi** (34 rooms) Viale L Petruzzi 30; ☎ 085 950235; e giardinodeiprincipi@tin.it; www. hotelgiardinodeiprincipi.it. Set in some lovely countryside in the lower town, Giardino dei Principi is a rather sweet little hotel with bright, decent-sized rooms. These are very clean with parquet floors & most have a balcony. The hotel also has a meeting room & restaurant. **$$$**

OTHER PRACTICALITIES As with many other towns in Abruzzo, amenities can be in short supply and most here are situated in the lower town. However, there are **ATMs** at Banca Popolare Dell'Adriatico (*Corso Vittorio Emanuele & Via Saline Est 9*) and Banca Caripe (*Via Diaz cnr Vico Gregoriano*). There is a **chemist** at Piazza Garibaldi (*Farmacia D'Addario*; ☎ 085 960206) and a **post office** (*Largo Trieste 1;* ☎ *085 96421*).

FESTIVALS AND EVENTS

6 January The Live Nativity. As with many other towns, on the day of the Epiphany Città Sant'Angelo puts on a live nativity display. It is particularly evocative here as it is held at night with the only light from burning torches. The whole town tends to participate, and it can be stunning if the streets are under a blanket of snow.

February Carnevale. Carnival time in Città Sant'Angelo is a colourful affair, with flamboyant costumes paraded through the town.

Summer From Etna to the Gran Sasso. This festival celebrates the town's twinning with the town of Nicolosi in Catania. It takes place for one week during summer with displays of traditional culture from both towns.

First week of August Enchanted Villages. This fair sees artists from the town and beyond set up shop along the town's medieval streets to sell their work.

Third week of August Festa in Corso. This festival takes place on the first weekend after 15 August and lasts three days. Music groups and bands from the region and further afield perform.

Third Monday of September Festival of San Michele. This festival is in honour of the town's patron saint, San Michele, and includes everything from special masses to displays of typical cuisine.

The Fair of the Grape, when carts of juicy grapes of all shapes and sizes line the streets, takes place at around the same time.

WHAT TO SEE AND DO The town's main church is the **Collegiate Church of San Michele Arcangelo**, whose belfry can be seen from miles away. It was reconstructed during the 14th century and restored in the 18th. The main entrance dates from 1326 while the belltower dates from the 15th century. Inside is the sarcophagus of Amico Buonamicizia (whose name can be translated as 'Friend Goodfriendship'), a bishop of Penne who died in the 15th century. There is also the noteworthy 14th-century statue of San Michele Arcangelo and frescoes from the same century.

The **Church of San Francesco** was restored in 1741 but is of 14th-century origin. Given the 18th-century restoration, the interior is largely Baroque. Other churches include the **Church of Sant'Agostino**, which is reportedly on the town's highest point, the **Church of San Bernardo,** and the **Church of Santa Chiara** with its interesting stucco work.

SPOLTORE

The historic centre of Spoltore, only 8km west of Pescara, is an easy half-day trip from the city, and well worth a visit. Ignore the new and rather over-developed town below and head straight for the old town. Small and compact, this medieval settlement is a hidden gem amongst the industry of the surrounding area. The pastel colours and terracotta rooftops of the houses combine with the narrow streets to make this an idyllic setting. The hilltop position gives views over the sea and mountains at the turn of every corner. You may even encounter a local guide: Nerone, the town's dog, often follows placidly at the heels of strangers and keeps you company while you meander the streets.

GETTING THERE ARPA operate about 25 services a day from Pescara bus station to Spoltore. The journey takes around 25 minutes. Be aware that some services will only stop at the new town below, so make sure to ask about this when purchasing your ticket at the ticket office.

By car, follow the SS16 out of Pescara and take the exit at Spoltore. Follow the signs to the *centro storico*.

 WHERE TO STAY

B&B Ottocento (4 rooms) Via Del Corso 10; m 3382 591 718; e ottocento2007@libero.it; www.bebottocento.it. The Ottocento exudes old-world charm and is perfect for those wanting to stay somewhere with the character of countryside Abruzzo. Situated right in the heart of the historic centre of Spoltore & therefore a meagre 5km from the conveniences of Pescara, owners Laura & Walter have created an idyllic atmosphere in this 19th-century house. The B&B features beautifully decorated rooms (1 even has its own delightful brick arches) with private bathrooms & benefits from a roof terrace with magnificent views spanning from Francavilla to Pescara & Città Sant'Angelo **$$$**

WHERE TO EAT

Locanda di Nonno Pez Via G di Marzio 4/6; 085 496 2206; ⊕ Tue–Sun. This popular eatery serves a wide variety of regional pasta & meat specialities. It is good value for money & only a stone's throw from the historic centre. Dishes are simple rather than elaborate & the main courses are not expensive. **$$**

WHAT TO SEE The town's major attraction is undoubtedly in its sleepy streets awash with colour and charm. Spend a few hours getting lost in them and enjoying the views of the nearby countryside. In addition, there are a few interesting churches, and the remains of an **ancient castle** can still be seen. Spoltore's main church, dedicated to **San Panfilo**, the town's patron saint, is situated in Piazza Q di Marzio and remains open throughout the year. It is an old, almost crumbling building hiding a newer 18th-century interior. Look out for the 16th-century statue of the *Madonna col Bambino*. Situated just outside the old town are the 15th-century **Convent of San Francesco d'Assisi** and its attached church, unfortunately usually closed to the public.

MOSCUFO

The town of Moscufo is known for its excellent olive-oil production, though the main reason people visit is for the stunning Romanesque **Church of Santa Maria del Lago** (usually closed, though ✎ 085 797668 to arrange a visit). It was built in the middle of the 12th century, probably on the site of an older structure that is mentioned in documents from AD969, although no trace remains of the pre-existing structure. The façade was restored in the 1730s. Those with some understanding of the Italian language might think that the church was dedicated to Holy Mary of the Lake. However, *lago* derives from the Latin *locus*, which later transformed to *lacum*, meaning 'woods'. The interior of the church houses an especially stunning ambo (early pulpit), sculpted in 1156 by Nicola da Guardiagrele (see page 255), and some breathtaking 12th-century frescoes of the *Last Judgement*.

The 17th-century **Church of San Cristoforo** (⊕ for services only) on Piazza Umberto I was restored in the 18th century and houses some interesting stuccowork. The church celebrated its 400th birthday in 2007. The piazza itself is lovely, with some charming small lanes running off it.

GETTING THERE There are around ten ARPA buses a day from Pescara, with the journey taking around 45 minutes. By car, the town can be reached from a turn-off on the SS151. It is approximately a 20-minute drive from Pescara.

PIANELLA

A short distance south of Moscufo is the town of Pianella, also at the forefront of olive-oil production in Abruzzo, and indeed all of Italy (it is otherwise known as La Terra dell'Olio, the 'Land of Oil'). The typically Mediterranean winding road between the two towns is lined with olive groves and makes for a very enjoyable drive. It is also a very pleasant walk; however, it is deceptively long and does take a few hours, so take plenty of water.

It is still possible to see parts of the medieval **wall** surrounding the town. Inside the walls lies the oldest part of town where you will find the **Church of San Domenico**, founded in the 15th century but entirely rebuilt in the 18th century. The main church of interest, however, is the **Church of Santa Maria Maggiore**, not far from the city centre. It has been altered over the centuries but was founded in the 12th century and has a striking entrance complete with a 13th-century rose window. Inside, there is yet another of Abruzzo's original and striking ambos. This one was completed in the 12th century, as were the frescoes adorning the church. The town also has a few good examples of civic architecture. Amongst these is the delightful **Palazzo Cipriani**, found along Via Cesare Battisti off Piazza della Vittoria. It has a charming doorway bearing an inscription dated 1625.

GETTING THERE From Pescara, there is a turn-off to the town from the SS81. Alternatively, head to Moscufo (see above) first and drive the picturesque road between the two towns. If you're happy to go on foot, the walk between Moscufo and Pianella is easy and very rewarding.

🏠 **WHERE TO STAY** There is only one hotel in town:

🏠 **Hotel Casa Bianca** (15 rooms) Via Catania 16; 📞085 972172; f 085 972173. Standard rooms with simple decoration. **$$$**

✖ **WHERE TO EAT** Of the few good restaurants in town, try:

✖ **La Locanda degli Artisti** Via Regina Margherita 58; 📞085 972670. Tasty pasta dishes. **$$**
✖ **Lu Piatt Call** Via S Lucia 120; 📞085 972335; ⊕ Wed–Mon. The name is Abruzzese & means 'the

hot plate'. Drop in here for typical Abruzzese dishes such as *pasta alla chitarra*. **$$**
✖ **Osteria Margherita** Via Regina Margherita 1; 📞085 972204; ⊕ Tue–Sun. Serves excellent pizzas. **$$**

OTHER PRACTICALITIES Unlike many of its neighbours, Pianella has few amenities. You will find ATMs at a few **banks** including Banca Caripe (*Via Regina Margherita 1*). There is also a **post office** (*Via Verrotti 12*; ⊕ *Mon–Fri 08.30–13.30, Sat 08.30–12.30*).

LORETO APRUTINO

Loreto Aprutino is the quintessential Pescara provincial town. Not only is it another important olive-oil town, but it is also picture-postcard pretty. The view from the road that winds around the front of the town is lovely: a mass of cluttered rooftops and belltowers dotted with the occasional pine tree and surrounded by thousands of olive groves.

The area has been inhabited since before the 6th century BC. The town was once the Roman town of Laurentum, and later the medieval Castrum Laureti. It was important during the Middle Ages, attested to by its rich artistic heritage. Its name was changed to Loreto, then, during the unification of Italy, the word Aprutino was added in order to differentiate it from other towns called Loreto throughout Italy.

LORETO'S OLIVE OIL

The production of oil in Loreto Aprutino is the mainstay of the town's economy. The conditions for growing olive groves in the hills surrounding the town are perfect and Loreto Aprutino alone is said to produce around 6,000 tonnes of olives per year, picked by hand between October and November. This translates to roughly around 20% of Pescara Province's entire production, and makes around 1,000 tonnes of extra virgin olive oil of very high quality with a fruity taste and slightly spicy undertone. When buying oil look for the DOC Aprutino-Pescarese mark.

There are 16 oil mills in the vicinity of Loreto Aprutino, including Agri-Oliva SNC (*Contrada Remartello 25*; 📞 *085 820 8544*), Belfiore Roberto (*Contrada Fontemaggio 1*; 📞*085 829 1753*), Bucan & C Sas (*Contrada Paterno 11*; 📞*085 829 0847*) and Di Simone Alfonso (*Contrada San Pellegrino*; 📞*085 828 9141*).

GETTING THERE

By car There are turn-offs to the town from the SS151. The town is a 25-minute drive from Pescara and ten minutes from Penne.

By bus ARPA runs services between Pescara and Penne which make stops in Loreto Aprutino. The journey takes around 40 minutes.

TOURIST INFORMATION

🛈 **IAT Loreto Aprutino** Piazza Garibaldi; ☎085 8290213. This new Abruzzo Tourist Board office is a testament to Loreto Aprutino's rising popularity with the domestic & international traveller. It is 1 of only 7 in the province.

🏠 WHERE TO STAY

🏠 **Hotel Castello Chiola** (36 rooms) Via degli Aquino 12; ☎085 829 0690; e info@castellochiolahotel.com; www.castellochiolahotel.com. A stunning luxury hotel set in a historic castle, this is 1 of the best places to stay in the province. This is not only because of the high quality of its rooms & amenities such as its wonderful pool, but also because of the setting. At the highest point in town, rooms have a view out to the hills & mountains. The building itself is a joy & lazing around by the pool is deeply relaxing. **$$$$$**

🏠 **Bed & Breakfast Laurentum** (6 rooms) Via del Baio 3; ☎085 829 2000; e info@bedbreakfastlauretum.com; www.bedbreakfastlauretum.com. This B&B is set in a beautiful old palazzo with a lovely courtyard & vaulted ceilings, right in the old town. Convenient & peaceful, it's a nicely atmospheric place to stay

& the elegant rooms are furnished in a way that's sensitive to the history of the palazzo. **$$$**

🏠 **Bed & Breakfast Loreblick** (4 rooms) Via Fiorano 42–44; ☎085 829 0319; e loreblick@inwind.it; www.bedbreakfastloreblick.com. This small B&B was dubbed the 'terrace of Abruzzo' by a local newspaper. It is set on a hill overlooking the town. The nicely appointed rooms are of decent size. Staff are extremely friendly & knowledgeable about the local area. **$$**

🏠 **Hotel Di Rocco** (18 rooms) Contrada Scannella Inferiore 18; ☎085 828 9179; www.hoteldirocco.it. The road it's situated on may not seem like much to write home about, but the Di Rocco is a warm & friendly family-run establishment with simple but clean rooms about a 10-min drive from town. The hotel has an excellent restaurant (see below). **$$**

✗ WHERE TO EAT AND DRINK

✗ **Il Melo Rosso** Contrada Collefreddo 29; ☎085 829 0122; ⊕ Wed–Mon. Everything from excellent pork to *arrosticini* is on offer at this typically Abruzzese eatery. It is bright, airy & simply decorated. **$$**

✗ **Ristorante di Rocco** Contrada Scannella Inferiore 18; ☎085 828 9179; www.hoteldirocco.it. This is actually the restaurant of Hotel Di Rocco (about 10-min drive from town) but is worth a separate entry. Beautifully presented dishes &

an intimate atmosphere make for a great dining experience. Try the homemade pasta dishes, such as *gnocchi*. The menu varies frequently so ask about the latest offerings. **$$**

✗ **Pizzeria Novecento** Via dei Normanni 61; ☎085 829 0061; ⊕ daily 17.00–23.00. Some excellent pizzas are made at this simple restaurant with slices or whole pizza to eat in or take away. The margherita is excellent. **$**

WHAT TO SEE AND DO
Churches

Church of Santa Maria in Piano (⊕ daily, closed for lunch) Though its current appearance is largely from the 16th century, the church dates back to the 12th and was probably founded on the site of a Roman temple. Its exterior (with the exception of the belfry) is a little plain but the interior houses a majestic fresco dating from the 1430s. Of the Last Judgement, it depicts God surrounded by angels and saints. It originally covered the entire wall though there are now missing sections.

Abbey of San Pietro Apostolo This church's appearance has altered somewhat due to restoration work over the centuries. However, it is particularly striking and houses some paintings of note from the mid 16th century by a local abbot as well as a wooden statue of St Thomas Aquinas in the chapel to the left of the main entrance. This chapel's floor is made from 16th-century ceramic tiles from Castelli (see page 233).

Church of San Francesco d'Assisi This rather weather-beaten church has a stunning stone entrance dating from the 13th century, and a 15th-century belltower built in the style of the belltower of Atri's Cathedral (see page 211). Due to later reconstruction the interior is largely Baroque and has some interesting stuccowork.

Museums
Museo Acerbo delle Ceramiche/Acerbo Museum of Ceramics (*Via del Baio 1;* \ *085 829 1589; www.museiciviciloretoaprutino.it;* ⊕ *Jun–Sep, Tue–Sun 10.30–12.30 & 17.00–19.00; Oct–May, Sat–Sun 10.30–12.30 & 15.30–17.30; admission €6, children €3)* The entrance to this museum is across from the Abbey of San Pietro. It houses a collection of ceramics from Castelli (see page 233) spread over six rooms. In the same building is the **Museo della Civiltà Contadina/ Museum of Farming Culture**, with a display of working tools and other artefacts from the peasant culture of the area.

Museo dell'Olio/Museum of Oil (*Castello Amorotto, Via Cesare Battisti;* \ *085 829 1589; www.museiciviciloretoaprutino.it;* ⊕ *Jun–Sep, Tue–Sun 10.30–12.30 & 17.00–19.00; Oct–May, Sat–Sun 10.30–12.30 & 15.30–17.30; admission €6, children €3)* A fitting museum for the town, full of the technology associated with the making of olive oil. It is housed in an evocative castle-cum-palace, with a locally typical corner tower and arched windows.

Museo Archeologico Antiquarium/Archaeological Museum (*Via dei Mille 8;* \ *085 829 1589; www.museiciviciloretoaprutino.it;* ⊕ *Jun–Sep, Tue–Sun 10.30–12.30 & 17.00–19.00; Oct–May, Sat–Sun 10.30–12.30 & 15.30–17.30; admission €6, children €3)* A small museum with local archaeological finds dating from the pre-Roman to the medieval.

Civic architecture If you wander the streets of Loreto Aprutino, you will come across a number of old *palazzi*. Among these are **Palazzo Amorotti** from the 15th century; the 17th-century Baroque **Palazzo Guanciali**; and the 19th-century **Palazzo Valentini** and **Palazzo Casamarte**.

AROUND LORETO APRUTINO
Picciano The town of Picciano, a ten-minute drive away, is not very interesting in itself, but it rates a mention for its lively **Sagra della Pizza e degli Arrosticini** which is held at the end of July to celebrate – well – pizza and *arrosticini!* The local fried pizza, served with a little salt, is an excellent companion to a handful of *arrosticini*. The town comes alive with bands and music groups travelling the streets decked out in local medieval costume.

PENNE

One of the oldest and most historically significant towns of the area, Penne is characterised by its ancient buildings and churches almost entirely made of brick, creating a unique townscape coloured beige and pink along its steep roads and lanes.

Around 300BC, the Vestini people invested the city, then called Pinna, with the seat of its government. As with the rest of the region, it came under the control of the Romans during the 1st century BC and was consequently given the status of a Roman *municipium*. During the medieval period, it came under the control of the Duchy of Spoleto and then the Kingdom of Sicily, and was even a regional capital. Nowadays, it relies on domestic tourism as a result of its rich cultural heritage.

GETTING THERE By car, Penne is on the SS81, a half-hour drive from Pescara. In terms of public transport there are about five buses a day from Pescara to Penne. The journey time is approximately one hour, though the 10.40 departure takes two hours. Buses go on from Penne to the town of Farindola.

TOURIST INFORMATION

Public Relations Office Town Hall, Piazzetta XX Settembre; 085 8216 7219; ⊕ Mon, Wed & Fri 08.30–12.00, Tue & Thu 08.30–12.00 & 15.30–17.30.

WHERE TO STAY

Hotel dei Vestini (53 rooms) Via A Caselli 37; 085 827 8200; e info@hoteldeivestini.com; www.hoteldeivestini.com. This is the only hotel actually in Penne. Although it looks a little dated the rooms are reasonable & have all you might need, & there's a lovely pool area as well as a good restaurant serving a host of local food. Try the excellent pork. HB & FB. $$$

Ferzetti Agriturismo (4 rooms) SS81, km96, Contrada Solagna 2; 085 827 0027; e info@fattoriaferzetti.it; www.fattoriaferzetti.it. This farmstay, about 3km north of Penne along the SS81, is surrounded by olive groves & some lovely Mediterranean countryside. The owners specialise in growing organic products & are always keen to show guests around. The accommodation is in lovely rooms, simply decorated but offering ample space, & the food is delicious (see below). $$

WHERE TO EAT

Ristorante Gran Sasso Via A Caselli 37; 085 827 8200. Although the décor at the Hotel dei Vestini's restaurant isn't to everyone's liking (it's a little 1980s), they serve excellent food, from meat to local pasta dishes. $$$

Ferzetti Agriturismo SS81, km96, Contrada Solagna 2; 085 827 0027; e info@fattoriaferzetti.it; www.fattoriaferzetti.it. An establishment dedicated to growing organic produce & cooking up local dishes using the highest-quality ingredients, including delicious & very fresh local lamb. They also offer farmstay accommodation. $$

Osteria Leone Piazzetta XX Settembre 3; 085 821 3224; ⊕ Tue–Sun. Osteria Leone is on the same square as the town hall, & is a convenient place for tasty meals local dishes such as *pasta alla chitarra*. $$

Ristorante La Grotta Via Pultone 8; 085 2312785; ⊕ all year Wed–Mon lunch & dinner, in summer only Tue dinner. Owner Mariana Laura's restaurant has a very rustic environment in which to try some excellent typical dishes of the area. Go for any of the meat-based dishes; they are so tender the meat melts in your mouth. $$

Ristorante Tatobbe Corso Alessandrini 37; 085 821 3293; ⊕ Tue–Sun dinner, Sun lunch; e ristorantetatobbe@virgilio.it; www.ristorantetatobbe.it. Decked out with redbrick arches & terracotta tiles so typical of the town of Penne, the Tatobbe provides one of the most authentic Abruzzese dining experiences for miles around & reasonable prices to boot. Try the mixed antipasto & the typical *maccheroni alla chitarra* (see page 40). $$

BRIONI

If you've ever seen or worn a Brioni suit then you've come into contact with one of Penne's most prestigious exports, as have the likes of Luciano Pavarotti, Pierce Brosnan and Nelson Mandela. Founded in 1945 in Rome, Brioni has provided quality suits worldwide for decades. Since its first fashion shows in Florence in 1952 and in New York two years later, Brioni has set up shop in many corners of the globe, including as far afield as Baku in Azerbaijan. Its headquarters and factory are found in Penne and its suits are all handmade by its local employees.

Gelateria La Regina Viale San Francesco 74; 085 827 0970; ⏱ after lunch until late. This humble little establishment makes lovely *gelato*.

Try the chocolate, & – when they have it – the yoghurt: it's delicious.

OTHER PRACTICALITIES There are numerous **ATMs**, including at Banca Caripe (*Piazza Luca da Penne*) and the Banca Popolare di Lanciano e Sulmona (*Largo San Nicola*). If you need a **chemist**, there's Farmacia Bianchini (*Corso Alessandrini 1;* 085 827 9543), and you'll find the **post office** at Via Aldo Moro 11 (085 821 0805).

EVENTS
Mid August Palio dei Sei Rioni. A festival which sees locals take part in various races. It is said to stem from a local legend which tells of the two daughters of Penne's founding father. The daughters, Rocca (a blonde) and Bruna (a brunette), are said to have been rivals who settled on two hills nearby. During the festival, the streets are lined with stalls selling food, arts and craft.

Mid August Pecora Nait. The 'slow food' movement has given rise to this recently established festival, which roughly translates as 'lamb night'. For four days the streets of Penne are filled with culinary specialities of the region. Various tastings, particularly of lamb's meat, and events make this a good time to visit the town.

August Sagra della Battitura e della Trebbiatura del Grano. The name of this festival – the Fair of the Smashing of the Grain – says it all; there are reconstructions of earlier ways of milling grain, as well as the usual food stalls and craft markets.

WHAT TO SEE AND DO
Churches Note that most churches in Penne are open to visitors during the day, although some will close for lunch.

Cathedral of Santa Maria degli Angeli e San Massimo Martire Penne's
main cathedral, or duomo, is found on Colle Sacro and dates back some thousand years. However, its appearance has changed over the years, with restoration work carried out in the 17th century, and following the damage it suffered during World War II. The striking crypt is adorned with restored frescoes dating back to before the 14th century. The belltower dates from the earliest period of the building's construction and inside the church you will find a 12th-century altar and a wooden statue of Jesus from the 13th century. Adjacent to the cathedral is the Diocesan Civic Museum of Sacred Art (see page 85).

Church of Sant'Agostino This church's current form dates back to the 1750s. Unfortunately it is often closed to the public, as is the adjacent Confraternity of the Cinturati. However, if you can get in, you'll find a charming complex, both overgrown and run-down. The church itself was built over an earlier medieval building and the belfry is in Atri-style with coloured tiles.

Parish Church of Sant'Annunciazione del Signore If you find this closed, call Don Celestino (✆ *085 821 1094*). This humble little church has a statue of Jesus on his tomb, encased in glass. There are interesting paintings dating from the 19th century on the church's walls.

Church of San Domenico Although of early medieval origins, this church has undergone many changes, especially during the 18th century. It contains a 15th-century relief of the Madonna on a throne and an entrance dated 1667.

Church of San Panfilo As above, if closed call Don Celestino (✆ *085 821 1094*). This is a tiny church with two exquisite wooden statues of the Madonna and Child. A peaceful spot to sit and recover from sightseeing.

Convent of Santa Maria in Colleromano Outside the city walls in the Penne countryside is this convent set inside a spectacular medieval building. It houses a gorgeous Baroque wooden high altar and a series of frescoes that date back 500 years.

Convent of Santa Maria del Carmine Also outside the historic centre is this 17th-century convent. Although Baroque in style, especially its fine façade, it is said to be built over a very old hermitage.

Civic architecture

Cortile Romano In the historic centre of Penne you will see a sign pointing you to this tiny cloister with its beautiful and romantic arches: one of the loveliest spots in the town. Once within the walls you can imagine you have been transported back a few hundred years. Although it is called the Roman Cloister it actually dates back to the early medieval period and is still remarkably well preserved.

The Renaissance Tower Across from the Church of San Panfilo is this delightful, somewhat understated palace built in around 1400. Its balconies and tower are particularly attractive.

Palazzo del Bono A brick-built palazzo dating back to the 1750s, the Palazzo del Bono is one of the most important examples of civic Baroque architecture in the area. It is stunning, from the brick pillars flanking the entrance to the stately window frames.

Palazzo Castiglione Another example of 18th-century civic architecture, the Palazzo Castiglione is the work of Francesco di Sio, an architect from Naples who probably also built the Palazzo del Bono. It is a three-storey palace characterised by the use of arches on the first- and second-floor terraces.

Other palazzos of note are the **Palazzo Picchetto-Pansa** (with its stunning stone doorway), the Baroque **Palazzo Gaudiosi** and the 18th-century **Palazzo Aliprandi**.

Museums Note that the museums below, including the Natural History Museum in the Lago di Penne Reserve (see below), can all be visited on one ticket.

Museo Archeologico G B Leopardi/G B Leopardi Archaeological Museum (*Piazza Duomo 7;* ✎ *085 821 1727;* ⊕ *Apr–Oct, Tue–Fri 09.00–13.30, Sat–Sun 10.00–1300 & 16.00–19.00; Nov–Mar, Tue–Fri 09.00–13.30, Sat 10.00–13.00 & 15.00–18.00, Sun 10.00–13.00; admission €3.50*) The area around Penne has been inhabited for such a long time that it is no wonder that its archaeological museum, adjacent to the Duomo, is brimming with artefacts. It occupies ten rooms and of particular note are the displays of local pottery.

Museo Civico-Diocesano di Arte Sacra/Diocesan Civic Museum of Sacred Art (*Piazza Duomo 8;* ✎ *085 821 0525; admission €4;* ⊕ *as Museo Archeologico G B Leopardi above*) This museum has displays of items from the duomo's crypt (which dates as far back as the 8th century) on the first floor, and religious objects and art from the 14th to the 18th century on the second floor.

AROUND PENNE
Riserva Naturale Regionale del Lago di Penne/Regional Natural Reserve of the Lake of Penne
Near the town is the Lago di Penne, a perfect spot to break the day's sightseeing with a picnic by the water. The reserve itself was established in 1989 and covers 150ha, and the protected area around it totals some 1,000ha. Inside the reserve is the **Nicola Da Leone Natural History Museum** (*Museo Naturalistico Nicola Da Leone; Contrada Collalto 1;* ✎ *085 827 9489;* ⊕ *daily 09.00–12.30 & 14.30–18.30; admission €3.50*), where there's an informative display on the flora and fauna of the park. This includes in particular the reserve's otters, who have their own dedicated **Otter Centre** (Centro Lontra). In addition there is a **playground** and the open-air **Butterfly Garden** (Giardino delle Farfalle).

Farindola This attractive town is set on a hillside about 20 minutes from Penne, on the edge of the Gran Sasso National Park. There isn't much to do here other than admire the location, with the buildings spread across the hillside, but there are some **castle ruins** that are worth a visit if you are already in the area. Buses from Pescara to Penne continue on to Farindola, taking a further 40 minutes. There are a number of walking paths that begin on the periphery of the town that will allow you to take in some of the spanning views of the area.

NORA RIVER VALLEY AND SURROUNDS

There are a number of pleasant little towns along the Nora River, which flows into the Pescara just past Cepagatti on the A25 *autostrada*. While these towns may not have the attractions to be found elsewhere in the province a few are still worth a look. Their slow pace and way of life is also a change from the busier city of Pescara, at most a 40-minute drive away. The biggest town in the area, and the only one with any amenities, is Cepagatti.

GETTING THERE Travelling all the way through the valley on public transport can be inconvenient. You can reach Cepagatti by bus from Pescara using ARPA services, which take approximately 45 minutes. However, having your own transport is ideal. The SS602 cuts through the Nora River valley and can be accessed from the SS81 and the A25.

CEPAGATTI There isn't a huge amount to see in Cepagatti, but it is the location of most of the few places to stay in the valley. Generally, though, you are better off basing yourself in Pescara, especially if you have your own transport.

The town is said to be of Roman origins, although this theory stems from the finding of one piece of Roman art. The town's churches are the **Church of Santi Lucia e Rocco**, the **Church of San Rocco** and the **Church of Santa Maria Assunta**. While none is particularly interesting, the last has the distinction of being founded in the 18th century by Albanian refugees.

Where to stay

Hotel La Rotonda (26 rooms) Via Nazionale 167, Villanova di Cepagatti; 085 977 1601; e info@hotel-larotonda.it; www.hotel-larotonda.it. Located outside the centre of Cepagatti in the area known as Villanova, this hotel is good value, especially for those rooms that have been renovated. The common areas need some updating but there a nice kidney-shaped swimming pool for those hot days & a decent restaurant serving some very tasty pasta dishes. **$$$**

NOCCIANO Nocciano is home to the **Church of Sant'Antonio da Padova**, which has a small 16th-century doorway. However, the **Church of San Lorenzo** is the highlight here. Now completely abandoned and generally ignored, this church is a real gem containing a series of frescoes from the early 1400s.

VICOLI The attraction here is not the modern town of Vicola but rather the **Old Vicoli** hamlet, a short distance away. The village's **fort** has stunning views over the area and is a great place to stop for a picnic.

CUGNOLI While a pleasant enough town for a quiet stroll, Cugnoli is known for its **Church of Santo Stefano**. From the outside the church doesn't appear interesting but the interior houses a famous **pulpit**, carved in 1166 and moved here in 1528.

CIVITELLA CASANOVA Though a fair way from Penne, about a half-hour's drive, Civitella Casanova rates a mention because of its **Church of Santa Maria della Cona** and its adjoining cemetery. It has a striking Renaissance doorway and the interior of the church contains a small but exquisite early 16th-century fresco of the *Madonna and Child*.

VILLA CELIERA Some 2km from this small town is the **Abbey of Santa Maria di Casanova**. It is now in ruins but worth a visit for its quiet, almost desolate setting. Despite its overgrown site, you can still make out the layout of the church and what would once have been an impressive tower.

CARPINETO DELLA NORA There isn't anything to attract the visitor to the centre of this town, but the beautifully sited **Abbey of San Bartolomeo**, about 2–3km away, is certainly worth a stop. It was founded as far back as AD962, though the tower, dating from the 12th century, is the oldest section of the building. The interior retains a 13th-century presbytery.

PESCARA RIVER VALLEY

The undulating hills flanking the Pescara River valley to the north of the A25 are home to some beautiful medieval towns and one of the most important abbeys in the region.

GETTING THERE

By car The A25 motorway and the SS5 (Via Tiburtina Valeria) cut through the Pescara River valley, making it one of the most accessible areas in the province.

By bus ARPA services connect Pescara with various towns in the valley. All the way over to the likes of Bussi you're looking at one hour by bus. There are about 11 services per day that make the trip from Pescara to Bussi, taking about an hour, with stops in the likes of Cepagatti, Torre de Passeri and Scafa.

By train The Pescara–Rome railway also travels through the valley. There are about 15 services a day costing roughly €4 from Pescara all the way to Popoli (the nearest station to Bussi). Not all services stop at every station so check that the train you want to take stops either at your town, or at a town where ARPA bus services are available to take you to your final destination.

ROSCIANO Rosciano's hilltop position gives wonderful views of the river valley. It is also home to the ruins of a **medieval fort** and the churches of **Santa Eurasia** and **San Nicola**. The latter contains some interesting 15th-century frescoes.

THE ORATORY OF MADONNA DELLE GRAZIE About 5km west of the town of Alanno (follow the signs), this is an excellent example of an Abruzzese late 15th-century rural church. It is said to have been built when locals claimed that the Virgin Mary appeared to them. The main doorway dates from the 16th century and the lunette above is adorned with a fresco. The interior is home to some striking frescoes depicting various religious scenes by an artist from Lombardy.

SCAFA There isn't much to bring the visitor to the heavily industrialised town of Scafa, close to the A25, but nearby is the **Parco delle Surgenti Sulferee del Lavino** (Sulphur Springs Territorial Park of Lavino), where the blue water has a clear and translucent quality. Follow the signs from outside the town to the east.

PIETRANICO Here the **Oratory of the Madonna della Croce**, founded in the 17th century, is worth a visit. Its ornate interior includes stuccowork, an interesting side chapel and paintings of religious scenes from the 17th century

TORRE DE' PASSERI Torre (for short) is one of the larger towns in the area and one of the least picturesque. However, it does have the large 18th-century **Palazzo Mazzara** and what is known as the **Gizzi Castle**. In the latter is the '**Fortunato Bellonzi' Dante Gallery** (*Pinacoteca Dantesca Fortunato Bellonzi; Via della Carrozza 1; ☏ 085 888 4220; www.muvi.org/bellonzi; admission €3; ⊕ Thu, Sat & Sun 09.00–12.00 & 15.00–18.00*), which contains books, prints and all manner of things relating to Dante's *Divine Comedy*.

ABBEY OF SAN CLEMENTE A CASAURIA (☏*0864 32849; www.sanclementeacasauria. beniculturali.it; admission free; ⊕ 08.00–14.00 Mon–Sat*) A short drive west of Torre de' Passeri, in the district called San Clemente, is one of Abruzzo's most important religious buildings. Its origins are shrouded in mystery and it is even said to have been built on what was then an island in the Pescara River. It is thought to have been founded in the 9th century and was an important religious centre from the 12th century onwards, largely due to the efforts of Abbot Leonate, who died in 1182. By the 19th century the church had fallen into obscurity and was relatively unknown

4

until it was declared a national monument in 1894. It has recently benefited from some much-needed maintenance.

The church's exterior is striking. Its main entrance arch is flanked by two pointed arches and gives way to three bronze doors which were completed at the end of the 12th century. The doors are surrounded by intricate carvings. Inside, much of the interior has been rebuilt over the centuries, some if it reusing the original materials. The church houses a sarcophagus that is said to have contained the remains of St Clement, to whom the abbey is dedicated. The ambo, dating from the 12th century, is particularly noteworthy.

CASTIGLIONE A CASAURIA Not far from the Abbey of San Clemente a Casauria, to the southwest, is the town of Castiglione a Casauria with its atmospheric streets and some old civic buildings. While wandering around, pay particular attention to the ornate entrances and windows of many of its buildings. The town is best known for the ancient **Palazzo de Petris Fraggiani**, which dominates views of the historic centre. Converted into a palace in the 17th century, its oldest sections date back to the 10th century.

PESCOSANSONESCO The settlement of Pescosansonesco includes the current, modern town and the now abandoned **Old Pescosansonesco**. As with many other towns in the region, the residents packed up and moved shop after it was hit by large earthquakes, especially those of 1917 and 1933.

Strolling around the abandoned town is a thought-provoking experience. At the top of the rocky spur you will find the ruins of the **medieval castle**, beautifully framed by the hills on the edge of the Gran Sasso National Park. There are two churches of significance here: the **Convent of Santa Maria degli Angeli** and the **Church of San Nicola**. The latter dates from the 12th century and is found near one of the old town entrances. The former has a lovely 16th-century doorway.

Where to stay and eat

🏠 **Ostello Petra** (4 apts, 24 beds) Via Colle della Guardia; m 3331756696; e ostellopetra@gmail.com; www.ostellopetra.it. This convenient hostel is situated inside an old Franciscan monastery & is excellent value for money. Rooms are clean & well appointed & the hostel offers FB options starting from only €44. The hostel even has a pool with some inspiring views of the surrounding area. **$$**

BUSSI SUL TIRINO Very close to Popoli is the pretty town of Bussi sul Tirino, a fairly large settlement by rural Abruzzo standards. It occupies a picturesque spot on the fringes of the Gran Sasso National Park. As its name suggests, it was founded on the banks of the Tirino River, around the 11th century, on the site of an earlier fortified settlement of which traces can still be seen.

Walking around you will notice the attractive main church on Via Progresso, and close by the turrets of the town's medieval **castle-mansion**. The castle, which has a lovely courtyard, is located on Piazza Tirino, dates from the 16th century and was supposedly built over an earlier fort. Bussi also boasts one of the two triangular towers in Abruzzo, the other being the tower of Montegualtieri in the town of the same name.

Heading north out of town on the SS153 you pass the remains of the church of **Santa Maria di Cartignano**, founded in the 11th century and restored in the 1960s. The church, with its pretty arches set against the surrounding hills, was home to some notable frescoes that are now in the National Museum in L'Aquila.

✕ Where to eat

✕ **Il Buongustai** Piazza Primo Maggio 8; ☏ 085 980 9545; ⏱ Tue–Sun dinner. Right in the heart of town, the Buongustaio serves some very decent seafood, particularly given its relative distance from the coast. There are also pizzas on the menu – including a particularly tasty margherita, with just the right mix of crust & tomato/cheese. It is an excellent restaurant & often busy on Sat evenings. **$$**

Events

4–5 August Sagra del Gambero e della Trota. To celebrate this feast dedicated to the prawn and the trout, the streets are lined with stalls selling tasty local trout and fresh prawns from the Adriatic Sea.

8 August Il Borgo Incantato. This fair, entitled The Enchanted Town in English, is a recent – 2007 – addition to the town's calendar. Artists display all manner of arts and crafts, and food stalls line the streets.

24–25 August La Collina del Sapere e Sapore/The Hill of Knowing and Flavours. Granted. The name of this event sounds a little strange when translated, but it is a real highlight of the year in Bussi. The surrounding area hosts sporting activities like canoeing and mountain biking, while the town centre comes alive with arts-and-crafts stalls and plenty of food.

MAJELLA NATIONAL PARK AND SURROUNDS

Just under a third of the Majella National Park falls within the province of Pescara. The towns here occupy lovely spots where the mountains of the national park give way to the hills around the Pescara River valley. See page 5 for a detailed look at the geology, flora and fauna of the park. For areas of the park that fall within the provinces of Chieti and L'Aquila, see pages 257 and 189 respectively.

TURRIVALIGNANI This small village is a short but very steep drive from Scafa. The road negotiates a series of sharp curves to bring you up the cliff and into town. Once there, make for the main square which is like a terrace overlooking the area below. The 12th-century **Church of San Vincenzo** is also worth checking out.

🏠 Where to stay

🏠 **Hotel Regis** (14 rooms) Via Mulino 6; ☏ 085 854 3118; e info@hotelregis.it; www.resortregis. it. This hotel, located below the town, is an ideal place to stay when exploring the area. It is set within an old but beautifully renovated building & the owners are very welcoming. The rooms are of a higher standard than those of other 4-star hotels in the region & the hotel restaurant serves up some wonderful food. It also has an excellent collection of wines in its cellar. It often hosts weddings & other religious festivities so it's well worth booking in advance. **$$$**

MANOPPELLO Many of Abruzzo's small villages have a speciality, whether to do with food, culture or a product of their natural surroundings. The last is the case for Manoppello, a town that is known for its 'Manoppello stone', from which many of its buildings are constructed. There are some fine examples of Baroque civic architecture here, most notably around Corso Santarelli. The town's most impressive monuments include the **Palazzo Verratti** and **Palazzo Bliasioli**. There is also the fine **Church of San Nicola**, which was rebuilt in the 18th century in the Baroque style, although the earlier church was built sometime around 1300. The **Church of Santissima Annunziata and Convent** houses a noteworthy 16th-century statue of the *Madonna with Child*. Other interesting churches in town are the **Convent of San Lorenzo** and the **Sanctuary of the Volto Santo**, the latter housing a holy shroud that is revered throughout the region and beyond. The image on the shroud is said to be that of Christ himself.

SERRAMONACESCA The main attraction here is the remains of the **Castel Menardo** (largely destroyed in the 15th century) which provide a stunning view of the area and the rooftops of the town. You will have to follow the signs out of the centre, leave your car at the foot of the hill and walk up.

However, do not leave Serramonacesca without visiting one of the most important churches in Abruzzo, a short drive south from the town centre.

The **Abbey of San Liberatore a Majella** (⊕ *Jul–Aug, Tue–Sun 09.30–13.00 & 15.00–19.00; Sep–Jun, Sat–Sun 09.30-13.00 & 15.00-19.00; if the site is closed,* ✆ *085 859279 for access*) occupies a quiet spot on the hills of the Majella. The original abbey was built as far back as the 850s and has interesting links to Charlemagne but has been restored many times, most recently during the late 1960s. The church has a nave-and-two-aisles layout, a memorable 13th-century mosaic floor and a series of 16th-century paintings that are said to cover older, 13th-century frescoes, including one depicting Charlemagne himself. The tiered belltower with its narrow arches was built sometime during the mid 12th century. There is a very peaceful garden area behind the church. The easily accessible **Alento River Gorge** runs adjacent to the church. Here there are tombs of medieval monks; to reach them cross the river by the first bridge you encounter.

The **Hermitage of Sant'Onofrio** (*to gain access use the key hung on the door for visitors; for a guide,* ✆ *085 922343*), founded by St Onofrius, is not far from the town of Serramonacesca, about a 15-minute walk from a parking area. The path to the hermitage is often steep and overgrown but it is a very pleasant walk, especially during the warmer months. This hermitage occupies a suitably secluded spot and it is thought to have been built at some point between the 11th and 14th centuries. On 12 June, the hermitage hosts the **Ricorrenza del Santo**. This sees pilgrims come from nearby towns to lie in the spot where the saint slept in order to cure illnesses such as stomach aches and high temperatures.

SAN VALENTINO IN ABRUZZO CITERIORE If you're driving along the A25 motorway from Pescara through this area you will notice to the south a hilltop town with two distinct belltowers; this is San Valentino. It is a pleasantly relaxed and picturesque little town that was once surrounded by defensive walls. There are still traces of its **castle** to be seen, though it has been largely incorporated into the surrounding residential buildings. The **Church of Santi Valentino e Damiano**, rebuilt in the 18th century, is the location of the two belltowers, which were added only in the 1920s.

ABBATEGGIO This is one of my childhood homes and family towns, just a five-minute drive from the village of San Valentino. The beauty of Abbateggio is in its setting. It is located on a hill to the left of the Lavino River, at an altitude of around 500m above sea level. The old town, supposedly already in existence by the 9th century, is peaceful and characterised by whitewashed narrow lanes and stone houses. The **Sanctuary of the Madonna dell'Elcina** occupies the highest spot in town with stunning views over the valley. It was built in the 15th century after a local inhabitant saw a vision of the Virgin Mary in a tree. The town also has the 15th-century **Parish Church of San Lorenzo**, which was later rebuilt in a Baroque style.

There is an excellent little cheese shop here, **Formaggi Tipici di Abbateggio** (*Piazza Trieste;* \ *085 468 1963*) that sells produce made in the area around Abbateggio.

Where to stay

Agriturismo Il Portone (9 rooms) Borgo San Martino; m 3479331082; e info@ borgosanmartino.eu; www.borgosanmartino. eu. Simply put, this is one of the most charming accommodation options in the province of Pescara. Family-run & beautifully kept, the *agriturismo* is set within the stone walls of an old farmhouse & the staff go that extra mile to make sure your stay is as comfortable as possible. Rooms are themed & include some of the original wooden beams of the house. As is usual for an *agriturismo*, Il Portone places emphasis on providing traditional cuisine using organic ingredients. You cannot go wrong with any of the homemade *pasta all'uovo*. The *agriturismo* also provides mountainbike tours of the area. **$$**

ROCCAMORICE This otherwise nondescript but pleasant enough town, a 10-minute drive from Abbateggio, has a stunning natural setting. It is most famous for the **Hermitage of Santo Spirito a Majella** (*to arrange a visit & for information, contact Roccamorice Town Hall,* \ *085 8572 1320*). The hermitage is about 8km south of Roccamorice and is signposted from the centre of town. It is most certainly worth the trip to see the impressive way the church and hermitage are carved into the rock face. The whole site comprises a church with a living-area annexe, the remains of an old convent and a further section that would once have been used to accommodate guests. It is said to date back more than a thousand years and has been greatly altered over the centuries. It was home to Pope Victor III in the 11th century and Pietro da Marrone, later Pope Celestine V (see page 101) in the 13th century. The latter is said to have paid for considerable work to be carried out here. It was further restored in the 16th century but later abandoned for a period of time until the 19th century. Further work during the 20th century restored it to its former glory. Don't miss the aerial stairway of the Maddalena Oratory: a narrow stairway with a sheer drop to one side and no railing – it is not for the faint-hearted.

The other hermitage of note in the area is the **Hermitage of San Bartolomeo in Legio** (*for details contact Roccamorice Town Hall,* \ *085 8572 1320*), an easy 4km walk from town. Another favourite hermitage of Pietro da Morrone, its date of origin is unknown, although we do know that Pietro rebuilt it during the 13th century. Its location is just as dramatic as that of the Hermitage of Santo Spirito.

In late August two processions are held at these locations. On 25 August, pilgrims drink water from a holy spring inside the Legio hermitage and then follow a statue

4

THE BOLOGNANO FALLS

A favourite spot with many locals, especially couples, in the Valle dell'Orta Nature Reserve is the Bolognano Falls. To get there by car, take the turn-off for Bolognano from the SS5. Once you reach the town, park on the road following the sharp bend in the road that acts as the main square and head into the small lane on the left. Turn right, keep going past the fountain and down a small path for about five minutes. From here, a long set of steps will take you to the bottom of the valley, just above the river. Take the steel ladder down to river level, and follow the river to your right. Eventually, after having waded through the water (an experience marred only by the slippery rocks), you will reach a raised area with a 'waterfall': in reality a trickle of water from the mountains above. This flows into a natural pool where you can swim in beautifully clear water. It is not unusual to have the place completely to yourself.

of St Bartholomew around town in holy procession. A similar event is held on 29 August for the Hermitage of Santo Spirito.

BOLOGNANO The easiest way to reach Bolognano is from its turn-off on the SS5. It's one of those towns in Abruzzo where time seems to have stood still. It sits on a hill in the Orta Valley and has managed to retain its medieval character and architecture. The town's focal point is the 16th-century **Palazzo Baronale**. The **Church of Santa Maria Entroterra**, nearby, retains its 16th-century exterior and a series of frescoes from the same century.

However, many people visit Bolognano because it sits at the entrance to the **Valle dell'Orta Nature Reserve**. At the heart of the reserve is a wonderful place to swim (see box above). It is also known for the **Grotta dei Piccioni**, a cave that has yielded some important archaeological finds, including Iron Age tools.

Around Bolognano
Musellaro This small town is strictly part of Bolognano, though around 3km away. It is now almost deserted but nonetheless striking, both for its layout and setting. The highest part of town has the ruins of the **Castello Tabassi** as well as a **chapel**.

TOCCO DA CASAURIA Inhabiting a hilltop, Tocco is a pleasant little town just off the SS5 and A25 *autostrada*, and very close to the boundaries of the Majella National Park. The Baroque, 18th-century **Church of Sant'Eustachio** has a belltower that can be seen for miles around (one of the best views of it is from the A25, just before the road cuts in between the Gran Sasso and Majella national parks). Just near the church are the **castle ruins**. Much of what you can see today dates from the rebuilding works of the 15th and 18th centuries, and wandering around the ruins gives you some idea of just how imposing this must have been in its heyday. Architecturally, it is similar to the castle at Celano (see page 129). The town is also home to the **Church of San Domenico**, which was built in the 1490s and has a charming and ornate doorway.

SALLE Salle is a largely modern town, having been rebuilt after the 1933 earthquake. **Salle Castle** (*www.castellodisalle.it*) is now home to the **Bourbon Medieval Museum** (*Il Castello e il Museo Medievale Borbonico; Via Salle Vecchia*

1; ✆ *085 928 265; admission €4, book at least 2 days in advance;* ◷ *1 May–15 Oct, Thu–Sat 15.00–19.30, Sun 10.00–13.00 & 15.00–19.00).* The impressive building is a sight in itself and the museum houses a collection of old weapons and armoury.

Around Salle
Salle Vecchia Salle Vecchia, a striking uninhabited medieval hamlet of the 11th century, is found a few kilometres from the modern town of Salle. Walking through the crumbling buildings, abandoned after the 1933 earthquake, is a rather eerie experience.

CARAMANICO TERME Caramanico is at the centre of the Majella National Park, forming both a gateway to the park itself and an attraction in its own right. Given its isolated position, it is a thriving little community and during the warmer months the town's shops are open on Sundays (a very rare thing indeed in Abruzzo).

Caramanico is the largest town in the area and well worth at least a few hours of your time, even if only to indulge yourself at the **Thermal Spas of Caramanico** (see box, page 94). Don't miss the breathtaking views of the terracotta rooftops and church spires along the SS487 on the approach to the town.

Getting there The town is situated on the SS487, which can be reached from a turn-off along the SS5. It is approximately an hour's drive from Pescara or Chieti. Alternatively, there are six bus services per day departing from Pescara and stopping along the way. The journey takes around 1½ hours and costs approximately €5.

Tourist information
🗌 **IAT Caramanico Terme** Via Fontegrande, 3; ✆085 922202. Caramanico's importance to the region's tourism industry means it has 1 of only 5 main tourist offices in the province.

 Where to stay and eat Because of Caramanico's popularity as a base for exploring the Majella National Park, there are many places to stay within the town or just outside. Most of the hotels listed below have excellent restaurants using the best of local ingredients. For a thermal break, see Hotel La Reserve in the box on page 94.

🏠 **Albergo Maiella e delle Terme** (107 rooms) Via Roma 29; ✆085 92301; e info@ albergomaiella.it; www.albergomaiella.it. A large but friendly hotel with fairly standard rooms. It has good facilities, such as a reading room, piano bar & a decent restaurant, & also offers comprehensive treatment packages for the thermal spa. **$$$**

🏠 **Hotel Cercone** (33 rooms) Viale Torre Alta 19; ✆085 922118; e hotelcercone@hotmail.com; www.hotelcercone.it. The Cercone is a pleasant establishment that looks more like someone's mountain villa than a hotel. The owner pays great attention to the little details that make your stay more pleasant & is always willing to help out with advice. The rooms are well furnished & there is also a pool & gym. **$$$**

🏠 **Hotel De Nardis** (24 rooms) Viale Roma 52; ✆085 92472; e hoteldenardis@hoteldenardis.

4

THE MAJELLA CARD

The Majella Card offers discounts on entry to museums and wildlife areas as well as hotels and restaurants within the national park. There are various pricing options depending on the number of people it is for and the length of time you are staying. Check out www.parcomajella.it for details, or approach any of the visitor information centres within the park.

Caramanico is home to the best-known thermal spa in Abruzzo. The spas here are particularly famous for their high sulphur content and they have been treating people for 400 years. Abruzzesi come from all over the region, sent by doctors, to help alleviate their respiratory problems, arthritis and digestive complaints. Treaments are doled out at the modern **Hotel La Reserve** (*72 rooms & suites; Località Santa Croce;* 085 92391; e *info@lareserve.it; www. lareserve.it; $$$$$*). It occupies an area of the old town over the thermal hotspot and has excellent rooms and facilities. There is a wealth of treatments and price plans. A simple day at the spa (without accommodation) will set you back €65 and will have you feeling as good as new. Half-day entrance (⊕ 09.00–13.00 or 13.00–17.00) will cost you €35.

it; www.hoteldenardis.it. This looks more like a modern residential apartment building than a hotel. However, the rooms are well-proportioned & comfortable, some with great views over the mountains, & there is also a lovely al fresco dining area. **$$$**

Hotel Ede (25 rooms) Viale della Libertà 59; 085 922121; e info@hotelede.it; www.hotelede. it. Ede is a good-value option & a 5-min walk from the centre of town. This is a well-run hotel with very friendly staff who will help you to feel at home. The rooms are simple but very comfortable & the bathrooms are spotless. HB & FB options available. **$$$**

Sporting Hotel Caramanico (33 rooms) Contrada San Nicolao 1; 085 923 1040; e info@sportinghotelcaramanico.it; www. sportinghotelcaramanico.tk. Previously known as the Hotel del Parco Principi di Caramanico, this recently redocorated hotel initially looks a bit forbidding from the outside but it has

comfortable rooms & a health centre that offers massages (a good way to wind down after sightseeing). It also has a pool, gym & tennis court. **$$$**

Hotel Di Fiore (18 rooms) Viale Roma 15; 085 922160; e info@albergodifiore.it; www.albergodifiore.it. An unpretentious 3-star establishment (easily mistaken for a residential apartment building) offering comfortable albeit simple, no-frills rooms. Staff are friendly & the coffee is excellent. **$$**

Hotel Iacobucci (34 rooms) Viale della Libertà 7; 085 922103; e info@hoteliacobucci. it; www.hoteliacobucci.it. Another hotel along Viale della Libertà, with a welcoming atmosphere & friendly staff. The rooms are good value for the price, & moderately decorated. The restaurant offers good local food in a relaxed atmosphere & makes the HB & FB prices particularly attractive. **$$**

Other practicalities There is an **ATM** at Banca Caripe (*Viale della Libertà 27*), a **post office** (*Via Dietro le Mura 21;* 085 929 0218) and a **chemist** (*Piazza Marconi 2;* 085 929 0228).

What to see and do

Church of Santa Maria Maggiore (⊕ *daily 08.30–18.00*) The highlight of this church, which was founded in the 15th century, is its outstanding entrance dating from 1452. Interestingly, the spot it currently occupies is not the spot on which it was originally built (it suffered extensive earthquake damage). The church has a nave with two aisles and has been restored over the centuries.

Church of San Nicola Found in Piazza Garibaldi alongside the Church of San Domenico (with its pretty doorways), this church has some excellent frescoes from the 16th century and some interesting wooden sculptures.

Museo della Fauna Abruzzese ed Italiana/Museum of the Fauna of Abruzzo and Italy (*Convento delle Clarisse;* ✆ *085 922343;* ⊕ *Jul–Sep, Tue–Sun 16.30–19.30*) This museum has a good display on the various animals found in Abruzzo and the rest of Italy. It is quite small but very informative, and the staff is extremely knowledgeable.

Centro di Visita and Museo Naturalistico ed Archeologico 'Paolo Barasso'/Visitor Centre and 'Paolo Barasso' Nature and Archaeological Museum (*Via del Vivaio;* ✆ *085 922343;* ⊕ *daily Oct–May 09.00–13.00; Jun–Sep 09.00–13.00 & 15.00–19.00; admission €4*) This information centre is just outside town and is an excellent reference point for those starting their exploration of the Majella National Park from Caramanico. The office can provide all sorts of information, from advice on accommodation to tours and wildlife spotting. The museum focuses on the geology of the area as well as archaeological finds from within the national park. There is also an **Otter Conservation Area**. At night it is possible to catch a glimpse of an otter or two. It is best to approach the area silently and have some patience as it can take a while for them to appear.

Around Caramanico
Church of San Tommaso San Tommaso Church, in the hamlet of the same name, is a drive of about 15 minutes from Caramanico. During the 13th century it was built on the site of an earlier temple from which there are a number of archaeological finds. Inside, there are some excellent 13th-century wall paintings. The church underwent major restoration during the mid 20th century. Not far from here in a spectacular position are the medieval remains of the **Castle of Luco**.

POPOLI Most of the Pescarese landscape is framed by the peaks of Gran Sasso to the north and Majella to the south, and Popoli lies just inside the Majella National Park. Situated on the A25 *autostrada* from Rome, it acts as the gateway to Pescara Province, and the ruins of its imposing hillside castle can be seen for miles.

The settlement has pre-Roman origins, though Popoli's current layout dates from the 13th century. It was a prosperous town during the Middle Ages, with a thriving wool industry and basking in the patronage of the wealthy families of the Kingdom of Naples. Because of its importance along the Rome–Pescara route, the British heavily bombed the town in 1944. While some of the ancient buildings were destroyed, enough has survived to justify a visit.

Getting there
By car Popoli has its own exit from the A25 and it also lies on the important SS5 (Via Tiburtina Valeria).

POPOLI THERMAL SPA

The town is set on the banks of the River Aterno and has an excellent thermal spa, second only to that of Caramanico (see box, opposite). Treatments are available at the **Stabilimento Termale** (*Località DeContra;* ✆ *085 987781; www.termedipopoli.it*), usually open all year round. Treatment options are many and varied but the staff are very knowledgeable and will be able to advise you.

By bus There are three direct daily services from Pescara to Popoli which take about 1½ hours and will set you back around €6. The other three services travel via Sulmona (which is only about 20 minutes from Popoli) and L'Aquila. Avoid the latter, as the trip takes over four hours. From nearby Sulmona, there are around 14 daily services taking around half an hour.

By train There are numerous departures to Popoli from Pescara Central station, taking anywhere between 48 minutes and 1½ hours. Tickets will set you back €3.60. The train journey from Rome can take anything up to four hours and costs around €10.

🏠 Where to stay and eat

🏠 **Hotel Tre Monti** (36 rooms) Via Tiburtina Valeria 1; 📞085 987 5059; e info@tremontihotel. it; www.tremontihotel.it. Very comfortable if rather unremarkable rooms are on offer at this hotel that lies a short distance from the centre of town. The hotel has an excellent restaurant with well-priced main courses, including a number of local dishes. **$$$**

Other practicalities There are two **banks** with ATMs along Corso Gramsci: Banca Caripe (*Corso Gramsci 13–15*) and Banco di Napoli (*Corso Gramsci 187*). The same road has two **chemists**, Farmacia Simoncelli (*Corso Gramsci, 164;* 📞085 98254) and Farmacia Violante (*Corso Gramsci, 8;* 📞085 98244). There is also a **post office** (*Via Marconi 13/17;* 📞085 98330; ⊕ *normal post office hours – see page 45 – but closed Fri*).

What to see and do

Medieval castle The ruins of Popoli's castle are very atmospheric, especially at night when they are lit up. Occupying a spot on the slopes of Mount Morrone just above the town, they contribute to the medieval feel of Popoli's townscape. The castle with its sturdy walls and towers dates back to the early 11th century and was once an important regional stronghold.

Taverna Ducale The intriguing 'Ducal Tavern' is one of the most important medieval buildings in the region. It was built over a period of four years during the 1370s to collect tolls and tithes for a nearby road. Bas-reliefs and other sculptures can be seen on its façade and the interior houses the **Ducal Tavern Museum** (*Museo Taverna Ducale di Popoli; Via Giuseppe Garibaldi;* 📞 *085 986701; www. tavernaducalepopoli.beniculturali.it; admission free;* ⊕ *Mon & Wed 09.00–13.00 & 15.00–16.30, Tue & Thu 09.00–13.00 & 14.00–15.00, Fri 09.00–13.00, Sat & Sun by appointment*).

Palazzo Ducale Used as a residence during the 15th century by the Cantelmo family (of importance in the area), this beautiful palazzo has a striking entrance and set of arches.

Church of San Francesco On the town's main square, Piazza della Libertà, the Church of San Francesco was founded in the late 13th century. Rebuilding took place in the 1450s and then again in the 15th, 18th and 20th centuries. The façade is rather impressive, with its rose window and statues at its top corners.

Church of the Santissima Trinità This church, dedicated to the Holy Trinity, was remodelled during the 18th century in a Baroque style. It has a particularly beautiful staircase leading up to its entrance. The interior houses some significant frescoes from the 16th century.

Around Popoli Two nature reserves lie in close proximity to Popoli. For information and guided tours in each reserve \085 980 8009.

La Riserva Naturale di Monte Rotondo/Monte Rotondo Natural Reserve
This nature reserve straddles the boundaries of the two national parks and is an excellent place for wildlife spotting, or simply to stop for a picnic. It's a 15-minute drive east of the town down an unnamed road; follow the signs.

La Riserva Sorgenti del Pescara/Sorgenti del Pescara Nature Reserve
The River Aterno flows into the River Pescara near Popoli, and this protected area gives you the opportunity to walk by the river and admire its clear waters (before it hits Pescara and becomes filthy). It's only a five-minute drive west of the town, along the SS17.

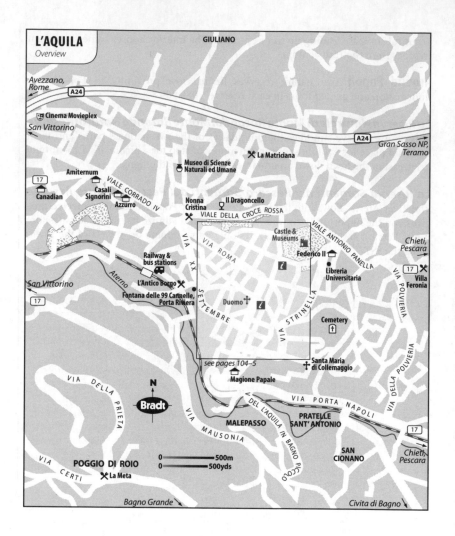

L'AQUILA
Overview

GIULIANO

Avezzano,
Rome

A24

🎭 Cinema Movieplex

San Vittorino

A24

Gran Sasso NP,
Teramo

✖ La Matriciana

Museo di Scienze
Naturali ed Umane

Amiternum

17

Canadian

Casali
Signorini

Azzurro

VIALE CORRADO IV

Nonna
Cristina

Il Dragoncello

VIALE DELLA CROCE ROSSA

Castle &
Museums

Federico II

Chieti,
Pescara

VIALE ANTIONIO PANELLA

VIA ROMA

Libreria
Universitaria

17 ✖

Villa
Feronia

VIA POLVIERIA

San Vittorino

17

Aterno

Railway &
bus stations

L'Antico Borgo ✖

Fontana delle 99 Cannelle,
Porta Riviera

VIA XX SETTEMBRE

Duomo ✝

VIA STRINELLA

Cemetery

VIA DELLA POLVIERIA

see pages 104–5

Santa Maria
di Collemaggio

Magione Papale

VIA DELLA PRIETA

N

Bradt

VIA MAUSONIA

MALEPASSO

DEL L'AQUILA IN BAGNO PICCOLO

VIA PORTA NAPOLI

PRATELLE
SANT'ANTONIO

17

VIA CERTI

POGGIO DI ROIO

✖ La Meta

0 ▭▭▭ 500m
0 ▭▭▭ 500yds

SAN
CIONANO

Chieti,
Pescara

Bagno Grande

Civita di Bagno

5

L'Aquila

At 03.32 on 6 April 2009, the ground beneath the city of L'Aquila shook violently. The earthquake, which measured no less than 6.3 on the Richter scale, caused severe and devastating loss to both human life and the artistic and cultural patrimony of L'Aquila, Abruzzo and – by extension – Italy. Awoken by severe jolts in the quiet dead of night, thousands of people found themselves trapped under rubble, and hundreds – almost 400 human souls – perished, many of them children and young students of the University of L'Aquila. More than 60,000 were made homeless in less than five minutes. For the weeks and months that followed, L'Aquila continued to shake, apparently without an end in sight. Aftershocks measured as high as 5 on the Richter scale, and many – including personal friends and family – described the difficulty of falling asleep knowing that such a horrific event could occur again.

Unfortunately for the traveller, L'Aquila still lies in a dormant state of ruin. Churches were damaged, some destroyed beyond repair; historic palazzos line the streets on which they stood for centuries in the form of crumbled stones. However, reconstruction and restoration will be forthcoming, even if not as quickly as was hoped immediately following the earthquake. Rebuilding in L'Aquila will require patience but will eventually result in the restoration of the city's ancient churches and cobblestone alleyways.

L'Aquila means 'The Eagle', which is fitting given the city's prominent position 714m above sea level, making it the highest regional capital in Italy. It is located on a slope not far from the left bank of the River Aterno in the region's northwest (almost at the geographical centre of Italy), with the jagged massif of the Gran Sasso d'Italia looming over the city.

L'Aquila was once the second most important city in the Kingdom of Naples. However, before the 13th century, the site was no more than a shoddy collection of 99 villages (more like tiny groups of houses) that were unified to create one prosperous city. In fact, the number 99 featured prominently in the city's history – from its 99 founding settlements and 99 squares to the 99 churches that once adorned its streets. But that number is almost a dim memory, along with a great many of the churches and squares. Before the catastrophic earthquake of 2009, it was a charming city still proud of its past prosperity and with enough evidence to justify such pride. It is home not only to an impressive fort containing a national museum, but more ancient churches than you could poke a cross at and one of the most unique monuments in the region, the Fountain of 99 Spouts, which suffered very little damage in the earthquake. The locals are also particularly proud of a history closely tied in with that of Pietro Angelieri, who commissioned the striking Basilica of Santa Maria di Collemaggio and who became the popular and controversial Pope Celestine V in 1294.

The city's ancient streets and alleyways branch out from the Piazza del Duomo and are dotted with old *palazzi* (the Italian world for 'buildings') that reflect centuries of city life in their crumbling lancet windows and arches. The relative survival of L'Aquila's architecture – with the imprint of centuries of wear and tear, earthquakes (most notably in 1703, 1915 and 2009), and a lack of money and attention – is something of a mystery. However, this is simply what has, over the last few centuries, made L'Aquila so authentic. When L'Aquila is finally restored to its former self, you will encounter no preened, manicured streets and perfectly preserved buildings like those in Tuscany or Umbria; and, as far as the no-nonsense Aquilani are concerned, if you don't like it you're quite welcome to head for the aforementioned tourist traps.

Despite a population of only 70,000, L'Aquila is actually quite lively, due, in part, to the throngs of students who come from all over Italy to attend the university (which reopened its doors on 19 October 2009) and populate its bars after dark. Its proximity to the most interesting areas of the Gran Sasso National Park (see page 119) means the city has for centuries been used as a convenient base for exploring the area, particularly in winter.

This buzz and cultural heritage, combined with access to the best skiing areas in the region and the sea only an hour away by car, mean that L'Aquila, when restored to former glory, will once again provide an excellent snapshot of the entire region.

HISTORY

The command to build Aquila – one large, prosperous city that grew from several hamlets and villages – changed the course of Abruzzo's history and gave it one of Italy's most dramatically situated and charming provincial capitals.

The city was born as a result of the amalgamation of a supposed 99 settlements of the Aquilan basin. Work was sanctioned and begun in the mid-1240s under the supervision of the Holy Roman Emperor and the king of Sicily, Frederick II, who wished to challenge the power of the Papal states in central Italy. The name Aquila was chosen as a result of the eagle adorning the coat of arms of the Hohenstaufen dynasty. It was altered to Aquila degli Abruzzi (Eagle of the Abruzzi) in the 1860s and to L'Aquila in 1939.

The city underwent its greatest period of expansion under Conrad IV and was completed in 1254. It became so significant that Pope Alexander IV transferred the bishopric from Forcona to L'Aquila and established the church of San Massimo and San Giorgio, which became the city's cathedral in the 18th century (see page 113). This was probably a symbolic gesture in order to re-establish the presence of the Church within a city held by a new Hohenstaufen king, Manfred.

In 1259, the king waged so fierce a campaign against the Papal states as to burn down and destroy the entire city upon discovering that his subjects chose to side with the Church. L'Aquila was consequently abandoned for a period of seven years before the commencement of the 1268 regeneration project attributed to Charles I of Anjou, king of Sicily. During this period, construction began on the city's impressive walls (completed in 1316) and the Basilica of Santa Maria di Collemaggio (see page 110), wherein Pope Peter of Morrone, later Pope Celestine V, celebrated his coronation as leader of the Church. This took place in 1294 and was an event which placed the city firmly on the map beyond the borders of the kingdom.

The early 14th century was a period of extensive growth and power as the kings of the Angevin dynasty bestowed great attention upon the city. This included privileges that removed certain taxes from activities related to sheep farming. Furthermore, in 1344 the city was granted its own mint.

Full of confidence and, some say, cocky and sure of their influence and power, the Aquilani often straddled both sides of the fence in the disputes between the House of Anjou and the Papal states during the early 14th century. It was in these feuds that the Papal states attempted to reassert their dominance over a city which they saw as too independent (see *History*, page 11). Despite skirmishes and sieges, the city remained prosperous.

However, the mid 14th century brought difficult times for the thriving settlement, as it was struck down by plagues and the wrath of Mother Nature in the form of various earthquakes which rattled and destroyed much of the city.

It didn't take the thick-skinned residents long to bounce back, however, and the following decades returned the city to its previous affluence. Attention was lavished upon it by the Franciscan order while Jewish families chose the city as home. Higher education was established and the city's first printing press began operations in 1482.

Yet all greatness has its time, and the city's revered independence was crushed after the French and Spanish battled for the throne of the Kingdom of Naples in the early 16th century, a feud that the Spanish won decisively. The Spanish, having destroyed parts of the city, established themselves in the surrounding countryside, and in 1532 the imposing castle, or Spanish Fort (see page 115), was erected. Once the Spanish established feudalism, the city never regained its quasi-autonomy. It was ruthlessly stripped of the various privileges that had allowed it to prosper over three centuries and development ground to a halt. The Aquilani rebelled against Spanish rule in 1647 but the Spanish responded quickly and ruthlessly, further impeding the city's freedom.

The 18th century was not kind to L'Aquila: it was once again destroyed in the chaotic earthquake of 1703, which left the majority of the citizens homeless and caused irrevocable damage to so many of the city's churches and monuments. As if this wasn't enough, the city was ransacked by French troops in 1799, under the rule of Napoleon. In the 1830s, the city took part in revolutionary efforts for a unified Italy and, upon the success of the unification in the 1860s, gained status as the capital of the Abruzzi. It is now the capital of the largest province in Abruzzo.

In the 20th century, L'Aquila once more found its footing with the building of much-needed transport links such as the A24 motorway connecting it with the country's capital. In 2009, an earthquake destroyed large parts of the city. Restoring the city to its former glory is estimated to take at least ten to 15 years.

BRIEF CHRONOLOGY

1245	Villages unite; work on the city begins.
1254	Work on the city is completed.
1256	Cathedral created by Pope as reward for siding against the Hohenstaufen.
1259	King Manfred razes the city.
1272	Work begins on the city's famed fountain.
1287	Basilica of Santa Maria of Collemaggio is founded.
1294	Celestine V celebrates coronation as Pope.
1311	Robert of Anjou bestows trading privileges.
1316	Work on city walls completed.
1344	City granted a mint.
1348	Plague epidemic.
1349	Major earthquake rattles the city, which is subsequently destroyed.
1363	Plague epidemic.
1376	Franciscan Order first bestows city as seat of the general chapters.
1424	Siege of the city, instigated by Queen Joanna II of Anjou.
1444	Bernardino of Siena first preaches in the city.
1461	City hit by earthquake.
1472	Body of Saint Bernardino is set up within namesake Basilica.
1482	Printing press created.
1532	Spanish rule ratified by building of castle.
1647	Aquila rebels against Spanish rule, to no avail.
1703	Worst earthquake in L'Aquila's history destroys the entire city.
1799	French troops raid the city.
1833	L'Aquila's first revolutionary efforts.
1860	Unification of Italy; city becomes capital of the region.
1939	Name changed from Aquila degli Abruzzi to L'Aquila.
2009	Earthquake measuring 6.3 on the Richter scale destroys the city.

GETTING THERE AND AWAY

BY CAR L'Aquila is easily reached on the A24 *autostrada* from Rome and Teramo, 115km and 60km away respectively. From Pescara and Chieti (both about 100km away), it is easiest to take the A25 to Bussi sul Tirino and follow the signs to L'Aquila via the SS17.

BY BUS ARPA has frequent scheduled services to L'Aquila from Pescara (1½ hours, approx €9.20), Teramo (1 hour 20 minutes, approx €6.60) and Rome (around 20 per day, 1½ hours, approx €11). If you are coming from Chieti, it is best to make your way to Pescara and take advantage of an ARPA service. Otherwise, Gruppo La Panoramica has a scheduled service from Chieti to L'Aquila but runs via Teramo

ROADS ACCESSIBLE TO THE PUBLIC

Due to the extensive damage caused to the city as a result of the 2009 earthquake, most roads and minor laneways in the historic centre are still classified as 'Zone Red' by the Italian military.

The following major roads and thoroughfares were open at the time of writing:

Viale di Collemaggio
Viale Crispi
Corso Vittorio Emanuele II
Via Rendina

Via Fontebraccio
Via XX Settembre
Via Fontesecco
Via Castello

and takes around two hours. Buses terminate at the city's central bus station, which is to the southeast of the city centre, just outside the walls.

BY TRAIN The train service between Pescara/Chieti and L'Aquila can take between two and three hours as it travels via Sulmona. There are about eight to ten services daily, which cost approximately €10. Despite Teramo's proximity to L'Aquila, there is still no railway track connecting the two cities and hence trains need to travel to Pescara before making their way on to Sulmona and L'Aquila, which is somewhat ridiculous. Thus the train journey from Teramo, a mere 60km away, can take around four to five hours; take the bus instead. Journey times from Rome are about three to four hours and cost a whopping €20. There are approximately ten services a day. L'Aquila railway station is to the northwest of the city centre, just beyond the walls.

GETTING AROUND

Unless you're travelling out to the nearby Roman ruins of Amiternum (see page 119), all of L'Aquila's sightseeing is within the historic centre and can therefore easily be enjoyed on foot.

BY BUS

Please note that at the time of writing, bus services were still limited due to the earthquake damage. Bus lines in operation on weekdays were as follows: 5, 8, 9, 10, 11, 12, 15, 16, 80, 83, 99, 101, 102, 104, 105, 106/108. Bus lines in operation on the weekends were as follows: 5, 99, 110, 111, 115, 116, 117.

L'Aquila's bus network is run by Azienda Mobilità Aquilana (AMA) (*www.ama. laquila.it*). This network of buses skirts the nucleus of the old town centre and extends into the modern city and beyond. The 3, M3 and M30 depart from the city's railway station, northwest of the town centre. Tickets are no more than about €1.

BY CAR If you are coming to L'Aquila with your own transport, there are plenty of car parks where you can leave your vehicle, and some hotels offer their own parking. However, you should leave the car parked, as driving to see the sights is futile.

L'Aquila GETTING AROUND

5

103

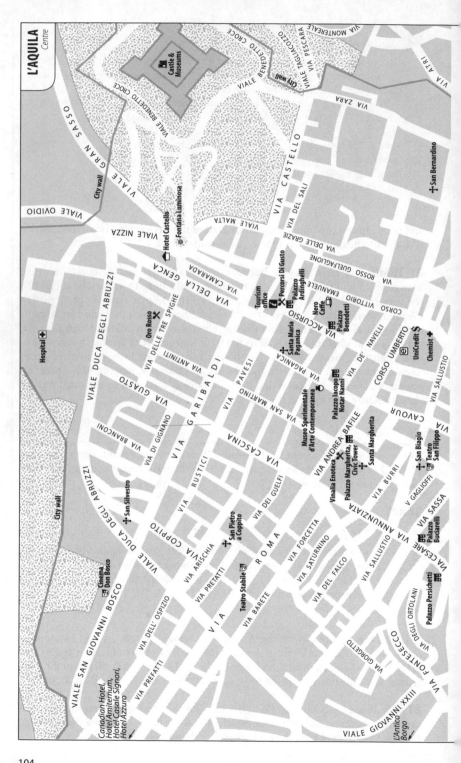

L'AQUILA
Centre

Castle & Museums

City wall

VIALE BENEDETTO CROCE

VIA MONTREALE

VIA PESCARA

VIA TAGLIACOZZO

VIA ATRI

VIA ZARA

✝ San Bernardino

VIALE GRAN SASSO

City wall

VIALE NIZZA

VIALE OVIDIO

VIA CASTELLO

VIA DEL SALI

VIALE MALTA

⚲ Fontana Luminosa

🏛 Hotel Castello

VIA DELLA GENCA

VIA CAMARADA

VIA ROSSO GUELFAGLIONE

VIA DELLE GRAZIE

Hospital ✚

VIALE DUCA DEGLI ABRUZZI

VIA DELLE TRE SPIGHE

✗ Oro Rosso

VIA ANTINITI

Tourism office ℹ

✗ Percorsi Di Gusto

🏛 Palazzo Ardinghelli

Nero Caffè

CORSO VITTORIO EMANUELE

VIA ACCURSIO

🏛 Palazzo Benedetti

VIA DE' NAVELLI

$ UniCredit
Chemist ✚

VIA GUASTO

VIA BRANCONI

VIA DI GIGNANO

VIA GARIBALDI

VIA PAVESI

✝ Santa Maria Paganica

VIA PAGANICA

VIA SAN MARTINO

🏛 Palazzo Iacopo Notar Nanni

VIA DE'

CORSO UMBERTO

CAVOUR

VIA SALLUSTIO

✚ San Silvestro

VIA RUSTICI

VIA CASCINA

Museo Sperimentale d'Arte Contemporanea

VIA ANDREA BAFILE

✗ Vinalia Enoteca

🏛 Palazzo Margherita, Civic Tower

✝ Santa Margherita

VIA BURRI

V GAGLIOFFI

✝ San Biagio

🎭 Teatro San Filippo

VIA COPPITO

VIA DEI GUELFI

✝ San Pietro a Coppito

R O M A

VIA FORCETTA

VIA ANNUNZIATA

VIA SALLUSTIO

VIA SASSA

VIA CESARE

🏛 Palazzo Bucarelli

VIALE DUCA DEGLI ABRUZZI

VIALE SAN GIOVANNI BOSCO

City wall

🎬 Cinema Don Bosco

VIA DELL' OSPIZIO

VIA ARISCHIA

VIA PREZATTI

🎭 Teatro Stabile

VIA BARETE

VIA SATURNINO

VIA DEL FALCO

Palazzo Persichetti

VIA DEGLI ORTOLANI

VIA GIORGETTO

VIA FONTESECCO

VIA PREFATTI

Canadian Hotel,
Hotel Amiternum,
Hotel Casale Signori,
Hotel Azzuro

L'Antico Borgo

VIALE GIOVANNI XXIII

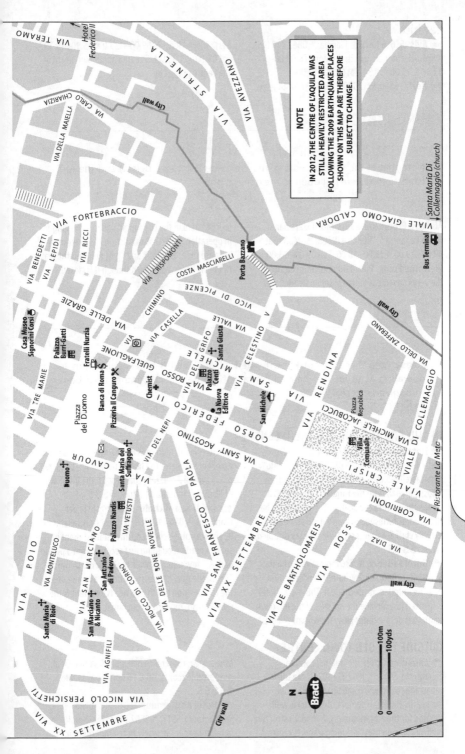

NOTE

IN 2012, THE CENTRE OF L'AQUILA WAS
STILL A HEAVILY RESTRICTED AREA
FOLLOWING THE 2009 EARTHQUAKE. PLACES
SHOWN ON THIS MAP ARE THEREFORE
SUBJECT TO CHANGE.

Car hire

🚗 **Avis** SS615 towards Pianola; ☎0862 410415; www.avisautonoleggio.it; ⏰ Mon–Fri 09.00–12.30 & 15.00–18.30, Sat 09.00–12.00
🚗 **Hertz** SS80, km 2320; ☎0862 319436; www. hertz.it; ⏰ Mon–Fri 09.00–13.00 & 15.30–19.30, Sat 09.00–13.00 Sat. Situated about 6km north of the centre of the city.

TOURIST INFORMATION

Note that at the time of writing, the Welcome Point (see below) and the APT tourist office were not open to the general public.

Abruzzo Promozione Turismo Piazza Santa Maria Paganica 5; ☎0862 410808; ⏰ Mon–Sat 09.00–13.00 & 15.00–18.00, Sun 09.00–13.00
Welcome Point Piazza Duomo. Unfortunately, the very convenient initiative set up by the local tourist board in the city's main square is no longer in operation. Note that this listing has been kept because there are still 1 or 2 signs pointing the way to the Welcome Point even though it is closed.

 ## WHERE TO STAY

Please note that it is not known when all of L'Aquila's hotels will return to operating as usual. It is best to contact the hotel directly, rather than book through an external website.

IN AND AROUND THE OLD TOWN CENTRE

🏠 **Hotel Castello** (50 rooms) Piazza Battaglione degli Alpini; ☎0862 419147; e info@ hotelcastelloaq.com; www.hotelcastelloaq.com. Across the road from the Fontana Luminosa & a stone's throw from the Spanish Fort, this hotel has clean rooms furnished to a very good standard, friendly staff & 4 rooms set aside for easy disabled access. **$$$$**
🏠 **Hotel Federico II** (36 rooms) Via Strinella, 6; ☎0862 22060; e info@hotelfedericosecondo. it; www.hotelfedericosecondo.it. This 4-star hotel is situated just outside the nucleus of the old town centre & is only seconds away from Spanish Fort.

Rooms offer all mod cons & are furnished to an excellent standard. The hotel's restaurant, Le Giare, offers typical Abruzzese cuisine with the influence of Abruzzo's mountain culture. **$$$$**
🏠 **Hotel San Michele** (32 rooms) Via dei Giardini 6; ☎0862 420260; e info@stmichelehotel. it; www.stmichelehotel.it. This establishment is set in a modern building just seconds from a public park & a few minutes' walk to Piazza del Duomo. The façade may not be as charming as some of the competition but the service is excellent & the rooms clean, modern & functional. **$$$**

OUTSIDE THE OLD TOWN CENTRE

🏠 **Canadian Hotel** (94 rooms) Località Casermette, SS17; ☎0862 317402; e canadian@ canadianhotel.it; www.canadianhotel.it. Like the nearby Hotel Amiternum, this hotel is well situated for the A24 motorway. A modern structure with all conveniences, including a sports centre &
fitness area, conference hall, pool & sauna. Clean, comfortable rooms. HB & FB options available. **$$$$$**
🏠 **Hotel Amiternum** (60 rooms) Bivio Sant'Antonio, SS17; ☎0862 315757; e hotel@ hotelamiternum.it; www.hotelamiternum.it.

Though the interior of the hotel seems in need of some redecoration, this is a functional hotel not far from the town centre. Own transport is advised. The hotel offers HB & FB options as well as B&B. **$$$**

🏠 **Hotel Azzurro** (9 rooms, 6 suites) Via G Di Vincenzo, corner of Viale Corrado IV; ☎0862 318054; e info@hotelazzurro.it; www. hotelazzurro.it Aptly named given its blue décor, Hotel Azzurro offers en-suite accommodation outside the city centre comprising 9 rooms, all with kitchenette & bathroom, furnished to a high standard. 6 larger suites are also available, along with ample parking & conference facilities. Great value. **$$$**

🏠 **Hotel Casale Signorini** (10 rooms) Località Cisternola, SS17; ☎0862 361184; e info@

casalesignorini.it; www.casalesignorini.it. Set on a hill within a 15th-century building, this hotel was modernised in the 1990s to offer accommodation with a personal touch in charismatic, rustic rooms. **$$$**

🏠 **Magione Papale** (17 rooms) Via Porta Napoli 67; ☎0862 414983; e info@ magionepapale.it; www.magionepapale.it. It is a testament to the Aquilani fighting spirit that there should be a new hotel in L'Aquila. Owned by the Hotel San Michele, the Magione Papale provides a country-style retreat just outside the city walls. The hotel has a pool and an excellent gourmet restaurant serving local specialities like *pasta alla chitarra*. The hotel has not been given a star rating yet but it is very similar quality to a 4-star hotel. **$$$**

✕ WHERE TO EAT AND DRINK

✕ **L'Antico Borgo** Piazza San Vito 1; ☎0862 22005; ⏰ daily lunch & dinner. This restaurant serves delicious traditional dishes with good-quality ingredients. It is situated near the Fountain of 99 Spouts. **$$$**

✕ **Oro Rosso** Via delle Tre Spighe, 3; ☎0862 207067; www.ororossoaq.it; ⏰ daily lunch & dinner. Although, with its three locations in and around L'Aquila, this restaurant is a chain, its food is excellent. The usual classic pizzas are available as well as a host of special pizzas such as the Oro Rosso, with mozzarella, saffron, mushrooms & pork sausage. Also try the Aragno, which comes with mozzarella, stracchino sausage meat & nuts. All pizzas are named after towns in L'Aquila Province. **$$$**

✕ **Ristorante La Matriciana** Via Tosto, 68B; ☎0862 26065; ⏰ daily lunch & dinner, closed Wed Aug–May. La Matriciana was centrally located off Piazza del Duomo but the earthquake of 2009 forced its operations to move just north of the old town. Despite its change, La Matriciana is as good value for money as it always was. The beauty of eating here is that often, you will not receive a menu but simply be told what dishes are available that day. **$$$**

✕ **Vinalia Enoteca Ristorante** Via Andrea Bafile 15; ☎0862 414545; e info@enotecavinalia.it; www. enotecavinalia.it; ⏰ Thu–Tue. Vinalia's reputation as the best restaurant in town is deserved. Oozing class & style, it offers a dining experience with an

elegance befitting an old regal town such as L'Aquila, as well as an extensive wine collection (at around 1,800 different labels) & friendly service. The food mixes an eclectic & creative collection of ingredients, bringing together the best traditions of the region, divinely presented. **$$$**

✕ **La Meta** Via della Pineta, Poggio Roio; ☎0862 602315; ⏰ daily lunch & dinner. Although this restaurant is several kilometres from the city centre, near the University's engineering faculty, it is worth a visit. It is a low-budget dining option where a 2-course meal will set you back no more than about €10. **$$**

✕ **Nonna Cristina** Via della Croce Rossa, 163; ☎0862 62371; ⏰ daily dinner only, from 20.00 until late. The Nonna Cristina was one of many casualties of the earthquake, which forced its move to the northern periphery of the town centre. Founded by Cristina's husband & dedicated to her (as attested to by her portrait inside the restaurant), Nonna Cristina was so named because of the couple's healthy number of grandchildren. The atmosphere here offers the rustic feel typical of so many restaurants in Abruzzo. Try the rather expensive steak, or alternatively, one of the restaurant's signature pizzas. **$$**

✕ **Percorsi di Gusto** Via Leosini, 7; ☎0862 411429; marziavinalia@yahoo.it; www. percorsidigusto.com; ⏰ daily lunch & dinner. A host of typical dishes from the region are on offer here, such as the sherry onion & hot peppers pizza & the scrumptious mozzarella, Norwegian cod, potatoes & saffron pizza. Try the lentil soup, a staple dish from nearby town Santo Stefano. Service is friendly & prompt. **$$**

✗ **Villa Feronia** Via Santa Veronica, 8; m3497 231 160; ⊕ Tue–Sat 12.30–14.30 & 20.00–22.00, Sun 12.30–14.30, closed Mon. Before the earthquake, the Villa Feronia was set within the stunning 15th-century building named Casa Jacopo Notar Nanni, which suffered extensive damage. The restaurant is now located a 10-min drive to the northwest of the town centre. The food here matches the authentically bucolic Abruzzo ambience & the dishes on offer are from all over the region. Try the excellent lamb. **$$**

♀ **Gelateria Duomo** Via della Croce Rossa; www.gelaterieduomo.it; ⊕ daily. This *gelateria* once occupied a spot along L'Aquila's busiest thoroughfare but was hit hard by the earthquake. The pioneering owners, however, decided L'Aquila could not do without their *gelato* & so set up shop in a mobile van. Specialising in producing

their own ice cream, this chain is also present in Avezzano & Rome. **$**

▭ **Nero Caffe** Corso Vittorio Emanuele, 43; ☎0862 401354; ⊕ daily 07.00–midnight. The buffet lunch is the draw card here at the Nero: it's perfect for a quick recharge after a day in & around the L'Aquila area. There is also an excellent set menu for €8.50, which comprises 2 courses, a side dish, water & bread. Excellent value. **$**

♀ **Il Dragoncello** Via della Croce Rossa, 42; ☎0862 64169; www.ildragoncello.it; ⊕ Mon–Sat 09.15–13.15 & 16.30–20.30, Sun closed. This charming wine & cheese bar may have changed location after the earthquake but its shelves are still filled with copious labels of wine & typical snacks from the region. Perfect for an aperitif before heading for one of the city's restaurants.

♀ **Fratelli Nurzia** Piazza Duomo, 74-75; ☎0862 21002; e torroneurzia@gmail.com. This is one of the few traditional *gelaterias* left in L'Aquila. Whilst its ice cream is delightful, it also sells traditional *torrone* (toblerone), with the dark chocolate variety made in & around the area since 1835.

ENTERTAINMENT

🎭 **Teatro Stabile d'Abruzzo** Palazzo Santa Teresa, Via Roma 54; ☎0862 413200; www.teatrostabile.abruzzo.it. Most of this theatre is now being restored, although a small section is open. Check the website for an up-to-date listing of shows.

🎬 **Cinema Movieplex** Via Leonardo Da Vinci 7; ☎0862 319773; www.movieplex.it. Due to the earthquake, this is now the only cinema in the city.

OTHER PRACTICALITIES

There is no shortage of **banks** within the old town centre. Banks such as San Paolo and Banca di Roma are located in Piazza del Duomo and have **ATMs**. Unicredit Banca is nearby on Corso Umberto. These banks also deal in currency exchange.

For a **medical emergency**, call ☎ 118. All of L'Aquila's **chemist shops** are now in temporary structures or vans throughout the city. There is one permanent pharmacy in operation in the Fontana Luminosa area (*Farmacia Moderna*, ☎0862 414569).

FORMER GLORY

Before the earthquake of 2009, the city's large student population meant that its nightlife centred around a few drinks at one of the numerous bars and pubs. These hangouts were mostly situated in the area between Via Cavour and Piazza San Margherita. However, L'Aquila's previously buzzing nightlight is now just a memory. Nevertheless, there is talk of some nightclub and bar operators returning to the scene in the next year or two, so do keep your eye out for news.

'The Forgiveness' is celebrated during the last week of August, but particularly 28–29 August, and is by far the most important event in the Aquilan calendar. And if you're an indifferent sinner and in L'Aquila during this important religious festival, there's no better opportunity to be shriven of all your mortal misdeeds and guaranteed entrance through the gates of paradise!

Pope Celestine V initiated this significant religious event in September 1294, right here in the city of L'Aquila. Over the centuries, but particularly in the 1900s, the event has become a spectacle of costumes and choreographed processions, providing entertainment for all who attend. The ritual consists of the transportation of the papal document decreeing the validity of the event from its permanent home in Piazza del Palazzo to the Basilica of Santa Maria of Collemaggio. This is usually (and in true Italian fashion) carried out by a striking young woman set to catch everyone's eye. Upon the reading of this historic document, the basilica's doors are flung open for the masses who eagerly await their chance to be forgiven for their misdeeds. There are only two conditions, upon which one is shriven of all earthly sins during this festival: entering the Basilica of Santa Maria of Collemaggio between the evenings of 28 and 29 August, and a true desire to repent and start anew.

HOSPITALS
✚ **San Salvatore Public Hospital** Via Vetoio, Località Coppito; ☎ 0862 3681

POST OFFICE
✉ **Central post office** Piazza del Duomo 39; ☎ 0862 637308; ⏰ Mon–Sat 08.00–18.30. The post office has now resumed full operation.

EVENTS AND FESTIVALS

Check with the tourist information office, if it is open by the time that you visit, for details of events and festivals as dates are likely to change.

5 JANUARY Feast of the Epiphany. The town's centre is lined with stalls of various kinds in celebration of the '*befana*', who some Italian children say is Santa's (very ugly) wife.

GOOD FRIDAY RELIGIOUS PROCESSION This event begins at the Basilica di San Bernardino and involves various crosses and statues of Christ in procession throughout the town. There is usually a very large turnout. It has been a major event, in some form, for hundreds of years, though its modern version began in the 1950s.

PENTECOST Processione dei Rosecci. A 14th-century cross is carried in procession and followed by groups of young ladies. Rose petals are thrown from windows as the cross passes.

MAY Il Maggio Celestino. The month of May is dedicated to celebrations – the Celestinian May – in honour of the city's two saints, St Pietro Celestino and St Bernardino di Siena.

END OF MAY–JUNE Festival of the Madonna delle Grazie and St Antonio Abate. Various places host stalls and other festivities in honour of the two saints.

1 JUNE Il Medievale a L'Aquila. Flag throwers from various cities take to Piazza del Duomo to display their skills. Essentially, it's a display of flag throwing, when flags on their thin poles are tossed into the air and caught on their way down. It's a lot harder than it sounds!

END OF AUGUST La Perdonanza (see page 109).

DECEMBER The month of December brings with it a whole host of Christmas events, from music festivals and Christmas shows to markets and light displays.

21 DECEMBER La Notte Noir. On the longest night of the year, a full programme of all things 'noir' entertains the locals and tourists. A programme is available at www.nottenoir.it.

WHAT TO SEE AND DO

Please note that most of the attractions below are still closed to the public. Original descriptions of all churches and monuments have been retained as a testament to their former glory.

CHURCHES
Basilica di Santa Maria di Collemaggio

> Level of damage sustained in 2009 earthquake: Major
> Approximate time to restoration: 6 years

The city's most popular religious building is the wonderful Basilica di Santa Maria di Collemaggio, founded in 1287 and consecrated in 1289. It's said to have been built as the result of a dream experienced by the Benedictine monk Pietro da Morrone, wherein the Virgin Mary appeared to him and instructed him that a church be built on that hill, which marked the very beginning of the

STUDYING IN L'AQUILA

L'Aquila has one of the region's best universities, with – among others – a particularly famed mathematics faculty. While the university itself was established only in 1964, its prelude spans some 500 years: from the citizens' requests of a *studium* to rooms set aside for higher education by religious orders.

The university has a number of other faculties: arts, biotechnologies, economics, educational science, engineering, medicine, psychology, sciences and sport sciences. In addition to offering a variety of Italian-language courses to the public, it has a reasonably developed population of international students, and offers courses that pertain to various European educational initiatives and programmes. Unfortunately, the university's enrolments have waned somewhat since the earthquake. For more information, contact the **International Affairs Office** (\ *0862 432762; www.univaq.it/inglese/eg-index.html*)

L'Aquila–Foggia sheep track (see page 147). Pietro da Morrone later celebrated his coronation as Pope Celestine V in this church in August 1294. The church's exterior features a typically Aquilan red-and-white stone pattern, which was completed in the 15th century and is one of its most striking features. The façade can be broken up into the upper section, which contains a particularly intricate 14th-century rose window, and the lower section, housing two smaller rose windows, the central portal (17th century) and two further lateral portals. The Porta Santa on the left-hand side was built in the 1400s and displays an outstanding lunette fresco by Antonio di Atri, dated 1397. It shows Mary and Jesus between John the Baptist and St Celestine.

The basilica has undergone major restoration over the centuries due to the devastating effects of earthquakes, particularly those in the 14th and 18th centuries. In the 1970s, the church was stripped bare of the Baroque decorations adorning the nave, aisles and pillars and hence the interior looks rather bare and sombre, with its tall arches and high timber ceiling. However, the aforementioned restoration works have uncovered some interesting frescoes, which include the *Crucifixion* and the *Madonna with Angels*.

The adjoining 16th-century cloister and 15th-century refectory have a pleasant atmosphere. The cloister, with its well and arches, remains open during the lunchtime period and is a wonderful spot to sit and take in the magic of the surroundings, accompanied by the music of the conservatory. The cloister also houses an information point and toilets. The grassed area in front of the basilica is a great spot for a picnic if you can avoid the smattering of youngsters playing soccer and others engaged in a spot of jogging.

Basilica di San Bernardino

Level of damage sustained in 2009 earthquake: Major
Approximate time to restoration: 6 years

The basilica is best approached from **Piazza Bariscianello** and its large wall-flanked 18th-century staircase, an arduous feat on a hot summer's day. The basilica itself was a rather significant undertaking that spanned the latter half of the 15th century from 1454 onwards. It houses the remains of St Bernardino (to whom the church was dedicated), which were transferred there some 20 years later. Its façade, constructed later in the 16th century by Cola dell'Amatrice, is an extremely important example of Renaissance building in the region, and the church itself is arguably the largest in Abruzzo. The interior of the basilica has a nave and two aisles. Of particular note are the extravagant wooden ceiling built by Ferdinando Mosca of Pescocostanzo in the 1720s; the lovely Baroque organ; the mausoleum of the basilica's patron, St Bernardino; a late 15th-century terracotta statue of the *Madonna with Child*; and some ornate frescoes from the 1600s.

Church of Santa Giusta

Level of damage sustained in 2009 earthquake: Major
Approximate time to restoration: 9 years

The sophisticated rose window and 16th-century frescoes by Giovanni Antonio of Lucoli make the 14th-century façade of this church in Piazza San Giusta quite special. This is further attested to by the unusual fountain, which makes it seem as if the water streams directly out of the façade. In typical Romanesque style, this is one of the few churches that did not suffer extensive damage due to the 1703 earthquake. Its single-nave interior dates from the early 17th century and houses an amazing 17th-century organ and 15th-century wooden choir stalls.

Church of San Marciano e Nicanto

Level of damage sustained in 2009 earthquake: Medium
Approximate time to restoration: 1 year

Built at the end of the 13th century, the white stone façade of this church befits the enchanting square, Piazza San Marciano, with its fountain and view of the mountains in the background. The church is an important example of Romanesque façades in Abruzzo and has some lovely ceiling paintings. Of the late 13th-century church on this site, only one stone wall remains; like so many other churches and buildings, its present form dates from the rebuilding after the earthquake of 1703.

Church of Sant'Antonio of Padova

> Level of damage sustained in 2009 earthquake: Medium
> Approximate time to restoration: 2 years

Not far from the church of San Marciano, this 17th-century church is of interest due to its Baroque decoration, including a 17th-century high altar made from Castelli ceramic tiles and a most impressive wooden ceiling.

Church of Santa Maria di Roio

> Level of damage sustained in 2009 earthquake: Medium
> Approximate time to restoration: 2 years

Dominating Piazza Santa Maria di Roio, this 14th-century church is similar in appearance to the Church of San Marciano and is another testament to the popularity of the Romanesque style in Abruzzo and L'Aquila. With an unassuming interior, the church has a lovely timber balcony above the entrance, and some interesting, though faded, paintings. It was rebuilt after the 1703 earthquake.

The Duomo: Cathedral of Sts Massimo and Giorgio

> Level of damage sustained in 2009 earthquake: Major
> Approximate time to restoration: 10 years

Although strictly speaking the principal church in the city, the duomo is certainly not the most intriguing. The cathedral was originally founded in the 13th century but the only testament to this ancient era is its right wall. It was rebuilt after the 1703 earthquake and the façade was completed as recently as 1928. The interior is built to a cross plane, with a nave and two aisles, and houses some interesting works, such as a 15th-century sepulchre, paintings and a wooden choir from the 1700s.

Sadly, the iconic dome of the cathedral suffered extensive damage in the 2009 earthquake and became the quintessential picture of the devastation, featured in newspapers across the country.

Church of Santa Maria del Suffraggio

> Level of damage sustained in 2009 earthquake: Major
> Approximate time to restoration: 4 years

On Piazza del Duomo, this church's façade was completed in 1770, although the work on the dome finished in the early 1800s. About as interesting as the duomo, the interior does house a noteworthy polyptych from the 16th century.

Church of Santa Margherita

> Level of damage sustained in 2009 earthquake: Medium
> Approximate time to restoration: 3 years

Situated in Piazza Santa Margherita, this church – built over an older 13th-century structure – has never been completed. Work began in 1636 and again after the 1703 earthquake. Inside the church is a marble sarcophagus wherein lie the remains of the patron saint of the city, St Equitius.

Church of San Pietro a Coppito

> Level of damage sustained in 2009 earthquake: Medium
> Approximate time to restoration: 2 years

Along Via Roma and a square with the same name, this 14th-century church is unique in that its rectangular shape makes it wide rather than long. The façade is actually a modern reconstruction using authentic restoration methods. Of note are the 14th-century frescoes depicting the life of St George.

Church of Santa Maria Paganica

> Level of damage sustained in 2009 earthquake: Major
> Approximate time to restoration: 4 years

On Piazza Santa Maria Paganica, the church's façade is the oldest in the city even though the church was almost entirely rebuilt following the devastating earthquake of 1703. Two late 13th-century portals survive from an older medieval church on this site and the single-nave interior of the church is largely 18th century.

Church of San Silvestro

> Level of damage sustained in 2009 earthquake: Medium
> Approximate time to restoration: 2 years

With the Gran Sasso mountain range in the background, this is one of the most evocative churches in the city. Built in the Romanesque style, it has been damaged by various earthquakes and its original founding date is unknown, although it is thought to be at least 14th century. The interior houses some excellent frescoes, particularly above the altar and next to the main church entrance, dating from the 14th–16th centuries. Also of note are a few works of art, such as the *Baptism of Constantine* by a pupil of Caravaggio named Baccio Ciarpi. The church once housed Raphael's *Visitation*, now at the Prado Museum in Madrid.

Other churches The Church of San Marco and Church of Sant'Agostino (medium-level earthquake damage, time to restoration 2½ years) are found on Piazza San Marco. The former, built from the 14th to 18th centuries, is largely unimpressive but stands over one of the first 13th-century churches to be built in the city. The latter, with its lovely façade, is now used as a theatre.

On **Piazza San Biagio** is the 18th-century **Church of San Biagio d'Amiterno** (medium-level earthquake damage, time to restoration 2½ years). The nearby Church of Santa Caterina was demolished after 1703 on the order of a fervent group of nuns who wished to build one from scratch.

CASTLE AND MUSEUMS

> The castle and museums were still closed indefinitely at the time of writing.

The Castle and Museo Nazionale d'Abruzzo/National Museum of Abruzzo

(*Viale Benedetto Croce;* \ *0862 633439/633440; www.museonazionaleabruzzo. beniculturali.it;* ⊕ *Tue–Sun 08.30–19.30, closed Mon; admission adults €4, 18–25yrs & teachers €2, under 18 & over 75yrs free for EU citizens. Tickets offer to Grotte di Stiffe & Museum-House Signorini Corsi*).

> Level of damage sustained in 2009 earthquake: Major
> Approximate time to restoration: 8 years

The **castle**, also known as the **Spanish Fort**, houses the National Museum of Abruzzo and is a ten-minute walk from the central square. While it is arguably one of the best-preserved castles in Abruzzo, if not Italy, it isn't exactly a 'beautiful' structure, as so many others in the region may be described. It is as impressive as it is downright ominous-looking, thick and impenetrable and reeking of military power. Approaching the castle's main entrance via the stone bridge gives one an impression of just how large and dominating this fort actually is.

Work on the castle was under way by the 1530s at the request of Viceroy Pedro da Toledo, who wished to make great displays of Spanish domination in the area. The castle, built using the latest techniques of the era, is a square structure with four stronghold bastions at its corners. The moat never actually contained any water and access to the keep was via a wooden drawbridge, which was demolished in 1833. The impenetrable walls range from 10m in thickness at the base to 5m above. Ironically, the castle was never involved in any significant battles or sieges.

The **museum** was opened in the early 1950s and contains important regional art and historic artefacts over two floors. The first floor houses a medieval collection of precious religious artefacts, of which a particular highlight is the Renaissance *Processional Cross* from 1434, by Nicola da Guardiagrele. Another noteworthy piece is the 15th-century wooden statue of St Sebastian by Silvestro dell'Aquila. The second floor displays a collection of religious paintings by artists such as Francesco Montereale and Pompeo Cesura, a follower of Raphael. The ground floor's archaeological display includes a particularly interesting fossil, *Archidiskodon Meridionalis Vestinus* (4m by 6m long), and also a large collection of remains and pieces from the nearby Roman city of Amiternum.

Born in 1825 in the northwestern corner of Germany, Ulrichs was later to become the world's first famous gay activist, choosing to spend his last decade in his beloved city of L'Aquila. Dr Ulrichs is thought to have been the first man to wave the public flag of gay rights and announce that homosexuality was neither a sin nor a disease. Writing under a pseudonym, his books were confiscated by the police in 1864 but the courts later lifted the ban, an event that marks what many gay activists see as the beginning of the modern-day movement. Coming out of the closet in 1868, aged 43, Ulrichs endured much persecution throughout Germany for his 'sinful' stance on homosexuality, including being jailed at various times. He settled in L'Aquila in 1883 and died there in 1895. His grave, in L'Aquila's cemetery, is marked 'Exile and Pauper'. Every year, gay activists from around the world gather here to honour his memory and pioneering efforts.

The **park area** outside the castle is pleasant for a wander and a spot of lunch, though it is probably a good idea not to walk around the area after dark.

Casa Museo Signorini Corsi/House-Museum Signorini Corsi (*Via Patini 42;* ☎ *0862 410900;* ☼ *Tue–Fri 16.00–19.00, w/ends & holidays 10.00–13.00 & 16.00– 19.00; admission €3.10*) The house belonged to a prominent family of merchants and contains some invaluable works of art, such as paintings from the 15th–17th centuries and Baroque furniture. The 16th- and 17th-century furnishings for which the House-Museum is also popular are both extravagant and decadent.

Museo di Scienze Naturali ed Umane/Museum of Natural and Human Sciences (*Via San Giuliano 56;* ☎ *0862 314201;* ☼ *Tue–Sun 10.00–13.00 & 16.00–19.00, closed Mon; admission €3*) Just outside the centre of town and housed within various rooms at the **Convent of San Giuliano**, this museum contains some important archaeological finds including the reconstruction of tombs dating to around the 7th century BC.

Museo Sperimentale d'Arte Contemporanea/Museum of Experimental Contemporary Art (*Via Paganica 17;* ☎ *0862 410505;* ☼ *daily 10.00–13.00 & 16.30–20.30; admission free*) As the name suggests, this is a museum exhibiting experimental contemporary art – from the region and beyond.

CIVIC ARCHITECTURE

All the buildings listed have sustained damage as a result of the 2009 earthquake. At the time of writing, access to the buildings was off-limits. Please see page 103 for a list of roads currently accessible to the public.

The hidden charms of L'Aquila are to be found in the double-lancet windows, the unadorned entrance portals and arched courtyards of its ancient noble residences. **Palazzo Buciarelli** (*Via Sassa 40*) is a fantastic example of one such building, attractive in its humility, with its stone medieval arches. Built between the 14th and the 16th centuries, it is now a mixture of residences and businesses, so do keep this in mind if the front entrance is open and you get to take a peek. It is truly amazing to comprehend that there are those of us who go about our daily lives in such a place during the 21st century.

The impressive 18th-century **Palazzo Ardinghelli** (*Piazza S Maria Paganica 15*), with its charming though well-worn entrance and regal windows, and the Baroque-style **Palazzo Centi** (*Piazza S Giusta 3*), with its wonderful balcony, are both examples of the grand 18th-century noble residences in L'Aquila. Even though the current **Palazzo Margherita** dates to the period of rebuilding after the 1703 earthquake, its appeal is still strong and its **Civic Tower** (*Piazza del Palazzo*) does have an interesting history. Built in around 1310, it featured only the third clock in the whole of Italy, after those in Ferrara and Florence. During Spanish rule, a cage was hung from the tower, and condemned men were left to rot there as punishment.

Tucked away with a largely unimpressive façade along Via Corso Umberto is **Palazzo Burri-Gatti** (*Via Corso Umberto 111*), built between the 16th and 18th centuries, with its captivating courtyard. If you find the entrance open, you may be lucky to take a peek into other courtyards at the 15th–16th-century **Palazzo Dragonetti** (*Via San Giusta 10*), the 15th-century **Palazzo Carli-Benedetti** (*Via Accursio 17*) and **Palazzo Franchi** (*Via Sassa 56*) from the 16th century. Other buildings of note include the 15th-century **Palazzo Nardis** (*Via San Marciano 14–16*), the **Casa Iacopo Notar Nanni** (*Via Bominaco 20–24*) built in the 15th century and featuring the city's oldest remaining courtyard, and the 18th-century **Palazzo Persichetti** (*Piazza Santa Maria di Roio 1*).

FOUNTAINS
Fontana delle 99 Cannelle

Level of damage sustained in 2009 earthquake: Very minor

The Fountain of 99 Spouts is almost completely intact following the 2009 earthquake. It is situated near **Porta Rivera**, and is arguably one of *the* highlights on any visit to L'Aquila.

The significance of this fountain is both architectural and cultural, and represents L'Aquila's 99 founding villages working as one to create a great new city. You can easily conjure images of medieval citizens hanging about the square a score of generations ago. The trapezoidal-shaped fountain has three walls, built in stages and characterised by the two-toned red-and-white chequered stone pattern, and 99 spouts, each built into its own mask and all now showing the effects of centuries of wear and tear. Commissioned and built in 1272 by Tancredi da Pentima, the fountain originally consisted of only 63 spouts on the central wall until the remaining two walls were built in the 16th and 18th centuries. The spouts on the fountain totalled 93 until 1871, when the remaining six were built. It suffered extensive damage as a result of the 1703 earthquake and various interventions were needed to return it to its former glory. The fountain received further attention in the 20th century, when, in the 1970s, a stamp was dedicated to the monument.

Fontana Luminosa In Piazza Battaglione Alpini L'Aquila, not far from the castle, this rather uninteresting fountain of two women carrying large jars is a significant example of the building boom in the second quarter of the 20th

5

century. It was sculpted by Nicola d'Antino of Caramanico and now acts as something of a meeting place.

CITY GATES
Porta Bazzano

Level of damage sustained in 2009 earthquake: Medium
Approximate time to restoration: 3 years

In the 1700s, this entrance point to the city replaced an older gate featuring double towers. The door leads to a triangular piazza and the view upon entering is of the red and pastel-coloured buildings that line the two streets leading off the square. One of these streets is the pretty **Costa Masciarelli** which winds its way towards the city's main square.

Porta Rivera

Level of damage sustained in 2009 earthquake: Medium
Approximate time to restoration: 3 years

This is one of the most evocative points of entry into the old city. The gate leads into the picturesque square of the 14th-century **Church of San Vito** and the nearby **Fontana delle 99 Cannelle**.

OTHER SIGHTS
Villa Comunale Facing the Grand Hotel e del Parco and the **Piazza della Repubblica** with the Council House (see *Government and politics*, page 15), Villa Comunale is a communal space in which the town's elderly gather *en masse* to discuss the latest gossip. The city's war monument is found here.

Cemetery Strange though it might seem to list a cemetery as a sight of interest, but L'Aquila's main cemetery, not far from the old town centre, contains the grave of Karl Heinrich Ulrichs (see box, page 116).

6

L'Aquila Province:
Gran Sasso National Park and Surrounds

Most of the area of the Gran Sasso National Park falls within the boundary of the province of Teramo (see page 231). However, the section of the park that falls within the province of L'Aquila contains some stunning areas, such as around Lago di Campotosto, and a handful of beautiful villages. Unfortunately, due to its proximity to the epicentre of the earthquake of 2009, the area has suffered some damage and residential buildings in all towns have been affected. Landmarks that were damaged have been pointed out below.

SUGGESTED ITINERARY

From L'Aquila, head north to the ruins of Amiternum. Double back and make your way on to the towns of Santo Stefano di Sessanio, Calascio (and the castle at Rocca Calascio), Castel del Monte and through Campo Imperatore. From here, head north to the Lago di Campotosto and while away some time in its peaceful surroundings.

AMITERNUM

The Roman ruins of Amiternum suffered a fair amount of damage during the recent earthquake. Restoration is estimated to take another three years and cost around €3.5 million.

Only a ten-minute drive from the city of L'Aquila are the ruins of the Roman town of Amiternum. The city was founded by the Sabines, though it became part of the Roman Empire in 290BC following the conquest of the area. By the 1st century BC, the town was a flourishing Roman colony.

The town is very close to the city of L'Aquila. Take the SS80 northwest out of the city and keep an eye out for the signs to the site. On the right-hand side of the road, you will eventually come across the ruins of the **theatre**, which you can see clearly from outside the gates. There is usually someone here to let you in during the day, but don't count on this: the hours they keep are very erratic. The theatre is set out over two levels and seated over 2,000 people; its size points to the wealth and importance of the city. It was built during the Augustan period in the second half of the 1st century BC. Nearby, and clearly visible from the gate, is a shed filled with sections of Roman pillars and columns, as well as a few statues and vases from the site.

To reach the **amphitheatre** (admission free), the more spectacular of the two surviving sites in Amiternum, you must drive further up the road and follow the

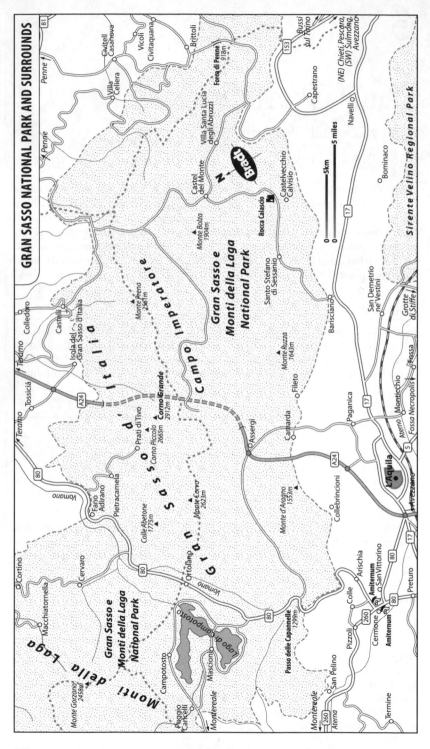

GRAN SASSO NATIONAL PARK AND SURROUNDS

120

signs left onto the SS80dir. After a few minutes, you will come to the amphitheatre. It is always open during the day for people to wander around, but beware of the dogs that roam the area. The amphitheatre dates from the 1st century AD and is extremely well preserved, retaining its red-brick arches and pillars. It could seat more than 6,000 people and was also built on two levels, though nothing remains of the upper storey.

SAN VITTORINO

Following the signs from either L'Aquila, or close to the ruins of Amiternum will lead you to the town of San Vittorino, known for the **Church of San Vittorino**. This beautiful place of worship (about to close for works at the time of writing) was built on the site of an earlier church, and there are unconfirmed reports that this sat on the site of an older temple. The church was consecrated in the 12th century and restored in 1528.

The interior houses some vividly coloured frescoes, particularly the *Christ Blessing*, which is supposedly the work of a local group of artists known as the Maestro di San Silvestro. There are also remains of an ambo and a 5th-century aedicule (small shrine). However, the catacombs below the church are even more interesting because of their complex and intricate nature. The works down here are being specially overseen by the Vatican, as the catacombs house the remains and tomb of St Vittorino the Martyr, who is believed to have founded the church.

LAGO DI CAMPOTOSTO

The 14km² manmade Campotosto Lake is at over 1,300m above sea level. Work began here in the 1930s, partly to alleviate the economic crisis that hit L'Aquila hard, but also to generate hydro-electric power for nearby areas.

Of the towns along the lake, the main ones are **Campotosto** itself, **Mascioni** and **Poggio Cancelli**. These are pleasant, with a bright and airy feel and, especially Mascioni, are well located, but are of little intrinsic interest.

GETTING THERE It is a very attractive drive on the SS80 from L'Aquila, past the ruins of Amiternum, and into the Gran Sasso National Park. The road rises steeply surrounded by dense forest and the summits and crags of the Gran Sasso mountains. Turn off onto the SS557 to reach the lake.

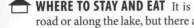 **WHERE TO STAY AND EAT** It is not unusual to see campervans parked up on the road or along the lake, but there are no official camping grounds in the area, though it is certainly a spectacular location.

🏠 **Albergo Ristorante Valle** (9 rooms) Via Roma 57; 📞 0862 900119; ⏰ May–Oct. This is an ideal place to base yourself to explore the lake & its surrounding area. It is located on the lake & has fantastic views. The rooms are basic but very clean & comfortable & the employees are friendly. The restaurant has some excellent local dishes. Try the lamb or the pasta with *ragù* sauce. **$$**

CYCLING AND WALKING The lake has a 50km-long trail around its perimeter. It is a popular place for locals to gather but also attracts joggers, hikers and cyclists. If you feel the entire length is too much for you to manage, you can cut across the Ponte delle Stecche, a bridge which crosses a narrow section of the water.

Perhaps the most popular walk is from the lake to the Monte di Mezzo. It is a 7km walk to the mountain peak and takes around 3½ hours. Begin the walk in the village of Campotosto, heading east on the SS80. Follow the Fucino river northbound (sticking to its right). There is a well-signed track. Note that this walk will probably be snowed under from late October through to April. Allow around seven hours for the full return trip.

NEAR LAGO DI CAMPOTOSTO

MONTEREALE You will only really pass through this town if you are making your way back to L'Aquila on the SS80 around the western side of Gran Sasso. The town's belltower, situated at its highest point, appears to be surrounded by forests and cliffs.

If you do find yourself here and have a taste for the macabre, visit the **Church of Beato Andrea**. It is dedicated to an Augustinian monk who died in 1480 and whose remains are on display here. The church is open for visitors. Interestingly, this town was one of the many originally destroyed in a series of three powerful earthquakes known as the Apennine earthquakes of 1703.

SANTO STEFANO DI SESSANIO

Please note that the watchtower in Santo Stefano, previously seen for miles around, was completely destroyed during the earthquake. However, the tower is to be rebuilt. Work will take at least another two to three years and cost almost €1 million.

About a half-hour drive east of L'Aquila and within the boundaries of the national park is one of the prettiest villages in Abruzzo. Established in the 11th century, this semi-abandoned settlement is quiet and largely undiscovered by tourists, living out an inconspicuous existence at more than 1,200m above sea level at the foot of the tallest mountain range in central Italy. The first sight of the village as you approach is of its elegant **watchtower** (but see note above), standing above the terracotta rooftops, stone houses and narrow lanes with their crumbling archways, all remarkably preserved.

EVENTS Visit at any time of year to wander quietly through the streets. However, during the first week of September the town livens up for its **Sagra delle Lenticchie** (Festival of Lentils). The village has long been known for the production of lentils (they really are excellent) and the festival has been going for many years.

 WHERE TO STAY

⌂ **La Locanda Sul Lago** (7 rooms) Via del Lago; ✆ 0862 899009; e info@lalocandasullago. it; www.lalocandasullago.it. This is 1 of my favourite accommodation options, in 1 of the prettiest villages in Abruzzo. The guesthouse is a no-fuss, family-run establishment. Rooms are themed (the 'Ancient', the 'Pine Room', the 'Tower Room', etc) & the decorations match. The hotel even runs cooking classes. At the time of

writing, a lentil-themed cooking class was booked out. **$$**

⌂ **Sextantio** (8 rooms) Contact through Via Vittoria Colonna, Pescara 65127; ✆ 08562 899112; e reservation@sextantio.it; www.sextantio.it. Known as a 'diffused' hotel, Sextantio offers accommodation of an unusual kind. The company has restored a number of rooms in several medieval buildings across the town, each of which has an antiquated charm. Painstaking attention is paid to detail & each of the spotless rooms preserves its original features

but with the added benefit of modern comforts. Only double rooms. **$$**

✕ WHERE TO EAT

✕ Agriturismo Il Borgo Piazza del Borgo; ✆086 289447; ⏲ Mon–Sat 12.15–22.00. This family-run establishment appears more like a cosy living room than a traditional restaurant. Don't be put off by the lack of written menu: you will simply be given a general idea of what is on offer, such as 'pasta' or 'meat' or 'lentils'. But whatever the options are you will be treated to some wonderful Abruzzese food. Meals are served with an abundance of bread & olive oil & finished off with a complimentary espresso. Inexpensive & highly recommended. **$$**

✕ La Locanda Sul Lago Via del Lago; ✆08562 899112; e info@lalocandasullago.it; www. lalocandasullago.it. This is a guesthouse restaurant that is deserving of its own entry. A charming and intimate dining experience awaits the very few who actually know of its existence. Try belly-bursting dishes such as pork in apple sauce & braised wild boar. A real highlight in the area, so do make sure you eat here at least once. **$$**

CASTEL DEL MONTE

Winner: Most Beautiful Villages in Italy; population 460

Strangely, most winners in the 'Most Beautiful Villages in Italy' programme are not bursting with famous landmarks or churches, and Castel del Monte, first settled around the 11th century, is no exception. Its charm lies in its picturesque streets and its location, at a height of 1,345m. However, the town does contain the interesting **Church of Madonna del Suffraggio**. This early 15th-century building houses a carved, wooden altar as well as a statue of the Madonna clad in local costume.

The oldest part of the town is around the **Church of San Marco**, which was previously a **lookout tower**. The town is known for dozens of varieties of pasta, and a spicy soup made of pasta with beans, potatoes and vegetables.

GETTING THERE The town, located to the northeast of Santo Stefano, is reached along the SS17.

 WHERE TO STAY AND EAT There is only one hotel in and around Castel del Monte.

⌂ Hotel Parco Gran Sasso (34 rooms, 6 apts) Via Campo Imperatore; ✆0862 938484; e htlparcogransasso@tiscali.it; www. hotelparcogransasso.it. The hotel is a short drive northwest of the town centre & is set in a modern building that resembles one of Pescara's numerous residential apartment buildings. However, the rooms are spacious & comfortable, & there's an excellent restaurant serving a wide range of local dishes, especially numerous pasta specialities. **$$$**

✕ La Locanda delle Streghe Via della Pineta; ✆0862 938911; ⏲ Mon–Sun 12.30–15.00 & 19.30–22.00. The aptly named 'Witches' Inn' is certainly bewitching: it looks like something out of the Addams family & approaching the stone building in the dim streetlight of the evening is eerie. However, that is certainly 1 of its drawcards, along with local *castellana* dishes of the area. The restaurant also runs themed witches evenings. Check website for details (but do be patient: it isn't updated very often). The hotel also has a handful of inn-style rooms that are basic but comfortable. **$$**

FORTRESS OF ROCCA CALASCIO

This great castle-fortress (admission free) is truly imposing and is perhaps one of the most magical sights in Abruzzo. Set at 1,500m above sea level, it's the

6

highest fortress in Italy and one of the highest in all of Europe. The exact date of construction is not known, but the castle (particularly the central tower) was reinforced in the mid 15th century. The stone fortress, a military stronghold, is notable for its symmetry and the quality of its construction, given the difficulties of building a castle in such an exposed and elevated location. The military reason for building a fort in this position was to give a sweeping view of Abruzzo, and it still has just about the best views to be had in the region, especially at dusk.

GETTING THERE

By car Follow the SS17bis east out of Santo Stefano di Sessanio. If coming from the SS17 proper, take the turn-off to Calascio and drive past Castelvecchio Calvisio (see below). From here, you will have to work to get to the fortress, even by car. The road that brings you to the car park is, in places, extremely narrow with very sharp drops. That it is a gravel two-way road with many pot-holes makes it especially hair-raising. However, no pain no gain, and here the pain (or rather fear) is definitely worth it. From the car park the road carries on through the deserted town of Rocca Calascio. It is at least a ten-minute walk and it is quite exposed and windswept, so it is advisable to bring a jumper, even on a warm day. Do not attempt to walk to the fortress wearing sandals or flip-flops.

At the **Church of Santa Maria della Pietà**, built on an octagonal plan at the end of the 16th century, the path swings round and takes you to the back of the fortress and into its main section. However, for an even more rewarding experience, leave the track and head up the hill to approach the fortress from the front.

On foot From Santo Stefano di Sessanio, it is about a two-hour walk to the fortress through some spectacular scenery, making this a popular way to get there, especially on summer weekends. Similarly, it is about two hours down the mountain to the SS17.

WHERE TO STAY AND EAT

🏠 Rifugio della Rocca (diffused hotel dorm room, apt, various rooms) Rocca Calascio; m 338 805 9430; www.roccacalascio.it. This is a very convenient 'refuge' situated in the abandoned town at the foot of the fortress. It features a comfortable 16-bed dorm room, an apartment & double & triple rooms scattered throughout the town (the number & configurations vary).

However, possibly the best thing about the refuge, apart from the stunning views from its bedrooms, is the excellent restaurant which specialises in traditional dishes. Start with the antipasti platters which consist of various meats & vegetables. Then try the lentil soup, & fusilli pasta with ricotta & saffron. **$$**

CASTELVECCHIO CALVISIO

Not far from Santo Stefano is the fascinating village of Castelvecchio Calvisio. It is a small place, the oldest part being the fortified section at its highest point. It is extremely well preserved and has maintained its original layout. Walking around through the numerous arches, you will notice many charming stairways, some leading to residents' front doors and many to – well, to absolutely nothing: entrances may no longer exist to earlier buildings but the stairways are very much intact. Quirky photo opportunities are to be had here.

GETTING THERE From the SS17, take the turn-off to San Pio and wind your way up the road to Castelvecchio Calvisio. To reach the oldest section of the village it is best to take the Via Borghi Archi Romani, which is found by coming through the gate after you have followed the signs to the *centro storico*. Park in the village car park, walk through the gate and simply wander around.

CAMPO IMPERATORE

Campo Imperatore, sometimes called the 'little Tibet' of Italy, is a large plateau at over 1,500m above sea level. It is about 30km long and just under 10km wide, and is overlooked by the tallest peak of the Gran Sasso National Park, the Corno Grande. The area is most popular for its winter skiing, though it's lovely to walk or drive here during the warmer months.

In 1943, Mussolini was imprisoned at what is now the Hotel Campo Imperatore (see box below). Please note that it is a complicated affair to drive around the area from around late October to March due to heavy snowfalls. Many of the roads are cleared, but it is advisable to take great care and drive with wheel-chains.

 WHERE TO STAY AND EAT

🏠 **Hotel Campo Imperatore** (50 rooms) Località Campo Imperatore, Assergi; ☎ 0862 760868; e info@hotelcampoimperatore.it; www. hotelcampoimperatore.it. Hotel Campo Imperatore is famous for having once been the prison of Benito Mussolini (between 28 Aug & 12 Sep 1943; see box below). Nowadays, it is a rather more luxurious resort. The public areas & rooms are modern as well as spacious, & the hotel has a heated pool for the colder months. If you feel like splurging, you can request the 'Mussolini Suite', the room where the dictator was hidden. The hotel has 2 separate restaurants, **La Taverna** & **Duca d'Aosta**. The latter is a restaurant in the 'sit down, order & have a nice long meal' sense, whereas the former is geared towards a quick bite between bouts of skiing. HB & FB. **$$$$**

WALKING There are a few, though not many, designated walking trails in the Campo Imperatore itself. However, it is easy to walk around the plateau – that is, until you find yourself at the foot of mountain peaks and can go no further! The walk from the nearby town of Assergi (see page 126) is quite pleasant. Head northeast from the town through Fonte Cerreto and beyond.

SKIING Campo Imperatore is one of the oldest ski resorts in the country. Though it is still well worth trying out the runs here, its popularity has waned in the face of competition from places such as Ovindoli (see page 134) and Pescocostanzo/ Roccaraso (see page 197).

THE GRAN SASSO RAID

In August 1943, Benito Mussolini was imprisoned under martial law at the Hotel Campo Imperatore, deep in the plains of Campo Imperatore, but the dictator made a remarkable escape. On 12 September, German commandos attempted a rather complex rescue mission. They came down onto Campo Imperatore aided by gliders and so surprised Mussolini's guards that they needed no gunfire to overpower them. Skorzeny, the man personally given command of the operation by Hitler, informed Mussolini that he had been sent by Hitler to free him. Mussolini supposedly replied that he knew his ally would not 'forsake' him. Mussolini and the German commandos were later flown to Vienna.

6

Ski passes Ski pass prices vary according to the day they are issued for. The following are weekend prices. A daily ski pass to the area costs €25 for an adult, while children go free. A two-day pass costs €38 whilst a three-day one will set you back €56. A weekly pass, for which you must supply photos, is available for €110.

For details of the Skipass to this and other areas, see page 48.

Ski runs

'EASY' (BLUE) RUNS		'MEDIUM-HARD' RUNS		RED RUNS	
Genziana	650m	Osservatorio	1,188m	Aquila Bianca	1,250m
Montanaro	710m	Del Parco	1,320m	Fontari	1,020m
		Narciso	710m	Agonistica	440m
		Mirtillo	1,130m		

ASSERGI

This pleasant small town is a quiet place in a very rural setting, framed by the mountain ranges of the Gran Sasso. Interestingly, though about 20km northeast of L'Aquila, it was part of the collection of towns which founded L'Aquila (see page 100). Those wishing to visit the southern side of the Calderone Glacier can access it from Fonte Cerreto in the Campo Imperatore, from where there's a chairlift up the mountain. For details, see page 235.

 WHERE TO STAY

Hotel Cristallo (19 rooms) Località Fonte Cerreto; ☎ 0862 606678; e info@ hotelcristallolaquila.it; www.hotelcristallolaquila. it. Though this hotel lacks a proper address, it is easy to find. It is a 10-min drive northeast of Assergi, first along the SR17bis & then east along the road to the district of Fonte Cerreto. Follow the road for another 500m & you will find the hotel on your left. The rooms are not that big, though you will have a wonderful sleep: the hotel is set in serene rural surroundings with little around it but trees & the mountain ranges of the Gran Sasso National Park. The restaurant is quite large & serves good local specialities such as gnocchi with asparagus & the excellent polenta. Both the quality of the hotel itself & the restaurant make it good value for money. HB & FB. **$$$**

7

L'Aquila Province:
Sirente Velino Regional Park and Surrounds

The Sirente Velino Regional Park, situated in the west of Abruzzo, occupies an area of around 50,000ha. Founded in 1989, the regional park has many attractions from wintersports and wildlife spotting to its attractive villages and towns, of which the park contains 21: Acciano, Aielli, Castel di Ieri, Castelvecchio Subequo, Celano, Cerchio, Collarmele, Fagnano Alto, Fontecchio, Gagliano Aterno, Goriano Sicoli, Magliano de' Marsi, Massa d'Albe, Molina Aterno, Ocre, Ovindoli, Pescina, Rocca di Cambio, Rocca di Mezzo, Secinaro and Tione degli Abruzzi. This chapter also includes towns and attractions close to the regional park. For the natural history of the regional park itself, see page 11.

> Quite a few of the towns in this region suffered damage during the L'Aquila earthquake of 2009 (see page 99). Most of the damage was sustained by residential buildings, which are slated for reconstruction. Details are given where extensive damage has occurred to specific landmarks. Restoration and rebuilding are still ongoing at the time of writing.

SUGGESTED ITINERARY

Start in the town of Celano. Head north along the SR5, cutting through the Sirente Velino Regional Park. Stop at Ovindoli (for skiing, if it's the right season!) and then north to the Grotte di Stiffe. Back on the SR5, head northwest to Ocre and its castle.

SKIING

The wintersports facilities in the Sirente Velino rival those of Abruzzo's three national parks. The skiing here centres on the peaks of Monte Magnola and Campo Felice. A full range of services such as ski schools, accommodation and equipment hire as well as detailed daily and seasonal information is found not only in the resorts but also in the surrounding towns such as Ovindoli, Rocca di Mezzo and Rocca di Cambio (see pages 134, 138 and 141).

CELANO

Celano's pastel-coloured houses and its castle – which, perched at 800m above sea level, can be seen from miles away – command extensive views of the Fucino Basin. And with one of the most dramatic landscapes in Abruzzo, the Celano Gorge, this is a highlight of any visit to Abruzzo.

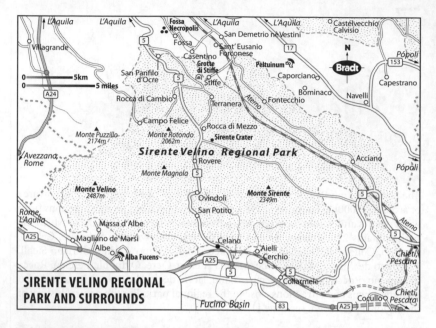

SIRENTE VELINO REGIONAL PARK AND SURROUNDS

A town has existed here for over 2,000 years. Before the Romans settled the area in the 1st century BC, the town is thought to have been the Aequi settlement of Cliternum. The site was especially important due to its strategic location, and over the years has been ransacked, fought over and invaded. During the post-Roman era, it came under the control of the Lombards and the Saracens. While most of the area was ruled later by the Duchy of Spoleto, the Marsica region, and thus Celano, was held by Charlemagne and his descendants in the 8th century AD.

Celano flourished, along with the Marsica area, during the Middle Ages. After a period under Norman rule, the area came under the control of the Swabians. The feudal governors of Celano became so powerful that they almost ruled Abruzzo and Molise entirely. So great was its regional power that, after some reshuffling of hierarchies by Frederick II, the city rebelled and was consequently raided and destroyed. Fortification works began in the late 14th century which saw the building of its imposing castle (commissioned by the then head of the town's prominent Piccolomini family), later damaged, along with a good deal of the town, in the earthquake of 1915. Restored during the 20th century, the city now houses an excellent museum with a collection of sacred art from the local area.

The town passed through the hands of the Angevins and Aragonese before being annexed into the Kingdom of Naples and then, from 1860, the Kingdom of Italy.

GETTING THERE

By car Celano is easily reached on the A25 motorway. It can also be approached along the regional SR5bis from L'Aquila. This is very picturesque as it cuts straight through the Regional Park of Sirente Velino.

By bus Arrive in Avezzano either by bus or train (around €9 by bus from Pescara) and catch the ARPA service to Celano. The service takes around 25 minutes and the town's bus stop is in the main square, from where the bus continues on to Rocca di Mezzo.

TOURIST INFORMATION (*Town Hall, Piazza IV Novembre 29;* ✆ *0863 79541; www. comune.celano.aq.it;* ⊕ *Mon–Fri 10.00–13.00, Tue–Thu 10.00–13.00 & 15.30–17.30*) The tourist information office is situated on the town's main square and can provide information on Celano as well as activities and sightseeing in the surrounding area.

🏠 WHERE TO STAY

🏠 **Hotel Le Gole** (40 rooms) Via Sardellino Aielli 2, Aiella; ✆ 0863 711009; e info@ hotellegole.it; www.hotellegole.it. Although not in the actual town of Celano but a short 2 mins away by car, this is by far the best hotel in the area. Approaching its driveway, you are presented with a typically rural property that is just as appealing inside as it is on the outside. The hotel's friendly owners are proud of their establishment & the reason for this is evident: rooms are comfortable & clean & the service is excellent. The hotel has a very good restaurant (see below). Check the website for special offers. **$$$**

🏠 **Hotel Lory** (34 rooms) Via O Ranelletti 279; ✆ 0863 793656; f 0863 793 055; e info@ loryhotel.it; www.loryhotel.it About a 7-min walk from the centre of the old town, this is a relatively new hotel with some good facilities, including a gym, & the excellent Ristorante Ferraro (see below). The décor won't knock your socks off (it's a little dated & tired) but the rooms are clean & comfortable. The hotel now runs tours of the local area & there are often great specials on their website. **$$$**

✕ WHERE TO EAT AND DRINK

✕ **Ristorante La Rosa dei Venti** Località Mazzare 27–9; ✆ 0863 611187; e info@larosa-deiventi.it; www.larosa-deiventi.it. Although a 5-min drive east of town, this restaurant mixes the best of Abruzzese cuisine with that of the rest of Italy. It is a fairly large place, decorated in the pastels & browns that are so common to country restaurants in Abruzzo. The antipasti (such as the typical Italian antipasto with hams & salamis) are particularly tasty, as are the traditional meat dishes. **$$$**

✕ **Ristorante Ferraro** Via O Ranelletti 279; ✆ 0863 793656; f 0863 793055; e info@loryhotel. it; www.loryhotel.it; ⊕ every day of the year. The Ferraro was a separate restaurant but recently transferred its operations to the Hotel Lory. The chef serves up a gourmet feast of local delicacies. Try the *vellutata di pollo con crostini*, the seafood ravioli & the refreshing apple sorbet for dessert.

Note that the restaurant offers both a seafood & a meat menu. **$$**

✕ **Ristorante Guerrinuccio** Via Sardellino Aielli, Aiella; ✆ 0863 711009; e info@hotellegole. it; www.hotellegole.it. Hotel Le Gole's restaurant is a delight. In keeping with the hotel's rustic look & feel, the chef cooks up typical Abruzzese dishes (as well as some international ones). Try the *chitarra al tartufo fresco*, which is not only extremely well priced but a real treat. Other pasta dishes, such as the ravioli, are also excellent. Finish off your meal with a lemon sorbet. **$$**

✕ **Pizzeria al Taglio** Piazza IV Novembre 40; ✆ 0863 792683; ⊕ Mon–Sat. No Italian town would be complete without a place to grab a slice of pizza. This is a cheap, convenient eatery right in the centre of the old town; it's basically fast food though the pizzas are good. **$**

OTHER PRACTICALITIES Celano runs to a couple of **banks**, both on the main piazza: Banca del Fucino (*Piazza IV Novembre 9/10*) and Carispaq (*Piazza IV Novembre 32*). There's a **post office** at Piazza Regina Margherita 1 (✆ *0863 795532*), and a **chemist**, Farmacia Baliva Dina, at Piazza Aia 96 (✆ *0863 792150*).

WHAT TO SEE AND DO

The Piccolomini Castle This imposing castle now houses the **National Museum of the Marsica** (*Largo Cavalieri di Vittorio Veneto;* ✆ *0863 792922; admission adult €3, 18–25 €1;* ⊕ *09.00–20.00 Tue–Sun, last entry 19.30*). The castle, built in various phases over 70 years from 1392, has suffered damage as a result of various earthquakes, the worst of which was that of 2009 (although no timetable for restoration has been announced). It was abandoned for the better part of 25 years before 20 years of restoration work began in 1940. The **main courtyard**, with its lovely arches, displays pictures of the restoration efforts following the damage of 1915. To the right of the entrance is the **portal of San Salvatore a Paterno**, dating from the 13th century. It is the only remaining part of this once important church. Another doorway nearby belongs to the church of San Nicola in Marano.

The museum's displays, spread over a number of rooms, feature important artworks and historical artefacts from the area. Of note are items from the **Church of San Pietro ad Alba Fucens** (see page 133); **wooden sculptures** from the Church of Santa Maria in Cellis in nearby Carsoli, dating as far back as 1132; **sculpted panels of wood and pearl** from the Church of San Nicola in Massa d'Albe, for a long time, kept in a national museum in Rome; 14th-century **chalices** and **crosses** which were also kept in a national museum in Rome before being handed back to Abruzzo; 17th-century **wooden sculptures of saints**; and a room of **ecclesiastical vestments** from the 15th to the 19th century.

After you are finished with the museum, have a walk around the castle and take in the views of the town and surrounding area. The cloisters are particularly charming.

Church of San Giovanni Battista
This is Celano's main cathedral. Its well-preserved entrance is decorated with a fresco and dates from the 15th century. The church has a pretty interior, especially the spectacular frescoes that embellish its arches.

Church of San Francesco
This church, founded by St Thomas of Celano (see box above) is open during the day for visitors. It is plain and simple with various plaques in Latin dating from the 1700s.

Church of San Michele Arcangelo
The highlight of this Romanesque church, founded in 1392, is its visually impressive 17th-century organ, above the main entrance, and the marble altar. The interior of the church is quite ornate, and decorated with paintings and wooden statues of the Madonna.

Church of Santa Maria
This is a small church with an interesting old, intricate altar and a lovely belltower.

Church of Santa Maria in Valleverde
This church, found outside of the historical centre, is important for its significant 16th-century paintings by local

artists. The paintings, most depicting religious scenes of some description, have been very well preserved. The nearby convent is slightly older, the church itself having been finished in 1509, according to the inscription above its entrance. The town's ruling family, the powerful Piccolomini, commissioned many of this church's works of art.

Piazza IV Novembre This is the old town's main square. On Fridays, from about 07.00 to 13.00, it comes alive with a market selling all manner of things. The square is also a bit of an evening hangout for the town's younger residents.

Celano Gorge Some have called the Celano Gorge the Grand Canyon of central Italy. This may be an exaggeration, but it is certainly one of the most spectacular gorges in the region – and one of the most visited in Italy. Created by the Foce River, its rocky walls reach as high as 190m, and in some places narrow to only 3m.

Further information on the gorge can be obtained from Celano's tourist office (see page 129) or from the offices of the Sirente Velino Regional Park (*Viale XXIV Maggio, Rocca di Mezzo;* \ *0862 9166;* e *info@sirentevelino.it; www.sirentevelino.it*).

Getting there The main entrance to the gorge is found to the east of Celano, a five–ten-minute drive. Follow the road down from the centre of the town to La Foce district of Celano, where there's a sign pointing the way to a car park that marks the beginning of the walking path to the gorge. Note that the gorge cannot be accessed during bad weather, including heavy rain, or in spring, when the winter snow is thawing.

Walking in the gorge The most scenic areas are found about a 1½-hour walk from the gorge's Celano entrance (or you can drive; see above). However, for a small taste of what the area has to offer, wander for ten minutes or so from the roadside towards the gorge.

A longer and more strenuous walk, taking around 2½ hours – or at least five hours there and back – starts around 5km south of Ovindoli. To get there, follow the signs for the Val d'Arano. When you reach the end of the asphalt road, take a right at the roundabout. After some 3km you will encounter a little fountain. Signs can be seen around here. The walk, which is not waymarked, offers some lovely views of the surrounding mountains, and is graded 'medium' in terms of difficulty.

ALBA FUCENS

If you take an interest in ancient Rome and its wonderfully convoluted history, Alba Fucens is a must-visit. Set on the hills and framed by the mountains of the Regional Park of Sirente Velino, this wonderfully well-preserved ancient city is an easy place to imagine Roman citizens going about their business. Nowadays, the Roman, medieval and modern town, all in close proximity to one another, show the various layers of settlement in Abruzzo.

HISTORY In its heyday, Alba Fucens was of great strategic importance, a fact that didn't escape the Romans who took it over in 304BC, overthrowing the Italic tribe of the Aequi (though some historians claim that due to its proximity to their land, it was actually a town belonging to the Marsi tribe). Situated along the famed Via Tiburtina Valeria, Rome's vital road link through Abruzzo to the

Adriatic Sea, the town prospered during the imperial period. During the Punic Wars, Alba strengthened its allegiance to Rome but later decided not to reinforce the Roman armies with troops from its city, a move that was punished by Rome's central government by way of physical force. Such a mistake was made during the Social Wars when the city paid its due as required by Roman convention. The town continued to thrive during the Middle Ages although it was sacked by the Saracens. It wasn't until the mid 20th century that excavations began at the site under the supervision of Belgian archaeologist Joseph Mertens, despite continuous knowledge of its presence and studies carried out by scholars such as Carlo Promis, an Italian architect and historian. The dig produced valuable ancient artefacts, as well as bringing to light a road structure and layout that would seem to date from around the time the town was founded in the late 4th century BC. However, the town's layout seems to suggest a new phase of building in the 2nd century BC, with the construction of many of its public buildings such as the theatre, the basilica and the sanctuary dedicated to Hercules.

GETTING THERE Take the A25 from Pescara (A24 from Rome *then* the A25) and exit at Avezzano. Follow the signs to Alba Fucense (as it is shown on the signposts).

TOURIST INFORMATION (*Piazza della Scuola 1;* \ *0863 449642;* e *albafucens@ virgilio.it; www.albafucens.info*) This tourist information point is found in the central square of the modern town. They provide guided tours of the area, accommodation advice and information on walks, and can arrange horseriding in the nearby hills, mountain biking and a whole host of other activities. The website has very questionable English.

WHERE TO STAY The best choice close to Alba Fucens is in the medieval Albavecchio (see opposite). For a wider selection, you might consider basing yourself in the city of Avezzano (see page 153).

Della Rocca Borgo Medievale Alba Fucens, Massa d'Albe; \ 0863 449662; e dellaroccaaurelia@ hotmail.com; www. ilborgomedioevale.com. This peaceful residence & hotel has various rooms & apartments at reasonable prices. The restaurant serves treats such as chickpea gnocchi, marinated trout & grilled lamb. For dessert, try the local spin on the *Sachertorte*, a chocolate dessert with a layer of apricot jam. It's delicious. **$$**

WHAT TO SEE AND DO Taking in the site of the ancient city at a relaxed pace requires at least a few hours. Start at the modern town beside the ruins, otherwise known as **Albe**, where you will find a road that leads to the **forum** area. From the forum, wander down through the remains of the **basilica**, built in the reign of Lucius Cornelius Sulla Felix, usually known as Sulla. Taking the Via dei Pilastri to the south, you encounter the remains of shops, including a tavern. Head back into the main area south of the basilica for the **macellum** and the **public baths**, which were open to men and women alike. Continuing south through the baths you will encounter the large **sanctuary** dedicated to Hercules. To its right, remains of various **domus** (wealthy residential buildings) can be seen. To the left is the **theatre**, which is not as interesting or evocative as the town's **ampitheatre**. This, a five-minute walk away, dates back to the first half of the 1st century BC and is in very good condition, with its oval layout completely preserved. Its magnificent entrance still retains its Latin inscriptions. Traces of the city's **walls**, covering a large area, can still be seen.

Titus Livius, or Livy as he is more commonly known in English, was a great Roman historian and writer. One of his most famous works, *Ab Urbe Condita* ('From the Founding of the City'), recounts the history of Rome and its empire. In this work, he mentions the founding and strategic importance of Alba Fucens. The historian writes, *'Soram atque Albam coloniae deductae. Albam in Aequos sex milia colonorum ...'* ('Colonies were established at Sora and Alba. Six thousand settlers were enrolled for Alba in the Aequian country ...'), confirming the presence of 6,000 settlers who descended upon the Aequi city.

Titi Livi, *Ab Urbe Condita*, Book 10:1

Looking down at the ground as you walk is a very good idea: some **mosaic floors** are still visible, though guides to the area usually cover them with pebbles in order to protect them from the elements.

The **Church of San Pietro ad Alba Fucens** (✆ *0863 23561;* m *340 625597*), a short walk uphill from the ampitheatre, is not usually open to the public, although you can contact either of the above telephone numbers and someone will open it for you. It is definitely worth the effort as it is one of the most striking ancient churches in Abruzzo. The museum in Celano hosts many of the artefacts found inside the church, which was an ancient temple dedicated to Apollo and converted into a church during the 3rd century AD. While most of its present appearance dates from the 12th century, you can still see traces of the ancient temple. The church became a Christian place of worship in the 4th century. It suffered extensive damage in the earthquake of 1915, but the nucleus of the ancient temple escaped, along with the church's arches. Major restoration work began in the 1950s.

Walking into the church through its gates, you will encounter scattered Roman ruins. Once inside, on the left, the church has a display of various pictures that show the damage caused by the earthquake, and it is hard to imagine the effort that was involved in carefully restoring the church bit by bit. However, one of the first things you will notice is the 13th-century ambo. It is a stunning work, made by Giovanni di Guidom, a sculptor from Rome. To the right, you will find various remains including a few large, ancient chalices.

Albavecchio   Albavecchio is the medieval core of the area. Situated about 300m from the archaeological site of Alba Fucens, it is best reached by car (follow the signs to 'Borgo Medievale' from outside Alba Fucens and the modern town). While the town is still inhabited by a small number of people, the ancient nucleus was completely destroyed by the earthquake of 1915. In fact, this part of the town was never reconstructed or restored, and strolling through the dilapidated and abandoned buildings is an eerie feeling. Keep walking through the town and past the 13th-century **castle** ruins and you will reach a **lookout** area with some lovely whitewashed ruins, which, along with the view onto the Roman ruins and the valleys, are a highlight of any visit. Look out for the **pillars** here: some are decorated with the remains of frescoes.

AROUND ALBA FUCENS
Magliano de' Marsi   Now not much more than a village, Magliano de' Marsi was once a thriving town complete with its own walls and towers, which have since

disappeared (the last section standing as late as the 20th century). The town was almost totally destroyed in the earthquake of 1915 and subsequently rebuilt.

The most interesting church is found at the highest part of town. The **Church of San Lucia** is in Romanesque style (though reconstructed after the earthquake), with three doors and a lavish entrance above which frescoes can be seen. If you happen to wander by at or around the 18.00 daily service, take a look inside. Although there is nothing particularly striking about the interior of the church, there is a baptistry dating to the 15th century.

Another church of note in the town, largely due to its 16th-century entrance, is the **Church of San Domenico**.

Getting there The town is a few kilometres northwest of Alba Fucens and just off the A25 motorway.

OVINDOLI

For more than a hundred years, this large town of medieval origins has been 'the' place in Abruzzo (if not in non-Alpine Italy) for skiing and snowboarding. During the colder months, Italians descend on this place with as much fervour as they would a *gelato* on a warm, July evening. In fact, the town's popularity as a summer holiday destination almost rivals its winter tourism due to the beauty of the surrounding landscape. It is situated at the southern end of the **Rocche plateau**, which connects the Sirente and Velino massifs, and sits at more than 1,250m above sea level.

HISTORY The 'whys' and 'hows' of Ovindoli's development are something of a mystery, though it is thought that perhaps a Marsi settlement arose around one of the tribe's ancient fortifications. It is known that the town was almost completely destroyed during the Social Wars and that it later prospered due to its proximity to the transhumance trails across Abruzzo. It therefore developed a pastoral way of life, in the strict sense of the word, and was a thriving township in the Middle Ages.

The town began to attract domestic tourists in the 1890s on the completion of the railway connecting Rome to Sulmona. However, it wasn't until after World War I that it became known for its ski slopes. Further development occurred in the 1960s with the opening of ski lifts and extensions to the trails. As with the rest of Abruzzo, the opening of the A25 *autostrada* connecting Rome to Pescara meant tourists from Rome and the central west coast of Italy could reach Ovindoli easily.

GETTING THERE
By car From Pescara, take the A25 *autostrada* and exit at Celano. From L'Aquila follow the SS5bis from L'Aquila or Celano.

By train The train from Pescara to Celano stops at Sulmona. From Celano, catch the ARPA bus to Rocca di Mezzo, which stops at Ovindoli in Piazza San Rocco.

By bus Aside from the above ARPA service that connects Rome to Rocca di Mezzo, stopping in Avezzano, Celano and Ovindoli, there is also a frequent line connecting Avezzano to L'Aquila via Ovindoli and various other towns in the regional park. From Pescara, take the ARPA service to Avezzano (around €9) and change. The journey will take approximately 1 hour 45minutes.

TOURIST INFORMATION

⚹ IAT Ovindoli Via O Moretti 9; ☎0863 706079; e iat.ovindoli@abruzzoturismo.it; ⊕ Mon–Sat 09.00–13.00 & 15.00–18.00. Found just off the main square outside the old town, this tourist information is amongst the most efficient & helpful in the region, & 1 of only 7 in the province. You can pick up information on just about everything, from ski trails to walking tours of the area.

🏠 **WHERE TO STAY** Due to Ovindoli's reputation as a ski resort, most of its accommodation is outside the old town nucleus.

🏠 **Rifugio Anfiteatro** (10 rooms) Località Monte Magnola; ☎0863 705059; www. ovindolichaletanfiteatro.it. With its location on Monte Magnola, the Rifugio Anfiteatro is is an ideal place to relax after a hard day of wintersports. The rooms, with modern furnishings, AC & heating, are available only Dec–Apr, but the restaurant also opens its doors Jul–Sep (ideal for the hiker). Forget any ideas of budget accommodation; this *rifugio* is by no means cheap. **$$$$$**

🏠 **Bed & Breakfast La Forestiera** (4 rooms) Via N Sebastiani 129; ☎0863 705476; m 333 440 7357; e nicola.liberatore@gmail.com; www. laforestiera.org. This B&B in the old town (Piazza della Fonte) has small but pleasant rooms. The owners are extremely friendly & try hard to help with requests from their guests. **$$$**

🏠 **Hotel Cavallino Bianco** (25 rooms) Via Moretti, 1; ☎0863 705544; e info@ cavallinobianco.net; www.cavallinobianco. net. The Cavallino Bianco ('White Pony') hotel is conveniently located in the centre of Ovindoli. Though it is a fairly small hotel, it is an excellent option for those wishing to take advantage of the skiing in the area while being close to the amenities of town. Rooms are simply decorated & have access to hotel WiFi. The hotel restaurant serves excellent cuts of grilled beef, among many other local specialities. **$$$**

🏠 **Hotel Cenzo** (10 rooms) Via Arano; ☎0863 705167; e info@hotelcenzo.it; www.hotelcenzo. it. Despite its shabby website & the fact that it appears more like a local apartment building, the pastel colours of this hotel combined with a warm & friendly atmosphere make it a good choice. A complimentary shuttle bus to Monte Magnola is available for guests in both winter & summer. **$$$**

🏠 **Hotel Moretti** (40 rooms) Via del Ceraso 48; ☎0863 705174; e info@hotelmorettiovindoli.it; www.hotelmorettiovindoli.it. Equidistant between the town's old centre & the Monte Magnola ski slopes, this large, family-run hotel has basic but comfortable rooms, a games room & bar. The interior gives the feel of a mountain chalet with its wooden beams & cosy ambience. The restaurant serves good food; try any of the fresh pasta dishes or a hearty meat dish with an Italian beer on a cold winter evening. **$$$**

🏠 **Magnola Palace Hotel** (78 rooms) Via del Ceraso 89; ☎0863 705144; e info@ magnolapalacehotel.com; www. magnolapalacehotel.com. Just outside town sits this large hotel with comfortable rooms & a convenient health & beauty centre. The hotel also provides excursions to the surrounding area, both in winter & summer, every day of the week. The knowledgeable guide, Arnaldo Botto, is contactable on m 333 190 8297. Tours from €6, children under 12 free. **$$$**

🏠 **Park Hotel Ovindoli** (60 rooms) Via del Ceraso 178; ☎0863 705221; e info@ parkhotelovindoli.com; www.parkhotelovindoli. com. With its unusual mixture of contemporary & '80s décor, Park Hotel Ovindoli is at least trying to present a more modern face to visitors. The rooms, containing all mod cons, are decent & there is a very good restaurant offering an excellent buffet breakfast & an extensive local wine list with dinner. **$$$**

🏠 **Hotel Mille Pini** (12 rooms) Via Dante Alighieri 6; ☎0863 706106; e info@hotelmillepini. it; www.hotelmillepini.it. The hotel's décor may not be for everyone (the exterior resembles a post-war Egyptian apartment block that has been involved in an unfortunate collision with a pastel-coloured chalet in the Swiss Alps), but this is a good budget option with well decked-out rooms, most with excellent views. **$$**

🏠 **Hotel Piccola Selva** (16 rooms) Via Dante Alighieri 8; ☎0863 705992; e info@ hotelpiccolaselva.it; www.hotelpiccolaselva. it. Situated next door to Hotel Mille Pini, Piccola

Selva's interior features brown hues wherever you look, but the rooms are comfortable & it has excellent amenities (such as a garden, tennis court & TV room) at very good prices. **$$**

🏠 **Pensione Ristorante La Torre** (10 rooms) Piazza Aia, Santa Iona di Ovindoli; 📞0863 792472; e lorenzo.liberatore@locandatorre.it; www. locandatorre.it. This *pensione* hotel is located around 3km south of the town of Ovindoli. It is a simple, no-frills affair run by a friendly family. The restaurant is well known for its excellent homemade pasta but also serves local meat dishes. **$$**

✕ WHERE TO EAT AND DRINK

✕ **La Lanterna di Brontolo** Via Sebastiani 35; m 3479297987. The Lanterna di Brontolo's main dining room is a typical rustic Abruzzese trattoria. The chef cooks up a storm of succulent cuts of lamb & beef & an antipasto comprising local hams & cheeses. Popular during peak tourist season. **$$**

✕ **Ristorante Creperie La Stozza** Via Ceraso 7; 📞0863 705633. Some very nice dishes are on offer here, courtesy of Osvaldo. These include excellent crêpes, including a chocolate crêpe that is particularly sinful. Savoury crêpes are also available. Extremely popular in the winter months. **$$**

✕ **Pizzeria Ristorante La Torre** Piazza Aia 1; 📞0863 792472; www.locandalatorre.it. Not far from the centre of Ovindoli, this pizzeria & restaurant is also a local pension with a handful of rooms. The restaurant is fairly simple, but it does serve some scrumptious pizzas. **$$**

✕ **Ristorante Hotel Il Ghiro** Via Mazzini 32; 📞0863 706092; e hotel-ilghiro@libero.it. The restaurant of Hotel Il Ghiro serves up dishes from the local area as well as those from elsewhere in Italy. Their simple spaghetti dishes are tasty, especially the one with a *ragù* sauce. **$$**

🍷 **Bellamy's Pub** Via del Ceraso 20; m 338 839 1994; ⏰ evenings until late. One of the main pubs around which Ovindoli's 'nightlife' is centred. As you might guess from the name, it's an Irish-themed establishment with a whole lot of Guinness.

🍷 **Birreria Brontolo** Via Sotto le Coste 4; 📞0863 705533; ⏰ evenings until late. Another good pub with a range of beers, though the décor is nondescript.

OTHER PRACTICALITIES There is a **bank**, Banca Toscana, at Piazza San Rocco 29, and a **chemist**, Farmacia di Iorio at Via Sebastiani 21 (📞 *0863 705417*). The **post office** is located on Via Sebastiani 19 (📞 *0863 705418*).

Useful telephone numbers Given the outdoor activities available in and around Ovindoli, it is worthwhile keeping these emergency telephone numbers to hand:

Emergency 📞113
Local police 📞0863 705037
Alpine police 📞0863 705058

Pharmacy 📞0863 705417
Town Hall 📞0863 706100

WHAT TO SEE AND DO Even if you are in town for the outdoor activities, a walk around the old town streets is worthwhile. Start from the main square at the bottom end of town, just outside the ruins of the **medieval walls**, which are clearly visible. The **parish church**, just through the gates and into the old town, holds a 1500s wooden statue of Mary. Head upwards to the surviving remains of the **12th-century keep** for spectacular views of the Rocche plain and the mountains.

SKIING: MONTE MAGNOLA Ovindoli is an excellent place from which to explore the surrounding Rocche plateau of the Sirente Velino Regional Park. However, the real highlight here is the skiing, and domestic tourists come from all over Italy to ski at **Monte Magnola**. The mountain peaks, at 2,223m above sea level, have skiing up to about 2,000m. The mountain is accessed from Piazzale Magnola, just outside Ovindoli's old town.

Ski schools It's not surprising that such a popular winter destination has so many ski schools. The following offer courses of varying difficulty and length to suit the needs of most visitors.

Scuola Sci Tre Nevi Piazzale Magnola 1; ☎0863 705347; e info@scuolascitreneviovindoli.it; www. scuolascitreneviovindoli.it. Courses range from €35 an hour for single students to €115 an hour for group classes, depending on the time of year. The school also offers ski equipment hire for personal use.

Scuola Sci 2000 Ovindoli Piazzale Magnola 3; ☎0863 705242; e info@scuolasci2000ovindoli. it; www.scuolasci2000ovindoli.it. With 40 years'

experience in ski training, courses are offered for either group or single students. Ski equipment also for hire.

Scuola Sci Magnola Piazzale Magnola 5; ☎0863 706081; e igis2007@gmail.com; www. scuolascimagnola.it. Just about the only school whose website is also in English. Courses are offered on an hourly basis for individual students, as well as over a longer period of time.

Ski passes Daily prices for adults range from around €25 for one day to €210 for ten days, depending on the season. There are also seasonal passes that allow you to ski the slopes from November until the end of the ski season. These are priced at around €490. There are discounts for children and senior citizens. For details of the ski pass, see page 48.

Ski runs The pistes are colour-coded according to difficulty, with blue being the easiest and black the hardest runs. There are various chairlifts to whisk you back

---

WALKING AND HIKING ITINERARIES

There are many hiking paths in and around Ovindoli. The most popular (and thus perhaps least consuming of time and effort) are outlined below. Note that the **estimated times** given here are based on going from A to B, and not for the round trip.

THE PEAK OF OVINDOLI
Height: 1,570m
Degree of difficulty: Easy
Time: Around 50 mins
From Ovindoli's Piazza San Rocco, take Via Faelli to the end. Here a path winds its way through the woods. Follow the red-and-white signs. Once at the top, there are marvellous views over the peak area.

THE TELESPAZIO REFUGE
Height: 1,980m
Degree of difficulty: Medium–hard
Time: around 2 hrs
This path begins at Piazzale Magnola. It largely follows the ski tracks until its arrival at the cable car, at around 1,800m. From here, head left through the ski trails to reach the Montefreddo chairlift, around 200m from the refuge. The views are simply stunning.

CELANO GORGE
See page 131.

and forth between the tracks and various mountain *rifugios*, or basic pension hotels, at which to catch your breath or even stay overnight.

'EASY' (BLUE) RUNS		'MEDIUM' (RED) RUNS		'DIFFICULT' (BLACK) RUNS	
Topolino	350m	Fontefredda	900m	Pistone	800m
Minnie	350m	Daino	1,000m	Vetrina	1,600m
Dolce Vita	600m	Anfiteatro	2,000m	Pistone	3,000m
Belvedere	1,100m	Genziane	1,000m	Direttissima	1,100m
Capanna Brinn	1,100m	Tomba	910m	Settebello	900m
Snow Park	950m	Canalone	1,800m		
		Panoramica	1,300m		

ROCCA DI MEZZO

Rocca di Mezzo, the home of the Sirento Velino National Park's headquarters, is a pleasant town in which to take a leisurely stroll and an excellent starting point for excursions around the park, with activities including horseriding, mountain biking and skiing. In fact, its wintersports rival those of Ovindoli just down the SS5, with its own popular ski resort nearby, **Campo Felice** (see page 142).

The town's name, roughly translated as 'rock in the middle', is said to refer to a castle that was built here, approximately halfway between Rovere and Rocca di Cambio. As with so many other towns in the area, it was held by various powerful feudal families who contributed to the founding of L'Aquila in 1253. The population of the town grew steadily until the 1920s, but has been in gradual decline over the last 80 years.

Young people here often complain that Rocca di Mezzo is the only town where summer is winter and winter is, well, winter. Indeed the climate is usually a few degrees cooler than the rest of the region in summer, but this can make it a perfect getaway from some of the stifling heat the region can experience during the months of July and August.

GETTING THERE Rocca di Mezzo is on the SS5bis, between Celano and L'Aquila, in the heart of the Sirente Velino National Park. The road can be accessed from both the A24 and A25 *autostradas*. Buses operated by ARPA to Ovindoli (see page 134) also stop here.

TOURIST INFORMATION The information centre is located in the **town hall** (*Piazza del Oratorio;* \ *0862 916125;* e *info@roccadimezzo.org; www.roccadimezzo. org;* ⊕ *Sat 10.00–13.00 & 16.00–19.00, Sun & public holidays 10.00–13.00*) The town's official website has a webcam on the main square.

The **headquarters** of the Sirente Velino Regional Park (*Via XXIV Maggio;* \ *0862 9166;* e *info@sirentevelino.it; www.parcosirentevelino.it*) are able to provide information on excursions and activities within the park.

🏠 WHERE TO STAY AND EAT

🏠 **Grand Hotel delle Rocche** (67 rooms) Via per Secinaro 1; \0863 917144; e info@grandhoteldellerocche.it; www. grandhoteldellerocche.it. The only 4-star hotel in the area occupies a picturesque setting & has benefited from a recent refurbishment. It is simply decorated & features modern comfortable rooms & good amenities, such as a pool & billiard room. Staff are friendly & serve up a feast in the hotel restaurant. **$$$**

🏠 **Hotel Caldora** (70 rooms) Via Colli della Mula 3; \0862 917174; e info@hotelcaldora.it;

www.hotelcaldora.it. After following the signs out of town to reach this hotel, you'll notice that its exterior is not everyone's cup of tea (it looks a bit like a communist apartment block). However, its no-nonsense rooms are comfortable, & the hotel offers wireless internet, a restaurant & what is hopefully described as a 'discothèque'. **$$$**

✗ Pizzeria Trattoria Antichi Sapori Via della Madonna 2; ☎ 0862 917360. This trattoria lives up to its name 'ancient flavours' with the use of a wood-fired oven to produce some excellent crusty pizzas with that characteristic 'smoky' taste. **$$**

✗ Ristorante Campacavallo Via della Madonna 2; ☎ 0862 917944. It's easy to miss the Campacavallo: it is nothing more than a tiny house on the side of the road. Don't let the shabby interior fool you. The food is simply amazing & the antipasti, which comprises local cured hams, meats & cheeses, is one of the highlights. Pasta dishes are simple but mouth-watering. A no-frills restaurant with matching prices but world-class food. **$$**

✗ Ristorante Pizzeria Santa Maria Via Passeg Santa Maria 2; ☎ 0862 917198. Another restaurant with a variety of options (including some excellent meat dishes) & good pizzas served in a friendly & pleasant environment. **$$**

OTHER PRACTICALITIES There's no bank in Rocca di Mezzo, but the town does have a **post office** (*Via Giorgeri 6;* ☎ *0862 916071*) and a **chemist**, Farmacia Betti (*Via D'Eramo 3;* ☎ *0862 917486*)

FESTIVALS AND EVENTS

May La Sagra del Narciso. Residents of the town and its neighbouring towns and villages come together to celebrate the narcissus in a display of colourful flowers (there are more than 390 species), with costumes, themed carts, food and drink and a whole lot more.

August Vicina(r)ti. Two evenings that see displays by artists, and musical groups performing in the centre of town.

August/September La Gara del Solco. This ploughing competition, or 'Race of the Furrow' is amongst the most venerable traditions of the area, dating back to the 15th century. The race takes place during the night, when teams, guided by very little light, must plough a furrow. The team that manages to create the straightest one wins.

WHAT TO SEE Although the town is of medieval origin, nowadays it is largely modern. Its highest point is home to the **Church of Santa Maria ad Nives**, restored in the 18th century and retaining its 16th-century doorway. Within the church complex is the entrance to the **Cardinal Agnifili Museum of Religious Art**, which is open upon request (☎ *0862 917429*) and houses a collection of art including a carved wardrobe from the 15th century and a 14th-century cross. Walking around the church you will notice the ruins of **ancient walls**, and around the belltower, a peaceful clearing with seating on which to relax and take in the views across the town and surrounding area.

Perhaps the prettiest sight in town is the 15th-century **Le Tre Archi** ('Three Arches'), where three roads cross. The light colours of the stonework, combined with the characteristic shuttered window above one of the arches, creates a lovely sight and is an excellent place to take photos.

In the lower and more modern part of town, a **paved pedestrian road** crosses the northern part of the main square, Piazza dell'Oratorio, and runs the length of the town. This is a popular gathering place for the town's residents and is great for a summer night's stroll with a *gelato* in hand.

SKIING **Campo Felice** (see page 142) is not far from Rocca di Mezzo and for this reason many tourists base themselves here. Information on the various skiing options is available from the regional park headquarters and the tourist information centre (see page 138).

For lovers of cross-country skiing, it is worth contacting the **Polisportiva Serra Candida** (*Via di Pezza 1;* m *338 6011298, or contact the tourist information centre*) who deal specifically with this.

AROUND ROCCA DI MEZZO

Sirente Crater This shallow seasonal lake is located on a small plateau west of Rocca di Mezzo. It's a rock-filled crater, the largest of a number of small craters scattered around the vicinity. It was not until the 1990s that these craters, known as the Sirente Group, were attributed to asteroid impacts with Earth during the Holocene period. Recent research and radiocarbon dating has placed its formation to the period of Imperial Roman control of the area, AD340–450. If confirmed this would mean that the crater is the only one known to have been formed during this historical period. Its relatively young age means that it is well preserved.

Getting there The crater can be reached by taking the first westbound road south of Rocca di Mezzo (the road is unnamed but sealed). After roughly 4km, the lake is on your right surrounded by extensive grassland.

Rovere Situated on the SS5 about halfway between Ovindoli and Rocca di Mezzo (by which it is actually governed) is the charming hamlet of Rovere. 'Steep' is the word here: it is quite a hike to the top of this pleasant town. Though not packed full of attractions, it is certainly worth a stop and a bit of a strenuous wander, particularly to take in the **castle ruins,** which offer commanding views of the mountains. In theory what is left of this castle is cordoned off, although there is very little left of the gate or fence either.

The town's central **Museum of Archaeology** (*Via dell'Arco della Chiesa 1;* \ *0862 914041; admission free;* ⊕ *on request*) contains a number of archaeological finds from the area.

The most interesting church is the **Church of San Pietro**, with its lovely Roman-style entrance and characteristic belltower.

Terranera The village of Terranera itself, situated on the SS5 about ten minutes from Rocca di Mezzo, is not much to speak of. However, just before you enter (when coming from Rocca di Mezzo) there is a very small, five-arched structure that appears to be a little temple built somewhat at random on the plateau. This is a great place for a photo, with the mountains and the village of Rocca di Cambio in the background.

ROCCA DI CAMBIO

At the foot of Mount Cagno is Rocca di Cambio, the highest town in the Apennine mountain range at 1,434m above sea level. Surrounded by the rocky landscape of the Rocche plateau and Campo Felice, it's no wonder that after World War II Rocca di Cambio developed a niche market for outdoor activities and active tourism. Given the peace and tranquillity of its location, this was a favourite place of the German emperor Otto II (AD955–983) who was said to have stayed here frequently during the summer.

The first mention of a town here, called Frustena, is from around AD100. This helped with the building of and oversaw the Via Valeria, an important Roman road. It later acquired the name Rocca di Cagno, which was Italianised to Rocca di Cambio in the Middle Ages. *Cambio* is the Italian word for 'change', as the town was a thoroughfare and horse-changing post for those on their way from L'Aquila down through the Marsica.

Nowadays, people come to Rocca di Cambio for two main reasons: for the skiing at **Campo Felice**, and for hiking and trekking. If you're already in the area visiting Ovindoli and Rocca di Mezzo, this little town is a short drive or bus ride away through the regional park towards L'Aquila.

TOURIST INFORMATION
Pro Loco Tourist Office Via Duca degli Abruzzi 2; ☎0862 918100; www.roccadicambio. it; ⊕ Wed–Mon 09.30–12.30 & 16.30–19.30, Tue 16.30–19.30

WHERE TO STAY AND EAT
Aurora Resort (11 rooms) Via del Rocchio 2; ☎0862 918377; e info@auroraresort.it; www.auroraresort.it. A recent addition to the accommodation options in Rocca di Cambio, this resort hotel is around 2km from the centre of town & only about 1km from the skiing at Campo Felice. Rooms are well decked out with good facilities, & there is even a health & spa centre on site, as well as a lovely restaurant. **$$$**

Cristall Hotel (20 rooms) Via Saas Fee 2; ☎0862 918119; www.cristallhotel.it. A hotel that will tend to all your needs, with good facilities & comfortable rooms. It has a good restaurant & offers extras such as a shuttle bus to the skiing areas, equipment hire & a TV room. The restaurant serves up excellent meals, particularly the hearty meat dishes in winter. **$$$**

Hotel Narciso Blu (10 rooms) Via della Crocetta; ☎0862 919007; www.hotelnarcisoblu. it. The Narciso Blu is very similar in both aesthetics & quality to most ski resorts in the area. It is a no-frills but very clean & comfortable B&B allowing quick access to the snow slopes in winter & the countryside in summer. It is fairly small & does not have a restaurant. **$$**

Apartment rental If you're planning to spend over a week in the area, you might consider renting an apartment. **Agenzia Immobiliare Elle** (*Piazzale Maggiore Lolli 4; ☎ 0862 918312; www.agenziaelle.it*) can help with rentals starting from around €280 per week or €2,000 for the entire winter season. It might sound a lot, but at a minimum of around €50 per night, hotel expenses can add up considerably over extended periods.

WHAT TO SEE AND DO The **Church of Santa Lucia**, just under 2km out of town, is arguably the prettiest of Rocca di Cambio's places of worship. It was founded sometime between the late 13th and early 14th centuries and restored in the late 1960s as well as in 1999. Aside from its ideal setting next to a small lake on the plateau, the church is worth a visit for its interior. This is of some importance due

7

to its large frescoes, including one of St Lucia herself and a notable portrayal of the *Last Supper*. The church sustained damage during the earthquake of 2009. It is estimated that this will take around two years to repair and the costs involved will be upwards of €2 million.

The small **Church of San Pietro** is at the highest point of town and has an interesting 10th-century wooden statue of St Peter. The exterior of the church was featured in the 1953 film, *The Return of Don Camillo*.

SKIING: CAMPO FELICE The town is well placed for easy access to Campo Felice (e *info@campofelice.it; www.campofelice.it*). Skiers have a choice of 20 downhill slopes spanning an area of around 40km². Cross-country skiers are also catered for.

Ski passes Prices will vary according to whether you wish to ski on a weekday or weekend and for how long. A full weekday pass will cost around €27 for an adult. Three-day passes are also available for around €82. A seven-day pass will set you back €172. The ski resort also has various season memberships that span multiple skiing areas in Abruzzo. Tickets are available on-site from the Campo Felice ticket office (*Piano di Campo Felice, Rocca di Cambio;* ✆ *0862 917143;* ⊕ *Dec–Apr, daily 08.30–16.00*).

For details of the ski pass, which also allows access to Campo Imperatore and Monte Magnola, see page 136.

Ski runs

'EASY' (BLUE) RUNS		'MEDIUM' (RED) RUNS		'DIFFICULT' (BLACK) RUNS	
Dello Scorpione (11%)	1,700m	Della Vergine (19%)	1,600m	Delle Aquile (26%)	2,500m
Dei Gemelli (10%)	1,300m	Delle Rondini (21%)	2,000m	Del Falco (27%)	2,400m
Del Sagittario (22%)	1,660m	Del Capricorno (21%)	1,300m	Gigi Panei (28%)	1,000m
Teaching slopes	450–600m	Della Volpe (22%)	1,600m	Del Lupo (27%)	1,300m
(x3) (9–12%)		Del Toro (17%)	2,200m	Dell'Orso (27%)	1,300m
		Dell'Ariete (20%)	1,000m	Del Leone (17%)	2,200m
		Degli Innamorati (16%)	2,500m		
		Teaching slope (13%)	420m		

Getting there

By car Follow the signs in and around Rocca di Mezzo. The area can also be accessed from the A24 *autostrada*, exit Tornimparte.

By bus During the winter season, Ski Bus (✆ *0677 591340; www.cegservizi.com, only in Italian*) offers a return service connecting Rome (from the S Giovanni metro station) with Campo Felice. A return ticket will set you back around €23. There's no equivalent service in the summer.

By chairlift The Brecciara chairlift is found around 4km south and west of Rocca di Cambio.

OCRE

The area known as Ocre, less than a half-hour south of L'Aquila on the SS5, is actually made up of five towns: San Panfilo d'Ocre (the principal town), San Felice d'Ocre, San Martino d'Ocre, Cavalletto and Valle.

The streets of **San Panfilo d'Ocre** are lined with colourful flowers and plants during the warmer months, and the town itself is dominated by the impressive **Castle of Ocre** in the Aterno Valley (see below). It's a very small, pretty town that is easily seen in a short time. Keep an eye out for the **Church of San Salvatore** as it has a lovely belltower.

Nearby, **San Felice d'Ocre** is a quaint village with a pleasant square which is home to the **Church of San Giacomo d'Apostolo**, dating from the early 11th-century.

WHAT TO SEE AND DO

Castello d'Ocre When I first visited this castle as a child, one question stuck in my mind: how on earth did they manage to build it? It is truly one of the most impressive fort ruins in the region, and certainly the highlight of any visit to the Ocre area.

The castle is actually a 12th-century fortified castle-village, laid out on a triangular plan with various defensive towers. Its structure meant that a number of people could survive quite happily in the knowledge that enemies below would have a very hard time breaking in, given its position high on a cliff (almost 1km above sea level), with a sheer drop down one side. Excavations here took place as recently as July 2007, at which time more residential housing was found within the walls of the castle. Aerial shots clearly show how well the fortress's layout has been preserved.

The inside of the castle is currently closed, although the real highlight here is walking around the outside and being impressed by its sheer dominance over the valley below. That, and the extraordinary views.

From the gate at the end of the road from which you enter the castle grounds, take the path to the left. This will take you past the daunting fortress walls and to a clearing with a stunning panorama over Abruzzo. It is possible to see the peaks of the Majella and Gran Sasso massifs from here, and there is an exceptional bird's-eye view of the town of Fossa (see page 144), right below the cliff. To the west, L'Aquila is clearly visible. On a clear day, you may even be able to make out the domes of individual churches such as San Bernardino. For an even better view of the castle as a whole, continue along the little ridge to your right.

If you take the path ahead of you from the gate (instead of the one to the left, as above) you will reach a rather broken-down staircase that leads right around the edge of the castle. It is quite overgrown and there are all manner of strange insects but the views of the castle and beyond are worth it.

Getting there The signs to the castle out of the town of San Panfilo d'Ocre will lead you to a gravel road that ends at a closed gate. You can walk into the castle grounds through the entrance to the left of the gate.

Convent of Sant'Angelo d'Ocre Along the same road that leads from San Panfilo d'Ocre to the castle you will find a turn-off for the peaceful Convent of Sant'Angelo d'Ocre, overlooking the Aterno Valley. A Franciscan abbey dating from the 15th-century (though originally built for Benedictine nuns), it became a church and convent complex in 1409, taking its present form in the 1480s, and later becoming a monastery.

There are still two monks living within the complex, so it is important to be mindful of this when visiting the site. The **main church's** interior is quite small with a compact side chapel and ornate altar.

FOSSA

Of the settlements in the area, Fossa is perhaps the best preserved of the medieval villages. It lies on the slopes of Mount Ocre and was known as Aveia in Roman times. Legend has it that in the 2nd century AD, St Massimo was hurled to his death from Mount Ocre onto Fossa below. It is also known for the missionary Cesidio da Fossa, who, on a mission in China during the Boxer Rebellion, was burnt alive in front of his church.

The village is best approached from San Panfilo d'Ocre via the road that has the turn-offs for the Castle of Ocre and the Convent of Sant'Angelo d'Ocre. The views of Fossa as you wind your way down the hills are stunning. You could easily spend two to three hours exploring the village, although you should stay away from the few scaffolded buildings that are still in the process of being rebuilt following the earthquake.

GETTING THERE Fossa is accessible by road, off the SS5 and SS261, following the signs from the SS17. By bus, Fossa is reached from L'Aquila on services run by the local bus company, AMA (*www.ama.laquila.it*). Route 16 travels from L'Aquila to Fossa and back, making various stops along the way. The trip takes around 20 minutes.

TOURIST INFORMATION The town's local council runs a **Pro Loco** (*Via Aveia, c/o Campo Sportivo;* \ *0862 755 1120;* e *info@prolocofossa.it; www.prolocofossa.it*) tourist office that can provide information on tours of the area.

 ## WHERE TO STAY AND EAT

⌂ Monastery Fortress of Santo Spirito (12 rooms) Via Santo Spirito SN; \ 0862 196 5538; e info@monasterosantospirito.it; www. monasterosantospirito.it. If you want to stay in the area, look no further than this monastery/fortress turned hotel. Back in the 13th century, it was the first & only monastery in the valley to be founded by the Cistercian Order. Nowadays, there are 12 rooms, each converted from parts of the old dormitory, with all mod cons. However, the highlight here is the enchanting setting & sheer peace the area offers. There is even a restaurant that claims the main ingredients of its food are 'memory' & 'identity'. Dishes include simple, hearty vegetable soups & homemade pasta. To get here, follow the road from Fossa's main car park (at the rear of town). **$$$**

WHAT TO SEE AND DO

Castle ruins The old castle stands tall over Fossa. All that is left of this once-grand fortress are the walls and the cylindrical tower – which houses a medieval dungeon – said to be the oldest part of the complex. It is currently closed to the public but can still be admired from the outside, especially from the road that leads down from the Castle of Ocre.

Parish Church of Assunta Though not as grand or ancient as Santa Maria ad Cryptas (see opposite) the town's principal church has a wooden ceiling and a 16th-century fresco of the *Wedding of St Catherine* that are well worth seeing. The ceiling dates from the 1600s and is decorated with religious scenes.

Santa Maria ad Cryptas (usually closed, though request key from house no 5, behind church) is a well-known church just outside Fossa. You will need a car to get here or be prepared for a walk of half an hour or so. The church's origins go back to the 8th century, but its current appearance dates from around the second half of the 13th century. This church's importance rivals that of Santa Maria di Ronzano and San Pellegrino in Bominaco. This is mainly due to its frescoes from the 13th century that adorn the inner walls and vault. They narrate various stories from both the Old and New Testaments of the Bible, and depict the lives of the saints. Among the most appealing are one of the Last Supper, and another in which St Martin is shown giving away his cloak. They are signed and dated by Gentile da Rocca, 1283, a painter from Rocca di Mezzo. The church also has a crypt which contains an ancient altar.

Fossa Necropolis (*closed to the public; bookings can be made on* m *348 474 7740*) Although they call this the Fossa Necropolis, it is a fair drive from the town, and is not even signposted from the village (but this is Abruzzo, after all). Coming from Fossa, take the first turn-off on the left straight after the railway track and crossing gates of Fossa station. Do not turn off the gravel road, but follow it beyond Colorificio d'Agostini and straight to the necropolis (which, again, is not signposted). Even though the gate is closed, it wouldn't be hard to break in – but it is best not to. Besides, this is one attraction that would make little sense without a guide to explain what you are looking at.

Thanks to an old farmer who discovered them in 1993, excavations have brought to light over 500 burial sites in an area of around half an acre, previously occupied by the Vestini tribe between 1000–800BC. There are countless funeral beds and chambers that are often lavishly decorated. The decorations and varying styles of burial show changes in funerary practices over a number of centuries. Some of the ivory decorations from here are amongst the most important archaeological finds relating to burial sites found in Abruzzo. The burial chambers housed multiple burials, often functioning as mausoleums for rich families. So far, 531 tombs have been discovered, their treasures now dispersed across the region's archaeological museums.

AROUND FOSSA
Casentino The charming town of Casentino, a two-minute drive from Fossa, is worth stopping at to visit the **Church of San Giovanni Evangelista**. It took its current form in the 18th century, and houses a spectacular terracotta statue of the *Madonna with Child*, near the altar. The church itself is beautifully located, with its stone belltower overshadowed by the hills behind.

Sant'Eusanio Forconese Another two minutes up the road, this town's **castle**, which also houses the **Church of Madonna del Castello**, sits peacefully atop a hill with views over the surrounding area. If you take the turn-off to the castle from the town below, leave your car before you reach the gravel road instead of driving; it is futile to try and get any further.

Back down in town is the **Church of Sant'Eusanio**, with an interesting doorway and square Romanesque façade. If you get a chance to enter, visit the church's crypt – it has a particularly old and eerie feel to it.

San Demetrio nè Vestini This little town is dominated by the 19th-century **Church of the Madonna dei Raccomandati**, which is currently undergoing restoration. Its belltower is very characteristic of the region.

There are two excellent examples of civic architecture in the town: the 15th-century **Palazzo Ducale** and the 18th-century **Palazzo Cappelli**. The Palazzo Cappelli is the more striking of the two and now houses a boarding school.

If you happen to pass by during the second week of August, stay around for the town's **Bread Festival**, held from 13 to 15 August. Numerous types of bread and other tasty bakery products are served up by the locals.

Around San Demetrio
Lago Sinizzo This lake and the park around make a perfect picnic area and a chance to catch your breath and relax. The lake itself is small but there is a children's play area on its shores, and it's popular during the warmer months. The water isn't fantastic but is fine for whiling away one of the typical scorching summer afternoons in Abruzzo.

To get there, follow the signs out of San Demetrio, which bring you out near the lake. Parking is around €3 per day (note that there is free parking just before the entrance to the lake and park but you will need some luck finding a space here on a hot day). You can hire a sunbed for about €3, or even a table, six chairs and a beach umbrella for just over €10.

LE GROTTE DI STIFFE

(\ *0862 86142;* e *info@grottestiffe.it; www.grottestiffe.it; admission adult €10, child €7.50;* ⊕ *daily 10.00–13.00 & 15.00–18.00 except Xmas day & New Year's Day; call ahead in case of bad weather*) As unfortunate as the name sounds in English (you will raise a few eyebrows when recounting stories to your friends back home), Le Grotte di Stiffe, just outside the town of Stiffe, are without a doubt the best caves open to the public in Abruzzo. During the 1980s plans were made to develop tourism in the area and allow the public to visit the caves, which were eventually opened in 1991. The Museum of Speleology (see opposite) opened later in 1996.

The caves comprise a network of passages leading 600m into the mountain. An underground spring flows through its interior (giving rise to the name, the 'river cave').

The entrance is situated at the base of a large overhanging rock face which rises 100m above it. A walkway of over 0.5km takes you from plunging waterfalls (the Waterfall Cave) to caverns such as the Concretion (or Flowstone) Room, where stalactites and stalagmites have formed over thousands of years. If you happen to be around during the Christmas period, the caves play host to a very atmospheric nativity scene.

You can only visit with a tour guide and the tour lasts 50 minutes. Be aware that the temperatures underground can plunge to around 10°C even if it is hot outside, so bring a jumper. It is also well worth wearing closed-toe shoes.

GETTING THERE
By car From Rome, leave the A24 *autostrada* at L'Aquila Est and follow the signs to Le Grotte di Stiffe. From Pescara, take the A25 and exit at Bussi sul Tirino, following the signs to L'Aquila and then to the grottoes. From L'Aquila it is a short drive, following the signs to San Demetrio nè Vestini and then to the grottoes.

By bus   Getting to le Grotte di Stiffe by bus is a bit of a chore. Paulibus runs a twice-daily service from L'Aquila to Stiffe (for approx €2), one bus departing at 07.30 and arriving in Stiffe at 08.00, and the second departing at 14.00 and arriving at 14.30. Herein lies the problem: if you're not interested in a walk around town there's a wait of around two hours before the first morning and afternoon admission into the caves.

WHERE TO STAY

Hotel Stiffe (20 rooms, 6 suites) Via del Mulino 3, Stiffe di San Demetrio; ℡ 0862 86218; e info@stiffehotel.it; www.hotelstiffe.it. A stone's throw from the caves' ticket office is this 3-star hotel, with perfectly comfortable & clean, though simple rooms, a kids' play area & mountain-bike hire nearby for exploring the local area. Special rates available on website for stays over 7 days. **$$$**

AROUND THE GROTTOES
Stiffe   The actual town of Stiffe is worth a quick visit, with its typical stone houses and alleys. The town has the tiny **Museo di Speologia/Museum of Speleology** (℡ 0862 86142; admission free; ⊕ daily 10.00–13.00 & 16.00–18.00) which features both human remains found in the caves, and the remains of a species of bear called *Ursus spelaeus*, or bear of the caves.

PELTUINUM

If Abruzzo's international tourism numbers rivalled the neighbouring regions of Tuscany and Umbria, Peltuinum, along with other ancient Roman cities in the region, would be a very different site altogether. But since this is untrodden Abruzzo, this priceless show of the might of Roman power and urbanisation is almost always devoid of tourists or visitors of any kind. There is no entrance fee and certainly no one 'guarding' the site, so anyone can just wander around what was once an important settlement along the Via Claudia Nova and ancient transhumance sheep track between L'Aquila and Foggia. There are some notable structures amongst what may seem like dilapidated walls and crumbling stone arches. Of these, look out for the **Temple of Apollo**, the Augustan **theatre**, and the **walls** and **gate**.

The setting of this ancient ruined city affords views over the nearby towns and, if you look carefully on a clear day, you may catch a glimpse of the castle of Rocca Calascio, one of the most impressive forts in the region (see page 123).

GETTING THERE   The site can only be reached by car. It is located around 20km from L'Aquila off the SS17, which can be accessed from both the A24 and A25 *autostrade*.

CAPORCIANO

Around ten minutes from Peltuinum and off the SS17, this fortified village, facing the Navelli plain, is dominated by its 11th-century tower (now the church's main belfry). There is an excellent view of the castle of nearby Bominaco. The village's walls were later absorbed by the spread of housing in the village though they are still visible in certain areas. The town has churches of varying interest, such as the 13th-century **Church of San Pietro** (follow the signs out of town), **Santa Maria of Cintorelli** and **San Benedetto Abate**.

> The walking-path signs from Caporciano claim that Bominaco is a ten-minute walk, but it is closer to half an hour, depending on your walking speed. However, the sign is correct in saying that Navelli is about a one-hour walk away.

WHERE TO STAY AND EAT

Agriturismo 4A (9 studio apts) Via San Pietro 6; ✆0862 931394. If this place simply appears to be someone's house, that's because it is. It is a small *agriturismo* with basic but very clean accommodation & friendly staff. The owners specialise in growing plants & herbs in their 20ha of land. Meals are simple but consist of excellent local produce. Good value for money. **$$**

BOMINACO

Two minutes further up the road from Caporciano is Bominaco, which is actually part of the same town. Previously known as Momenaco, this little settlement boasts a castle that occupies a prime position on Monte Buscito, around 1,170m above sea level, with views over the surrounding mountains and the Navelli plateau. The castle itself comprises a cylindrical tower that is similar to other fortified towers in the province.

However, the village's main attraction for art and history lovers is the Benedictine church and oratory complex of **Santa Maria Assunta e San Pellegrino** that can be visited upon request (*contact Caporciano Town Hall, Via Roma 24;* ✆ *0862 93731*). The **church**, whose humble exterior gives no indication of the value of the treasures found inside, is one of the main Romanesque churches of the region and dates back to around the early 1100s, although there was an older monastery from the 10th century. The church's main nave and aisles are complemented by rows of round arches, frescoes and a stunning ambo and throne (for the abbot) both dating from the 1180s. The altar, constructed in 1223, is also of particular note and houses a beautiful candelabrum.

San Pellegrino's **oratory's** current appearance dates back to its reconstruction in 1263. The three-arched entrance is delightful, as is the portico added in the 17th century using fragments of the building on which it was founded. Art lovers should look out for the oratory's 13th-century frescoes, one of the three most important groups of frescoes in the region after the churches of Santa Maria of Ronzano (see page 230) and Santa Maria ad Cryptas (see page 145). These depict, among other things, celebrations of key religious festivals such as Easter and Christmas. Along with the church, the oratory has thankfully escaped extensive damage by earthquakes and pillaging over the centuries and was declared a UNESCO World Heritage Site in 1996. If you plan to stay in the area, **Agriturismo 4A** (see *Where to stay and eat*, above) is your best option.

WHERE TO EAT

A Bominaco Via della Madonnella 2; ✆0862 93623. It's a typically Abruzzese experience that the most amazing meals are to be found by heading out of the cities & deep into the countryside. A Bominaco is a sheer delight. All its dishes are to die for, but the real reason for coming is the wood-fired pizza. Try the 'Bominaco' with its homemade tomato sauce, mozzarella, sausage & truffle. If pizza isn't what you're looking for, the antipasto followed by the *chitarra pasta al ragù* is a sure bet. Warning: you may leave feeling considerably 'heavier' than when you arrived. **$$**

EVENTS

8 May La Festa di San Michele Arcangelo. The town really comes into its own for the Feast of St Michael the Archangel. The festivities begin inside the church of

Santa Maria Assunta and proceed (literally) to the Sanctuary of St Michael in the nearby mountains. This particular sanctuary is of note due to the incisions found on rocks close by which are said to have been made by the saint as he died.

NAVELLI

Back on the SS17, between Caporciano and Capestrano, is this peaceful, picture-postcard-pretty town, situated on a hill that overlooks the plain of Navelli dotted with bales of hay and olive groves.

GETTING THERE

By car For the most striking approach by car, arrive from the Bussi side of the SS153. To reach the top of the town, don't take your car through the centre. Instead, follow the signs to the Palazzo Santucci. Alternatively, you could park and walk, though it is quite an effort due to the steep streets.

On foot There is a pleasant path between Navelli and the nearby town of Capestrano, taking about an hour.

 ## Where to stay

Abruzzo Segreto (4 rooms) Via San Girolamo 3; 0862 959447; www.abruzzo-segreto.it. Owners Francesca & Jimmy provide very personal & attentive service to make sure your stay at their small B&B & in the Navelli area is a pleasant one. Check website for details of packages. **$$**

EVENTS

May Festa della Madonna del Gondalone. A religious festival with a ritual procession and offering of the bread.

First weekend after Aug 15 Sagra dei Ceci e lo Zafferano. As you might expect from the Fair of the Chickpea and Saffron, stands through the town offer chickpeas and saffron from the local area.

A PRECIOUS COMMODITY: THE SAFFRON OF THE NAVELLI PLAINS

At first glance, there isn't much more to this town than pretty alleys, a fort and a few Renaissance churches. However, this humble town is renowned for the production of the highest-quality saffron (from the plant *Crocus sativus*) in the world, known as *Zafferano dell'Aquila* ('Saffron of L'Aquila'). The saffron from here has been lauded for its properties and delicate taste by many writers and historians, including Homer and Hippocrates. Nowadays, the saffron produced on the Navelli plains is exported the world over.

The cultivation of this flower is both expensive and time-consuming. It takes around 200,000 saffron flowers to make a single kilogramme of saffron. Presently, Navelli produces around 80kg of saffron per year. If this doesn't sound like much, it is probably because only the stamen of the flower can be used for making saffron powder, and this needs to be separated by hand.

A restaurant in L'Aquila used to serve a simply stunning *risotto allo zafferano di Navelli*: risotto with saffron from the Navelli plains – but it has now closed due to the earthquake. Perhaps another chef will take it on.

What to see The town itself is dominated by the fortified **Palazzo Santucci** (closed to the public), built in the 16th century over an older fort. There are two churches by the Palazzo: the 15th-century **Church of St Sebastian** and the 18th-century **Chapel of the Madonna**.

CAPESTRANO

This tranquil and delightful little town, once owned by the famed Medici family, is best approached from its turn-off on the SS153. There are some lovely chances to take photos if you take this route: the typically Mediterranean fields of Abruzzo with their round bundles of hay lie in front of the town's impressive fort and old houses scattered across the hillside.

The town itself is not built for driving, so leave your car in the car park near the castle and wander through its old lanes to discover its mix of medieval, Renaissance and Baroque architecture. The town is most noted for the discovery of the *Warrior of Capestrano* (see box, page 22) and for being the birthplace of St John of Capestrano, an important Franciscan saint. Although there is a place to eat, there's nowhere that leaps out at you.

GETTING THERE Take the A24 or A25 *autostrade* then follow the SS17 (L'Aquila–Pescara). Approach from the SS153 for a lovely view of the town, which is also reachable by bus a few times a day on ARPA's L'Aquila–Pescara route.

 WHERE TO STAY

🏠 **B&B Paparella** (3 rooms) Nucleo Collelungo 15; ☎0862 954209. It's easy to miss the Paparella, a small B&B accessed through a gate on the side of a narrow road. You will, however, be delighted with what it offers if you are after cheap accommodation: 3 basic & small but comfortable rooms with their own bathrooms & even bunk beds for the kids. There are lovely views of the surrounding countryside from its grounds & everything in the area is easily accessible. **$$**

EVENTS

15 July Sagra del Terzo Paese. The 'Fair of the Third Country' is a rather bizarre celebration of 'country and western' – and cowboys.

August Once a year the town's castle hosts a medieval-themed dinner, for which bookings are essential (*contact the town hall,* ☎ *0862 95227 or* m *349 395 5914*).

10 August La Cocomerata. Watch the annual display of meteoroids from the town's main square.

11–12 August Sagra della Trota. Fishermen celebrate the feast of the trout by selling fresh local trout from stalls around the town.

13 August The Pizza Show. A celebration of the local bread and pizza.

WHAT TO SEE AND DO Put the guidebook away and stroll through the town's narrow streets. Its position overlooking the plains of the Tirino River, a tributary of the Pescara, gives great views of the surrounding area. If you have your own transport, make sure you don't miss the nearby Church of San Pietro ad Oratorium (see opposite).

Piccolomini (or Medici) Castle The castle now houses the town hall (✆ *0862 95227; www.comunedicapestrano.it;* ⊕ *Mon–Fri 10.00–13.00, Sat 10.00–12.00*) which, when open, allows access to the rest of the castle's impressive grounds. The fortress was heavily restored in the 17th century and major modifications were undertaken in the 1920s, including the addition of the castle's main entrance, which was previously just a solitary wall. Despite the fiddling, the castle maintains its medieval charm and, wandering through its grounds, it is apparent that this is one of the region's best. The castle itself is open to the public as above, as well as, somewhat sporadically, on summer afternoons. Contact the town hall to visit outside these times.

Church of Santa Maria of the Peace On the town's main square, this Baroque church's interior is a little worse for wear but has some lovely ceiling paintings and a number of interesting statues. It was founded in 1643 on the site of a pre-existing church but not consecrated until the second half of the 18th century. The belfry is a relatively recent addition, completed in 1857.

Civic architecture When walking around the town, look out for Baroque buildings such as Palazzo Cataldi, Palazzo Capponi and Palazzo Carlitecca.

NEAR CAPESTRANO
Convent of San Francesco and Church of San Giovanni This convent complex includes the impressive Church of San Giovanni. To get here, follow the road out of Capestrano's main square. The church has some interesting wooden statues of various saints and a striking gold-plated ceiling. The adjacent cemetery, with its little chapels, is very peaceful. The convent itself was founded in the 15th century and occupies a very picturesque spot.

Church of San Pietro ad Oratorium About ten minutes on the SS153 from Capestrano towards Bussi sul Tirino is the important Church of San Pietro ad Oratorium. This ancient church was founded, according to tradition, by the Lombard king Desiderius as far back as the 8th century, and was subsequently restored in the 12th and 20th centuries. It features the nave and two aisles layout so

---

THE MAGIC SQUARE

```
R  O  T  A  S
O  P  E  R  A
T  E  N  E  T
A  R  E  P  O
S  A  T  O  R
```

The church of San Pietro ad Oratorium contains a historical conundrum that has been a bone of contention amongst historians for years. The 'magic square' is a set of five words: *rotas, opera, tenet, arepo* and *sator*. These words can be translated, at face value, as 'everywhere', 'operates', 'holds', 'plough' and 'sower' respectively. Interestingly, the words can be read vertically or horizontally in each direction: from left to right and right to left, from top to bottom and vice versa (see above). Historians have long argued over their intended meaning and some have thought it to be an anagram of the *Pater Noster*.

characteristic of Romanesque churches in the region. The ciborium (container for the Host), apparently built over a pagan altar and suggesting the presence of a place of worship here before the 8th century, is in excellent condition and dates from the 13th century. However, the 12th-century frescoes are probably the most impressive of the church's attractions.

Despite being a little overgrown, the area surrounding the church is ideal for picnics. However, do keep an eye on children: the nearby Tirino River flows extremely quickly. Stand on the bridge over the river for a pleasant view.

Getting there The turn-off for the church is on the SS153 between Bussi sul Tirino and Capestrano (on the left if coming from Bussi and on the right if coming from Capestrano).

Castel del Monte lies at 1,345m, with stunning views over Gran Sasso National Park; the Church of San Marco at its centre was once used as a lookout tower (I/A) page 123

left The prominent towers of Pacentro's Cantelmo Castle can be seen for miles (SMG/A) page 195

below Set 1,500m above sea level, the mighty castle-fortress of Rocca Calascio is one of the highest in Europe; its elevation was a vital part of its defences in the late Middle Ages (LC/D) page 123

bottom Founded by the Sabines and later a Roman colony, the town of Amiternum is remarkably well preserved to this day (L/D) page 119

above Framed by the mountains of the Sirente Velino Regional Park, the archaeological site of Alba Fucens has been excavated to reveal various layers of settlement in Abruzzo (VA/A) page 131

below The Fontana delle 99 Cannelle in L'Aquila was built to represent the province's 99 founding villages; each has its own mask (SS) page 117

above   Montepulciano grapes are grown throughout Abruzzo, and the region's wine has become one of its most famous exports (BA/A) page 43

left   *Confetti* on sale in Sulmona: these sugared almonds are used nationwide to celebrate events from baptisms to weddings (M101/D) page 193

below   The traditional costume of a black dress and a distinctive headdress has been worn by the women of Scanno since the 17th century (SS) page 184

top left   Monte Piselli: over two-thirds of Abruzzo's terrain is covered by rugged mountains (A/D) page 3

above left   Pineto's Blue Flag beach is separated from the buzz of town by a pine grove (LDG) page 212

above right   The Camosciara Reserve is replete with trekking paths and waterfalls, and was the original core of the National Park of Abruzzo (B/D) page 178

below   Prati di Tivo is one of Abruzzo's most popular ski resorts, with 18km of pistes and some of the highest peaks in the region (W) page 233

above The Lago di Scanno's pebble beaches are a popular retreat in the summer months (AI/S) page 186

right The alpine plateaux, steep valleys and wildflower-swathed meadows of the Majella National Park make it a major draw for hikers (SS) page 10

below Created in 1951, the manmade Lago di Barrea is now one of Abruzzo's prime beauty spots (AV/D) page 180

above **Orsini's viper (*Vipera ursinii*)** (W/A) page 11

left **Mariscan brown bear (*Ursus arctos marsicanus*)** (FB/B/FLPA) page 7

below left **Apennine chamois (*Rupicapra pyrenaica ornata*)** (GF/FLPA) page 8

below right **Eurasian lynx (*Lynx lynx*)** (MB/B/FLPA) page 9

8

L'Aquila Province:
Southwest Abruzzo

The southwest of Abruzzo comprises a number of different geographical areas, from the Fucino Basin to the Roveto Valley, most of which are located in the greater area known as the Marsica. From a historic battle to earthquakes and lakes that refused to drain, the area has a fascinating history that combines Marsi settlements and Roman towns with some exceptional medieval architecture. Don't be fooled by towns that on the surface seem to be uninspiring; dig a little further and you will find thousands of years of history and medieval towns completely abandoned after the devastating earthquake of 1915.

SUGGESTED ITINERARY

Start at Oricola, in the region's far west. Visit the towns of Pereto and Colli di Montebove. Head east to wonderful Tagliacozzo. Further east near the A25 motorway, visit the ruins of the ancient Roman town of Alba Fucens. From here, keep heading east (avoiding Avezzano altogether if possible) and visit the towns of Pescina and Lecce dei Marsi (the latter only for the abandoned old town).

AVEZZANO

There is little to occupy your time in this run-of-the-mill and fairly industrial city, though it rates a mention for being one of the larger places in the region. It makes a good base from which to explore the surrounding area, including the ruins of Alba Fucens (see page 131). The town's modern appearance is explained, in large part, by the various earthquakes that have rocked the area, most significantly that of 1915. That, combined with the extensive bombing it suffered in 1944, meant that it was largely rebuilt during the 20th century.

HISTORY Historians have long argued over the origins of the name Avezzano, with two theories prevailing. One – more commonly accepted by the locals – is that the name derives from 'Ave Jane', the name of a temple dedicated to the Roman god, Janus. Another, perhaps more likely theory has it that it derives from the phrase 'Ad Vetianum', dedicated to the noble Vetia family from nearby Alba Fucens, who owned the earliest settlements in the area. Regardless of which is correct, it is known that more than a thousand years ago several hamlets were grouped to form a larger town. Documents attesting to the existence of a single town with the name Avezzano date from the 14th century, though it was not until the 15th century that clear boundaries were established and set in statute.

The town, though ruled by dukes from the surrounding area, enjoyed a certain amount of economic autonomy. Its history has long been linked to the history of

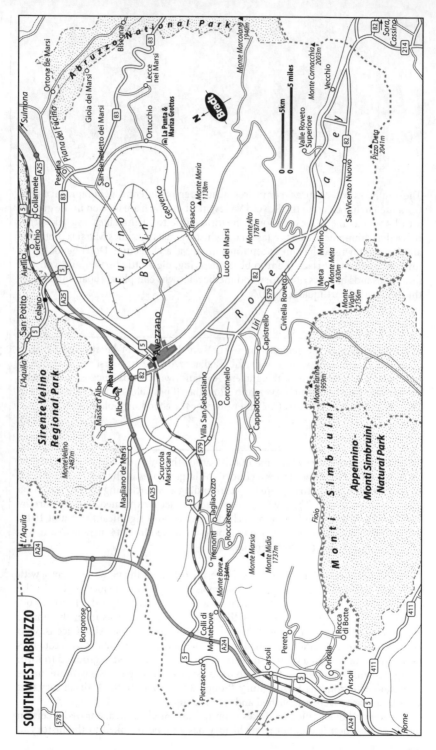

SOUTHWEST ABRUZZO

Abruzzo National Park

Ortona de Marsi

Bisegna

Lecce nei Marsi

Gioia dei Marsi

San Benedetto dei Marsi

Ortucchio

La Punta & Mariza Grottos

Monte Marcolano 1940m

Monte Cornacchia 2003m

Vecchio

Valle Roveto Superiore

Pizzo Deta 2041m

Sulmona

Piana del Fucino

Pescina

Collarmele

Geovenco

Fucino Basin

Trasacco

Monte Meria 1138m

Luco dei Marsi

Monte Alto 1787m

San Vincenzo Nuovo

Aielllo

Cerchio

Celano

San Potitto

L'Aquila

Meta

Monte Meta 1630m

Morino

Monte Tarino 1959m

Monte Viglio 2156m

Roveto Valley

Civitella Roveto

Capistrello

Liri

Avezzano

Alba Fucens

Massa d'Albe

Albe

Villa San Sebastiano

Corcomello

Cappadocia

Monti Simbruini

Appennino - Monti Simbruini Natural Park

Sirente Velino Regional Park

Monte Velino 2487m

Scurcola Marsicana

Magliano de'Marsi

Tagliacozzo

Roccacerro

Tremonti

Monte Marsia

Monte Midia 1737m

Fioio

L'Aquila

Borgorose

Colli di Montebove

Monte Bove 1344m

Casoli

Pietrasecca

Pereto

Oricola

Rocca di Botte

Arsoli

Rome

5km

5 miles

North

Lake Fucino, and it wasn't until the draining of the lake during the 19th century that Avezzano really came into its own, prospering as the economic powerhouse and largest settlement of the area. However, this was brought to an end by the 1915 earthquake that obliterated much of the town. Part of the Orsini Castle survived, though more than 12,000 people, a huge proportion of the town's population, were buried by rubble and lost their lives. When Avezzano was rebuilt the medieval street plan was abandoned and the town laid out along a system of straight and parallel roads.

GETTING THERE There is a turn-off for the city from the A25 motorway. If you're coming by bus, ARPA (*www.arpaonline.it*) runs services from Pescara, L'Aquila and Sulmona to Avezzano on a daily basis; there are at least two services a day. Tickets from Pescara, travelling via Chieti, will set you back €9 and the journey will take approximately 1½ hours. Buses arrive at the bus station north of the city centre. The train station is in the centre of town and operates on the Pescara–Rome line. Most trains that stop in Avezzano are likely to stop at most stations between Pescara and Rome, making it a long and arduous journey.

GETTING AROUND SCAV (*www.scavautolinee.com*) is the local bus company. Single-journey tickets within the town are around €1 and can be bought from any *tabbacchino*.

TOURIST INFORMATION
🛈 **The Municipio** Town Hall, Via Benedetto Cairoli; ☎0863 413397; www.comune.avezzano. aq.it

🏠 WHERE TO STAY
🏠 **Hotel dei Marsi** (112 rooms) Via Cavour 79B; ☎0863 4601; e info@hoteldeimarsi.it; www. hoteldeimarsi.it. Despite its Mussolini-style fascist appearance, this central hotel with functionally furnished & clean rooms has a conference centre & is geared towards business travellers. The good-value restaurant serves regional & pan-Italian dishes as well as daily specials that you can check on the menu updated on the website every day. The hotel offers some tours of the local area. **$$$**
🏠 **Hotel Velino** (22 rooms) Via Montello 9; ☎0863 412696; e info@hotelvelino.it; www. hotelvelino.it. The Velino is very conveniently

located across the road from Avezzano's train station. Rooms are clean & pleasantly decorated in navy & pastels. There is no pool & no restaurant. **$$$**
🏠 **Motel Belvedere** (12 rooms) Via XX Settembre 484; ☎0863 599555; e info@ motelbelvedere.it; www.motelbelvedere.it. More of a 3-star hotel than a motel, the Belvedere offers simple but attractive rooms about 2km from the centre of town. The restaurant serves some typical regional cuisine; give any of the meat dishes, such as the lamb, a try. **$$$**

✕ WHERE TO EAT
✕ **Minghino Cadadia** Via Crispi 71; ☎0863 414 412687; ⏱ daily 12.30–23.30. The Minghino Cadadia is a relatively classy affair in a city that is otherwise not really known for its chic. Chefs take great care to serve scrumptious dishes that are well presented. The lamb shank is a real treat, as are the ricotta gnocchi. **$$$**

✕ **Le Jardin Via** Sabotino 40; ☎0863 414710; ⏱ Thu–Tue. One of the few restaurants in Avezzano that is worth eating at, with a friendly environment & slightly French ambience. It serves simple, traditional dishes of which the best are the meaty ones, particularly the lamb & beef. **$$**

OTHER PRACTICALITIES

Banks
$ **Banca di Credito Cooperativo di Roma** Via Garibaldi 111–113
$ **Banca Nazionale del Lavoro** Piazza Municipio 3
$ **Banca Toscana** Via Monte Zebio 23

Chemists
✚ **Farmacia d'Eramo** Via Marconi 21; ☎ 0863 413118

✚ **Farmacia Rizzi** Via Sturzo 17; ☎ 0863 444291
✚ **Farmacia de Bernardinis** Via Garibaldi 114; ☎ 0863 413830

Post office
✉ Piazza Matteotti 1; ☎ 0863 413590

Hospital
✚ Via G di Vittorio; ☎ 0863 4991

WHAT TO SEE There are very few tourist attractions in Avezzano. However, if you are based in town in order to explore the surrounding area, you might consider visiting the outside of the **Orsini Castle**. Founded in 1490 and now a converted theatre, it is an excellent example of Abruzzo's military architecture. The castle suffered extensive damage in the earthquake of 1915. To get there from the city's main square, face the cathedral and take the road to its right until its end. Then turn right and take a left at the first major intersection.

AROUND AVEZZANO

THE FUCINO BASIN
Getting there The basin, easily accessible from Avezzano, is best visited by car and is well serviced by a network of regional roads; just follow the signs out of town to Luco dei Marsi. If coming from the A25 motorway, exit at Pescina, cross the SS83 and follow the signs for San Benedetto dei Marsi.

Luco dei Marsi Developed during the Middle Ages, Luco dei Marsi was a town on the shores of Lake Fucino (hence its strung-out configuration). Its current street plan maintains the medieval layout but the town was largely destroyed by the earthquake in 1915. However, a few buildings remain, such as the stunning **Church of Santa Maria delle Grazie**, with its harmonious architecture. It was founded in the 10th century and rebuilt in the 13th century, undergoing various phases of addition to its interior (where several side-chapels were added). The church's façade had to be partly rebuilt after the earthquake, including the belfry. Also standing the test of time is the elegant 18th-century Baroque **Church of San Giovanni Battista**.

Trasacco Trasacco is another of the handful of towns that developed along the shores of Lake Fucino and was, needless to say, destroyed by the 1915 earthquake. It is situated 685m above sea level at the foot of Monte Alto and seems at first to be rather uninteresting. However, Trasacco is renowned for its most obvious attraction, the **defence tower** which dominates the town and overlooks the surrounding area. The tower (which is currently not open to the public) has an unusual quirk: its lower part (thought to be older) is square, while above it sits a round upper storey, making it unique to the area.

The town's principal **Church of Santi Cesidio e Rufino** acquired its current layout in the late 1610s, though it actually dates from before the 13th century. An unusual feature of its architecture is the façade, which incorporates a smaller 'women's' door and a 15th-century 'men's' entrance.

You wouldn't expect to find one of the most important space telecommunications centres in the world in an isolated little town in rural Abruzzo. However, just outside Ortucchio, the Fucino Telespazio centre, inaugurated in the 1960s, is just that: the world's biggest space centre dedicated to civilian use. It operates some 90 antennas and 14 control rooms over an area of more than 37ha, and is part of a company with many other sites (*www.telespazio.it*). One of its tasks is to guide satellites from their launch rockets to their eventual orbital position. In May 2012, the Telespazio centre held a significant conference in Rome that was attended by some 300 renowned geospacial professionals from all over the world.

Ortucchio Further to the east is the town of Ortucchio, the most interesting settlement in the Fucino Basin. It is known for its impressive **castle** that in its heyday was accessible only by water (which became a moot point after the draining of the lake). The castle, which can be admired from the outside, was built by the Piccolominis (whose other notable castle is the one in Celano, which was damaged as a result of the 2009 earthquake) sometime in the 15th century and restored in the 20th century following the earthquake of 1915. Aside from the medieval frescoes on display at the **Church of Sant'Orante** (restored in the 1960s), the town is also a starting point for visits to the nearby grottoes of **Maritza** and **La Punta**.

Grottoes of Maritza and La Punta The grottoes are accessible by taking the road back towards Trasacco and then proceeding on foot from the signposts. They are the lowest of the grottoes in this area, of which there are a few. However, La Punta and Maritza are the most important from a historical perspective. La Punta, the older of the two, was used as far back as the Palaeolithic period and they were both put firmly on the map with the discovery in the early 20th century of *Homo sapiens* remains, which suggests that the area was inhabited thousands of years ago. Hiking further up the Monte Meria you'll also discover the grottoes of **Piana, Gambarile** and **Zengare**.

San Benedetto dei Marsi A short drive north from Ortucchio is the ancient town of San Benedetto dei Marsi. It dates back to Roman times, and is known to have gained the high status of a Roman *municipium* sometime before the beginning of the empire (27BC).

Much of the town was destroyed due to the 1915 earthquake, though the **Church of Santa Sabina** preserves a large and intricately carved doorway dating from the 14th century. Ruins of the Roman baths can still be seen in the small town centre and it is thought that the Roman forum was located somewhere near the church of Santa Sabina.

PESCINA At first glance, Pescina's attractions seem understated but a little exploration will bring to light some fascinating places. Situated just to the east of the Fucino Basin on the Giovenco River, Pescina was – like everywhere else in the region – largely destroyed by the earthquake of 1915, although it still retains its **tower** and **castle**, situated high on a hill dominating the town. The town had an earlier defence tower, known as *castrum* by the Romans. Piscina owes its name to

LAGO DI FUCINO

Sometimes known in English as the Fucine Lake, this erstwhile body of water has an interesting history. During the Roman Social Wars it was the site of a fierce battle between an army led by Cato and rebels from the surrounding area. The lake was a mixed blessing, often flooding the surrounding area, though it was brimming with fish and provided the locals with fertile soil. Two Roman emperors attempted to control the size of this lake and expand the area of agricultural land. Emperor Claudius's bid saw the building of a tunnel measuring over 5.5km in length, laid at a depth of over 7m. Though it required tens of thousands of workers to complete, it was not a hugely successful undertaking, only reducing the size of the lake from approximately 140km² to around 90km². Half a century later, Emperor Hadrian was a little more successful and managed to knock another 30km² or so off the efforts of Claudius, reducing the lake to just under 60km².

However, with the decline of the Roman Empire the works were ignored. Sediment and vegetation blocked the Roman drain and the lake returned to its former glory over the next few centuries. In the 1860s, a Swiss engineer was commissioned to undertake a project that would see the entire lake drained. Within a decade and a half, this had been achieved, providing Abruzzo with one of the most fertile areas of land in the entire country.

the various *piscinae* found in the area, pools that the Romans used for washing and keeping ducks and trout.

The town has two churches of interest, the 16th-century **Cathedral of Santa Maria delle Grazie** and the **Church of Sant'Antonio**. Both have wonderful façades with the latter sporting a 14th-century doorway. Both churches were restored after the earthquake. The main square is named after one of the town's most revered citizens, Cardinal Mazarin (see box, opposite), as is the **Civic Museum** (*Museo Civico Cardinale Mazzarino; Viale Francia;* \ *0863 842156;* ☉ *summer, Sat–Tue 09.00–12.00 & 16.00–19.00; winter, Sat & Sun 09.00–12.00 & 15.00–18.00*), which houses a collection of all things Cardinal Mazarin.

ORTONA DEI MARSI This small town lies just inside the boundary of the National Park of Abruzzo. It still preserves its medieval layout, unlike most of the other towns in this area. Approaching Ortona dei Marsi, its **castle ruins** and **tower**, at the highest point in the village, are still visible. The town's main **church** still retains its 13th-century façade, although its interior is not that interesting except for the intricate work of the pulpit.

LECCE NEI MARSI Although a modern town, developed (like a few of its neighbours, such as Gioia dei Marsi) after the 1915 earthquake, the town's previous incarnation, **Lecce Vecchia** (Old Lecce), is nearby. It is now a collection of abandoned buildings that evoke a sense of eeriness and desolation. Amongst the ruins it is still possible to see parts of the **fortified walls** and the old **castle**, worth a look if you are in the area. The town is only a minute's drive south from Ortucchio and the Fucino Basin.

Nearby The town of **Sperone**, partially destroyed and abandoned after the earthquake, has a round and distinctive tower, with views over the valley.

SCURCOLA MARSICANA Although it's an attractive little town, the only real draw at Scurcola Marsicana is the Orsini Fortress, which was closed to the public at the time of writing. However, it is definitely worth a look, even if only to examine its outer walls; follow the signs leading up from the bottom of the town.

If you're looking for somewhere to base yourself to explore the surrounding area and are not keen on the industrial city of Avezzano, Scurcola is a good choice – although there is only one hotel in the immediate vicinity.

Getting there
By car The town is about 15 minutes from Avezzano along the SS578, or take the SS5 off the A25 motorway.

By train The main Pescara–Rome railway line has a stop near the town at Villa San Sebastiano. From Pescara you will have to change at Avezzano; the total journey time is close to three hours. Tickets cost around €8.

By bus There are regular ARPA services from Avezzano, generally heading in the direction of Tagliacozzo.

Where to stay and eat

🏠 **Hotel Olimpia** (76 rooms) Via Tiburtina Valeria, Cappelle dei Marsi; ☎0863 4521; e info@hotelolimpia.it; www.hotelolimpia.it. This hotel is not in the centre of Scurcola Marsicana but in the local authority of Cappelle dei Marsi (still part of Scurcola Marsicana). It is very close to the turn-off from the A25 motorway. Its elegant & modern rooms are comfortable & all have AC. The hotel features a pool & health-cum-beauty centre with various pampering options. Its restaurant serves a decent mixture of local & international dishes. **$$$**

✗ **Ristorante Antica Taverna del Cors** Corso Vittorio Emanuele III 12; ☎0863 561308; ⏰ Wed–Mon. This restaurant, with an appealing rustic ambience, is one of the more popular venues in town. The owners serve up a veritable feast of pasta & meat dishes (including some excellent spaghetti & lamb), both from Abruzzo & beyond. The ingredients are fresh, simple & full of flavour. **$$**

Other practicalities For a little town, Scurcola Marsicana has reasonable amenities, boasting a **bank** (*Banca di Credito Cooperativo di Roma; Corso Vittorio Emanuele III 9*; ☎*0863 561031*), a **post office** (*Via della Vittoria*; ☎*0863 561045*) and a **chemist** (*Farmacia Ferrari; Piazza Risorgimento 19*; ☎*0863 561780*).

FAMOUS PESCINA LOCALS

Pescina was the birthplace of to two notable figures. One is the writer Ignazio Silone (see page 21) and the other is Cardinal Jules Mazarin.

Although **Cardinal Jules Mazarin**, or Giulio Raimondo Mazzarino, was born in Pescina in the 17th century he was to make a significant impact on the history of France. He rose to become an important statesman and entered the service of the French crown after he offered his services to Richelieu. Following the death of Louis XIII, the king's son – Louis XIV – was initially too young to rule, so Mazarin helped Queen Anne of Austria to rule in his stead, making him the effective ruler of France during the mid-1600s. The two were rather intimate and rumours circulated that the Dauphin, the young Louis XIV, was their child.

THE 1915 EARTHQUAKE

Generally known as the 'earthquake of Avezzano', this took place on 13 January 1915, wreaking havoc in the area and felt throughout central Italy.

The earthquake was originally measured using the Mercalli scale, which – unlike the Richter scale's measurement of an earthquake's ground motion – measures an earthquake's intensity through the destruction it causes. Its degree on this scale was a whopping XI (11), described as 'very disastrous'. Converted to the more commonly used Richter scale, the earthquake came in at a frightening magnitude of 8.1. To put this into perspective, the Chinese earthquake of 12 May 2008 in Sichuan measured 8.0 and claimed more than 80,000 lives.

The earthquake occurred at 07.48 local time and numerous aftershocks were felt during the following months. It claimed around 120,000 lives in the region of Abruzzo alone, and some towns, such as Avezzano and the smaller Pescina (where 5,000 of the 6,000 residents were killed), were almost completely levelled.

In the months after the quake various theories began to circulate through the local population as people searched for a reason to explain the devastation. One rumour blamed the draining of Lake Fucino for triggering the earthquake. The Italian government was also the target of criticism for not being prepared to deal with such a major disaster.

The recent earthquake in L'Aquila, measured at 6.3 on the Richter scale, has caused some minor damage in and around southwest Abruzzo. Mostly, however, it caused a panic amongst the older generation who grew up listening to their parents' stories about the 1915 earthquake.

What to see There have been obvious renovations to the **Orsini Fortress** over the years, but it retains an air of rather neglected antiquity. Standing at the foot of one of the towers near the adjacent Sanctuary of Santa Maria della Vittoria gives you a sense of its imposing stature and just how daunting and impenetrable this fort would have been to attack. Its unique architecture, laid out on a triangular plan, gave the occupants' enemies one less side to attack.

The 16th-century **Sanctuary of Santa Maria della Vittoria** (⊕ usually during daylight hours) is of interest for those wandering through. Not just because of its charming 13th-century doorway imported from the abbey of Santa Maria della Vittoria, but also due to its fine altar and several side chapels.

Situated in the lower part of town, **Piazza del Mercato** has a delightful whitewashed church with a particularly striking Baroque staircase and adjacent chapel. Climbing the first few steps of the staircase you will notice a plaque dating from 1631 and attesting to the church's foundation.

THE ROVETO VALLEY

Officially recognised as a geographical area by statute in 1976, the Roveto Valley has seven main towns, all of which were completely destroyed by the 1915 earthquake so hold little of interest for the traveller. Some of the outlying villages, however, such as Cività d'Antino, are worth a visit. The valley, surrounded by the bare rock sides of the neighbouring mountains, occupies an area of around 300km². The main settlement is Civitella Roveto, about a 20-minute drive south of Avezzano.

GETTING THERE The SS690 cuts straight through the valley. There is also a railway line that connects Avezzano to Lazio and the south, with has numerous stops along the valley.

CIVITÀ D'ANTINO Travelling south from Scurcola and Avezzano will eventually bring you to Cività d'Antino, in the Roveto Valley and in close proximity to the River Liri. It is not only a pleasant town to visit but also has evidence of a couple of thousand years of habitation. It was once a very important centre for the Marsi tribe, after which it became the Roman town of **Antinum**, from which a **wall** is still visible (from the road into town) dating back to the 5th century BC. Cività d'Antino was the only Roman *municipium* in the Roveto Valley, gaining this status after the Social Wars.

The centre of the current town is **Piazza del Banco**, on which stands the **Church of Santo Stefano** and below which the ancient **Roman forum** is located. There are also some old examples of civil architecture in town, such as the medieval **Palazzo Ferrante** and **Casa Cerroni**.

CIVITELLA ROVETO Most of the buildings in this town date from after 1915. However, a charming medieval quarter has been preserved to the east of the town near the walls. The architecturally stunning **Church of San Giovanni Battista** has a collection of frescoes dating back to the 1600s.

Near Civitella Roveto
Meta Located at the foot of Monte Meta, the village that existed here before 1915 has been completely abandoned, with the residents moving out to establish a new settlement after the earthquake. However, the ruins here, including an old church, are worth wandering around.

BALSORANO This is another town that packed up and moved out after the earthquake in 1915. Balsorano's new settlement isn't much to speak of but the old centre, now abandoned, is just as thought-provoking as any other. Another attraction is one of the most impressive castles in the region, the **Piccolomini Castle** of Balsorano. It was built on the site of a pre-existing fort to keep a close watch on the happenings, comings and goings in the area during the late 15th century. And this is a prime spot for such a purpose: the views from the castle are spectacular. You also get a sense of its sheer domination over the territory when the castle is viewed from the area below. Restoration work took place in the 1930s and the castle is now privately owned.

TAGLIACOZZO

A picturesque town of serene laneways and alleys, Tagliacozzo is dotted with medieval and Baroque *palazzi*. One of the larger settlements in the area, it is renowned for its fairly intact medieval core. The town is not far from Abruzzo's westernmost border with Lazio and is dramatically situated, as the name suggests (*taglia* means 'cut'), cut sharply into the side of a hill. This means that its streets, most of which cars dare not try to navigate let alone fit into, can be very steep, which makes the town all the more captivating.

HISTORY Tagliacozzo's name is said to derive – perhaps fancifully – from the phrase *collina tagliata*, or 'hill that is cut'. The precise date of its founding is a little obscure, as documents are available only from the early medieval period onwards. The town acquired a degree of fame because of the battle fought there between the House of Anjou and the Swabians (see box below). It enjoyed a period of wealth and prosperity in the later Middle Ages, and became a centre of some importance again during the 1860s, when Abruzzo belonged to the Kingdom of Italy and the independent Papal States were right next door, functioning as a significant border town. Today it is an attractive town much frequented by the inhabitants of Rome, who, despite being in a different region, live only 89km away.

GETTING THERE
By car Take the A24 from Rome (exit Tagliacozzo) or the A25 from Pescara. The town is situated along the SS5, and is actually closer to Rome than it is to coastal Abruzzo.

By train Tagliacozzo is on the main train line between Pescara and Rome. The journey from Pescara costs around €8 and takes 2–2½ hours. From Rome, the fare is around €6 and takes about 1½ hours. The station is situated northeast of the town.

By bus ARPA runs a service from Avezzano to Carsoli via Tagliacozzo. However, there are only two services a day taking over an hour, so you are better off taking the train.

TOURIST INFORMATION
Informazioni Accoglienza Turistica Abruzzo (Tagliacozzo) Piazza Obelisco 49; ☎0863 610318; e iat.tagliacozzo@abruzzoturismo. it. One of about 20 or so official information points run by Abruzzo Promozione Turismo, found in the lower town's main square.

 ## WHERE TO STAY
Hotel Park (60 rooms) Via Tiburtina Valeria, km 99; ☎0863 66822; e info@parkhoteltagliacozzo.it; www. hotelparktagliacozzo.it. A hotel, as well as

A BATTLE TO END ALL BATTLES

Tagliacozzo, like Hastings in England, is known for a significant battle: the Battle of Tagliacozzo, fought not far from the current town on 23 August 1268. On this day, the French troops of Charles of Anjou fought against the armies of the young duke of the Swabians, Conradin, who was only 16 years old. Conradin not only laid claim to the throne of Sicily, as did all members of Germany's House of Hohenstaufen (otherwise known as the Swabians) from 1194, but was also King of Jerusalem from 1254 to 1268.

Just when it seemed as though the battle had been won by Conradin – who in a moment of seeming victory had dispersed his armies into the area in order to loot and plunder – Charles of Anjou lured Conradin into a trap. Battalions of French reinforcements attacked the Swabian army as their troops diffused in a moment of faux victory. The battle finally saw the collapse of Swabian rule over southern Italy. Young Conradin fled to Rome where he attempted to board a ship to Sicily. Instead he was arrested and turned over to Charles, who had him imprisoned in Naples, where, on 29 October 1268, two months after the fatal battle, he was beheaded along with his comrade, Frederick of Baden.

a restaurant & bar, this is the only 4-star establishment in town, although the rating seems a bit generous given the rather basic amenities. It is, admittedly, a great place to relax & get some sun, with a massive pool area complete with kids' pool & water slide. And the rooms are clean & good value. The large restaurant, decorated in marble & pastel colours, is excellent value; staff will make you feel at home & serve up hearty meals of pasta & meats. **$$$**

⌂ **Albergo Ristorante Marina** (35 rooms) Via G Matteotti 14; ✆0863 619627; e info@ albergomarina.it; www.albergomarina.it. The Marina is a well-located family-run establishment with very friendly staff. Its rooms are quite spacious & well equipped, with AC (particularly important as Tagliacozzo can become very hot during summer). The hotel also has a bar & a perfectly acceptable small restaurant, largely meant for the FB & HB clientele. **$$**

⌂ **Hotel La Lucciola** (13 rooms) Via Variante Tiburtina 61; ✆0863 6501. This is a small hotel offering clean & simple rooms at a reasonable price. The staff will welcome you with open arms & strive to answer any queries or requests. Note that the hotel is closed during the first 2 weeks of Sep. **$$**

✗ WHERE TO EAT AND DRINK

✗ **Ristorante La Vecchia Posta** Piazza dell'Obelisco 22; ✆0863 66611; e info@ lavecchiaposta.it; www.lavecchiaposta.it. An imposing entranceway leads you into this popular restaurant set in an old *palazzo* on the main square. It serves up excellent local specialities, such as *gnocchetti con ceci* & *polenta con salsiccia*, using high-quality ingredients, & has a wine list to impress even the most knowledgeable. **$$$$**

✗ **Ristorante Al Corradino di Svevia** Piazza dell'Obelisco 48; ✆0863 68246; www. alcorradinodisvevia.it. Also on the main square, this restaurant is named after Conradin of Swabia (see box opposite), who brought death & destruction to the town. Regardless, it is a prize eatery serving a host of dishes from Abruzzo (such staples as *pasta alla chitarra*) & beyond. **$$$**

✗ **Pizzeria Al Solito Posto** Piazza Obelisco 39; ✆0863 610748. Cleverly named (you can just imagine people saying, 'Do you want to eat at The Usual Place?'), this pizzeria's friendly staff serve very good pizza. It is particularly popular amongst locals in a hurry. **$$**

♀ **Pub Duca 33** Piazza degli Abruzzi 33; m 344 813 8071. A pub with a friendly atmosphere & a range of beers as well as snacks.

OTHER PRACTICALITIES There are a couple of **banks** in and around Piazza Duca degli Abruzzi, found just outside the eastern entrance to the old town: Banca Toscana (*Piazza Duca degli Abruzzi 37*) and Carispaq (*Piazza Duca degli Abruzzi 3*). There's also a **chemist** here (*Farmacia Pellacchi; Piazza Duca degli Abruzzi 70;* ✆*0863 610287*). The **post office** is at Viale dei Giardini 1 (✆*0863 698220*).

EVENTS AND FESTIVALS

July Ascanio. Usually the first weekend of July, this festival is in remembrance of a local, Ascanio Mari, who in the 16th century was a disciple of the Florentine artist Benvenuti Cellini. Early music ensembles, bands and various displays line the streets.

August Sagra della Salsiccia. The 'Feast of the Sausage' is just about what you would expect: a thousand types of sausages with a thousand types of seasoning for thousands of hungry Abruzzesi.

WHAT TO SEE Put the guidebook in your bag and lose yourself in the winding streets of this medieval gem: centuries-old buildings without names, mysterious doorways and more churches than are possible to visit in a week transport you back in time. It is best to enter the old town from Piazza Duca degli Abruzzo, through the captivating medieval gateway, **Porta dei Marsi**. The town's main square is **Piazza**

dell'Obelisco, named because of its fountain with an obelisk. Other entrances into the old town are the **Porta San Rocco** (or **Pulcina**), next to the Palazzo Ducale (see below); the **Porta Romana**, close to the Church of Santa Maria del Soccorso, with **Porta Valeria** just opposite; the **Porta da Piede**; and – near the river – **Porta Corazza**.

Churches
As one elderly man said to me in Tagliacozzo: 'There are more churches here than there are Christians!' This might well be true, and many little churches aren't even signposted. The following is a handful of the more significant.

Church of San Giovanni Battista
Found on the Piazza dell'Obelisco, right at the eastern entrance to the old town, this church has an elaborate portal, although the interior is a little less impressive.

Church of San Francesco
This church is found by following the Via del Municipio Vecchio from Piazza dell'Obelisco. Its doorway is humble, though characteristic of many churches in the town, with the rose window above dating from the 15th century. The interior of the church houses the remains of Tommaso da Celano.

Church of Santa Cosma and San Damiano
Found in the upper part of town, this church preserves its original façade and boasts an excellent example of a Renaissance entrance. It is actually part of a larger convent complex, whose first mention dates from 872.

Church of Santa Maria del Soccorso
Outside Porta del Soccorso, this church's portal and belltower date from the 15th–16th centuries, though the church was built on the site of an older 12th-century church, Santa Maria in Furca.

Church of San Francesco d'Assisi
This is found on Largo San Francesco and is built in Romanesque style with a particularly elaborate entrance portal.

Santuario della Madonna dell'Oriente
Five minutes from town is the Sanctuary of the Madonna of the Orient. Its highlight is a 13th-century painting of the *Madonna and Child*.

Palazzo Ducale
(closed for restoration at the time of writing) Situated about a five-minute walk west and north of Piazza dell'Obelisco (the main piazza at the foot of the old town), the Palazzo Ducale is an important example of Abruzzesi civil

---

A TASTE OF THE LOCAL

This part of the region has a few signature dishes: *gnocchetti con ceci* and *polenta con salsiccia*. The former is a plate of gnocchi with chickpeas, which are so loved by Abruzzesi, especially the older generation. Although it may seem a surprising combination they go very well in this pasta dish. The latter is a polenta dish with chopped-up sausage, one of my personal favourites. Traditionally, this dish is served in a *scifelletta*, or a wooden dish. You can try these dishes at many of the eateries in town. Ristorante La Vecchia Posta (see page 163) serves both.

architecture. It was started in the 14th century by the Orsini family, who built many of the important buildings of the surrounding area. What you see today is the result of a number of restoration programmes that have tried to bring the building back to its former glory. The double lancet windows of the first floor, which was severely damaged in the 1915 earthquake, are the highlight of the building's façade, which is neither intricate nor elaborate but modest and unassuming. Also on the first floor is a set of 15th-century frescoes. Its second floor houses a chapel that was once home to frescoes of some importance, but which are now housed in the main museum in the castle in Celano.

The Fortress Tagliacozzo's fortress ruins stand watch over the town. The remains include the castle's towers and walls and a little of the internal residence. From here, there are sweeping views across the valley to nearby towns; the castles of Castiglione di San Donato and Tremonti are visible to the east and west respectively.

AROUND TAGLIACOZZO
Roccacerro While there are no specific sights to attract the visitor, this is a quaint little village that occupies a gorgeous spot facing the surrounding mountains.

Colli di Montebove The sandstone colours of this tiny hamlet create a lovely contrast with the darker surrounding mountains and hills. The view as you arrive from the S5 is especially pretty, with the village's old **belltower** dominating the panorama. There isn't much to do here but take in the postcard views and perhaps walk around the **castle ruins**. Nearby, there is a turn-off for **Monte Marsia**.

Tremonti The real attraction here is the ruined **castle**, high on a hill above the town. It is not just the castle that has views over the surrounding mountains; due to the town's wonderful position, nearly every single bedroom window must share the panorama. There is a charming 14th-century church in Largo Don Pietro Manfredi.

Carsoli This is not the prettiest town in Abruzzo by any means, but the **Church of Santa Vittoria** is certainly striking. It dates from the 16th century and has an impressive and imposing stone altar and some exceptional wall paintings. Its **castle**, built by the Angevins, is little more than a pile of rubble.

Oricola Certainly prettier than its neighbour, Carsoli, Oricola has a small **castle**, typical of the area, as well as a quaint staircase that leads up to the council offices and a post office. It is worth wandering up to the castle, which is at the highest point in town, if only for the area in front which has a lookout from where you can see for miles across Abruzzo and the neighbouring region of Lazio. There are a few churches in town, including that of **Santa Restituta** with an interesting fresco dating from the 13th century, and the 18th-century **Church of Santissimo Salvatore**, with an early 19th-century organ.

Pietrasecca Magnificently situated on a rocky cliff (its name literally means 'dry rock'), this little town is worth wandering around. Its oldest part preserves much of its 15th-century layout. However, the highlight here is of the natural variety: the **Grottoes of Pietrasecca** (*for information, visit Carsoli Town Hall, Piazza della Libertà 1; ⧄ 0863 9051*). Opened to the public in 1992, the grottoes are situated a five-minute drive northeast of the town. They cover a rather large area of around 110ha, and are replete with underground streams and lakes.

Pereto Undoubtedly the prettiest village in these parts, Pereto sits precariously on a rocky spur called the Piano del Cavaliere. This is one of many towns in Abruzzo that make you wonder how, hundreds of years ago, people successfully managed to build houses in such inaccessible spots. From its approach roads, views of the town are breathtaking. Because of the steep terrain of the area around the town, don't be surprised to see elderly men and women hitchhiking back to town after wandering down the hill to visit friends or pick berries. It is the accepted practice to pick them up. I have paid my community dues to the elderly here on at least three occasions and it is a great way to get to know the locals.

Because of the steep and narrow streets you will have to park your car at the foot of the town and climb up. Before you do this, take a walk around the first piazza you encounter when arriving; it is a wonderful hub of activity for young and old alike.

Getting there The town is reached from the A24 (exit Carsoli-Oricola) or from a turn-off on the SS5.

What to see
The castle The castle, at one stage belonging to the Orsini family, was originally built to keep a close eye on the border between Lazio and Abruzzo and was therefore one of the most strategically important castles in the region. Apart from being a spectacular sight in itself, with the 14th-century walls and towers dominating the town below, it is built around the oldest quarter of Pereto, evident from the narrow and winding lanes. Its largest tower is said to be even older, probably dating from the 12th century, and is now privately owned.

9

L'Aquila Province:
National Park of Abruzzo and Surrounds

Fresh mountain air, an abundance of wildlife and ancient towns perched high above lakes: these are just some of the reasons to visit the **Parco Nazionale d'Abruzzo**. Officially, it is called the National Park of Abruzzo, Lazio and Molise as it spans the border with the neighbouring regions. However, the greater part of it lies within the region of Abruzzo. The park occupies an area of around 50,000ha at between 900m and 2,200m above sea level and its landscape is varied and exceptionally attractive.

There's something for everyone here: from walking and trekking to wildlife spotting and skiing or simply relaxing by a lake. See page 10 for a detailed look at the park's flora, fauna and geology.

SUGGESTED ITINERARY

Take the exit for the park on the A25 motorway at Pescina. Travel through the towns of Ortona dei Marsi and Bisegna to Pescassèroli. From here, visit Opi, the Val Fondillo, Villetta Barrea and Civitella Alfedena before stopping at Barrea and its lake. Travel back towards Villetta Barrea and up the stunning SS479 through Scanno, Villalago and finally, Anversa degli Abruzzi. Although this could be done in a day, allowing two to three days would be far more relaxing.

GETTING THERE AND AROUND

BY CAR The national park can be reached from the A25 motorway coming from Rome or Pescara. The SS83 cuts straight through the park and the park's eastern border is defined by the SR479. Most of the towns are found along the SS83.

BY BUS Pescassèroli (the park's headquarters), Opi, Villetta Barrea and Barrea are all on ARPA (*www.arpaonline.it*) services that run between Avezzano and Castel di Sangro. There are about seven departures per day from Avezzano to Pescassèroli (roughly 1½ hours) and around six per day between Pescassèroli and Castel di Sangro (about 1¼ hours). The buses stop at all towns along the way, including a request stop at Val Fondillo.

PESCASSEROLI

Pescassèroli is one of the most isolated towns of importance in the region. It is situated on an area of flat ground, making it hard to believe that it stands more than 1,150m above sea level. Tucked away in the depths of the National Park of Abruzzo, of which it is the headquarters, this town offers a range of different experiences. To some, it is a haven of relaxation within the national park, offering a chance

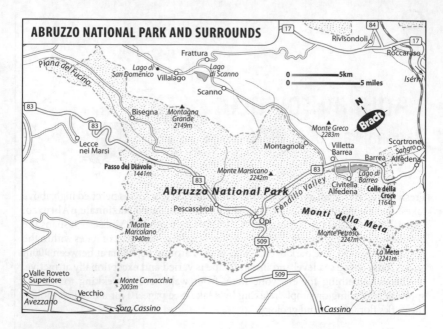

ABRUZZO NATIONAL PARK AND SURROUNDS

to wander around a charming town, eat good food and laze about in a hotel. To others, Pescassèroli is a good place for an action-packed break in an area offering everything from wildlife spotting to cycling, hiking and skiing.

TOURIST INFORMATION

APTR Pescassèroli Head Office Via Principe di Napoli; ✆0864 69351; e presidio.pescasseroli@abruzzoturismo.it; www.abruzzoturismo.it. Attesting to the town's importance as a tourist centre is the presence of an Abruzzo Turismo head office; the only others are located in the region's provincial capitals. The office can provide

information on Pescassèroli & is the main information point for the National Park of Abruzzo.

Ente Parco Nazionale d'Abruzzo, Lazio e Molise Viale S Lucia; ✆0863 91131; e info@parcoabruzzo.it. This is the national park's head office, where information on the park is readily available.

 ## WHERE TO STAY
Upmarket

Villa Mon Repos (14 rooms) Via S Lucia 2; ✆0863 912858; e villamonrepos@villamonrepos.it; www.villamonrepos.it. One of the few 5-star hotels in the region & arguably the prettiest hotel in the area is fittingly named 'My Rest'. It's a gorgeous castle-like manor constructed in the early 20th century, with friendly owners who will do all they can to make sure your stay is supremely relaxing. Rooms are well decorated & fitted with all mod cons. Don't be surprised to see the odd bride & groom around the place: the hotel also has an excellent restaurant (see page 170), which sees its fair share of weddings, & a recently renovated hammam-style Turkish baths, a sauna & massage services. **$$$$$**

Albergo Villino Quintiliani (11 rooms, 4 chalets) Viale S Lucia 1; ✆0863 910755; e villino@villinoquintiliani.it; www.villinoquintiliani.it. Another of the town's stunning little villas that is just as attractive on the inside as it is on the outside (if not more so). Beautiful décor, in a local traditional style, offsets relaxing rooms with all mod cons. The hotel often offers some excellent special deals (based on season & weather) which are updated on the website. The owners can also provide a knowledgeable guide to the area. Early bookings advised, particularly in summer. **$$$$**

Club Primula Hotel Residence (140 rooms) Via della Pineta 1; ✆0863 9141; e info@primula.it; www.primula.it. This hotel residence draws in a healthy number of young people &, as such, is a fun & friendly place to stay. It offers good-value accommodation, with several different room configurations, including apartments, & a variety of activities & excursions. There's a health & spa centre for guests, who pay for a compulsory membership card of €35 (although this is sometimes included in the room price). Frequent offers & promotions on website. FB & self-catering options available. **$$$$**

🏠 **Hotel Bamby** (38 rooms) Via Castel Mancino 4; 📞 0863 911818; e hotel.bamby@tiscali.it; www. bamby-iris.it. See Hotel Garnì Posta, below. **$$$$**

🏠 **Hotel Edelweiss** (21 rooms) Viale Colli dell'Oro 10; 📞 0863 912577; e edelw89@libero.it; www.edelweisshotel.biz. A very short drive from the centre of town & in an attractive rural setting near the town's skiing area is Hotel Edelweiss. Though it resembles a functional Swiss chalet, it occupies a picturesque spot with lovely mountain views & comprises good-sized rooms as well as a bar, games room & even a private disco. **$$$$**

🏠 **Hotel Garnì Posta** (24 rooms) Via Principe di Napoli 19; 📞 0863 911017; e info@garniposta. it; www.garniposta.it. A good-value choice, centrally located & offering comfortable & clean rooms (triple & family rooms also available) with mod cons including satellite TV. B/fast is particularly good. HB options available. The hotel also offers excursion packages during the summer. Under the same ownership are the Bamby & Iris, with similar accommodation & service. HB & FB. **$$$$**

🏠 **Hotel Iris** (27 rooms) Via Fontana Difesa 1; 📞 0863 91900; e hotel.iris@tiscali.it; www.bamby-iris.it. See Hotel Garnì Posta, below. **$$$$**

🏠 **Hotel Pagnani** (36 rooms) Via Colli dell'Oro 5; 📞 0863 912866; e h.pagnani@ermes.it; www. hotelpagnani.it. A solid accommodation option with comfortable, clean rooms decorated in pastel greens, a games room, bar, restaurant & swimming pool (with attached jacuzzi). **$$$$**

🏠 **Hotel Sport Daniel** (16 rooms, 3 apts) Via Colli dell'Oro 1; 📞 0863 912896; e info@ hoteldaniel.it; www.hoteldaniel.it. Aside from the questionable name, this hotel is good value & offers comfortable rooms that are modern & tastefully decorated (2 of them adapted for the disabled), a swimming pool & a decent restaurant. **$$$$**

Mid range

🏠 **Albergo Paradiso** (18 rooms) Via Fonte Fracassi 4; 📞 0863 910422; e info@albergo-paradiso.it; www.albergo-paradiso.it. Set in lovely surroundings, the Paradiso arguably lives up to its name & does so at prices that won't break the bank. With a slightly kitsch attempt at a mock-traditional interior it features rooms with mod cons, a children's play area, & a bar & restaurant. HB & FB options available. **$$$**

🏠 **Grand Hotel del Parco** (114 rooms) Viale S Lucia 3; 📞 0863 912745; e info@bluhotels.it; www.bluhotels.it. This 4-star hotel just south of the old town centre features clean, comfortable rooms decorated in a rustic mountain style. There is a good restaurant serving some excellent homemade pasta dishes, & even a swimming pool, although this is open only during the warmer months. **$$$**

🏠 **Hotel Basel** (21 rooms) Via della Cabinovia; 📞 0863 91875; www.hotelbasel.it. A good choice for 2-star accommodation, although for HB & FB options it may seem a little pricy for its rating. (Their B&B rate is more in keeping with the norm.) It's a simple though pleasant hotel with functional, rather old-fashioned rooms & a good restaurant. **$$$**

🏠 **Hotel Cocoon** (33 rooms) Via Cabinovia 1; 📞 0863 910477; e Info@hotelcocoon.it; www. hotelcocoon.it. Surrounded by forested hills, Hotel Cocoon is about a minute's drive northwest of the town centre. Featuring 20 rooms with balconies, 1 suite & 12 'attic rooms', it offers clean & functional accommodation close to the attractions of Pescassèroli & the surrounding area. The restaurant dishes up a number of local specialities. **$$$**

🏠 **Hotel Corona** (29 rooms, 10 suites) Via Collacchi 2; 📞 0863 91731; e info@coronahotel. it; www.coronahotel.it. Another impressive hotel that's ideal for a little R&R, complete with health & spa centre (including a pool & gym), a decent restaurant & comfortable rooms. It looks a little dated from the outside but the interior has been spruced up & modernised, albeit in a corporate sort of way. Particularly popular during ski season. FB & HB options available. **$$$**

🏠 **Hotel Cristiania** (12 rooms) Via Collacchi 5; 📞 0863 910795; e info@hotelcristiania.com; www. hotelcristiania.com. The friendly owner, Enrico, markets this property as his own home & provides accommodation fitting to a homestay. Views over the area & the look of an alpine hotel make this an appealing choice for a little relaxation. Rooms are spacious & tastefully decorated in rustic style with a country cottage feel. **$$$**

🏠 **Hotel Duca degli Abruzzi** (8 rooms) Piazza Duca degli Abruzzi 5; ✆0863 911075; www. pescasseroli.biz/hotelducadegliabruzzi. A small 2-star hotel in an excellent location on a very pretty square. The rather dark rooms are simple but have en-suite bathrooms, TV & phone. The restaurant is intimate & serves good traditional food. **$$$**

🏠 **Hotel Il Picchio** (56 rooms) Via Valle dell'Oro; ✆0863 910760; e ilpicchio@ilpicchio. com; www.ilpicchio.com. Il Picchio is situated not far from the town centre in a lovely rural setting. The hotel comprises comfortable, functional rooms with plain but adequate decoration & furniture, & extras such as a 'disco' & even a bowling alley. The hotel's restaurant is very accommodating, with menu options for vegetarians & coeliacs; they will happily take requests for food to be cooked/served according to religious preferences. **$$$**

🏠 **Hotel Valle del Lupo** (11 rooms) Via Collacchi 1; ✆0863 910534; e valledelupo@ virgilio.it; www.valledelupo.it. About 1km from the centre of Pescassèroli this mountain chalet offers comfortable accommodation with pretty, wood-panelled & good-sized rooms. There is even a private guide (at a fee) who will show you the trekking sites in summer & the skiing in winter. **$$$**

Agritourism

🏠 **Agriturismo Valle Cupa** (13 rooms) Via Fontana della Difesa; ✆0863 910444; www. agriturismomaneggiovallecupa.it. A family-owned country escape, with all the warmth befitting a true Abruzzese welcome & pleasantly simple traditional rooms. It is situated at about a 10-min drive south of town. It is an excellent complex, providing a whole host of information on the local area as well as summer & winter activities such as horseriding (they certainly have enough horses). Note that the minimum stay during high season is 1 week. **$$$**

Camping There are a few campsites in the area. The following, all within a short distance of the town (follow the signs), have decent but basic facilities and allow both tents and caravans. All offer camping at less than €10 per person per night. At the time of writing, none offered cabins or chalets. Arguably the most attractive is La Panoramica, for its location on the edge of the old town.

⛺ **Campeggio Aquila Reale** Via San Donato, 1; ✆0863 910641

⛺ **Campeggio S Andrea** Località S Andrea; ✆0863 912173

⛺ **Campeggio La Panoramica** Viale Cabinovia 19; ✆0863 910750

✗ **WHERE TO EAT AND DRINK** Most of the hotels above have their own restaurant and it is worth remembering that, unlike in many other parts of the world, most – however small – will serve food that is of good to excellent quality.

✗ **La Buvette Wine Bar, Tea & Chocolate Room** Viale Principe di Napoli 19; ✆0863 910787. Hotel Garnì Posta is the location of this well-loved restaurant & bar, frequented by both tourists & locals alike. It's a great place for a hot chocolate during the winter months & its food menu includes small snacks such as cheeses & cakes. The wine list is extensive. **$$$**

✗ **Ristorante Pizzeria La Baita** Piazzale della Cabinovia 20; ✆0863 910434. This alpine-inspired building, appropriate for the depths of mountainous Abruzzo, serves up a decent pizza

cooked in the restaurant's wood-fired oven, as well as regional pasta & meat dishes & pan-Italian favourites. **$$$**

✗ **Villa Mon Repos** Via S Lucia 2; ✆0863 912858; www.villamonrepos.it. Hotel Villa Mon Repos's restaurant is a fine dining choice. A warm & friendly atmosphere accompanies some excellent food, such as its pasta dishes (the non-tomato based ones are especially good). It is quite popular for weddings & other functions, so it is worth booking in advance or at least checking whether they expect to be busy. **$$$**

✗ Osteria A Cavu't Piazza Vittorio Veneto 17; ☎0863 91816. The brown hues & timber beams of this place create a rustic, authentic Abruzzese setting. Try any of the excellent pasta dishes (particularly the homemade spaghetti). Meat dishes are also excellent, particularly the lamb. There is an extensive wine list. **$$**

✗ Pizzeria Ristorante San Francesco Via Isonzo 1; ☎0863 910650. This restaurant's speciality is its pizza, of which the best is probably the deliciously simple margherita & the *capricciosa*. **$$**

✗ Ristorante Agriturismo Valle Cupa Via Fontana della Difesa; ☎0863 910444; www. agriturismomaneggiovallecupa.it. Though part of the agritourism covered above, this is one restaurant that is worth a separate mention. The food here is typically Abruzzese. High-quality ingredients are used in simple though tasty dishes, such as their scrumptious *spaghetti alla chitarra*. **$$**

OTHER PRACTICALITIES

Banks Most of the banks in town are situated on Via Principe di Napoli:

$ Banca Credito Cooperativo Via Principe di Napoli 48; ☎0863 911086

$ Banca Toscana Via Principe di Napoli 2; ☎0863 911126

$ Banca Popolare dell'Adriatico Via Principe di Napoli 28; ☎0863 91951

Post office

✉ Via Piave 1; ☎0863 910731; ⏰ Mon–Fri 08.00–13.30, Sat 08.00–12.30

Chemists

✚ Farmacia Comunale Viale S Lucia 1; ☎0863 910481

✚ Farmacia del Parco Piazza Vittorio Emanuele III 12; ☎0863 910753

Local tour operator

Ecotur Via Piave 7; ☎0863 912760; e informazioni@ecotur.org; www.ecotur.org. An excellent one-stop shop for all your touring needs in the area. Ecotur offer tours of Pescassèroli & excursions to the surrounding area. There are various itineraries including themed treks & walking tours, depending on the time of year & what you wish to accomplish.

WHAT TO SEE AND DO The beauty of Pescassèroli now lies in its setting and its narrow street pattern. Many buildings were destroyed in the 1915 earthquake (see box, page 160) and as such not a whole lot remains of its former glory. However, there are some things worth seeing, even if you are principally in the area to take advantage of its outdoor activities.

Little remains of the **Mancino Castle**, on a hill high above Pescassèroli, which has slowly decayed over time and suffered particularly during the 1915 earthquake. However, it offers excellent views of the town below and the surrounding area.

The parish **Church of Santi Pietro and Paolo** (⏰ during the day) is mentioned in documents as far back as the 1100s, and still preserves some medieval features despite having had to be restored during the 20th century. These include one of its right-hand doorways and the window above the main portal which dates from the 16th century. The altar supports an ancient wooden statue of Mary that is much revered by the locals. In front of the church there is a small garden with a war memorial built in the 1920s. Another church of interest in the town is that of the **Madonna del Carmine,** founded in the 18th century by a local family. It has a lovely Baroque altar and an important 17th-century crucifix. The church underwent restoration in the 1980s. Nearby is the **Sanctuary of the Madonna di Monte Tranquillo**, the Madonna of the Tranquil Mountain, dating back to the early Middle Ages. There is a procession to this sanctuary every year on the last Sunday in July.

The 18th-century **Palazzo Sipari**, found on Piazza Benedetto Croce is an excellent example of civil architecture. It has a charmingly simple façade.

Museo Naturalistico/Nature Centre and Museum (*Viale Colli dell'Oro 1;* ✆ *0863 91131;* ⊕ *daily 09.00–19.30; admission adult €6, child €4*) This museum and nature park is one of the highlights of the area. It includes various displays of flora and fauna found in the national park (see page 10 for a summary of the national park's vegetation and wildlife). Of particular interest is a 2,500-year-old pre-Roman tomb found in a nearby excavation site. The nature centre, however, houses the real attraction, a number of brown bears (see page 7). A conservation project managed by the national park, the nature centre is not strictly a zoo, but rather a place where animals that have suffered injuries (and are in danger of extinction) are looked after in natural surroundings and subsequently released back into the wild.

SKIING AROUND PESCASSEROLI The skiing around Pescassèroli is some of the best in the region. It is spread over four areas: **Monte Ceraso** (1,814m), **Monte Vitelle** (1,945m), **Monte Schiena Cavallo** (1,962m) and **Rifugio Pesco di Iorio** (1,870m). There are around 14 downhill ski slopes totalling approximately 20km in length, and other amenities including three chairlifts. The slopes are reached by following the signs out of town to a large square, Piazzale Cabinovia, which is home to various ski schools and equipment-hire centres.

Ski schools Skiing schools such as **Scuola Italiana Sci La Lince** (*Piazzale Cabinovia;* ✆ *0863 912864*) offer private lessons from €40 for an hour per person to €70 for four people. Group lessons occur from 11.00–13.00 and you can buy slots ranging from two hours over one day for €25 to 12 hours over six days for €120. Similar arrangements are offered by the nearby **Scuola Italiana Sci Pescassèroli** (*Piazzale Cabinovia;* ✆ *0863 912796*).

For further details, contact **Direzione Impianti** (*Piazzale Cabinovia;* ✆ *0863 911118*), the authority which manages the skiing area. Information can also be found on www.sciareapescasseroli.it.

Ski passes Daily pass prices begin at around €22 for adults, but half days are cheaper. Weekend and three–six-day passes are also available from around €59. Seasonal passes will set you back €300 for adults, or €200 for children.

Ski runs

'EASY' (BLUE) RUNS		'MEDIUM' (RED) RUNS		'DIFFICULT' (BLACK) RUNS	
Campo scuola		Stazzetto	632m	Direttissima	1,328m
(skiing school)	300m	Camoscio	486m	Aquila	610m
Orsetta	200m	Lupo	782m		
Raccordo	640m	Volpe	798m		
Vallone	1,069m	Variante Volpe	175m		
Stradello	383m	Aceretta	779m		
Panoramica	491m				

OPI

Winner: Most Beautiful Villages in Italy; population around 500

Rising from a rocky spur is the striking old town of Opi, whose narrow, medieval alleyways are as pretty as a picture whether doused with snow or drenched in sunshine. It is one of the highest settlements in the national park and its popularity as a tourist resort is only overshadowed by the liveliness and accommodation on offer in nearby Pescassèroli. As far as towns go, however, Opi is definitely the prettier of the two.

HISTORY There are two possible origins for the town's peculiar name. One is that Opi derives from the name of the Roman goddess and wife of the god Saturn, Ops. However, it is more likely that the name evolved from the Roman word *oppidum* which means 'fortified castle'.

The village preserves its early medieval layout, even though there is evidence that a settlement has existed in and around the present site of the town since Italic times. It is known that in the early medieval period, residents relocated further up the rocky spur in attempts to block the attacks of enemy raiders.

For just under 40 years during the 19th century, the town joined with nearby Pescassèroli in a union that was intended to create greater wealth and status for the area. The town slowly declined, however, with the beginning of emigration to the Americas. It is said that around 500 residents of Opi migrated over a period spanning a decade and a half; rather a lot considering that the population of the town at the time was only around 800. In 1901, Opi suffered extensive damage, especially on a human level, when an earthquake struck the area. In recent years, the town has come to wider attention as a result of important local archaeological findings, the most significant of which is the Necropolis of Val Fondillo (see box, page 176).

GETTING THERE
By car and bus See *Getting there and around*, page 167.

On foot The 6km road between Pescassèroli and Opi makes for a pleasant short walk taking around 1¼ hours. When you see the town on a rocky spur take the stairs to the left of the road, which take you up to the town.

TOURIST INFORMATION
🧭 **Ufficio Turistico Pro Loco Opi** Opi Municipio, Via San Giovanni 30; ☏ 0863 916073; m 347 888 7056; ⏱ high season (June–Sep), daily 09.30– 13.00 & 16.00–19.00; low season (Oct–Jun), Thu–Tue 09.30–12.30 & 15.30–18.30

 WHERE TO STAY

🏠 **Antica Rua B&B** (4 rooms) Via Salita la Croce; ☏ 0863 91856; e anticarua@opionline. it; www.anticarua.it. Antica Rua is a charismatic B&B set within a building of medieval origin & decorated with traditional fittings. Benefiting from a recent refurbishment, it now offers practical rooms with some quirky decoration (such as little animal statuettes & floral vases), a TV & games room, & a kitchen where b/fast is served. Friendly owners & staff. HB & FB options available. **$$$**
🏠 **Hotel La Pieja** (12 rooms) Via Salita la Croce 1; ☏ 0863 910772; e info@lapieja.it; www.lapieja. it. While the décor might not be to everyone's liking (rooms look more like camping log cabins with their wooden walls & green, patterned bedspreads), the hotel is in a scenic position & its

rooms are functional & clean. There is also a good restaurant. Check the website for seasonal specials. HB options available. **$$$**
🏠 **Pensione Fresilia** (7 rooms) Via San Giovanni; ☏ 0863 916072; info@fresilia.net; www. fresilia.net. Just near the council buildings on the main road, this is a friendly, family-run hotel set in a 17th-century building & offering good-value accommodation with rooms of a decent size. There's also an excellent hotel restaurant. HB options available. **$$$**
🏠 **Affittacamere Ursitti** (5 rooms) Via Torre 3; ☏ 0863 912805; e ursitti@opionline.it. Making use of a popular surname from the area – Ursitti – this small lodging is set in a historic building. This does, however, mean that amenities are basic, with

only 2 bathrooms between the 5 rooms, which are simple though comfortable & well laid out. **$$**

🏠 **Il Giglio B&B** (3 apts) SS83, km49; 📞0863 916011; e ilgiglio@opionline.it. In a rural setting south of town on the SS83, this B&B overlooks the mountains & is surrounded by hills & trees. Apartments have their own kitchenette & bathroom as well as heating & hot water. Rooms are simply decorated though spacious & comfortable. **$$**

🏠 **La Sosta B&B** (6 rooms) Via Marsicana 17; 📞0863 916057; e lasosta@opionline.it; www. pescasseroli.biz/lasosta. This B&B with lovely views over the surrounding mountains & valley has tastefully decorated rooms & elegant public areas. An excellent b/fast consists of homemade breads, cakes & jams. Staff are very accommodating & will go the extra measure to make your stay pleasant. **$$**

Camping Both the following campsites are in very peaceful locations, and charge around €8 per person per night.

🏕 **Campeggio Le Foci** Via Fonte dei Cementi; 📞0863 912233; e lefoci@opionline.it. A good choice for campers, a short drive northeast of town, with 125 tent pitches & 7 chalets.

🏕 **Campeggio Il Vecchio Mulino** SS83, km52; 📞0863 912232; e vecchiomulino@opionline.it. This campsite is a 5-min drive east of town near the Val Fondillo & has 90 places for tents as well as space for caravans.

✖ WHERE TO EAT

✖ **Ristorante La Vecchia Locanda** SS83, km49 + 600; 📞0863 91936. Just outside town, on the SS83, this is pretty much the only restaurant in Opi.

It serves up delicious meals (its meat, particularly the lamb, is fantastic) using fine ingredients. Some excellent local house wine is also available. **$$**

OTHER PRACTICALITIES Other than the **chemist**, Farmacia Catallo (*Via San Giovanni 6; tel 0863 912758*), there are very few amenities in the town. Head to Pescasseroli instead.

EVENTS

August La Sagra dei Gnocchi. If you are in town during the gnocchi festival, you are indeed lucky! Try gnocchi with various sauces, though personally I think one of the best is the traditional gnocchi with *ragù* sauce.

October Festa dei Sapori d'Autunno. For the Feast of Autumn Flavours the town is decorated with the colours of autumn and various local dishes are on offer, such as *arrosticini* (see page 42), locally grown chestnuts, and cakes such as the *ciambella* (a round, simple but tasty sponge cake).

WHAT TO SEE AND DO The simple **Parish Church of Santa Maria Assunta** (📞 *0863 910653;* ⊕ *daily;*) was built in the 12th century and preserves its old belfry, though everything has required restoration due to earthquake damage. Above the main entrance is a plaque dated 1656 and the views through its side windows to the rooftops of the main road below are charming. The other church in town is the small, Baroque **Chapel of San Giovanni Battista** with an elegant altar made of marble.

At the end of the town's main road, Via San Giovanni, there is a **defence tower**. Don't be fooled: it's not that old (the plaque reads 1903).

Museums

Museo del Camoscio/Museum of the Chamois (*Via Torre;* 📞 *0863 910715; www.opionline.it/museo.html;* ⊕ *summer, daily 9.00–13.00 & 15.00–19.00; winter,* depending on level of tourism; admission €1) This little, four-room museum has lots of information on the chamois (see page 8), which is native to Abruzzo. Displays recreate such things as its habitat and even a sample of its droppings. Ideal for kids.

Museo dello Sci/Ski Museum (*Opi Municipio, Via San Giovanni 30; tourist office* ☎*0863 916073; admission free;* ⊕ *Mon–Fri 09.00–14.00*) This tiny museum has only one room, decked out with ski equipment from throughout the 20th century.

SKIING IN OPI Skiing in the immediate area is mostly of the cross-country variety. The **Macchiarvana Plateau** is the main location, and **Sci Club Opi** (*Via Domenico Ursitti 2;* ☎ *0863 910622;* e *sciclubopi@opionline.it*) hosts competitions here. They can also provide further information on skiing in the local area, as can the tourist office in the town hall. However, most people head for the skiing in and around Pescassèroli due to the better amenities, equipment hire and ski schools.

FONDILLO VALLEY

The Val Fondillo is a must-see on any visit to the national park, especially for nature lovers and those in search of the outdoors. Its thick forests contain a rich selection of flora and fauna and kilometres of walking tracks. The entrance to the valley is relatively developed and amenities range from bike hire and picnic equipment hire (see page 177) to horseriding and parking for cars, caravans and motorbikes (€3, €5, €1 respectively). You will need to take your own food supplies, drink and hiking gear.

Accommodation is scarce in the immediate area, but since the valley is close to the towns of Opi, Pescassèroli and Villetta Barrea, most people tend to use one of these as a base.

GETTING THERE
By car The Fondillo Valley is off the SS83 and is well signposted.

By bus The valley has a request bus stop at the entrance. The ARPA route that links the towns of the national park, beginning in either Avezzano or Castel di Sangro, passes this stop. See page 167 for more information on getting around.

ACTIVITIES
Hiking and cycling trails Various trails branch out from the valley entrance (known as the Centro Foresta) into the depths of the valley and its surrounding mountains. While maps are available at the entrance to the valley, at the time of writing there was no tourist information available in English so the main hiking tracks are described below. Estimated times are based on one way. It is also possible to buy an excellent map of the national park, which sets out the valley in some detail. You can purchase this at the valley entrance or directly from the park's head office (see *Tourist information*, page 168).

The valley's main trails are marked with the letter 'F', followed by a number. While there is bicycle hire at the entrance to the valley (see below), F2 and F4 are the only bike-friendly trails – and even then there are sections where you will need to alight and walk.

F1: Grotta Fondillo to Monte Amaro (medium difficulty; 2½ hours) The trail, which winds its way up to the Amaro peak at just under 1,900m above sea level, can be a little testing and is best done in summer. It is especially good if you are hoping to catch a glimpse of Abruzzo's chamois.

F2: *Centro Foresta to Passo dell'Orso* (medium difficulty; 3 hours) While this is the longest continuous trail in the park, it is actually relatively easy. It begins at the Centro Foresta and continues to the Passo dell'Orso. Large sections of this trail can be covered on a bicycle (at least theoretically; it is often overgrown and strewn with pot-holes, so take care).

F3: *Centro Foresta to Opi (Le Casette)* (easy; 45 minutes) This short, easy trail takes you from the valley to close by the town of Opi.

F4: *Colle Frasinetto to Alta Valle Fredda* (easy; 1 hour) This actually starts at the **Grotte di Fondillo** and winds its way up to the Valle Fredda ('Cold Valley'). It is possible to follow this track on a bicycle, although the same warnings apply as those to the F2.

F5: *Acquasfranatara to Valico Gravare* (medium difficulty; 3 hours) Branching off from the F2 trail, this route ascends to around 1,900m with some excellent views to be had through the trees, though it can be a little testing as it is often quite steep.

F6: *Valle Sfranatara to Valico Inguagnera* (medium difficulty; 1 hour) This trail branches off from the F5 and also reaches over 1,900m above sea level but is relatively short.

F7: *Alta Valle Fredda to Il Coppo* (easy; 30 minutes) Not far from the end of the F4 trail is the start of the F7. It is short and relatively flat, making for a pleasant stroll.

F8: *Alta Valle Fredda to Monte la Felcia* (medium difficulty; 1 hour) Again, another short trail – beginning at the end of the F4 – and winding its way up to around 1,900m.

F9: *Alta Valle Fredda to Valle Inguagnera* (medium difficulty; 3 hours) Starting at the junction of the F4 and F8 trails, the distances covered on this trail aren't huge but it can be demanding, particularly since you will have already walked for an hour to get to the starting point. It does offer some good opportunities to spot wildlife such as the chamois.

F10: Ponte Forcone to Monte Marsicano (medium difficulty; 4 hours) This track begins outside the valley, just off the SS83 at the 53rd km. It's a long hike and climb so if you plan to do it in a day it is best to start early. The perfect time for the hike is on a sunny autumn or spring day when the temperatures are neither too hot nor cold.

Picnic equipment hire You will need to bring most of your own equipment, though the larger stuff is available for hire. A picnic table will cost €6, a grill (or barbecue) is €4 (not including the wood, which is €2).

Bicycle hire There are bikes for hire at the Centro Foresta: half-hour, €2 (which wouldn't allow you to get very far); 1 hour, €3; half day, €8; one day €15

Horseriding (15 minutes (children only) €6; half-hour €11; one hour €15; half day €50; one day €90) Riding a horse is an excellent way to give your sore legs a break, cover a lot of ground and have some fun. Please note that a guide is provided

PAIESE ME' BY ARTURO URSITTI

Arturo Ursitti was a 20th-century local poet who dedicated many poems to his home town. The one below, *Paiese Me'*, is written in the local dialect. It is also translated into both standard Italian and English (although the translation cannot do it justice).

PAIESE ME' (LOCAL DIALECT)	PAIESE ME' (ITALIAN)	PAIESE ME' (ENGLISH)
Ddù file de case 'ngiallite, ddù vie che mezzane i'fiate, ddù chiese pe' tanta peccate, tre funde, tre funde seccate.	Due file di case ingiallite, due vie che mozzano il fiato, due chiese per tanti peccati, tre fonti, tre fonti seccate.	Two rows of yellow-hued houses, two roads that take away your breath, two churches for many sins, three springs, three springs, dry
sott'a 'nne colle de vènde.	sopra un colle di vento.	atop a windy hill.
La Foce: 'na conca sfennata, 'na conca 'i sedore sedate 'mmes'a ddù valle fierite: 'na loggia pe' quacc'affaciata,	La Foce: una conca sfondata una conca di tanto sudore, in mezzo a due valli fiorite: una loggia per qualche affacciata	The mouth: a worn-out basin, a basin of much sweating, in the midst of a flowering valley: a lodging for someone appearing
sott'a 'nne ciele pelite.	sotto un cielo pulito.	beneath a clean sky.

with every horse, and hard hats are available. Approach the Centro Foresta for details and a guide.

AROUND THE FONDILLO VALLEY

La Camosciara (*www.camosciara.com*) The Camosciara is another reserve a few kilometres from the Fondillo Valley. Amongst the highlights are an **old steam train** (€5 return) that whisks you from the car park area to the Piazza Camosciara. Other attractions include the area's fauna and various trekking paths, which all start from the same piazza. Along with the Fondillo Valley, this area was the original nucleus of the national park, founded in 1921.

Bike hire (1 hour, €4; 2 or more hours, €6) is available here from stands in Piazza Camosciara.

VILLETTA BARREA

Lying between Mount Mattone (1,814m) and the western end of the **Lago di Barrea**, Villetta Barrea sneaks just within the boundaries of the national park. It is found on the SS83 about halfway between Opi and Barrea and is an ideal place to use as a base for exploring the area around Lake Barrea. The lake, nearby, is in a dramatic location hundreds of metres above sea level, nestled amongst the mountains. Villetta Barrea is not the most fascinating or attractive village in the region – its buildings are not particularly old or characteristic of the region and there is little to do in town – but its amenities are manifold.

TOURIST INFORMATION

⛏ Pro Loco Tourist Information Via B Virgilio 1; ☎0864 89333; ☺ daily. This tourist office is one of the best in the national park. They can provide information on accommodation in the area, as well as excursions & tours. It is managed & run by **Scuola di Escursionismo Naturalistico 'I Camosci'** (*www.camminatura.com*) who run walks (including night-time walks), excursions, trekking & educational programmes for people of all ages.

WHERE TO STAY

⌂ Hotel degli Olmi (32 rooms) Via Fossato 8/B; ☎0864 89159; ℮ info@hotel-olmi.it; www.hotel-olmi.it. This hotel is a little closer to town than Hotel del Lago & the accommodation is a little more attractive & spacious. The staff are friendly, & there is access to a gym, kids' play area & a particularly nice swimming pool. **$$$**

⌂ Hotel del Lago (34 rooms) Via Roma 1; ☎0864 89388; ℮ info@albergodellago.com; www.albergodellago.com. A short drive from town & set facing the lake, Hotel del Lago's rooms are comfortable if straightforward & utilitarian. The hotel has a restaurant & bar area & the friendly staff can provide information on the area's attractions. HB & FB options available. **$$$**

⌂ Hotel Il Pescatore (30 rooms) Via Roma 80; ☎0864 89347; ℮ geampesc@virgilio.it; www.albergoristorantepescatore.com. This hotel next to the API petrol station has good-sized, bright & airy rooms; those with a balcony are particularly appealing. The hotel also has its own restaurant, bar & TV room. There is even a 'disco', as well as a spa offering massages & treatments, & a sauna. **$$$**

⌂ De Sanctis Apartments (6 apts) Via Casette 58; ☎0864 89298; ℮ info@appartamentidesanctis.it; www.appartamentidesanctis.it. Found conveniently near the tourist office, these attractive & clean apartments have double or triple bedrooms, & all have a private bathroom & provide bed linen. Pets are allowed. **$$**

WHERE TO EAT

✕ Il Pescatore Via Roma 80; ☎0864 89347; www.albergoristorantepescatore.com. This large hotel restaurant serves up some tasty dishes (ranging from homemade pasta to excellent fish from the Adriatic) & is popular with the locals. Since it is a rather large restaurant, it tends to host its fair share of wedding banquets. Tables can be booked online under 'Prenotazione Ristorante' (a very unusual feature for a restaurant in Abruzzo). $$

✕ **Ristorante Parco Nazionale D'Abruzzo** Via B Virgilio 53; ☎0864 89493. Very well located at the foot of the old town, this restaurant serves tasty dishes at good prices. The pizzas are very good, as are the meat dishes (both the beef & the lamb are excellent). $$

✕ **Ristorante Pizzeria La Lanterna** Via B Virgilio 52; ☎0864 89165; ⊕ daily 12.30–15.00 & 19.30–22.30, pizzas only 19.30–midnight. At the foot of the town's centre, this great-value restaurant serves some excellent pizzas as well as pasta & meat dishes. Note that the pizza menu is only available for dinner. It is popular with locals, who come not only for the food but also the friendly, intimate atmosphere. $

WHAT TO SEE AND DO The remains of the old **castle tower** can be seen in the residential area at the highest part of town. The tower has now been absorbed into the surrounding residential structures. The parish **Church of Santa Maria Assunta** has been rebuilt since World War II after it suffered extensive damage during both the 1915 earthquake and bombing during the war. It retains an 18th-century doorway and a few paintings from the same era. The town's other two churches, the **Church of San Michele** and the **Church of San Rocco**, have also both been rebuilt and restored during the 20th century.

The **Transhumance Museum** (*Il Museo della Transumanza, Via Roma; tourist office* ☎ *0864 89333; admission free;* ⊕ *winter only, usually from Jan onwards*) is a testament to the importance of the transhumance (see page 5) in the national park. The **Museum of Water** (Il Museo dell'Acqua) was closed at the time of writing though it is interesting to take a wander near the grounds of the modern hydro-electric power plant nearby.

AROUND VILLETTA BARREA

Civitella Alfedena On a clear, sunny day, the views from this town are magical. Not only do they take in Lake Barrea and the surrounding villages, but also the dazzling whitewashed walls and terracotta roofs of the town itself, framed by hills and mountains. The town is particularly well known for the flora and fauna found in the surrounding area and for its Museum of the Wolf and related enclosure.

Tourist information
🇮 **Pro Loco Ufficio Turistico** Piazza Plebiscito; ☎0864 890194; ⊕ usually Mon–Fri 16.00–19.00, Sat–Sun 10.00–13.00 & 16.00–19.00

 **Where to stay and eat**
🏠 **Albergo Al Luparo** (10 rooms) Via Colle Pizzuto 1; ☎0864 890504; e info@alluparo. com; www.alluparo.com. The combination of an attractive building & the fact that most rooms here have a balcony with a fantastic view of the lake & surrounding area makes this a worthwhile place to stay. The restaurant serves up some particularly tasty pasta dishes (such as the gnocchi with wild spinach). HB & FB options available. $$$

🏠 **Albergo Ai 4 Camosci** (26 rooms) Via Nazionale 25; ☎0864 890262; e aicamosci@tiscali.

it; www.geocities.com/ai4camosci. Set in the old town, this is a good place to base yourself. The hotel has simply decorated, no-frills rooms, as well as a relaxing outdoor area & a good restaurant serving local dishes. $$

🏠 **Albergo Antico Borgo La Torre** (20 rooms) Via Castello 3; ☎0864 890121; e info@ albergolatorre.com; www.albergolatorre.com. This is 1 of the nicest places to stay in town, set within the pretty historical centre & offering very reasonable prices for what is available. The

9

rooms are pleasant even if the look & feel of some of the décor (such as the colours of curtains & bedspreads) is a little dated. There is a restaurant & a lovely garden, decked out with sunloungers & umbrellas. **$$**

✕ Ristorante Il Transumante Via Santa Lucia, 1; ☎0864 890183. Good, simple food & fresh ingredients are the order of the day here. They serve up some excellent local meat dishes, such as lamb brochettes. **$$**

Shopping It is worth coming to Civitella Alfedena to buy a product or two at the intimate **La Betulla** (*Piazza Plebiscito;* ☎ *0864 890215;* e *info@labetullaonline.com; www.labetullaonline.com;* ⊕ *winter, Mon–Sat 09.30–13.00 & 16.00–19.30; summer, daily 09.00–24.00*), a cute shop dealing in all of kinds of local products, from honey, sweets and nuts to hams, cheeses and oils. Of particular interest are the various types of honey, including the artisan honey of Civitella Alfedena and others such as eucalyptus honey and sunflower honey. Opened around 15 years ago, this was the first shop dedicated to local produce in the national park. The knowledgeable owner, Pietro Santucci, is a professionally recognised tour guide who runs guided excursions of the area, most of which have a particular theme (such as their wildlife-watching tour, called the Lord of the Forest). Check their website for details.

What to see
Museo del Lupo/Museum of the Wolf (*Via Santa Lucia;* ☎ *0864 890141; admission adult €4, child €2;* ⊕ *summer daily 10.00–13.00 & 15.00–18.00; winter, Tue–Sun*) is dedicated to the Apennine, wolf and welcomes a steady stream of visitors to its educational displays. These shed light on the behaviour of this protected animal and there are displays recreating its habitat, as well as explanations on its diet, history and where the wolf is most commonly found. The dedicated staff here are very enthusiastic about protecting the wolf and can answer just about any question you throw at them.

Take the road beside the museum and you will reach the **Wolf Sanctuary**. Here, you might be lucky enough to spot a wolf or two that has been brought into the sanctuary to be looked after having been found injured, before being released back into the wild.

Other attractions If you continue further up this road you come to the **Belvedere San Lucia**, a square that has a panoramic view of the lake and surrounding area. The town's main **Church of San Nicola** has a choir and frescoes dating back to the Baroque period.

BARREA AND LAGO DI BARREA

This is arguably one of the most awe-inspiring spots in the whole of the region of Abruzzo. The view from Barrea's main car park (just outside the old town) down to Lake Barrea, over to the surrounding mountains and across the town's terracotta roofs really brings home the beauty of Abruzzo and its landscape. The fact that the lake itself is manmade (work began after World War II) takes nothing away from its dramatic setting and jagged shoreline.

There isn't a whole lot to do in Barrea, besides absorbing the atmosphere of the old streets and lanes of its historic centre and gazing out upon the lake.

TOURIST INFORMATION
◪ Pro Loco Ufficio Turistico Via Roma 1; ☎0864 88227. Provides information on Barrea & the surrounding area.

WHERE TO STAY

⌂ **Hotel Holidays** (25 rooms) Via Palombara Nuova 133; ☏0864 88370; e admin@hotel-holidays.it; www.hotel-holidays.it. The décor isn't to everyone's taste (lots of '80s furniture with dubious colours) & the website is arguably not very user-friendly, but the hotel provides good accommodation with its comfortable rooms. The restaurant here is good (despite the décor) & serves simple but delicious spaghetti with *ragù*. **$$$**

⌂ **Hotel Lago Verde** (40 rooms) Via Sarentina Inferiore 154; ☏0864 88522; e info@hotellagoverde.it; www.hotellagoverde.it. You will find this hotel at the foot of town, on the shores of the lake. The views from the hotel, whilst not as sweeping as those from the town above, are still grand. Rooms offer most mod cons, & while a bit on the chintzy side are comfortable & clean. The hotel's restaurant is known for its excellent dishes using local produce. **$$$**

⌂ **Hotel La Poiana** (7 rooms) Spiaggia 'La Gravara', Località Masseria 1; ☏0864 88106; e info@albergolapoiana.it; www.albergolapoiana.it. This small rural hotel, with lovely rooms decorated in soft rustic browns & wall paintings, is situated on the shores of Lake Barrea. There's a perfectly good hotel restaurant. **$$**

Camping

⛺ **Camping La Genziana** Loc Tre Croci; ☏0864 88101; e pasettanet@tiscali.it; www.campinglagenzianapasetta.it. 'Peace, quiet & tranquillity' is the motto at this campsite 1km south of town, & that is what you get. It's quite a large site, situated about 1,100m above sea level, & comprises a picturesque camping area & a cooking area. *€8 pp*

✕ WHERE TO EAT

✕ **Ristorante Pizzeria Il Giardino** Via Roma 39; m 347 9543561. Conveniently situated in the town near the tourist information desk is this restaurant & pizzeria, with a warm & friendly atmosphere & excellent pizzas & pasta dishes to boot. The staff are often ready for a chat. **$$**

✕ **Ristorante Pizzeria La Tana dell'Orso** Via P San Rocco 60; ☏0864 88125. 'The Bear's Cave' restaurant dishes out some hearty meat dishes that are very satisfying after a full day of sightseeing. Simple décor with a bucolic edge lends an intimate ambience. **$$**

SHOPPING There are a few very worthwhile local produce shops in the old town, amongst them the excellent **D'Amico Italo Alimentari Diversi** (*Viale Duca degli Abruzzi 16*; ☏ *0864 88140*; ⊕ *Fri–Wed 09.00–13.00 & 17.00–20.00, Thu 09.00–13.00*) with their shop window full of grappa and local limoncello in quirky lady's shoe bottles. Another one to try is **Sapori d'Abruzzo**, a little further down the road.

WHAT TO SEE AND DO The best thing to do in Barrea is to simply wander around. The steep alleyways are dotted with medieval buildings and each rooftop is framed by views of the lake and mountains.

BAR OR OLD CAR YARD?

CINE LOCANDA (*Belvedere Il Colle, Barrea*; ☏ *328 6952273*; ⊕ *11.00–late*) For such a small town, it is rare to find a bar of this calibre. The interior is decked out with old car parts and bits of traffic lights and – although this doesn't sound promising – it is all tastefully arranged by owner Luca Cirasola. The bar has access to the terrace above and a lovely garden, which also houses the town's nativity scene during Christmas (the statues are actually left there all year). Cine Locanda also sells locally made products such as biscuits, and is definitely the grooviest place for miles to sit, have a drink & relax.

The first thing to do when you arrive in town is to stop at the circular car park with its **lookout point**, which has a sign to explain exactly what you are looking at across the lake, town and mountains.

From here, follow the road that leads directly to the old town. As you pass the main **archway** into the medieval town, follow Via Castello on the right; this leads to the town's **castle ruins,** which are usually closed, though the remaining walls and tower are visible. The main church in town is that of **San Tommaso** (⏲ usually closed to public; open for services around 16.00–16.30), with a belltower that is visible from the lake and surrounding area. The interior is Baroque and is worth a stop if you are around during Mass.

The **lake** has enough picnic areas, playgrounds and 'beaches' to entertain the whole family, yet it rarely gets crowded, even at the height of summer. Though it's possible to walk to the lake, the route is along the main road so it's not the most scenic of options.

AROUND BARREA
Alfedena Situated just outside the boundaries of the national park, Alfedena is a nondescript modern town. However, it has particularly striking **castle ruins** that can be reached on foot. The town is situated on the SS83, a short drive from Barrea.

Scontrone A rocky cliff is home to the small village of Scontrone, whose medieval layout is preserved alongside **defence towers** and the 13th-century **Church of Santa Maria Assunta**, which retains old frescoes alongside numerous modern paintings from the 1990s.

SCANNO

Winner: Most Beautiful Villages in Italy; population around 2,000
Densely packed medieval palazzi, terracotta rooftops, church spires and quirky ancient doors: this is Scanno. It is a picturesque, relatively secluded village in the upper Saggitario Valley and is one of the highlights of any visit to the area. Its architecture mixes the eccentric and the classic, and the injunction to ditch the guidebook applies here more than to any other village in the area. Scanno – well known for cheese, cheese and more cheese (think *pecorino classico*, *ricotta*, *gregoriano*, etc) – lies at 1,050m.

HISTORY The presence of a pre-Roman settlement here has been confirmed by various archaeological finds in the area. Found in a nearby abbey, the first document attesting to Scanno's presence dates from 1067. Its name still resembles those given to the town over the centuries: from Scageum to Scannum to Scamnum. Despite the town's growth during the Middle Ages, it was not until the 17th and 18th centuries that it reached the height of its wealth. Much of this was derived from its natural resources, the woodlands and pasture for herds of animals, and its extensive production of wool thanks to large flocks of sheep. Brigands and emigration took their toll on the town's population during the 19th century, but today the population seems on a slow but steady increase thanks to the local tourism industry and the nearby national park.

GETTING THERE
By car From Pescara or Rome, leave the A25 motorway at Cocullo and follow the SS479 (a beautiful drive) through Anversa degli Abruzzi, Villalago and eventually to Scanno.

By train Catch a train from Pescara (around 1½ hours) or Rome (up to 3 hours) to either Sulmona or Anversa and then the ARPA bus to Scanno, which will take around 50 minutes.

By bus ARPA runs a service beginning at Rome's Tiburtina station and continuing on to Sulmona and then Scanno, stopping at various villages along the way. From Rome, it is a lengthy trip at just under three hours, and will set you back around €15. It is quicker and more comfortable to take the train.

TOURIST INFORMATION

🄸 IAT Scanno Piazza S Maria della Valle 12; ☏0864 74317; e scanno@abruzzoturismo.it.

Located just outside the old town across the road from the Church of Santa Maria della Valle.

🏠 WHERE TO STAY

🏠 Hotel Acquevive (33 rooms) Via Circumlacuale; ☏0864 74388; www.hotelacquevivescanno.com. In a pretty spot by the water, Hotel Acquevive offers decent & well-appointed rooms. It has a good restaurant, & is quite popular with Italian holidaymakers due to its position; relaxation on the shores of the lake is the order of the day. $$$

🏠 Hotel Belvedere (40 rooms) Piazza S Maria della Valle 3; ☏0864 747420; e info@belvederescanno.it; www.belvederescanno.it. In a convenient location near the main church in town & the tourist office, & belying first appearances, Belvedere has comfortable rooms with good views in a great location. Book in advance, particularly during the winter months. HB & FB options available. $$$

🏠 Hotel del Lago (24 rooms) Via del Lago 202; ☏0864 74343; info@hoteldellagoscanno.com; www.hoteldellagoscanno.com. Situated in a pretty spot on the shores of Lake Scanno near to a charming little church, Hotel del Lago has good-sized & spotlessly clean, if rather plain, rooms. There is also a bar & TV room. HB & FB available. $$$

🏠 Hotel Garden (30 rooms, 5 suites) Viale del Lago 79; ☏0864 747475; e info@hotelclubscanno.it; www.hotelclubscanno.it/garden. A good-value hotel given its 4-star rating (the only 1 in Scanno), the Garden is a modern block perched above the town. It has well-maintained, modern-ish rooms with private bathrooms. The public areas are elegant & there's a good restaurant, games room & TV room. HB & FB. $$$

🏠 Hotel Grotta dei Colombi (16 rooms) Viale dei Caduti 64; ☏0864 74393; e grottadeicolombi2002@libero.it; www.

grottadeicolombi.it. This is a good option not far from the historic town, & with a suitably bucolic interior design. The rooms are simple & comfortable with attractive wooden furniture. $$$

🏠 Hotel Mille Pini (25 rooms) Via Pescara 2; ☏0864 74387; e informazioni@millepiniscanno.it; www.millepiniscanno.it. A friendly, family-run hotel about 0.5km from the old town. The alpine-style building has a rustic feel, with simply decorated but comfortable rooms, & a decent restaurant & b/fast room serving up a tasty start to the day. The hotel offers various themed packages that include trekking, mountain biking & well-being weekends. Check website for updates. $$$

🏠 La Baita B&B (7 rooms) Via Pescara; ☏0864 747826; e info@labaitadiscanno.it; www.labaitadiscanno.com. This is a B&B with a twist: it has its own restaurant & even a bar, with a good selection of beers. It was refurbished in 2012. The rooms are simple but cosy & full of character. One of the best options for good-value accommodation in Scanno. $$

🏠 B&B La Casa di Costanza (5 rooms) Via Napoli 27; ☏0864 747821; e info@lacasadicostanza.com; www.lacasadicostanza.com. Friendly owner Costanza provides a warm, typically Abruzzese welcome in her home, with old-fashioned but well-furnished & comfortable rooms & a great b/fast. Costanza & her husband also own Il Palazzo (see below). $$

🏠 Il Palazzo B&B (3 rooms) Via Ciorla 25; ☏0864 747860. Costanza & her husband (see above) also own this place set in a historic townhouse. $$

🍴 WHERE TO EAT

Because of the well-established domestic tourist market in Scanno, most hotels offer half- and full-board options and therefore have good restaurants

Scanno is particularly well known in Italy because of its women's fashion. No, we're not talking about the latest in Prada heels or the Louis Vuitton Speedy 30 bag (which seems to be so popular in Pescara), but a different kind of dress. During the 17th–18th centuries, the women of Scanno developed a traditional costume consisting of a black dress adorned with homemade lace and an often-colourful apron, and topped with a distinctive flat headdress.

The fashion arose alongside the growth of the wool and dyeing industries. During the 1700s, the women whose business it was to make these garments were renowned throughout the Kingdom of Naples for their aptitude in weaving cloth.

Whilst you can't fault Scanno for making use of this colourful attire for the purposes of drawing in a crowd or two, there are still many women today who wear the garment on a day-to-day basis and it is not unusual to see a local woman going about her business in this archaic costume.

serving the best local dishes made from the freshest ingredients (reputation is paramount). Also try:

✕ **Ristorante Agli Archetti** Via Silla 8; ☎0864 74645. Situated in an early 20th-century *palazzo* this restaurant is noted for its good vegetarian dishes. In particular try the *maccheroncini Agli Archetti*, a little arch-shaped pasta. **$$**

✕ **Ristorante Alla Fonte** Via Fontana Saracco 3; ☎0864 747390. Alla Fonte is a simply decorated restaurant with a friendly atmosphere that is fostered by its excellent staff. It is a good choice, with some very tasty local dishes & a good selection of drinks. Try the *chitarra con ragù d'agnello* (pasta with lamb sauce). **$$**

✕ **Ristorante Costanza e Roberto** Via Roma 15; ☎0864 74345; www.lacasadicostanza.com. Owner Costanza (who also owns a couple of B&Bs in town,

see above) cooks up a feast in her little restaurant, making the best use of the town's speciality – cheese. Try the excellent *pasta alla chitarra*. A good selection of regional wines is also on the menu. **$$**

✕ **Ristorante da Mirella** Via del Lago 123; ☎0864 74552. This place has good food, especially the pasta dishes, & drinks, as well as friendly staff. Decoration is simple & the atmosphere no frills. **$$**

🍰 **Bar Pasticceria Pan dell'Orso** Viale del Lago 20; ☎0864 74475; www.deliziepandellorso. com. This is arguably the best pastry & sweets shop in town, loved by locals. Once inside, past the flowers around the entrance, you are overwhelmed with the choice of cakes, tarts & all manner of sweet things. **$**

OTHER PRACTICALITIES
Banks
$ **Banca Toscana ATM** Piazza S Maria della Valle 1
$ **Banca di Credito Coop di Roma** Via Napoli 19
$ **Carispaq** Via Fuori Porta S Maria 4

Chemist
✚ **Farmacia Mancinelli** Via Abramo 13; ☎0864 74348

Post office
✉ **Central post office** Via Napoli 19; ☎0864 747715; ⊕ Mon–Fri 08.00–13.30, Sat 08.00–12.30

EVENTS
5 January Le Chezzette. This event takes place on the evening of Epiphany. Young men, dressed in traditional black capes and hats, wander the streets singing at the windows of the young women of town.

First Sunday in July Madonna delle Grazie. A procession honouring the Virgin Mary. Hundreds of men, women and children accompany an effigy of the Madonna around the town.

14 August Il Catenaccio. In somewhat unreconstructed style, couples marry in traditional costume and the grooms line the streets as the women are accompanied from their homes to the church, then head back to the man's house, where they will start their new life.

10 November Le Glorie di San Martino. An evening honouring the legend of San Martino who, in an act of kindness, cut his cloak in half on a cold, rainy night to share with a beggar on the road. Large fires are lit and stalls offer many types of local dishes.

Christmas One of the most notable Christmas events in Scanno is its live nativity set. Residents of the town and people from elsewhere in the region recreate scenes thoughout the town centre that tell the story of Christmas.

WHAT TO SEE AND DO As in many other towns in Abruzzo, the best way to explore is simply to wander around, up, down and through the steep and narrow alleyways of picturesque Scanno.

Churches
Parish Church of Santa Maria della Valle (⊕ during the day excluding lunchtime) This nave and two-aisle church is located right at the entrance to the old town centre, across from the tourist information centre. It contains some lovely frescoes, especially on its pillars, discovered after restorers removed the church's Baroque decoration. (They are now behind glass for preservation.) The doorway is noteworthy, built in 1563, and the church has a striking marble altar dating from 1732. The belltower dates from the 16th century.

Church and Convent of Santa Maria delle Grazie (⊕ during the day) This Baroque church is neat and compact, although its interior is quite ornate, especially the altar with its statue of the Madonna. It is not old by Scanno standards, having been founded in 1733.

Church of San Giovanni (⊕ during the day) Although the building of this church itself is not especially interesting, it does have a display of 18 wooden religious statues, some over 300 years old. These were once housed in various other churches across the town.

Church of Santa Maria di Constantinopoli (⊕ during the day) Found in Piazza San Rocco, this church is famous for housing its striking, detailed and colourful fresco dating back to 1418, the *Enthroned Madonna and Child.*

Museums
Museo della Lana/Wool Museum (*Via Calata Sant'Antonio;* ☎ *0864 747203; www.muvi.org/museodellalana;* ⊕ *Jun–Sep, daily 10.00–12.30 & 16.30–19.00; winter, on request*) This little museum, inaugurated in the mid-90s, outlines in some detail the history of pastoralism and the wool industry of Abruzzo. Of particular interest are the displays of old looms and tools used to produce the yarn.

Scanno is situated along the SS479, a road whose southern end marks the border of the Abruzzo National Park. Cutting through the Montana Peligna area from Villetta Barrea all the way to Anversa degli Abruzzi, it makes for a drive through spectacular scenery where keeping your eyes on the road can be a chore. During summer, the peach-hued hills are the epitome of a Mediterranean landscape, and it is not unusual to find wandering flocks of sheep making their way from one pasture to the next. Adding to the experience are Scanno, Villalago and Anversa degli Abruzzi – three of Abruzzo's 19 'most beautiful villages in Italy' (see box, page 25).

Civic buildings The town of Scanno has some notable and interesting examples of civic architecture dating back centuries. These include: **Palazzo Nardillo, Palazzo Mosca, Palazzo di Rienzo, Palazzo Serafini Ciancarelli, Palazzo Colarissi** and **Palazzo de Angelis**. Most, but particularly Nardillo, Mosca and de Angelis, have striking and imposing portals. Keep an eye out for these portals framing wooden doors with their intricate handles.

SKIING IN THE AREA Scanno is close to Monterotondo and Passo Godi, two of the region's most popular ski slopes. **Monterotondo** is reached by a chairlift that will whisk you from the outskirts of town to the slopes. The runs here are not numerous (there are around six), but it's a good place to ski if you don't wish to venture too far from town.

Passo Godi Passo Godi is, by far, the better of the two skiing areas. It is around 10km from Scanno along the SS479 towards Villetta Barrea. A daily ski pass here will set you back around €16, while a seasonal pass will cost around €110.

There are eight slopes (five easy, two medium and one hard) and four chairlifts. There is also tobogganning here. For more information, contact the park's managing authority (*Monte Godi SRL;* \ *0864 74480;* e *info@scannopassogodi.com; www.scannopassogodi.com*).

AROUND SCANNO
Lago di Scanno Lake Scanno is found to the north of the town and is a popular destination during the summer months. The lake has an artificial pebble beach, various kiosks and bike hire.

Where to stay See *Where to stay* in Scanno, page 183, for accommodation options. There is also a campsite here:

Å **Villa Lago Riviera** \ 0864 740100. A mid-
sized camping ground that offers basic amenities.
€10 pp

Lago di San Domenico This small manmade lake north of Lake Scanno is worth a mention for its crystal-clear water. It doesn't really have an accessible shoreline, so you will have to park the car along the SS479 and reach it along one of the few access paths created by others who, like yourself, couldn't resist the lure of the blue water.

VILLALAGO

Winner: Most Beautiful Villages in Italy; population around 600

Charming Villalago, founded around AD1000, is one of 19 towns and villages in Abruzzo considered as the country's most beautiful villages under the 'I Borghi Più Belli d'Italia' programme. The village sits peacefully at 930m on Mount Argonetta, its ancient buildings clinging onto the cliff face.

There are no 'sights' as such and the real attractions are the narrow streets and alleys of its medieval street pattern. However, the **Church of Santa Maria di Loreto** is a hidden gem, with its striking 15th-century doorway. Inside is the 16th-century painting of the *Madonna of the Rosary*, which is definitely worth a look. The town's other church of note is that of **San Michele Arcangelo**, founded in the 18th century.

For foodies, it's worth noting that Villalago specialises in *pacchiarozze*, a *fettucine*-style pasta with lamb and *pecorino* cheese sauce.

 WHERE TO STAY

🏠 **Hotel Stella Alpina** (28 rooms) Via Roma 1; ✆0864 740132; e stellalpinahotel@libero.it; www.hotelclubscanno.it. This hotel offers sound, basic accommodation. Rooms are clean & comfortable, some large family ones with bunk beds as well as a double. There's also a restaurant, TV room & games room. HB & FB available. **$$$**

ANVERSA DEGLI ABRUZZI

Winner: Most Beautiful Villages in Italy; population around 400

Approach this very attractive small village on the SS479 from Villalago for truly breathtaking and memorable views. Anversa is one of the loveliest villages in Abruzzo. It is situated almost 600m above sea level on a spur that overlooks the Sagittario Gorge, carved, as the name suggests, by the river of the same name. Some of the first documents relating to the town date back to the 12th century, when the town – which was founded around AD1000 – already possessed its own courthouse. It prospered until the 17th century before it was devastated by a plague that spread from Naples. The town was later partly destroyed by the earthquake of 1706. However, careful restoration works over subsequent centuries have returned it to its former glory. Today, Anversa degli Abruzzi is known locally for its smoked ricotta cheese.

TOURIST INFORMATION

🛈 **Tourist information point** Piazza Roma 1; ✆0864 49286. Publishes a comprehensive information pack on the village.
🛈 **Infopoint Natural Reserve of the Sagittario Gorge** Cooperative Dafne, Piazza Roma 1; ✆0864 49587; e golesaggitario@interfree.it. This provides information on the nearby Sagittario Gorge, including walks & excursions.

 WHERE TO STAY

🏠 **Bioagriturismo La Porta dei Parchi** Loc Fonte di Curzio; ✆0864 49354; e info@laportadeiparchi.it; www.laportadeiparchi.it. This welcoming agritourism establishment & 'diffused' hotel is greatly concerned with the preservation of the culture & the surrounding countryside (even inviting you to 'adopt' a sheep). Rooms are spotlessly clean, if simple. Their menu is excellent, & features the best of local cuisine using many natural & organic ingredients. They also produce & sell a wide variety of local cheese, ham, oil & honey. **$$**

✗ WHERE TO EAT

✗ **La Fiaccola** Via Duca degli Abruzzi 12; ☎0864 49474. A good restaurant with a friendly atmosphere & rustic feel serving some excellent local dishes (try the *quagliatelli e fagioli*, a minestrone-style soup made with pasta). $$

WHAT TO SEE AND DO The village's **castle** is now no more than a handful of ruins, having been decimated by earthquakes. That said, you can still see its square stone tower and the remains of its walls.

At the foot of town on Piazza Roma is the **Church of Santa Maria delle Grazie** (currently closed to public, though ⊕ for weekday services 17.00). Its Renaissance doorway, made from limestone, dates back to 1540. The interior of the church, housing an interesting terracotta statue of St Roche, is laid out in the typical nave and two-aisle formation found elsewhere in the region.

Next to one of the village's gates you'll find the **Church of San Marcello**, which boasts both a noteworthy entrance and a fresco of the *Madonna with Child* dating back to the 1400s. Not far from this church is a **gateway** dating from 1666. Note the sculptures of a fish, a snake and a sword, images connected with San Domenico (after whom the nearby lake is named). Relatively close again are the local **houses of the Lombards**, built during the 15th and 16th centuries.

Sagittario Gorge This nearby gorge is a favourite spot with locals and is great for a stroll or picnic. It is actually a nature reserve and home to an abundance of flora and fauna. It also has its own botanic garden. To get there, drive east out of town along the main road for about five minutes; you can't miss it!

10

L'Aquila Province:
Majella National Park
and Surrounds

The L'Aquila side of the Majella National Park is as peaceful as it is picturesque. The Majella mountain range rises sharply immediately east of the flat valley that houses the ancient city of Sulmona, making the scenery dramatically beautiful. The area houses some charming towns such as Pacentro and Pescocostanzo and has some of the best skiing in the region during the winter months. See *Chapter 1* for details on the Majella National Park, including flora and fauna.

SUGGESTED ITINERARY

Start in the old city of Sulmona. Travel down the SS17 to the town of Pescocostanzo. If you're here during the winter months, some skiing (or an attempt at it!) is recommended. From here, wind your way back up through the edge of the Majella mountain range to the town of Pacentro. It is then only a short drive back to Sulmona. While you could do this in one day, allow two to three days to take in all the sights.

SULMONA

The small city of Sulmona is the prettiest of its size in Abruzzo. With an impressive array of churches and Roman ruins, and a number of quirky museums, there is enough to keep you occupied for at least a full day's sightseeing. Although it only has a population of around 25,000, it acquired its importance and wealth as a result of its position on the SS17 and its proximity to the Via Tiburtina. The Abruzzesi descend on the town during its Giostra Cavalleresca, a jousting festival held in summer.

HISTORY Little is known about Sulmona before the Romans arrived. However, it was one of the most important cities of the Peligni tribe, one of the Italic pre-Roman peoples who settled in the area. During this period it was probably known as Sulmo, and it seems to have largely escaped the destruction that accompanied Hannibal's attack on the region in the Second Punic War. It wasn't until the Social War (91–89BC) that Rome recognised the strategic and commercial value of the city, and around 49BC it was captured by the Roman general Domitius Calvinus. Sulmona thrived under the Romans, and was the birthplace of Ovid (43BC–AD17 or 18), the Roman poet.

After the fall of Rome, the city's importance waned. Then, in the 12th century, it began to thrive once more; the city expanded and an aqueduct was built to ensure a reliable supply of water. During this time, the city also acquired numerous churches and its fortified walls.

As with much of the surrounding area, Sulmona suffered greatly from a series of earthquakes in the early 1700s (most notably in 1706), though quite a few of

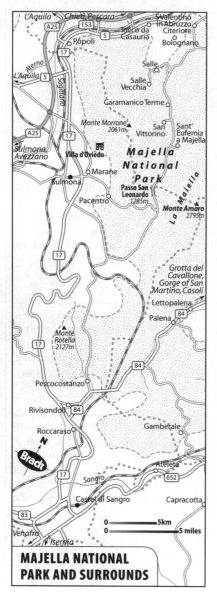

its landmark religious buildings escaped harm, as well as the city gates and aqueduct. With the coming of the railway connecting the city to Rome in the 19th century there was another period of growth and the city expanded considerably. A more grim side to Sulmona came to the fore in the 20th century with the building of Campo 78, a prisoner-of-war camp that was in use during both world wars. Today, Sulmona is the most important producer of *confetti* (sugared almonds) in Italy, and sees a considerable amount of domestic tourism, see box, page 193.

GETTING THERE

By car The city can be reached from the A25 motorway from either Rome or Pescara (take the turn-off for Sulmona), and is also on the important SS17 that runs through the middle of the region.

By bus Buses run by ARPA and Concapeligna (*www.concapeligna.it*) connect Sulmona to smaller towns as well as to Pescara, Rome and Naples. The journey to or from Pescara takes an hour and costs around €7. Services from L'Aquila take 1¼ hours and cost around €9.

By train Sulmona's railway station is connected to Rome and Pescara, but the train to Rome takes 2½–3 hours, and tickets are approximately €9. Trains from Pescara take from 1–1½ hours and cost around €4. The train journeys are not worth the time. The station is located southwest of town, and numerous buses run from here to the city centre.

TOURIST INFORMATION

🛈 **Abruzzo Promozione Turismo** Corso Ovidio 208; 📞0864 53276; e iat.sulmona@ abruzzoturismo.it

🏠 WHERE TO STAY

🏠 **Hotel Armando's** (21 rooms) Via Montenero 15; 📞0864 210783; e infoarmandos@ libero.it; www.hotelarmandos.it. This attractive

small hotel is set in tranquil surroundings not too far from the centre. The rooms are straightforward, modern & clean, & as a family-

Bus & railway station

Hotel Meeting (6km)

VIA LE STAZIONE CENTRALE
VIA PESCARA
VIA GENNARO SARDI

† Cathedral of San Panfilo

Ovidius

Museum of Image & Documentation

VIA G GALILEI

VIA COSTANZA

VIA DELLA CORNACCHIOLA

VIA GIACOMO MATTEOTTI

VIA FILIPPO TURATI

VIA CARSO

Parco Fluviale del Vella

VIALE ROOSEVELT

VIA IAPASSERI

VIALE PAPA GIOVANNI XXIII

Vella

Banca Caripe S

Santuario Ercole Curino →

VIA CIRCONVALLAZIONE OCCIDENTALE

✕ Clemente

VIA PORTA ROMANA

VIA SOLIMO

VIA VELLA

VIA CIRCONVALLAZIONE ORIENTALE

VIA GIOVANNI PANSA

VIA TRATTURO

VIA BARBATO

VIA ARAGONA

VIA GRAMSCI

VIA MORRONE

VIA CORFINIO

VIA STELLA

VIA PAOLINA

Santa Annunziata Complex ✚

i

VIA A DE NINO

Palazzo Sardi & Natural History Museum

VIA TORRONE

VIA E CIOFANO

VIA DELL'OSPEDALE

CORSO OVIDIO

VIA ARABONA

Piazza XX Settembre

VIA ROMA

VIA MARSELLI

VIA PELIGNA

San Filippo Neri ✚

Piazza Garibaldi

VIA CORFINIO

VIA QUATRARIO

VIA PANFILO MAZARA

† San Francesco della Scarpa

❖❖ Aqueduct

VIA CIRCONVALLAZIONE ORIENTALE

Santa Chiara Monastery & Diocesan Museum

Gallery of Modern & Contemporary Art

CORSO OVIDIO

VICO DELLE CONCIERIE

† Santa Maria of the Tomb

Piazza Plebiscito

VIALE TEOFILO PATINI

VIA DELLA CONA

N
Bradt

VIA VENEZIAN

Porta Napoli

V MAIELLA

Banca S di Roma

Hotel Armando's

0 ——— 100m
0 ——— 100yds

VIA TRIESTE

Museum of Sugared Almond Production ↓

run business the service has a nicely personal touch. **$$$**

🏠 **Hotel Meeting** (78 rooms) SS17, km95 + 500; 📞0864 251696; e meeting@arc.it; meeting. hotelsantacroce.com. This spacious hotel, found on the SS17 not far from the centre of town, is 1 of only 2 4-star establishments in Sulmona. It has spacious grounds, a swimming pool & comfortable if slightly old-fashioned rooms. Staff are extremely friendly & the owner is often there to greet guests. It is advisable to have your own transport. **$$$**

🏠 **Hotel Ovidius** (29 rooms) Via Circonvallazione Occidentale 177; 📞0864 53824; e info@ hotelovidius.it; www.hotelovidius.it. The Ovidius, named after the Roman poet, is on the city's ring road not far from the old centre. The owners & staff are helpful & attentive, taking great care to ensure the hotel runs smoothly. Rooms are pristine & well decorated, despite the somewhat questionable small dark floor tiles. Guests have access to a lounge & gym. Great value for money for a 4-star hotel. HB & FB. **$$$**

✖ WHERE TO EAT

✖ **Ristorante Clemente** Vico Quercia 5; 📞0864 52284. If there's one place you must eat at in Sulmona, it's Ristorante Clemente. The peach-hued arches & the wooden furniture of the interior create a wonderfully rustic dining experience. The house speciality is meat, though the pasta dishes & soups (such as the tasty potato, lentil &

chestnut soup) are also delicious. You must try the *cuoratello d'agnello* (a local lamb stew with onion) & the local *salsicce di fegato* (liver sausages) – they may not sound particularly appetising but they are scrumptious. For dessert, don't look past the *tiramisù* or the *panna cotta*. **$$$**

OTHER PRACTICALITIES

Banks
$ **Banca di Roma** Piazza Vittorio Veneto 7
$ **Banca Caripe** Piazza Tresca 3

Chemists
✚ **Farmacia Centrale** Piazza Vittorio Veneto 14; 📞0864 52645

✚ **Farmacia del Corso** Corso Ovidio 225; 📞0864 210830

Post office
✉ Piazza Brigata Majella 2/3; 📞0864 247237; 🕐 Mon–Fri 08.00–18.30, Sat 08.00–12.30

WHAT TO SEE AND DO

Medieval Sulmona Sulmona's medieval core is very compact and can easily be seen on foot. The majority of the town's significant monuments are clustered around **Corso Ovidio**, the focal point of the city since the Middle Ages.

The **Basilica Cathedral of San Panfilo Vescovo** (*Piazza del Duomo;* 📞 *0864 34739;* 🕐 *daily*), or duomo, is the main religious building in town, and an important example of 11th-century Romanesque architecture. It is supposedly built on the site of an ancient temple dedicated to Apollo with a nave and two aisles separated by round pillars. As with so many important religious monuments in Abruzzo, the cathedral was rebuilt in the Baroque style following the 1706 earthquake. The interior of the entrance is flanked by two 15th-century sarcophagi, and a fresco depicting Mary and Joseph, one each side of a crucifix. Two of the most important artefacts of the church are the 14th-century wooden crucifix, found halfway up the right-hand aisle, and a wooden choir dating from the 1700s. However, the real highlight is the church's crypt, built in around the 8th century and last restored as far back as 1075. The 12th-century relief of the *Madonna with Child* is particularly striking.

Piazza XX Settembre is the location of a monument to Ovid (see page 21) and the curiously named **Palazzo Giovanni dalle Palle** (Palazzo of John from the Balls), built in the late 1400s by a Venetian merchant of the same name. The building has been heavily modified and its striking entrance dates from the 18th century. The square gives a charming view of the dome and tower of the Santa Annunziata Complex.

The **Church of San Francesco della Scarpa** (St Francis of the Shoe), whose name derives from the resident monks' tradition of wearing shoes to church instead of clogs, is just off the southern end of Corso Ovidio. Building work on the church began during the late 13th century but it was ruined by the earthquake of 1706. However, the church façade still features a late 14th-century doorway by Nicola Salvitti. The dome paintings inside the church are of particular note because of their complexity. Also look out for the ate 14th-century frescoes, a wooden crucifix dating from the 15th century and a striking organ built around 1700.

The **Church of Santa Maria della Tomba** (Santa Maria of the Tomb) faces onto **Piazza Plebiscito** and dates from the 13th century, though its Gothic façade with a charming rose window is thought to have been added in the 15th century.

Porta Napoli is the most intact of Sulmona's old city gates, dating from the 14th century and incorporating Roman fragments.

The Santa Annunziata Complex This is perhaps the most architecturally and culturally significant monument in the old town centre. The complex has served many functions over the centuries, including as an orphanage, a church and, since the 1960s, a hospital. It was founded in 1320 and the current façade is a result of rebuilding over the years, especially during the 15th and 16th centuries. The extensions were added in the 1960s. The complex also houses a number of museums.

The **Civic Museum** (*Museo Civico; Palazzo dell'Annunziata;* \ *0864 210216;* ⊕ *Tue–Sun 09.00–13.00; admission €2, tickets also valid at the Diocesan Museum*) is set around a picturesque cloister and courtyard (with a rather incongruous-looking pair of palm trees), and contains a solid collection of historical artefacts such as bowls, tools, cooking implements and clothes, mainly from the valley of Peligno.

The **Archaeological Museum 'in Situ'**, or 'on site', displays the remains of a Roman residential complex which came to light during archaeological excavations on the site. The museum comprises a series of walking paths that allow the visitor to take in the remains without damaging them.

The small **Museum of Abruzzo-Molise Costume and Transhumance** (*Museo del Costume Abruzzese-Molisano e della Transumanza; Palazzo dell'Annunziata;* \ *0864 212962;* ⊕ *only on request; admission free*) is set in the room known as the Sala del Campanile, or Room of the Belltower, and has a collection of prints and paintings of historical costumes.

Piazza Garibaldi An excellent place to wrap up a day's sightseeing in Sulmona is the wonderful Piazza Garibaldi, which sits on the edge of the Majella National

---

CONFETTI

In Italian, *confetti* refers to the sugared almonds that are a nationwide confectionery used at events from baptisms to weddings. The almonds are coated with a thick layer of sugar (usually in white, light blue or pink), perfect for those who have a sweet tooth. The production of these sugared almonds is big business in Italy, and Sulmona is at the forefront of this sector, producing much of the nation's share. The Museum of the Art and Technology of Sugared Almond Production (see page 194) is a great way to explore methods and equipment used in the making of *confetti*.

Park, backed by the Majella mountain range. The square is the home of the city's marketplace and its main feature is the prominent **medieval aqueduct** with its 21 Gothic arches, built in 1256.

Don't let the aqueduct draw your attention away from the wealth of 16th–18th century buildings that line the square, such as the **Church of San Filippo Neri**, with its 14th-century doorway (taken from the erstwhile church of Sant'Agostino), and the **Monastery of Santa Chiara** with its Baroque interior featuring a number of striking paintings. The monastic complex also houses two other places of interest. The **Diocesan Museum of Sulmona** (*Museo Diocesano di Arte Sacra;* e *museodiocesanosulmona@muvi.org; www.muvi.org/museodiocesanosulmona*) hosts a collection of local religious artefacts and works of art, and the **Municipal Gallery of Modern and Contemporary Art** (*Pinacoteca Comunale di Arte Moderna e Contemporanea;* e *pinacotecasulmona@muvi.org; www.muvi.org/ pinacotecasulmona*), which contains paintings and sculptures from the last century. Both share a telephone number, entrance prices and opening hours (📞 *0864 212962; admission €1 to both;* ⊕ *Tue–Sun 09.30–13.00 & 15.30–19.30*).

Other museums Other museums in the city include:

Museo di Storia Naturale/Museum of Natural History (*Via Giuseppe Andrea Angeloni 11;* m *347 7228038;* ⊕ *Tue & Fri–Sat 10.00–13.00 & 16.00–19.30, outside these times, by appointment; admission €3*) Housed in the 16th-century **Palazzo Sardi**, this museum features displays on local geology and flora and fauna species.

Museo dell'Arte e della Tecnologia Confettiera/Museum of the Art and Technology of Sugared Almond Production (*Via Stazione Introdacqua 55;* 📞 *0864 210047;* ⊕ *Mon–Sat 08.30–12.30 & 15.00–18.30; admission free*) Full marks for originality here, but the idea of a museum to sugared almonds (*confetti*, in Italian) is not in any way unusual to the locals, for Sulmona is well known for the Pelino Sugared Almond factory. This museum is right next door, and the collection ranges from machinery to memorabilia dating from the 18th to 20th centuries.

Museo dell'Immagine e della Documentazione/Museum of Image and Documentation (*Rotonda San Francesco, Corso Ovidio;* 📞 *0864 211035;* ⊕ *Mon–Sat 16.00–20.00; admission free*) This museum has an excellent collection of photographic equipment used in the region in the last century.

AROUND SULMONA
The Santuario Ercole Curino The Roman sanctuary of Hercules Curino is situated on the western hills of the Majella National Park, a ten-minute drive east of Sulmona. As with all of Abruzzo's Roman sites, it can be visited any time of day and there is no entrance fee. The site is often overlooked and you will probably have it to yourself. Admittedly, there isn't much left of the complex, which dates back to around AD90. The most interesting part is a large section of intact staircase, from where the view over the valley is stunning. Excavations began in the 1950s and the site was, at first, thought to be Ovid's villa, but was later found to have been a Christian sanctuary.

Getting there Reaching the sanctuary can be tricky, despite the fact that it is clearly visible on the side of a mountain. Take the SS17 from Sulmona, exiting at Bugnara, then follow the signs for Badia. You will soon arrive at a monastic complex. From here, take the left-hand road and follow it to the end. Park your car and walk to the sanctuary (around ten minutes).

PACENTRO

Winner: Most Beautiful Villages in Italy; population around 1,300
The pretty town of Pacentro, east of Sulmona, was first settled around the 8th century, and occupies a lovely setting at 650m on the western hills of the Majella National Park. Aside from the castle, there isn't a particularly famous church or landmark; the town's real charms lie in its steep streets and abundant examples of medieval housing. Pacentro has gained some questionable celebrity as the home town of pop-queen Madonna's parents and grandparents. More usefully, it is renowned for its excellent meat dishes, and the 'peasant's dish', *La Polta*: fried peppers with oil, garlic, potatoes and beans.

 WHERE TO STAY AND EAT There is nowhere to stay in the town; it is best to base yourself in Sulmona, which is only 15 minutes away by car.

✕ **Ristorante Taverna de li Caldora di Pacentro** Piazza Umberto I 13; ☎ 0864 41139. This country-style restaurant is set in a 15th-century building in the heart of the old town. The owners cook up a feast of local food & it is excellent. The menu varies from season to season, but you might be lucky enough to be able to try *La Polta* (see above). Also good is the veal with peppers & truffles. $$$

WHAT TO SEE The **Cantelmo Castle** (closed at time of writing) manages to be both imposing and charming at the same time. Its two prominent towers, which can be seen from miles away, have become something of an icon of the Majella National Park. The structure retains its protective wall, and the interior layout dates back to at least the 13th century. Over the years, sections were added and restoration work carried out. Parts of the oldest tower, at the castle's northeast corner, date from as far back as the 9th century.

PESCOCOSTANZO

Pescocostanzo is widely held to be one of the most striking towns in central Italy. Its architectural and artistic gems include centuries-old houses and public buildings, set on a peaceful plateau in a southern corner of the Majella National Park.

HISTORY The town first appears in records of the 11th century as Pescus Constantii, but little is known of its early history. However, Roman burial sites from the 3rd century BC have been discovered in the area, which has led historians to believe that there was a considerable Roman presence here.

During the Middle Ages, particularly the 13th century, the town's population began to increase, partly because of civic works such as the building of the town's defensive walls. As with so many towns in Abruzzo, Pescocostanzo was largely destroyed by an earthquake in 1456, but the townspeople were quick to rebuild. As part of these rebuilding efforts a road, known as the Via degli Abruzzi, was constructed linking the area south to Naples and north as far as Florence. The town acquired considerable wealth from farming during the 16th–18th centuries but nowadays it largely survives on income from tourism.

GETTING THERE

By car Pescocostanzo's turn-off is on the SS17 (which can be reached via the A25 *autostrada*). It is also possible to reach the town through the Majella National Park along the SS84 and SS487.

By train The town's station is about 1km southeast of the old centre and is also shared with the neighbouring town of Rivisondoli. From Pescara, the journey takes around two hours (as opposed to around an hour by car) and costs around €6. Please note that you must change trains at Sulmona.

🏠 WHERE TO STAY

🏠 **Hotel Le Torri** (22 rooms) Via Vallone 4; 🔧0864 642040; e info@letorrihotel.it; www. letorrihotel.it. 'The Towers' hotel is beautifully set in a 17th-century stone building with corner turrets. It occupies a very peaceful location in the town's historic centre. Rooms are comfortable & well maintained. There are few 'extras' (such as a pool) but given the compact size of the historic centre everything is on your doorstep. Book well in advance, particularly during the ski season. **$$$$**

🏠 **Hotel Archi del Sole** (20 rooms) Largo Porta di Berardo 9; 🔧0864 640007; e booking@virgilio. it; www.archidelsole.it. Friendly owners Gabriella & Marco offer spacious rooms decorated in a rustic style in an attractive old building in the historic centre. There is a communal lounge & a garden for guests' use. B/fast is particularly good. **$$$**

🍴 WHERE TO EAT

🍴 **LT Restaurant** Via Vallone 4; 🔧0864 642040; www.letorrihotel.it. Hotel Le Torri's restaurant deserves a separate mention as it is 1 of the finest places for a meal in town. The atmosphere is relaxed & the food is fresh & tasty. Try the pasta dishes & the dessert crêpes. **$$$**

🍴 **Ristorante Da Paolino** Strada Vulpes 34; 🔧0864 640080; e info@ristorantedapaolino.com; www.ristorantedapaolino.com. Owner Paolino is a renowned restaurateur in the area, having founded

this eatery almost 30 years ago. His place is rustic in décor but oozes elegance & style, right down to the presentation of its dishes – such as ravioli or *agnello con salsa di prugna* (veal with prune sauce). **$$$**

🍴 **Lo Spizzico** Corso Roma 11; 🔧0864 642515; ⏰ Tue–Sun. Lo Spizzico is the town's most popular little pizza haunt. Their slices of pizza are delicious; try the margherita or the potato-topped one. **$$**

OTHER PRACTICALITIES Despite its popularity, there are few amenities in Pescocostanzo, though it does have a **bank** (*Banca Popolare dell'Adriatico; Via Fontana Maggiore 26*), a **post office** (*Via Sabatini 3;* 🔧*0864 641194*) and a **pharmacy** (*Farmacia Caruso Alessia, Via Ottavio Colecchi 10;* 🔧*0864 640818*).

WHAT TO SEE

Collegiate Church of Santa Maria del Colle (⏰ daily 07.00–12.00 & 17.00–19.30) This is the town's principal church and one of the most important religious buildings in Abruzzo. A church has existed on this site since at least the 11th century. The building was largely destroyed by the earthquake of 1456 but was reconstructed a decade later. The main entrance here is striking and dates from 1580.

Inside, the church houses a number of wooden statues, including the notable 12th-century *Madonna del Colle*, beautifully carved and painted in vibrant colours. The church is one of the very few in Abruzzo to have embraced information technology, providing a touch-screen kiosk to the side of the entrance that details its history in some depth.

Church of Santa Maria del Suffraggio del Morti (⊕ only for Mass, Sun 10.00)

Although the church has been an important part of the town since the 16th century, it has been destroyed and rebuilt various times throughout its history. The interior houses various sculptures in wood and marble, and its stunning ceiling, decorated with carvings and paintings, dates back to the mid-1630s. The main altarpiece and its paintings also date from the mid 17th century while the side altars are later, from 1749. While the church is closed outside of services, it is possible to view the interior through the metal grille at the entrance.

Civic architecture The town's streets are lined with medieval buildings, of which a few stand out. One is the **Palazzo Grilli**, which houses the Hotel Le Torri (see opposite), dating from the early 17th century and with a charming little turret at each of its corners. The **Palazzo Comunale**, near the main square, has a 15th-century floorplan but its appearance has changed over the years, having been reconstructed in 1600, 1700 and 1932. It is found across from the **Palazzo del Governatore**, which was the residency of the town's governor. In front of these buildings is an old **fountain**. Also nearby is the **Palazzo Mosca**, which has been a private residence since the 16th century but also doubled as a school of philosophy until the mid 19th century.

SKIING AROUND PESCOCOSTANZO The skiing around Pescocostanzo is some of the most exciting in the region, with the three towns of Pescocostanzo, Roccaraso and Rivisondoli forming the hub. Roccaraso and Rivisondoli are largely uninteresting, so many people choose to base themselves in the much prettier town of Pescocostanzo, only five minutes away.

Ski passes Skiing starts at €25 for a half day per adult. A day pass will cost you €33. There are also multiple-day passes starting with two-day passes (€63) and three-day passes (€92), all the way up to 12-day passes at €308. A seasonal pass will set you back €480.

Ski schools One of the best ski schools in the area is Roccaraso's **Scuola Sci** (*Via Circonvallazione 2–6;* \ *0864 62736; e info@scuolasci.com; www.scuolasci. com*) A morning's lesson will cost you €25, and a five-day course from around €100, depending on the time of day of the lessons. The school also hires out ski equipment, starting from €15 for one-day ski hire with boots.

Ski runs There are numerous ski runs, reached from any of the three towns. Please note that some runs encompass more than one degree of difficulty.

'EASY' (BLUE) RUNS		'MEDIUM' (RED) RUNS		'DIFFICULT' (BLACK) RUNS	
Doppia Paradiso 1	476m	Doppia Paradiso 2	476m	Lago d'Avoli-Orso	546m
Nuovo Baby-Orsetto	472m	Lago d'Avoli-Orso	546m	Triposto del Prato	1,180m
Valloncello	383m	Doppia Crete Rosse	468m	Orsa Maggiore	1,360m
La Valletta	650m	Pratelletto	653m		
Roccalta	453m	Valloncello	383m		
Montecalvario	245m	Roccalta	453m		
Skiing School	307m	Valle Fradda	1,198m		
Raccordo	313m				
Stazzetto	562m				
Valle Fradda	1,200m				

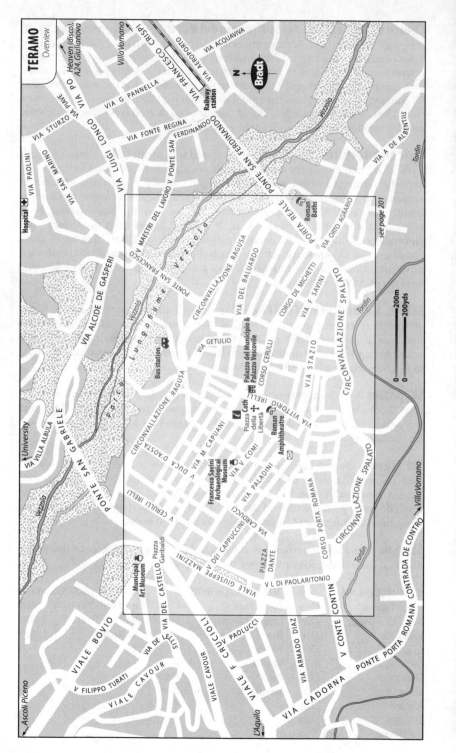

TERAMO
Overview

Bradt

Heaven (disco), A24, Giulianova

Villa Vomano

VIA ACQUAVIVA

VIA AEROPORTO

VIA FRANCESCO CRISPI

Railway station

VIA PO
VIA G PANNELLA
VIA STURZO
VIA PINE
VIA FONTE REGINA
PONTE SAN FERDINANDO
V PONTE SAN FERDINANDO
V MAESTRI DEL LAVORO
PONTE SAN FRANCESCO
Vezzola

VIA LUIGI LONGO
VIA SAN MARINO
VIA PAOLINI
Hospital

VIA ALCIDE DE GASPERI

University
VIA VILLA ALBULA
PONTE SAN GABRIELE
Parco
Vezzola
Lungofiume Vezzola

VIA A DE ALBENTIIS

Tordin

see page 201

Roman Baths

PORTA REALE

VIA ORTO AGRARIO

CORSO DE MICHETTI
VIA F SAVINI
CIRCONVALLAZIONE SPALATO
Tordin

CIRCONVALLAZIONE RAGUSA

VIA DEL BALUARDO

GETULIO

Bus station

CIRCONVALLAZIONE RAGUSA

VIA DUCA D'AOSTA
V CERULLI IRELLI
V VIA M CAPUANI

Palazzo del Municipio & Palazzo Vescovile
CORSO CERULLI
VIA STAZIO
VIA VITTORIO

Piazza Cath della Libertà
Roman Amphitheatre

Francesco Savini Archaeological Museum
V V COMI
VIA PALADINI
VIA CARDUCCI
VIA DEI CAPPUCCINI

CORSO PORTA ROMANA
CIRCONVALLAZIONE SPALATO

Municipal Art Museum
Piazza Garibaldi
VIA DEL CASTELLO
VIALE GIUSEPPE MAZZINI

PIAZZA DANTE
V L DI PAOLARITONIO

Tordin

VIALE BOVIO
VIA DE VIA CRUCIOLI
VIALE F CRUCIOLI
VIA F PAOLUCCI
VIALE CAVOUR
V FILIPPO TURATI

VIA ARMADO DIAZ
V CONTE CONTIN
PONTE PORTA ROMANA CONTRADA DE CONTRO

Ascoli Piceno
L'Aquila
Villa Vomano
VIA CADORNA

0 200m
0 200yds

198

11

Teramo

Teramo's location on a plateau between the Tordino and Vezzola rivers is a neat mirror of its status as neither a city of the mountains nor of the sea. At roughly 265m above sea level, it is the capital of the province of the same name. Teramo at once faces the dominating peaks of the Gran Sasso and is swept by the winds of the nearby Adriatic. Of the four provincial capitals in the region of Abruzzo, it is the one that brings together both coastal and mountain culture, from cooking to household traditions. It is also the region's smallest city, and has more of the feel of a large town.

HISTORY

Archaeological excavations suggest that the area has been inhabited since around 3000BC. The ancient city, known as Pretut, was founded in a position of strategic importance by the central Italian tribe known as the Praetutii, believed to have had strong connections with the Phoenicians. Later known by the Latin Interamnia (meaning 'between two rivers'), Teramo was annexed as a Roman municipality when it was conquered by Manius Curis Dentatus in 290BC. However, it later lost this status after fighting against the Romans during the Social War. Reinstated as a municipality by the emperor Julius Caesar, the city is mentioned by writers such as Claudius Ptolemy and Frontius, the latter referring to the inhabitants of the area as Internamnates Praetutiani. That it was a place of some importance, probably because of its geographical location, is shown in its wealth of Roman artefacts and architecture. Excavations have revealed an ancient theatre, baths, statues and mosaics.

Following the fall of the Western Roman Empire, the city fell within the territories of the Duchy of Spoleto, but was later destroyed by the invading Normans. Rebuilt thanks to the efforts of one Bishop Guido II, it became, in the 14th and 15th centuries, the site of much bloodshed between the feuding Melatino and Antonelli familes as they vied for control and power of the region. Later, under Aragonese rule followed by that of the Kingdom of Naples, the city became a hive of artistic activity and was eventually absorbed into the Kingdom of Italy in 1860.

Due to the difficulty of travelling between Teramo and both the rest of the region and the country, the city has remained in relative isolation. In 1984, however, a 10km tunnel was bored through the Gran Sasso mountain range, connecting Teramo to Rome for the first time ever. Fuelled in part by its relatively popular university, Teramo is now a thriving little city with a healthy student population.

GETTING THERE

BY TRAIN There are around 12 daily train services from Pescara (€4.50 one way) to Teramo's railway station, about 2km east of the city, making various stops along the way. It takes approximately just over an hour if you don't have to change at Giulianova. Trains from L'Aquila to Teramo can take upwards of five hours as they must travel via Sulmona and Pescara.

BY BUS ARPA operates four services daily from Chieti to Teramo, via Pescara. The journey will set you back around €7. The Teramo to Rome service (via L'Aquila, around €16) departs six times daily during the week with a reduced service at weekends. Several other routes operate to towns in the area, such as Isola Gran Sasso, Civitella del Tronto and Giulianova. The bus terminus is at the railway station.

BY CAR The A24 from Rome via L'Aquila ends in Teramo. If you are coming from Rome directly to Teramo, you must stay on the A24 at the junction with the A25 shortly after Carsoli, in Abruzzo. From Pescara, take the A14 in the direction of Ancona and follow the turn-off for Teramo. From the *autostrada* exit it is approximately 18km into the centre of town. Follow the signs onto the SS80.

GETTING AROUND

Teramo's historic centre is relatively small and walking is your best bet for getting around. However, the local bus company, **Staur** (*www.staur.it*), operates seven lines that criss-cross the city.

BY CAR Driving, and particularly parking, in Teramo is a nightmare, especially in the city centre. It was not built to sustain the number of cars that fill every inch of the narrow streets. For convenience, park on or around the ring road, or *circonvallazione*. Large parking areas are at Piazza Dante and Piazza Francesco.

TOURIST INFORMATION

Abruzzo Promozione Turismo (APTR) Via Guglielmo Oberdan 16; 0861 244222. The official tourist office is a short walk from Piazzale Martini della Libertà & its cathedral.

WHERE TO STAY

The options for accommodation in Teramo are not as wide-ranging as they are in Pescara or along the coast. Many prefer to stay in one of the charming nearby towns and villages such as Campli, Civitella del Tronto or on the coast at Giulianova. However, there are a few places worth considering.

Hotel Abruzzi (50 rooms) Viale Mazzini 18; 0861 241043; e info@abruzzihotel.it; www. abruzzihotel.it. Situated on the outskirts of the old town centre, offering basic but clean rooms at what is a good price for the convenient location. It has a restaurant serving simple but tasty food & the staff are very friendly. **$$$**

Hotel Gran Sasso (43 rooms) Via Vinciguerra 12; 0861 245897; e info@hotelgransassoteramo. it; www.hotelgransassoteramo.it. Situated in the northern part of the old town centre. The décor is a little dated but the rooms are comfortable &

functional. There's a lounge, a games room & a bar. It's well located for exploring Teramo's historic centre & good value for money. **$$$**

Hotel Sporting (55 rooms) Via A de Gasperi 41; 0861 414723; e info@hotelsportingteramo. it; www.hotelsportingteramo.it. The only 4-star hotel in Teramo, the rooms & facilities are well maintained & located within easy reach of the town centre. The rooms are colourfully decorated & spacious & the hotel also offers a games room, conference room & sauna. There is an excellent restaurant here, Il Carpaccio. **$$$**

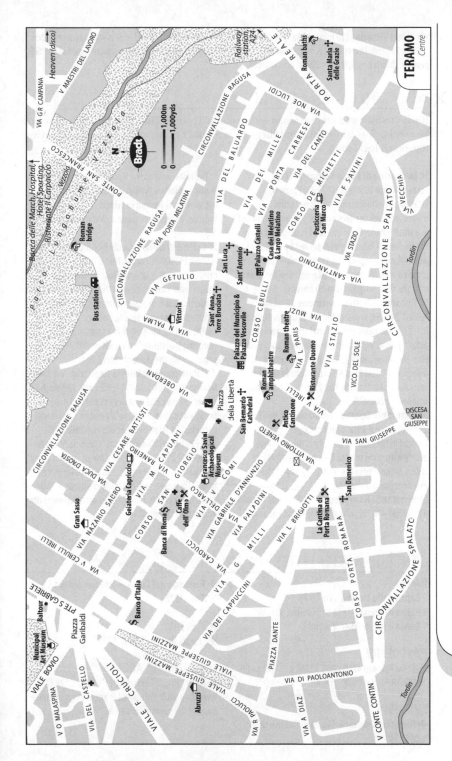

Heaven (disco)

V MAESTRI DEL LAVORO

V GR CAMPANA

VIA GR CAMPANA

Banca delle March, Hospital,
Hotel Sporting,
Ristorante Il Carpaccio

PONTE SAN FRANCESCO

Lungofiume Vezzola

Vezzola

Parco

fiume Vezzola

Roman
bridge

Bus station

Bradt

N

0   1,000m
0   1,000yds

Railway
station,
A24

Santa Maria
delle Grazie

Roman baths

PORTA REALE

VIA NOE LUCIDI

CIRCONVALLAZIONE RAGUSA

VIA DEL BALUARDO

VIA DEI MILLE

PORTA CARRESE

VIA DEL CANTO

CORSO DE MICHETTI

VIA F SAVINI

VIA VECCHIA

CIRCONVALLAZIONE SPALATO

Pasticceria
San Marco

Casa del Melatino
& Largo Melatino

Palazzo Castelli

San Luca

Sant' Antonio

VIA SANT'ANTONIO

VIA STAZIO

CIRCONVALLAZIONE RAGUSA

VIA PORTA MELATINA

VIA GETULIO

Sant' Anna,
Torre Bruciata

Vittoria

VIA N PALMA

Palazzo del Municipio &
Palazzo Vescovile

CORSO CERULLI

VIA MUZII

Roman theatre

VIA L PARIS

Ristorante Duomo

VIA STAZIO

VIA OBERDAN

Piazza
della Libertà

San Bernardo
Cathedral

Roman
amphitheatre

VIA V IRELLI

Antico
Cantinone

VICO DEL SOLE

CIRCONVALLAZIONE SPALATO

Tordin

DISCESA
SAN
GIUSEPPE

CIRCONVALLAZIONE RAGUSA

VIA V CERULLI IRELLI

Gran Sasso

VIA NAZARIO SACRO

VIA DUCA D'AOSTA

VIA CESARE BATTISTI

VIA RANIERO

VIA M CAPUANI

CORSO SAN GIORGIO

Gelateria Capriccio

Francesco Savini
Archaeological
Museum

V DELL'ARCO

Banca di Roma

Caffè
dell'Olmo

COMI

VIA GABRIELE D'ANNUNZIO

VIA FALPADINI

VIA G MILLI

VIA VITTORIO VENETO

VIA SAN GIUSEPPE

San Domenico

La Cantina di
Porta Romana

CORSO PORTA ROMANA

VIA L BRIGIOTTI

Banco d'Italia

VIA CARDUCCI

VIA DEI CAPPUCCINI

VIALE GIUSEPPE MAZZINI

VIALE GIUSEPPE MAZZINI

PIAZZA DANTE

VIA DI PAOLOANTONIO

V CONTE CONTIN

CIRCONVALLAZIONE SPALATO

Tordin

VIA A DIAZ

V R PAOLUCCI

PTE S GABRIELE

VIALE BOVIO

Municipal
Art Museum

Baltour

Piazza
Garibaldi

VIALE F CRUCIOLI

VIA DEL CASTELLO

V O MALASPINA

Abruzzi

⌂ **Hotel Vittoria** (10 rooms) Via Pretuzio 12; ✆0861 242250. The Vittoria is more akin to a pension than a hotel. It has clean rooms with an excellent b/fast included & is well situated within minutes' walk of the main square. Good value. **$$**

✕ WHERE TO EAT AND DRINK

It pays to pick and choose when eating out in Teramo. The culinary scene may not be as varied as in Pescara, but there are a number of excellent restaurants serving top-notch local food.

✕ **La Cantina di Porta Romana** Corso Porta Romana 105; ✆0861 252257; www. lacantinadiportaromana.it. This beautiful restaurant gives the feeling that you are eating out in a small village. Excellent food is prepared from the freshest of ingredients & served by staff who will make it an experience to remember. The menu is varied with all kinds of pasta, fish & meat. Don't miss the seafood gnocchi with mussels. **$$**

✕ **Ristorante Antico Cantinone** Via Ciotti 5; ✆0861 248863; www.ristoranteanticocantinone. it. It's not hard to recognise that the owners value a dining experience that is wholesome above all else. The restaurant's '(s)low cost' menu takes the principles of slow food & successfully keeps the costs down. Particularly tasty are the traditional *scrippelle 'mbusse*. **$$**

✕ **Ristorante Duomo** Via Stazio 9; ✆0861 241774; www.ristoranteduomo.com; ☉ Mon–Sat. Located in the heart of the city is this spacious eatery with good service & even better food. It is very popular with the locals. Try any of the excellent pasta dishes. **$$**

✕ **Ristorante Il Carpaccio** Via Alcide de Gasperi 41; ✆0861 414723; www.hotelsportingteramo. it. The restaurant of the Hotel Sporting specialises in dishes that are typical not only of Abruzzo, but specific to Teramo Province. Try the *scripelle 'mbusse*, a crêpe-like pasta rolled in a light sauce. **$$**

✕ **Caffè dell'Olmo** Via del Fico Melchiorre 56; ✆0861 248600; ☉ daily. This is one of the chicest cafés in town. It is situated just off the main square with a lovely view of the cathedral. Its modern décor is in stark contrast to the medieval architecture surrounding the piazza. This is an excellent place for a drink & a spot of people-watching (particularly on a Sat night). It's quite popular with the student crowd. **$**

⌷ **Pasticceria Gelateria Capriccio** Via Sauro Nazario 65; ✆0861 248617; ☉ daily. Although this serves scrumptious pastries, it's better known for being a good place to grab a *gelato* on a summer evening. The strawberry *gelato* is excellent. **$**

⌷ **Pasticceria San Marco** Corso de Michetti 40; ✆0861 254818; ☉ daily. One of Teramo's best pastry shops, San Marco is also a popular place for b/fast. Their sweets & cakes are delicious & their speciality seems to be anything with (an unhealthy amount of) cream. **$**

OTHER PRACTICALITIES

BANKS
$ **Banca delle Marche** Via Po 18
$ **Banca di Roma** Corso San Giorgio 60
$ **Banca d'Italia** Viale Mazzini 1

POST OFFICE
✉ Via Paladini 42; ✆0861 323601; ☉ Mon–Fri 08.00–18.30, Sat 08.00–12.30.

CHEMISTS
✚ **Farmacia Cerasani** Piazza della Libertà 34; ✆0861 248826

✚ **Farmacia del Corso** Corso San Giorgio 81; ✆0861 244272

HOSPITAL
⊞ Piazza Italia 1; ✆0861 4291

LOCAL TRAVEL AGENTS
Baltour Piazza Garibaldi 59; ✆0861 252817; www.baltour.it. This popular agency can organise tours of the surrounding area.

EVENTS

MAY Before the onslaught of the hot summer weather, Teramo hosts a spate of events, otherwise known as the **May festivities**. These include music, theatre, dance, film festivals and also the interesting Teramo Comics Exhibition. Details are available on the council website (*www.comune.teramo.it*).

JULY–SEPTEMBER During the summer months, Teramo comes alive with the 'estaTE' programme, a host of events that tend to differ from year to year, but which incorporate concerts, plays and food tasting. One such event, for example, is the relatively new 'Li Chiacchier'. It involves the cooking of a savoury waffle called *li chiacchier*, accompanied by copious types of hams and cheeses, as well as music and dancing. Again, check the council website for programmes and full details.

ENTERTAINMENT AND NIGHTLIFE

Although this is a large university town, and as such has a sizeable population of young people, nightlife is a little thin on the ground. During summer, the fun shifts to the beachside towns along the province's coast, from Martinsicuro to Silvi Marina. The vibrant summer nightlife of Pescara and also San Benedetto del Tronto (actually in the neighbouring region of Le Marche) is also within easy reach. There is, however, a funky club called **Heaven** (*Villa Pavone, Teramo*; m *349 466 1511*). On warm nights, groups of friends gather in the central square, Piazzale della Libertà, where the **Caffè dell'Olmo** (see opposite) is an ideal place for a drink and a chat.

WHAT TO SEE AND DO

ROMAN TERAMO All that remains of the town's 1st-century BC **Roman ampitheatre**, an impressive 70m wide, is situated near the cathedral along Via Vincenzo Irelli, where its large brick walls are visible. The Augustan **theatre**, the more impressive of the two given its good state of preservation, is best viewed from Largo Amfiteatro or Via Teatro Antico. Able to accommodate up to 3,000 spectators, the theatre's *cavea* (seating area) consisted of two levels of arches, of which only the lower level has survived. Further important Roman-era remains can be seen, including the **Largo Torre Bruciata** ('Burnt Tower') constructed in the 4th century and preserving fragments of frescoes and decoration. Remains of the Roman public baths can be seen in **Largo Madonna delle Grazie**.

CHURCHES
Cathedral of San Bernardo (⊕ daily) The cathedral, one of the city's highlights, is situated on the main square. Built on the site of a Roman temple, it is thought to have been constructed between 1158 and 1174 on the orders of Bishop Guido II. Following an extension in the 1330s and various modifications during the 16th century, a reconstruction of the interior was begun in the 1730s, when the church was given a Baroque appearance. Further renovation in 1932–5 restored the interior to its original state.

The church's main façade shows evidence of the different stages of construction over the centuries. Its main entrance, dating back to 1332, is the work of Roman artist Deodato di Cosma, and the two sculptures at either side that of Nicola da Guardiagrele. The belfry, similar in appearance to the one belonging to Atri's main cathedral, was begun towards the end of the 12th century but not completed until the 1490s by Antonio da Lodi. Inside, the oldest section of the church (on the eastern side) consists of a nave and two aisles while the 14th-century extension was built on the western side comprising six bays with Gothic arches. Of note within the church are the high altar's 15th-century silver frontal, also by Nicola da Guardiagrele and restored in the 1700s; a wooden crucifix dating from the beginning of the 15th century (currently in the left aisle); Antonio da Lodi's 15th-century marble shrine; and a late 16th-century wooden altar.

Church of Sant'Antonio This church on Largo Melatini, with its 18th-century interior, was originally built in the 13th century. The only surviving features from this earlier structure, its doorway and windows, are found on the left-hand side of the church.

Church of Sant'Anna dei Pompetti or San Getulio This church, on a piazza to the east of the town hall, is what remains of the ancient cathedral of Santa Maria Aprutiensis, founded in the 6th century over a Roman *domus*. The current church is a result of rebuilding over the centuries, particularly after the Normans demolished the structure entirely in the 12th century. The floor of the church contains glass panels through which you can see the foundations of the earlier building.

Church of San Domenico Found on Corso di Porta Romana, San Domenico dates from the 14th century and, although renovated many times since, is worth a look for its traces of 14th- to 16th-century frescoes.

Church of San Luca While more of a prayer room than a church, this place of worship, reached from Largo Melatini or Via del Baluardo, is worth popping into for its humble 14th-century charm.

Church of Santa Maria delle Grazie Outside the main old-town nucleus and beyond the public gardens outside the Porta Reale, is the renovated Church of Santa Maria delle Grazie, which was once the church of a Benedictine convent. The structure contains various 19th-century frescoes and a pleasant cloister that was rebuilt during the 1800s.

CIVIC BUILDINGS The **Casa dei Melatino** along Largo Melatini dates back to the 13th century and was the residence of the Melatino family, one of the two families that fought for control of the city for over a century. The main façade of the building retains a charming, medieval double lancet window.

The **Palazzo del Municipio**, the town's city hall on **Piazza Orsini**, dates from the 15th century, while nearby is the 14th-century **Palazzo Vescovile**, or Bishop's Palace. Across the road from the Church of Sant'Antonio is the **Palazzo Castelli**, which represents a fine example of Art Nouveau architecture.

MUSEUMS
Museo Archeologico Francesco Savini/Francesco Savini Archaeological Museum (*Via Delfico 30;* ✆ *0861 247772;* ⊕ *Tue–Sun 09.00–13.00 & 16.00–19.00; admission €5 including entry to Municipal Art Museum*) This is the place to look for archaeological finds from the city that span some 20-odd centuries. From earthenware to funeral objects, the items on display are well worth your time. Don't miss the wonderful headless statue of Aphrodite.

Municipal Art Museum (*Pinacoteca Civica; Viale Bovio 4;* ✆ *0861 250873;* ⊕ *Tue–Sun 09.00–13.00 & 16.00–19.00; admission €3*) This small museum is set within the **Villa Comunale** gardens, the city's main park, and displays paintings, sculptures and ceramics from around 1600 to the present day.

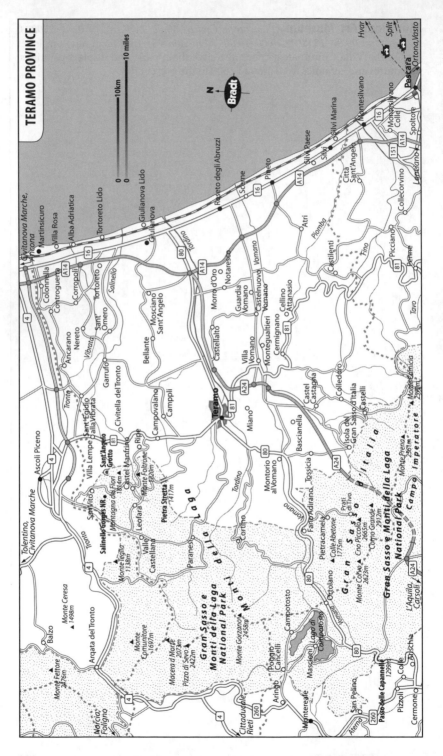

12

Teramo Province

The province of Teramo may not be as diverse as other parts of Abruzzo, though it offers some of the most convenient coastline in terms of amenities, not to mention the beautiful mountain scenery of the interior of the province. The beach-resort towns are a great place for a summer holiday, while the winding roads and medieval towns of the hills make for excellent day trips. You could easily while away several days making your way from one town to the next.

SUGGESTED ITINERARY

To explore the coast, wind your way up the SS16 through the coastal towns of the province, with side trips to the old towns of Giulianova and Tortoreto. Inland, travel from Teramo to the towns of Campli and Civitella del Tronto. Drive through the hills of the interior towards the coast (preferably staying off the main roads) with visits to any of the charming towns in this chapter.

COASTAL TERAMO

GETTING THERE

By car The SS16 'Adriatica' runs the length of the coast of Abruzzo. Alternatively take the A14 *autostrada*, which can be more convenient for the longer journey from Pescara to the northern coast. From the interior of the province the SS80 will take you from Teramo to the coast, meeting the SS16 just before Giulianova.

By train The line that runs from southern Italy to Milan runs along the whole of Abruzzo's coastline, and hence the province of Teramo's coastline, making the train a much more convenient way to travel than by bus. The journey from Pescara to the northern coastal towns takes only 40 minutes (€3.60), while the bus trip will take you upwards of 1½ hours. There is also a line from Teramo, which joins the main north–south railway at Giulianova. The journey to Giulianova takes about half an hour and costs €2.40.

By bus There are about 30 buses a day from Pescara's bus station to the coastal towns of Teramo. The journey to Martinsicuro (the last town before you enter the region of Le Marche) takes about 1½ hours and costs around €6. There is a bus service from Teramo to the coastal towns, but because the SS16 can often become congested as it passes through the town centres, this, too, takes longer than the train.

SILVI MARINA Silvi Marina is the location of one of Abruzzo's 22 Blue Flag beaches. The lovely beaches here are essentially the only attraction in an otherwise modern town with little in the way of sights. However, as the residents from nearby inland towns began to move down to the coast during the late 19th century, they built some impressive villas. Keep your eyes peeled as you walk around town.

Tourist information
☑ IAT Silvi Marina Via Garibaldi 208; ☎085 930343; e iat.silvi@abruzzoturismo.it

 **Where to stay** Silvi is popular with Italian tourists and the handful of Germans and British who have discovered the delights of Abruzzo. Hence there is a good selection of high-quality hotels, and most have a section of private beach for guests. Almost all places offer half-board and full-board options and have decent restaurants. These usually serve excellent seafood, such as tasty prawn-based dishes. See page 71 for an explanation of the 'Tessera Club', which applies to most hotels in Silvi.

Upmarket
⌂ Abruzzo Marina Hotel (115 rooms) Via Garibaldi 196; ☎085 930397; e info@ hotelabruzzomarina.it; www.hotelabruzzomarina. it. This is an exceptionally well-run, modern, glossy-design hotel. Great attention to detail means the rooms are beautifully decorated & pristine, the restaurant world-class, & the numerous facilities (such as its large swimming pool) excellent. This is one of the most popular hotels in the area & it is therefore advisable to book early. **$$$$$**
⌂ Grand Hotel Berti (118 rooms) Via della Marina, 19; ☎085 935 0760; e info@bertihotels. it; www.bertihotels.it. This large 5-star hotel has very comfortable rooms with sea views from their balconies, a great outdoor pool area & an excellent restaurant. It is 1 of 2 hotels in Silvi that are part of the Berti chain. **$$$$$**
⌂ Hotel Cirillo (45 rooms) Via Garibaldi 238; ☎085 930404; e info@hotelcirillo.it; www. hotelcirillo.it. A simple & pleasant hotel with very pretty rooms (some of them have balconies which you should request when booking). The bathrooms are somewhat functional but spotless & there is a relaxing terrace area outside. HB & FB. **$$$$**
⌂ Hotel Parco delle Rose (63 rooms) Via Garibaldi 36; ☎085 935 0989; e info@ parcodellerose.it; www.parcodellerose.it. A whitewashed 4-star hotel in a pleasant location with 43 of its rooms looking out onto the beach. The rooms themselves are comfortable if slightly old-fashioned. You will have to book in advance & specify whether you want a sea view, for which you'll pay more. HB & FB. **$$$$**

⌂ Hotel President (252 rooms) Via Leonardo da Vinci 19; ☎085 935 0760; e info@bertihotels.it; www.bertihotels.it. This 4-star hotel is Silvi's other member of the Berti chain. **$$$$**
⌂ Mion Hotel (64 rooms) Via Garibaldi 22; ☎085 935 0935; e info@mionhotel.com; www. mionhotel.com. The Mion's slightly overblown motto is 'charme & relax', & to be fair it does live up to it. Once you're past the questionable green colour scheme of the rooms, you'll find modern accommodation with good facilities such as a palm-strewn outdoor pool area with tented gazebos, tables & chairs. HB & FB. **$$$$**

Mid range
⌂ Hotel Hermitage (110 rooms) Via Dante Alighieri 1; ☎085 935 3565; e info@ hermitagesilvi.com; www.hermitagesilvi. com. A good-value hotel with attractive & very comfortable rooms, all with beach views at no extra cost. It has a large private beach for guests as well as a health & spa centre that offers various treatments from massage to hammam-style baths & a full-body steam treatment. Often at full capacity in the warmer months. **$$$**
⌂ Hotel Riviera (21 rooms) Via Garibaldi 316; ☎085 930095; www.hotelrivierasilvi.com. The 2-star Riviera is in a white, funky modern building & is excellent value. The rooms are pristine, with a definite seaside feel to them (all blues & whites), but only some have sea views (for which you pay a supplement). HB & FB. **$$$**
⌂ Hotel Silvi (43 rooms) Via A Rossi 95; ☎085 930405; e info@hotelsilvi.it; www.hotelsilvi.it.

Although there is not much in the way of extra services (such as a health centre & spa), the Silvi is a well-priced beachfront hotel with bright & airy rooms, as well as private beach facilities & a restaurant. The palm-lined pool is seconds away from the beach. HB & FB. **$$$**

Camping

⅄ Lake Placid Camping Via Leonardo da Vinci 13; ☎085 932567; e info@campinglakeplacid. it; www.campinglakeplacid.it. This is actually a fairly large tourist resort with good camping facilities. The fixed accommodation is in a series of simple cabins but there are pitches for tents as well as caravans & all basic amenities are on hand. *Camping €7–10; caravan €12–16 pp.*

✗ Where to eat

✗ Il Guazzetto Via della Marina 19; ☎085 935 0760; ⊕ May–Sep. The restaurant at the Grand Hotel Berti is a great place to eat & deserves to be singled out from the hotel entry. Dishes are cooked to perfection (the pasta is amongst the best in town) & beautifully presented. All this & it's good value too. **$$$**

✗ Ristorante Pizzeria Gli Antenati Via Santo Stefano 56; ☎085 930888; www.gliantenati.com; ⊕ daily. A typically Abruzzese family-run affair with a wide variety of choices all based around the 'peasant' food that the locals are so proud of. This is one of the few places that serve variations of Abruzzo's popular *arrosticini* (see page 42): try the chicken or liver versions. Pizzas are also excellent. **$$$**

✗ Ristorante Vecchia Silvi Circ Boreale 22; ☎085 930141; e info@ristorantevecchiasilvi.com; www.ristorantevecchiasilvi.com; ⊕ summer, daily lunch & dinner; winter, Wed–Mon lunch & dinner, Tue dinner. This traditional restaurant is in Silvi Alta, a 10-min drive from Silvi Marina. It's worth making the trip for the typical Abruzzese cuisine & the warm atmosphere. Try the *tagliatella di nonna finuccia*, a pasta dish made with local ingredients. **$$$**

✗ Velvet Via Cristoforo Colombo 7; ☎085 935 0692; www.ristorantevelvet.it; ⊕ daily. With its own online booking engine – something that is very unusual for Abruzzo – it is clear that Velvet means business. Not just in service and presentation, but in the sheer quality of the fresh seafood. Try the excellent swordfish. **$$$**

Other practicalities There are a few **banks** in town with ATMs, including Banca di Castiglione M Re Pianella (*Via Roma 285*); Banca Popolare dell'Adriatico (*Via A Rossi 1*) and Banca Toscana (*Via Nazionale Adriatica Sud 59*). **Chemists** can be found at Farmacia Comunale (*Via Leonardo da Vinci 28,* ☎ *085 935 3375*) and Farmacia Laviano Francesca (*Via A Rossi 20;* ☎*085 930259*). The **post office** is at Via Carducci 8 (☎ *085 936 7011*).

Around Silvi

Silvi Alta Silvi Alta (or 'High Silvi') is the medieval nucleus of the town and commune of Silvi Marina. It is set on a spur overlooking the coast, a ten-minute drive from the marina and certainly worth a look (although take care on the road up to the town as it is in a state of disrepair). The views up and down the coast are stunning, certainly the best in the area. It's the highest town in the district, and walking up the main road of the medieval centre (Corso Umberto I) feels a long way above the bustle of the coast. **Piazza Largo Della Porta** is the main square, while the main church is the **Church of San Salvatore**, dating back to the 12th century.

Where to stay If you want to stay away from the buzz of the newer Silvi below, an excellent option is **Locanda del Frate** (*5 rooms; Via San Rocco 1;* ☎ *085 935 2039;* e *info@locandadelfrate.it; www.locandadelfrate.it;* **$$**), an intimate family-run hotel that has a lovely rustic restaurant (⊕ *Thursday–Tuesday*). Try the excellent handmade *pasta all'uovo*.

ATRI The tranquil town of Atri, with its reputation for art and culture, is set on the hills a few kilometres from the Teramo coastline.

History Recent evidence suggests that the town was of some importance in the pre-Roman times of the Italic tribes. Before the Romans settled here, it was one of a handful of major Greek harbour cities along the Adriatic coast. However, in the late 3rd century BC, it became known as a prosperous Roman colony by the name of Hatria, which some historians believe to be the origin of the name of the Adriatic (others claim the Etruscan city of Adria in the Veneto region of Italy actually gave its name to the sea). During the Punic Wars of the early 3rd century BC, the city remained loyal to Rome and was subsequently the recipient of much grateful beneficence. Its status fell somewhat after the reign of Augustus and it was Hadrian who breathed life into the colony once more (it is possible that Hadrian's family was originally from here). As with many other parts of Abruzzo, the Middle Ages were a period of instability and the town changed hands between rulers many times.

Tourist information

🛈 **IAT** Piazza Duchi d'Acquaviva 1; ☎085 879 8864

🛈 **Associazione Pro Loco Hatria** Piazza Marconi 8; ☎085 878 0085

🏠 Where to stay

🏠 **Hotel du Parc** (49 rooms) Viale Umberto I 6; ☎085 870260; e info@hotelduparc.it; www. hotelduparc.it. For a town so rich in sights, it's surprising that this is the only hotel. The décor in this place is a little dated (the peach hues combined with the furniture give it a real early-'90s look), but the rooms are spacious & the hotel has a swimming pool (which, while the beach is only about 10km away, is very convenient during those hot summer months). **$$$**

✕ Where to eat

✕ **Locanda del Duca d'Atri** Via San Domenico 54; ☎085 879 7586; ⊕ Wed–Mon. This excellent restaurant is a lovely place to sit down, relax & eat good food that won't break the bank. It has a rustic feel & is very well looked after by the owner. There are some tasty pasta dishes (particularly those with a tomato-based sauce) & an excellent house wine. **$$**

✕ **Trattoria alla Corte** Corso Adriano 40; ☎085 870305; ⊕ Tue–Sun. This is cheap eating at its best. The food here is excellent quality, & prices very reasonable. The meat dishes here are particularly good, especially the traditional *arrosticini*, & the desserts are great: if they have it, try the *tiramisù*. **$$**

Shopping Termo has a bakery (more like a sweet shop) that's certainly worth a visit. **Pan Ducale** (*Viale Risorgimento I*; ☎ *085 87774*; ⊕ *Mon–Fri 09.00–13.00 & 16.00–20.00*) was first opened in 1967 and since then has become locally famous. Try their *pan ducale*, a sweet hazelnut bread (whence comes its name). There are also various kinds of *biscotti* which you might be tempted to stock up on for home.

Other practicalities There are three banks in town with **ATMs**.

Banks
$ **Tercas** Piazza Duomo 5
$ **Banca Popolare dell'Adriatic** Via Roma 17
$ **Banca Toscana** Via Umberto I 11

Post office
✉ Largo San Pietro 1; ☎085 879 2631; ⊕ Mon, Wed & Fri 08.30–13.30, Tue & Thu 08.00–18.30, Sat 08.30–12.30

What to see and do

Churches Due to Atri's architectural and historical importance most of its churches normally welcome visitors during the day, particularly the three listed below.

Cathedral of Santa Maria Assunta This architecturally interesting building will probably be the very first place you visit in Atri, given its position on the main road into town. First mentioned in a papal bull from the year 1140, it was rebuilt at the end of the 13th and beginning of the 14th century and was given the status of a minor basilica six centuries later in 1964. Its construction, unusually for Abruzzo, has been irregular and haphazard, which shows in its layout. There are clear differences between the church's east and west sections, the former having been constructed on a Roman cistern. The cathedral's belltower is famous throughout the region, and was the model for the belltowers of many town churches during the Middle Ages. Inside, the church contains some very fine works of art, including the apse frescoes of the *Life of the Virgin* by Andrea Delitio, arguably Abruzzo's most important painter of the 15th century.

Church of Sant'Agostino Founded in the 15th century, this small church with a simple interior hides a beautifully conserved fresco, also by Andrea Delitio. The main belfry is modelled on that of the Cathedral of Santa Maria Assunta. It is worth visiting this church if only to see its intricate 15th-century doorway.

Church of San Nicola di Bari The first mention of this church is from the year 1181. It was rebuilt in 1256, though it retains much of its original layout. Its Gothic interior contains some frescoes by Andrea Delitio and a painting of the *Madonna with Child* by one of his students. Behind this church there is a lookout point with sweeping views.

Roman theatre You could be forgiven for not realising that Atri is home to the ruins of a Roman theatre. They can be found on Via del Teatro Romano, on the site of Palazzo Cicada, since the theatre was used as part of the foundations for later buildings. There isn't a whole lot to see, and what there is is officially closed. However, if you go around to the back of the site, you will reach an area that is gated off (and the wire ripped away); you can see some of the ruins from there.

Museums

Museo Archeologico Civico/Archaeological Museum (*Via dei Musei 1;* ☎ *085 879 7875;* ⊕ *Tue–Sun 10.30–12.30 & 16.00–19.00, Mon 16.00–19.00; admission €3.20*) This small archaeological museum is full of artefacts from the immediate area. It is broken up into three main sections from the prehistoric to the Roman and beyond. Items on display include pottery, tools, cups and Roman ornaments. There are also two 4th-century BC skeletons that were unearthed in 1900: one is of a man who was found with his tools and the other a woman with decorative bracelets and a pot. Unfortunately, none of the labels is in English.

Teramo Province COASTAL TERAMO

12

Museo Capitolare/Chapter Museum (*Piazza del Duomo;* \ *085 879 8140;* ⊕ *Oct–May, Thu–Tue 10.00–12.00 & 15.00–17.00; Jun–Sep, daily 10.00–12.00 & 16.00–20.00; admission €3*) There are ten rooms at this museum, crammed with displays of all things religious, from paintings and crosses to busts and pottery. One of the highlights, however, is the charming cloister in which the museum is set, with its double row of arches surrounding a large well. Beneath this Romanesque cloister, it is possible to visit the original Roman cloister which contained baths. It's rather cold and eerie down there, an impression reinforced by the dim lighting. The walls of the outer cloister are lined with fragments of Roman buildings and large sections of mosaic.

Museo Civico Etnografico/Ethnographic Museum (*Piazza San Pietro 1;* \ *085 87721;* ⊕ *Oct–May, Tue–Sat 10.00–13.00; Jun–Sep, Tue–Sun 16.30–19.30; admission €2*) Dedicated to everyday life around Atri, this small museum houses collections of agricultural and industrial machinery from the town. There are also various mock-ups of rooms, among them a bedroom from the early 1800s, a peasant's kitchen from the early 20th century and various workshops from the last century and a half.

Calanchi di Atri Nature Reserve (*www.riservacalanchidiatri.it*) Erosion of the cliff face has resulted in some dramatic scenery at this reserve, founded in 1995. It occupies around 380ha of 'badland', formed through the erosion of soft rock and soils with a high content of clay. Walking to the reserve from Atri takes around half an hour along the main road south of town.

PINETO The amiable town of Pineto is arguably one of the prettiest on the Teramo coast. Outside of the hectic summer season it is peaceful and an excellent place to lounge around and recharge your batteries. In 2008 its **beach** was awarded a Blue Flag, but it narrowly missed out in 2012.

Unlike in many other coastal towns here, the town does not extend to the coast itself, but is separated from the beach by a railway line and a **pine grove** (from which the town gets its name) planted by Luigi Filiani. This lack of beachfront development combines with the dry Mediterranean hills that frame the town to make it both attractive and serene.

Tourist information
🗗 **IAT Pineto** Villa Filiani Pineto, Via D'Annunzio; \085 949 1745; e iat.pineto@abruzzoturismo.it

🏠 Where to stay and eat
Upmarket
🏠 **Hotel Ambasciatori** (31 rooms) Via XXV Aprile 5; \085 949 2900; e ambasc@tin.it; www.pineto.it. This beachfront hotel, with its palm trees & peaceful outdoor pool area, looks as though it should be in somewhere like Fiji. The rooms are spacious & comfortable, the staff very friendly & the service impeccable. The restaurant serves excellent food; try any of the pasta dishes. **$$$$**

Mid range
🏠 **Hotel Abruzzo** Viale Abruzzo 2; \085 949 1699; e hotel.abruzzo@tin.it; www. abruzzohotelvacanze.com. Although it may not look like much from the outside (looking more like a block of residential apartments than a hotel), the Abruzzo is set amongst the pines behind the beach & is bright & airy. It offers clean rooms with plenty of space, & private beach facilities. **$$$**
🏠 **Hotel Caravel** (40 rooms) Via Jugoslavia 15; \085 949 1291; www.caravelpineto.com.

This family-run, rather simple hotel is situated away from the beach. The rooms are quite plain but comfortable & guests have access to a pool, a tennis court & even a mini-soccer field. HB. **$$$**

🛏 **Hotel Corallo** (18 rooms) Via Roma 72; 📞085 949 1563; e info@hotelcorallo-pineto.it; www.hotelcorallo-pineto.it. A well-maintained, no-fuss hotel with straightforward but attractive, clean rooms & recently renovated bathrooms. It is situated off the main road & away from the beach for that extra little bit of peace & quiet during the summer months. **$$$**

🛏 **Hotel Costa Verde** (40 rooms) Lungomare dei Pini 5; 📞085 949 1633; e info@hotelcostaverdepineto; www. hotelcostaverdepineto.com. Another whitewashed, modern block of a hotel set on the beach with its own private beach facilities for guests. It's worth staying here even if just for the restaurant, which specialises in fish. A swimming pool, terrace & games room make it especially attractive for families. HB & FB. **$$$**

🛏 **Hotel Ester Safer** (30 rooms) Via Venezia 12; e info@hotelestersafer.it; www.hotelestersafer.it; 📞085 949 2276. This classic Mediterranean-yellow building offers very basic but functional rooms. The hotel's only unusual feature is an external glass lift. HB & FB. **$$$**

🛏 **Hotel Felicioni** (66 rooms) Via della Rampa 30; 📞085 949 1512; e info@hotelfelicioni.com; www.hotelfelicioni.com. The Felicioni offers simply decorated, almost austere rooms, a private beach for guests & friendly staff who will go to great lengths to make their guests' stay as pleasant as possible. The 6th floor has a spa area, & the hotel can arrange tours of the surrounding countryside. FB. **$$$**

🛏 **Hotel Jean Pierre** (27 rooms) Via F P Michetti 70; 📞085 949 0587; e info@ hoteljeanpierre.it; www.hoteljeanpierre.it. The somewhat plain, brown exterior of this hotel might be enough to put off some travellers, & the rooms themselves feature some rather questionable bright-blue & green décor, but it's a comfortable & more tranquil alternative to the beachfront establishments as it's set towards the hills. Even so, it does offer guests the use of private beach facilities. HB & FB. **$$$**

🛏 **Hotel La Pineta** (57 rooms) Via G D'Annunzio 193; 📞085 949 1406; e info@ hotellapineta.eu; www.hotellapineta.eu. This

clean, convenient hotel close to the beach doubles as a local hangout for elderly people to sit & play cards. The friendly owner makes sure all his rooms are well maintained & comfortable. It is a great place to mingle with the locals. HB & FB. **$$$**

🛏 **Hotel Lunik** (54 rooms) Via C de Titta 124; 📞085 949 1497; e info@hotellunik.com; www. hotellunik.com. This funky-looking round building has been recently restored. The rooms & bathrooms are clean & decent enough, if a bit basic, & there is a bar, restaurant & the use of a private beach. HB & FB. **$$$**

🛏 **Hotel Mare Blu** (20 rooms) Via Francia 1; 📞085 949 0545; e info@hotelmareblu.com; www. hotelmareblu.com. A little way out of town, this hotel offers a peaceful stay with comfortable if somewhat spartan rooms, a restaurant & even free transport between the hotel & railway station & airport (which is a plus as the airport is located in Pescara). There is a minimum stay of 7 nights during summer. HB & FB. **$$$**

Budget
🛏 **Pensione Franco** (15 rooms) Via G D'Annunzio 45; 📞085 949 1784. This pension hotel only allows FB stays but is excellent value, at around only €60 pp per night. It's set a little away from the beach but is ideal for families as it has a lovely, safe courtyard where children can play. **$$**

🛏 **B&B Pensione Oasi** (9 rooms) Via Primo Maggio 16; 📞085 949 3521; e info@pensioneoasi. it; www.pensioneoasi.it. Oasi is an interesting & quirky B&B run by a friendly elderly couple. Each room has its own colour & theme. The single room is cute with its massive wall map. The restaurant is also very good. **$$**

Other places to eat and drink
✗ **Bacucco d'Oro** Via del Pozzo 8, Località Mutignano; 📞085 936 227; www.bacuccodoro. com; ⊙ Thu–Tue. Around 5km out of town, this simply decorated restaurant – in a lovely setting – is a favourite among locals. Its typically Abruzzese dishes are delicious, particularly the pasta. It also has an excellent wine list. **$$$**

✗ **The Beach** Villaggio Pineto Beach, entrance on Via XXV Aprile; 📞085 867 3535; www. ristobeach.it; ⊙ Apr–Sep, 07.00–01.00. As its name suggests, the location of this restaurant right on beach makes it a draw card for locals & tourists. As one of the few restaurants in Abruzzo that is actually open from breakfast, its menu is extensive. Listen to the sound of the waves at dusk & enjoy one of the restaurant's excellent pizzas. **$$$**

♀ **Bar Sportivo** Via G D'Annunzio 48; ☎ 085 949 3403. Bar Sportivo is a typical Abruzzese bar but it also serves basic lunchtime dishes such as lasagne. There is a set menu, which gets you a main dish & a drink, for €7.50. **$$**

Other practicalities There are a few **banks** in town with ATM facilities. Amongst them are Banca San Paolo Intesa (*Via G D'Annunzio 191*); Banca Toscana (*Via G D'Annunzio 91*); and Cassa di Risparmio (*Piazza della Libertà 1*).

Chemists are Farmacia di Febo Camilla (*Via Trieste 1;* ☎ *085 949 1436*) and Farmacia di Pietro Bruno (*Via Leopardi 16;* ☎ *085 949 5755*).

The **post office** is at Viale Mazzini 42 (☎ *085 94985;* ⊕ *Mon–Fri 08.00–18.30, Sat 08.00–12.30*).

Around Pineto

Scerne di Pineto Scerne di Pineto is, to all intents and purposes, just an extension of Pineto's hotels and residential buildings. However, it does have one breathtaking beach that is worth a visit. To get there, take the SS16 from Pineto and turn off at the sign 'Mare' after the Mercatone Uno shopping centre. Here you will find an attractive little promenade and crystal-clear water. There are always fewer people here because of the lack of sand. It attracts the local LGBT crowds on a Sunday.

Torre di Cerrano The Cerrano tower, built in 1568, occupies what would once have been a small promontory just above the sea. It was a watchtower for over two centuries and has undergone restoration at various times during its history, most recently during the 1980s. The **beach** here, about a five-minute drive south of the town, is wide and less crowded than at Silvi or Pineto. It's an excellent place to while away a day at the coast. Bring plenty of sunscreen as it is not equipped with umbrellas or deckchairs.

ROSETO DEGLI ABRUZZI

Although less developed than the much larger city of Pescara, Roseto is more of an urban centre than its neighbour, Pineto. In fact, the outskirts of the town, before the district of Giulianova, are downright industrial. However, Roseto has a beach that is consistently awarded Blue Flag status, an excellent coastline and good facilities. Lungomare Roma is the prettiest of its beachfronts, though if you want peace and quiet you're probably better off heading to Pineto. Like its neighbour, Roseto has a handful of attractive villas from the late 19th century, but there isn't much else to see here.

In early July, the town hosts the **Bontà di Mare** (Abundance of the Sea) fair, at the Palazzetto dello Sport. Many wonderful food stands line the building, and there is also live music.

Tourist information

🖿 **IAT Roseto degli Abruzzo** Piazza Libertà 37/39; ☎ 085 899 1157; e iat.roseto@ abruzzoturismo.it. Located opposite the railway station.

Where to stay and eat

Upmarket

🛏 **Hotel Bellavista** (92 rooms) Lungomare Trento 75; ☎ 085 893 0425; e hotel@ bellavistahotel.net; www.bellavistahotel.net. Bellavista is one of Roseto's best, even if it is not so attractive from the outside. The rooms are comfortable with balconies & sea views. There are also good amenities such as a pool, bar & private beach. Check the website for offers. HB & FB. **$$$$**

⌂ **Hotel Liberty** (34 rooms) Lungomare Roma 8; ☎ 085 893 6319; e info@libertyroseto.it; www.libertyroseto.it. Attention to detail is what makes this 2yr-old 4-star property an excellent place to stay. The property has elegant, spacious rooms, modern bathrooms, a gym, ice-cream parlour & private beach facilities. There is a cool little café outside, the Liberty Fashion Café, with funky leather seats. HB & FB. **$$$$**

⌂ **Hotel Roma Sul Mare** (22 rooms) Lungomare Trento; ☎ 085 893 6319; e info@hotelromasulmare.com; www.hotelromasulmare.com. The Roma is one of the very few hotels to open its doors in Abruzzo since before the global financial crisis. Its excellent service, bright & airy rooms with sea view, garden & private beach facilities mean that it has quickly established itself as one of the best accommodation options in the area. **$$$$**

⌂ **Hotel La Tartaruga** (30 rooms) Via Marcantonio 3; ☎ 085 899 2188; e info@hoteltartaruga.it; www.hoteltartaruga.it. Though this is a 2-star hotel, it has the feel of a much higher-priced establishment and has been recently spruced up. More of a resort than just a hotel, it is set around a gorgeous bay. The rooms are clean & comfortable but it does have a tendency to get very busy during the summer months. HB & FB. **$$$$**

⌂ **Villaggio Lido d'Abruzzo** (150 bungalows, 18 apts, 50 mobile homes, camping) Viale Makarska; ☎ 085 894 2643; e info@villaggiolidodabruzzo.it; www.villaggiolidodabruzzo.it. This very large village resort has just about everything you could possibly need & is an ideal place to stay for families or large groups. Apartments & bungalows are of a good size, & the amenities for campers are excellent, with 80 tent pitches, & electricity for campervans. There are also various equipped play areas for kids. **$$$$**. *Camping €7–11pp*

Mid range

⌂ **Hotel Clorinda** (26 rooms) Lungomare Roma 30; ☎ 085 893 0803; e info@clorindahotel.it; www.clorindahotel.it. The Clorinda's green-&-orange façade might be enough to scare you off, but inside it features bright, airy rooms, a good restaurant & even an ice-cream parlour. It is a good place to stay for those with young children & there are also private beach facilities. HB & FB. **$$$**

⌂ **Hotel Radar** (58 rooms) Lungomare Roma 14; ☎ 085 899 9700; e hotelradar@tiscali.it; www.radarhotel.it. The Radar is a good-value option, even if its décor is more than a little dated. Rooms are of a good size & very simply decorated; those at the front all have sea views (it is worth requesting one). There are private beach facilities. HB & FB. **$$$**

⌂ **Hotel Mion** (85 rooms) Lungomare Trento 101; ☎ 085 899 2290; e info@hotelmion.it; www.hotelmion.it. The exterior of the building is not much to speak of (actually it rather looks like a prison) but it is rather more flash inside. Ignoring the questionable taste of the extravagant chandeliers & suchlike you will find some of the biggest rooms in town, as well as excellent service from very friendly staff. HB & FB. **$$$**

⌂ **Hotel Palmarosa** (61 rooms) Lungomare Trento 3; ☎ 085 894 1615; e info@hotelpalmarosa.it; www.hotelpalmarosa.it. Simple though modern rooms can be found at this classic Euro-beach resort hotel, alongside a large private beach, garden, & 'American' bar (though just what makes it so 'American' is hard to see). HB & FB. **$$$**

⌂ **Residence Felicioni** (69 apts) Lungomare Trieste; ☎ 085 894 4163; e info@residencefelicioni.com; www.residencefelicioni.com. For everything that is included in the price, this huge residence is an ideal place to stay, especially for longer periods. Apartments all include kitchens & AC, & there is private parking & beach facilities. HB & FB. **$$$**

Other restaurants

✗ **Ristorante da Peppe** Lungomare Roma 14; ☎ 085 899 2140; ⊕ Tue–Sun. This relaxed & friendly restaurant specialises in fish & seafood, & does it well. Try the refreshing cold seafood dishes; they're great on a hot summer night. **$$**

✗ **Locanda di Jezz** Via Grottaferrata, 3; ☎ 085 915 0092; ⊕ Wed–Mon. The owners here really cook up a feast for you, with seafood featuring prominently. In a region where vegetarianism hasn't really taken off, the restaurant prides itself on including a number of tasty vegetarian dishes on its menu. **$$**

Other practicalities Most of the town's amenities are located on Via Nazionale (SS16). There are a few banks in town with **ATM** facilities,

Banks
$ **Banca delle Marche** Via Nazionale 330
$ **Banca Popolare dell'Adriatico** Via Nazionale 426
$ **Banca Antonveneta** Via Nazionale 453
$ **Banca Toscana** Via Nazionale 458

Chemists
✚ **Farmacia Chicco Antonio** Via Nazionale 495; 📞085 899 8187
✚ **Farmacia Eredi** Via Nazionale 98; 📞085 899 0237
✚ **Farmacia Candelori** Via Tevere 1; 📞085 899 2161

Post office
✉ Via Nazionale 229; 📞085 894 4211

GIULIANOVA The medieval town of Giulianova, situated on a hill overlooking the coast, has more substance than its neighbours, Roseto degli Abruzzi and Pineto. While the beaches may not be as fine as those of, say, Pineto, there is much more to see away from them. Thus it effectively enjoys the best of both worlds: wide beaches overlooked by the domes and spires of the attractive old town above.

The two parts of the city are the old town, known as Giulianova Città (Giulianova City), and the beachfront, known as Giulianova Lido. Note that the central and northern coasts of Giulianova Lido have better stretches of beach than the southern coast.

Tourist information
🎫 **IAT Giulianova** Via Nazario Sauro; 📞085 800 3013; e iat.giulianova@abruzzoturismo.it. The town's main tourist information point is found in the lower town, Giulianova Lido.

 Where to stay All the places listed below are in Giulianova Lido.

Upmarket
⌂ **Grand Hotel Don Juan** (148 rooms) Lungomare Zara 97; 📞085 800 8341; e info@ grandhoteldonjuan.it; www.grandhoteldonjuan. it. Similar in quality to the Cristallo below, the Don Juan is impeccably decorated & deserves to be given a 'boutique hotel' label. A whitewashed building, it features modern rooms with all mod cons, a private beach, & a health & spa centre with all manner of treatments. HB & FB. **$$$$**
⌂ **Hotel Cristallo** (55 rooms) Lungomare Zara 73; 📞085 800 3780; e info@hcristallo.it; www. hcristallo.it. A stylish & modern 4-star property with beautifully decorated rooms & lobby. The owners have paid great attention to detail & it really pays off. The clean-cut lines of shiny floorboards & new leather sofas give it the feel of a big city hotel with a seaside edge. The restaurant is amazing & is often used for private functions such as weddings or company meetings. There are also private beach facilities for guests & excellent views

from the sun deck at the top of the building. HB & FB. **$$$$**
⌂ **Parco dei Principi** (87 rooms) Lungomare Zara; 📞085 800 8935;
e info@ giulianovaparcodeiprincipi.it; www. giulianovaparcodeiprincipi.it; ⊕ May–Sep. The Parco dei Principi is aptly named. It looks as though it belongs in an oil-rich Arab state as the residence of a wealthy family. Apart from contemporary & brightly lit rooms, the hotel has a large outdoor pool area flanked by Roman-style statues as well as private beach facilities. HB & FB. **$$$$**

Mid range
⌂ **Hotel Europa** (72 rooms) Lungomare Zara 57; 📞085 800 3600; e info@htleuropa.it; www. htleuropa.it. This nice Best Western hotel is rather well done, with modern rooms (some with excellent views), a good restaurant & a pleasant outdoor pool area. HB & FB. **$$$**

🏨 **Hotel Miramare** (57 rooms) Lungomare Spalato 82; ✆ 085 800 5320; e info@hmiramare.it; www.hmiramare.it. A bright & airy hotel featuring decently sized rooms with lovely views from their balconies & a big, simply decorated restaurant with some very good food (particularly the meat dishes). HB & FB. **$$$**

🏨 **Hotel Ritz** (40 rooms) Via Quinto 3; ✆ 085 800 8470; e info@hotelritz.it; www.hotelritz.it; ⊕ May–Sep. Don't be fooled by the name; this hotel doesn't match up to the hotels of the same name in London & Paris. It is, though, still a pleasant place to stay, considerably cheaper than its 5-star namesakes, with a relatively modern interior & well-proportioned rooms, a restaurant, pool & private beach facilities. HB & FB. **$$$**

🏨 **Albergo Garden** (9 rooms) Via Montefalcone 53; ✆ 085 800 4961; e albergogarden@gmail.com; www.hotelgardengiulianova.it. This small hotel, set back from the beach, features rather basic but perfectly adequate accommodation at good prices. The restaurant's friendly staff will serve up a host of good local dishes. Try the pasta with *ragù* sauce. HB & FB. **$$**

✖ **Where to eat** In addition to the hotels above, there are a couple of recommended restaurants in the town.

✖ **Ristorante Beccaceci** Via Zola 28; ✆ 085 800 3550; ⊕ Tue–Sat. Beccaceci is a locally famous, family-run restaurant. People come from towns nearby to eat the excellent seafood, & the large & varied wine list is also worth perusing. The staff are welcoming & the atmosphere conducive to a relaxed dinner. **$$$**

✖ **Terrazza Buozzi** Piazza Buozzi; ✆ 392 402 2802; ⊕ daily. The spanning views from its sun terrace are as much a drawcard here as the food itself. There's nothing quite like watching dusk settle on the Adriatic with a glass of red in hand. Try the mixed *bruschetta* & the varied meats of the mixed antipasti. **$$$**

✖ **Ristorante The Fool** Largo del Forno 1; ✆ 085 802 8500; e the_fool@hotmail.it. You certainly wouldn't be a fool for eating here. Located on a piazza in the old town, this eatery serves very tasty Sardinian food. The mixed *bruschetta* is a must & so are the Sardinian sausages (*salsiccia sarda*). **$$**

Other practicalities

Giulianova Lido There are **banks** with ATMs at Banca Popolare dell'Adriatico (*Via Turati 48*); Banca Nazionale del Lavoro (*Via G Galilei 188*); and UniCredit Banca (*Via G Galilei 3*).

Chemists can be found at Farmacia Ielo Fiammetta (*Via Orsini 103;* ✆ *085 800 7712*) and Farmacia Comunale (*Via Trieste 159;* ✆ *085 802 6965*), and there's a **post office** at Via dell'Annunziata 72 (✆ *085 800 0646;* ⊕ *Mon, Wed & Fri 08.00–13.30, Tue & Thu 08.00–18.30, Sat 08.00–12.30*).

Giulianova Città For **banks**, try Tercas (*Corso Garibaldi 1*). The town's **hospital** (*Ospedale Civile;* ✆ *085 80201*) is at Via Gramsci in the upper part of the town. There are also a couple of **chemists** in this part of town: Farmacia Dr Marcelli Tito (*Piazza della Libertà 35;* ✆ *085 800 3204*) and Farmacia Galli (*Via A Gramsci 45;* ✆ *085 800 3349*).

The **post office** in Giulianova Città is at Via Gramsci 1 (✆ *085 800 3445*) and has the same opening hours as the one in Giulianova Lido.

Events

July I Tesori di Fattoria. The Farmhouse Treasures festival, held in late July, sees one of the largest turnouts in all Abruzzo for a town fair. It is held in the old town's Piazza della Libertà (see page 218) and features a market, local dishes and music.

August Sagra del Pesce. In mid-August the town hosts an annual Seafood Fair at the amphitheatre on the southern coast. A wide variety of seafood is served and the fair culminates in a special dish (the recipe varies from year to year) that is served on 15 August. As with any other fair, there is music, dancing and shopping.

What to see and do

Church of San Flaviano The dome of this church, colloquially named 'La Rotonda', dominates the view of the city for miles around. It was built in the 16th century just after construction had begun on the city of Giulianova, and has a distinctive northern Italian feel thanks to the Lombard architects who worked on it. The church has been restored and although its interior doesn't contain any artefacts of importance it is still worth a look.

Il Bianco Tower This solid, imposing tower was once part of the larger fortifications that surrounded the old city. It is now the only visible remnant of this wall, with other sections incorporated into nearby residential buildings. Inside is the **Archaeological Museum** (*Museo Archeologico; Torrone Il Bianco, Via del Popolo, cnr Via Acquaviva;* ✎ *085 802 1215;* ⊕ *sporadically, call for information; admission free*).

Splendore Museum of Art (*Museo d'Arte dello Splendore; Via dello Splendore 112;* ✎ *085 800 7157; www.museodellosplendore.it;* ⊕ *Tue–Sun 17.00–20.00; admission free*) This museum features an extensive collection of contemporary art including works by Bruno, Galligani, Valentini and Zotti. The courtyard is a little paradise, full of greenery, and even contains a chicken pen.

Piazza della Libertà Giulianova's terrace is the Piazza della Libertà, a big square with great views over Giulianova Lido and its port.

TORTORETO Like Giulianova, the beachside town of Tortoreto Lido has the added benefit of being overlooked by the older, medieval town (sometimes known as Tortoreto Alto) with a few pleasant churches. Below this attractive little town you will find another of Abruzzo's gorgeous Blue Flag beaches. The town's relaxed atmosphere is partly due to the slow pace of life, not to mention the countless palm trees, which lend a slightly tropical feel.

Tourist information

🄸 **IAT Tortoreto** Via Archimede 15; ✎ 0861 787 726; e iat.tortoreto@abruzzoturismo.it

 ## Where to stay

Upmarket

🏠 **Hotel Ambassador** (79 rooms) Lungomare Sirena 598; ✎ 0861 777399; e info@h-ambassador. com; www.h-ambassador.com. This classy 4-star hotel has a striking appearance & is one of the best places to stay in the area. Apart from beautifully decorated rooms & excellent beach facilities, it has a fantastic roof-garden terrace complete with its own stage & entertainment. This is also popular with locals for private parties & functions. Staff are helpful & enthusiastic. HB & FB. **$$$$**

🏠 **Residence Playa** (26 apts) Lungomare Sirena 106; ✎ 0861 788980; e info@ residenceplaya.it;

www.residenceplaya.it. This low-key hotel is nicely turned out & has a bit of class, particularly its public areas. It has good rooms & a beautiful outdoor pool area dotted with palm trees, & lies just across the road from the beach. **$$$$**

Mid range

🏠 **Hotel Clara** (48 rooms) Via Archimede 80; ✎ 0861 787782; e info@hclara.it; www.hclara.it. A comfortable, straightforward hotel not far from the beach, with simple though modern rooms, a lovely spa, terrace & private beach facilities. Group discounts apply. HB & FB. **$$$**

🏠 **Hotel Continental** (50 rooms) Lungomare Sirena, 30; ☎0861 787020; e info@hcontinental.com; www.hcontinental.com; ⊕ May–Sep. The rooms are a bit small but simple & unfussy in this 3-star establishment. On the plus side, it is clean, with attentive staff, & there's a private beach for guests. HB & FB. **$$$**

🏠 **Hotel Lady G** (36 rooms) Via Vespucci 21/23; ☎0861 788008; e info@ladyg.it; www.ladyg.it; ⊕ Apr–Sep. Set about 100m from the beach, this attractive, no-fuss hotel offers simple but spotless modern rooms, a pool & restaurant. HB & FB. **$$$**

🏠 **Verdemare B&B** (4 rooms) Lungomare Sirena 620–622; m 347 885 2157; e info@verdemaretortoreto.it; www.verdemaretortoreto.it. This beautiful modern B&B, across the road from the beach, is set in its own verdant grounds with a pretty landscaped front garden. The rooms are colourful, the staff friendly & an excellent b/fast is on offer. **$$$**

🏠 **Villa Elena** (39 rooms) Viale Adriatico 136/138; ☎0861 774408; e info@hotelvillaelena.it; www.hotelvillaelena.it. A very pleasant hotel not too far from the beach. It is ideal for families as it features large rooms (apparently soundproofed) & a kids' play area. The pool area is conducive to a spot of rest & relaxation. The restaurant, decorated in pastel colours, is small but welcoming. Pasta dishes are fantastic. HB & FB. **$$$**

🏠 **Residence Hèlène** (15 rooms) Via Nizza 10; ☎0861 787 819; e info@residencehelene.com; www.residencehelene.com; ⊕ May–Sep. A good-value-for-money, 1-star hotel with clean, no-fuss rooms, a restaurant serving simply presented though excellent food (try the lamb), friendly staff, & all just a stone's throw from the beach. HB & FB. **$$**

✕ **Where to eat and drink** As elsewhere along this coast, all the hotels above have their own restaurants, but the old town above also has a few excellent restaurants:

✕ **Anchise** Via XX Settembre 60; ☎0861 786587; ⊕ Tue–Sun. An authentic local dining experience is to be had at the Anchise, a few doors down from the Cantina del Nonno (above). Pasta is homemade & the pizzas are simple but scrumptious. The restaurant has a perfectly situated terrace overlooking the surrounding hills. **$$$**

✕ **La Cantina Del Nonno** Via XX Settembre 37; ☎0861 788315; ⊕ daily except Wed in winter. This rustic cantina is in the heart of the old town overlooking the coast. Fuss is kept to a minimum & the food is the simple fare you would expect from a traditional Abruzzese restaurant. The lamb is delicious & for those with a sweet tooth, the *tiramlsù* is one of the best for miles. **$$$**

Other practicalities The town's amenities are all found in Tortorero Lido.

Banks
$ **Banca Caripe** Via Nazionale Adriatica 41
$ **Banca di Teramo** Via Nazionale Adriatica 146
$ **Banca Picena Truentina** Via Trieste 144

Chemists
✚ **Farmacia Gasparroni** Via Carducci 145; ☎0861 787039

✚ **Farmacia Comunale** Piazza della Libertà 12; ☎0861 774785
✚ **Farmacia Misantone** Via Nazionale Adriatica 106; ☎0861 787274

Post office
✉ Via Archimede 17; ☎0861 788588

What to see and do The medieval town of Tortoreto, a short but pleasant drive from the beach, is certainly worth exploring. The road between the two is lined with olive groves and is steep, so walking would take about an hour.

Tortoreto Like its neighbours that occupy a scenic spot above the coast, the old town of Tortoreto also has a lovely viewpoint: **Belvedere**. It is a great place for a family picnic and on a clear day you can see right down the coast as far as Pineto. The town has several churches, and in the nearby district of Le Muracche are the interesting remains of a **Roman villa**. You can walk there from Tortoreto in about 45 minutes, but they're not strictly open to the public.

Church of Santa Maria della Misericordia This little gem of a church on Via Terranova was built towards the end of the 14th century in honour of the Virgin Mary who, apparently, saved the town from the plague of 1348. To the left of the entrance there is an interesting set of frescoes depicting this. Most of the frescoes are the work of Giacomo Bonfini; look for his signature and the date on the frescoes of 16 September 1526.

The most interesting of the set is to the right of the entrance: an extremely well-preserved depiction of a nativity scene. The apse has a fresco of Jesus nailed to the cross, but more interesting is the portrayal of the old town of Tortoreto in the background. This fresco was restored during the 1970s.

Church of San Nicola di Bari The first church on this site dates from about the year 1000, although the current one was erected in 1534, shown by a plaque on the side of the building. The paintings inside are the work of a local artist, Marcello Liberati.

Church of Sant'Agostino The most interesting part of this 17th-century church is its doors: one has a depiction of a bishop with his crozier and another a bishop folding his hands in prayer.

Tortoreto Lido While Tortoreto Lido is a typical beach town, with little in the way of tourist attractions other than a wide, sandy beach, it does boast the tiny **Museum of Marine Culture** (*Museo della Cultura Marinara; Via Nazionale Nord 1;* \ *0861 789180;* ⊕ *Tue–Fri 15.00–19.00, morning on request; admission free*). It's located in the lower beach area of town and has a collection of sea life found along the coast.

Just five minutes by car from Tortoreto Lido is **AcquaPark Onda Blù** (*SP8, km0 +700;* \ *0861 7791; www.acquaparkondablu.it;* ⊕ *daily during warmer months 10.00–18.30; admission adult €20, child €15*), a water theme park with all the usual waterslides and pools that was once the only one in Abruzzo. It has seen better days, although it can still be a fun day out, especially if you have children. Be mindful that it can get rather crowded on Sundays.

ALBA ADRIATICA The modern seaside resort town of Alba Adriatica (whose name translates as 'Adriatic Sunrise') probably has more hotel rooms and beds than residents. Its beachfront development resembles more that of Pescara than its provincial neighbours, and it caters to those who want a busier, more crowded beach holiday. The town itself is rather uninspiring and there isn't much to do apart from lounge around on the beach and come back and eat at your hotel. That said, it's by no means an unpleasant place. The huge pine plantation on the central section of the coast is quite lovely and has picnic facilities and a kids' playground.

Alba (for short) is popular with the German tourists who drive along the coast in search of idyllic weather and beaches and decide that Martinsicuro (the first town in Abruzzo coming from the north) is a little too low-key.

Tourist information
🛈 **IAT Alba Adriatica** Lungomare Marconi; \ 0861 712426; e iat.albaadriatica@ abruzzoturismo.it

⌂ Where to stay

Upmarket

⌂ **Hotel Doge** (60 rooms) Lungomare Marconi 292; 📞0861 712508; e info@hoteldoge.it; www. hoteldoge.it; ⏱ May–Sep. This efficient, family-run hotel is another place that doesn't look much from the outside, but it has good rooms, a great pool area & is right on the beach. Facilities include bicycle hire. HB & FB. **$$$$**

⌂ **Hotel Eden** (56 rooms) Lungomare Marconi 328; 📞0861 714251; e info@hoteleden.it; www. hoteleden.it; ⏱ Apr–Sep. Alfredo Ricci's Hotel Eden might not look like much from the outside but it is arguably the best hotel in the area. Very comfortable, clean & decently sized rooms are accompanied by an excellent restaurant serving a plethora of meat & pasta dishes (try the lamb), good facilities (such as a lovely pool) & a private beach for guests. HB & FB. **$$$$**

⌂ **Hotel Excelsior** (56 rooms) Lungomare Marconi 238; 📞0861 712345; e info@ excelsioralba.com; www.excelsioralba.com; ⏱ May–Sep. The owners of the 3-star Excelsior have created a modern & comfortable atmosphere for their guests. Rooms are very light & airy, all with a balcony overlooking the sea, & there is ample parking. The buffet b/fast here is memorable. HB & FB. **$$$$**

⌂ **Hotel Meripol** (51 rooms) Lungomare Marconi 290; 📞0861 714744; e info@ hotelmeripol.it; www.hotelmeripol.it. Another top-notch 4-star hotel, though this 1 is open all year round. Rooms are modern, bright & airy. The private beach is excellent, as are the service & restaurants. HB & FB. **$$$$**

⌂ **Hotel Sporting** (50 rooms) Lungomare Marconi 308; 📞0861 712510; e info@hsporting. it; www.hsporting.it; ⏱ May–Sep. Hotel Sporting is great for a family or group stay. The rooms are comfortable & there are bigger apartments for larger parties. Aside from its private beach facilities, there are 2 attractive pools & a tennis court. Restaurant staff are friendly & the food is good. HB & FB. **$$$$**

⌂ **Hotel Tassoni** (40 rooms) Lungomare Marconi 28; 📞0861 712530; e info@hoteltassoni. it; www.hoteltassoni.it; ⏱ May–Sep. Although this hotel is a bit pricy for its class, it is still a good option. It has excellent, spacious rooms, a very big swimming pool & a handy fitness area. It's all complemented by great staff who really seem to care about the place. HB & FB. **$$$$**

Mid range

⌂ **Hotel Astor** (30 rooms) Via Reno 6; 📞0861 714207; e info@hotelastor.it; www.hotelastor. it; ⏱ May–Sep. Set away from the beach, the Astor has rooms that are more than comfortable & the private beach facilities are not far away. If the décor (such as the suede bar bench) can be a little odd, the bar is a good place to while away a few hours, & the restaurant (decorated in pastel blues, yellows & oranges) serves some great local pasta dishes. HB & FB. **$$$**

⌂ **Hotel Atlas** (35 rooms) Lungomare Marconi 314; 📞0861 712393; e info@hotelatlas.it; www. hotelatlas.it. The Atlas is a beachfront, 3-star establishment whose rooftop terrace & al fresco dining & drinking area make it a great place for a drink. The rooms are of a good standard & the staff are helpful. HB & FB. **$$$**

⌂ **Hotel Baltic** (35 rooms) Lungomare Marconi 310; 📞0861 714693; e info@hotelbaltic.it; www. hotelbaltic.it; ⏱ May–Sep. You will find, as I did, that there's nothing even remotely Baltic about this beachfront hotel; it is a purely Mediterranean experience. All rooms all have sea views (which is an added benefit) & there is free use of hotel bicycles (very handy). The restaurant is not bad value for money, either. HB & FB. **$$$**

Budget

⌂ **Hotel Adria** (26 rooms) Via Calabria 20; 📞0861 712453; e info@adria-hotel.it; www. adria-hotel.it. The décor in some rooms of this discreet 2-star hotel is a little dated, but it is not far from the beach & offers good value in reasonably comfortable rooms. HB & FB. **$$**

⌂ **Hotel Euro** (19 rooms) Via Trento 14A; 📞0861 752092; e info@hoteleuro.info; www. hoteleuro.info; ⏱ May–Sep. A simple, modern hotel, recently upgraded to 2 stars. Very clean & uncluttered with simple rooms on offer, it also has a pleasant al fresco seating area & a restaurant. HB & FB. **$$**

⌂ **Hotel Lidia** (7 rooms) Via dei Tigli 15; 📞0861 714441; e info@hotel-lidia.it; www.hotel-lidia. it. The Lidia's looking a little worse for wear, & its exterior (it looks like a Russian communist shed) might cause you to flee, but this small hotel offers very good value for money. Accommodation is in simple, clean rooms; AC & beach facilities are extra. HB & FB. **$$**

🏠 **Hotel Naxos** (22 rooms) Via C Battisti 156; 📞0861 751666; e info@enzotavoni.it; www. enzotavoni.it; ⊕ Apr–Sep. The Naxos might look like a run-of-the-mill apartment building with some dated décor, but the rooms are comfortable if functional, not to mention very well priced, & it's not far from the beach. **$$**

✖ Where to eat
If you're looking for somewhere different to eat, beyond the hotels, there are several possibilities.

✖ **Hostaria Arca** Viale Mazzini 109; 📞0861 714647; www.hostariaarca.it; ⊕ Wed–Mon. This boutique restaurant is one of the city's best & a great favourite with locals & visitors alike. The dishes mix modern creativity with local traditions & recipes. Come especially for the pasta dishes & the seafood. The pork stuffed with rabbit is an excellent, belly-bursting dinner option. **$$$**

✖ **Osteria Carlo V** Torre della Vibrata, Via Cavour 20; 📞0861 710225. Set within an old medieval watchtower, this is an excellent alternative to eating at your hotel. The food, mostly local dishes, is tasty & the restaurant has an ample selection of beers as well as a very good-value fixed menu. **$$**

✖ **Ristorante Casa Rossa** Via Ascolana 58; 📞0861 711899; www.hotelristorantecasarossa. it; ⊕ Thu–Tue. Set within the Hotel Casa Rossa is this gorgeous rustic restaurant, with a variety of traditional local dishes, as well as international fare. Try the pizza: it is made in the owner's wood-fired oven. Friendly staff & a relaxing atmosphere add to the experience. **$$**

✖ **Ristorante Cinese Giardino del Mare** Lungomare Marconi 236; 📞0861 711481. The only Chinese restaurant for miles, the Giardino del Mare offers a variety of Chinese dishes including some nice seafood options. Chinese food is not all that popular in Italy so this place is never quite packed to the gunwales. The ambience is relaxing & the service good. **$$**

Other practicalities The town's **banks** are Banca delle Marche (*Via Mazzini 24*), Banca Picena Truentina (*Via Mazzini 45*) and Banca Popolare dell'Adriatico (*Via Roma 125*). A **chemist** can be found at either Farmacia Bruni Massimo (*Via Trieste 15B,* 📞*0861 719153*) or Farmacia Parere Arnaldo (*Via Roma 42,* 📞*0861 712352*).
The **post office** is at Via Risorgimento 4 (📞*0861 727031*).

MARTINSICURO Martinsicuro is Abruzzo's northernmost town and beachside resort. It is a quieter alternative to the neighbouring Alba Adriatica, with fewer hotels and a shorter coastline (including a Blue Flag beach). There is not very much to do in town, but one site of note is the 16th-century **Tower of Charles V**. It is easy to wander into the tower's grounds, though the tower itself was closed at the time of writing; a museum is being set up here displaying archaeological finds from the local area.

Tourist information
🔲 **IAT Martinsicuro** Via Aldo Moro 32/A; 📞0861 762336

🏠 **Where to stay** Many of the town's hotels are in the area of Villa Rosa, 2km to the south but still part of Martinsicuro.

Upmarket
🏠 **Hotel Villa Truentum** (20 rooms, 35 apts) Via dei Colli 3; 📞0861 762191; e hvt@libero. it; www.hotelvillatruentum.com. This rather uncharismatic modern block seems somewhat overpriced. Its rooms & apartments are pretty standard, though they are clean & comfortable. There is a gym, meeting rooms, a snack bar & even wireless internet for which you might be thankful as there are no internet cafés around. **$$$$**

Mid range

🏠 **Hotel Corallo Abruzzo** (40 rooms)
Lungomare Italia 60, Villa Rosa; ✆0861
714126; e info@ hotelcoralloabruzzo.it; www.
hotelcoralloabruzzo.it; ⏰ Apr–Sep. An excellent
beachfront hotel with a beautiful garden & pool
area. The rooms are very light & quite large with
tasteful décor, & the restaurant offers up some
decent seafood. HB & FB. **$$$**

🏠 **Hotel Haway** (44 rooms) Lungomare
Italia 62, Villa Rosa; ✆0861 712649; e info@
hotelhaway.it; www.hotelhaway.it; ⏰ May–Sep.
The Haway is a great place for families, priding
itself on the variety of its kids' activities & its
special afternoon snacks – consisting of one of
the country's favourites, Nutella on bread. It may
not sound like much but parents who are after
a bit of R&R will be thankful that their children
are kept happy & busy. Rooms are spacious &
guests have access to a pool area & private beach
facilities. HB & FB. **$$$**

🏠 **Hotel Olimpic** (56 rooms) Lungomare
Italia 72, Villa Rosa; ✆0861 712390; e olimpic@
hotelolimpic.it; www.hotelolimpic.it;
⏰ May–Sep. The family-run Olimpic is a

standard, fairly simple beachfront hotel with
bright & colourful rooms accompanied by a large
pool area, restaurant & private beach facilities.
HB & FB. **$$$**

🏠 **Hotel Riva d'Oro** (40 rooms) Via Riva
d'Oro 3; ✆0861 761258; e info@rivadoro.it;
www.rivadoro.it; ⏰ May–Sep. The Riva d'Oro
is a recently refurbished hotel which features
tastefully decorated, modern rooms with
spacious bathrooms. The pool area is a great spot
in which to lounge around & relax. The gym,
unusually for a hotel, actually has some good,
new equipment & the private beach area does
not get too crowded (a plus in summer). HB &
FB. **$$$**

🏠 **Hotel Sympathy** (40 rooms) Lungomare
Europa 26; ✆0861 760222; e info@sympathyhotel.
it; www.sympathyhotel.it; ⏰ Apr–Sep. Emalia
Ciaralli's colourful family-run hotel offers bright &
airy rooms, some with excellent views, & a private
beach across the road. The restaurant features a
relaxed dining ambience & the food (such as the
excellent pasta dishes) is tasty but not pretentious.
$$$

✖️ **Where to eat** For a break from the hotel restaurants, try:

✖ **Pasqualò** Via Colle di Marzio 40; ✆0861
760321; ⏰ Tue–Sun. Away from the beachfront
establishments, Pasqualò is one of the most
popular places in town for a good dish of seafood.
It's a simple, relaxed place, & the prawns are
fantastic. **$$$**

✖ **Ristorante Minerva** Via Franchi 77; ✆0861
71440; ⏰ Tue–Sun. The Minerva serves up a
seafood feast only a stone's throw from the popular
beaches of the town. A perfect meal: the *antipasto
misto freddo* (cold seafood antipasto) followed by
the *spaghetti vongole* washed down with a local
white. **$$$**

Other practicalities Martinsicuro boasts both a couple of **banks**, Banca Toscana
(*Via Roma 186*) and Banca Popolare dell'Adriatico (*Via Roma, cnr Via del Vignola*)
and two **chemists**: Farmacia Bruni Parere Maria Teresa (*Via Roma 162;* ✆ *0861
797560*) and Farmacia del Principe Palmina (*Via Tordino 1;* ✆ *0861 762126*). The
post office is on Via Piemonte 13 (✆ *0861 795332*).

VIBRATA RIVER VALLEY

The Vibrata River runs from the province's northeastern mountains down to the
Adriatic. It is a relatively short river, rising at around 1,700m above sea level and
flowing for only around 30km. However, it passes by or through some of the most
spectacular towns in the province of Teramo.

The valley is relatively small so it is best to base yourself at one of the towns along
the coast, particularly if you have your own transport. The farthest reaches of the
valley are never more than a 45-minute drive from the coast.

GETTING THERE AND AROUND

By car Various provincial roads run along the valley, as well as the SS259 from the coast. From Teramo, take the SS81 and turn off onto the SS259.

By bus ARPA run services from Giulianova and Tortoreto, through Alba Adriatica and on to Civitella del Tronto, stopping at all the major towns in the valley. The journey from Alba Adriatica to Civitella del Tronto takes approximately an hour.

COLONNELLA The delightful town of Colonnella is a few short kilometres from Martinsicuro, though the road between them is quite steep. This leads you into the historic centre, where you will find yourself at the bottom of a long **staircase** leading to the town's main church. On the second level of this staircase there is a **war memorial** erected in 1928, and on the third level an interesting little **tower** of unknown use and origin.

At the top the **Church of Santi Cipriano e Giustina** (⊕ daily 09.00–18.30) was built in the 18th century. The interior houses an interesting sculpture of Jesus lying atop a tomb and an 18th-century statue of the Madonna. There is also a fine 19th-century organ.

The **clock** and **belltower** are reached by following a little road beside the church. The tower has great views over the surrounding countryside, stretching all the way to the Majella National Park. There are also fantastic views of the coast from Piazza del Popolo.

CONTROGUERRA Controguerra (its name literally means 'against war') is best reached by road from Colonnella, a beautiful drive through the olive groves of the nearby hills. The town is usually only visited for the frescoes that adorn the walls of its **Church of San Benedetto Abate**. If you take a walk through the town you will also come across the **Palazzo Ducale**, at the highest point of town. The streets are unusually lively for rural Abruzzo, thanks to a healthy population of young people.

CORROPOLI This unassuming little town is set out around the very pleasant **Piazza Piedicorte**, with its delightful fountain surrounded by 12 palm trees and overlooked by the belltower of the **Church of Sant'Agnese**. The church itself has a simple façade which hides a marvellously ornate interior.

However, the highlight of Corropoli is the **Abbey of Santa Maria a Mejulano**, about 1km from the centre of town. The complex, beautifully set in its own grounds with a pine tree-lined driveway, has an impressive brick façade. The cloister has been rebuilt, and the interior now houses a school, and (at the time of writing) the offices of the town hall.

NERETO Nereto is largely industrial, although its centre contains some interesting buildings. One is the **Town Hall Building** on Piazza della Republica. Although it may look medieval it was actually built in the early 20th century. The most interesting church in Nereto is the 12th-century **Church of San Martino**, apparently the oldest in the town. It has been restored over the years, but it still retains its charm, and the surrounding parkland makes a nice spot for a picnic.

ANCARANO Ancarano is one of the prettiest villages in the area, with stunning views over the province. It is a sleepy little place with a few interesting sites, especially the village's surviving gateways: the 16th-century **Porta de Monte**, and the **Porta da Mare**. The former is found off **Belvederc Cecco d'Ascoli**, with its sweeping views of Gran Sasso and over to Le Marche. The latter gateway has an inscription dating back to the 17th century; its tower has now been absorbed into the surrounding buildings. Near this gate is the 16th-century **Palazzo della Comunità** as well as the ruins of an old **tower**.

The **Parish Church of the Madonna della Pace** is a modern building, though it houses a wooden statue of the Madonna and Child, which dates back to the 15th century.

FARAONE ANTICO The deserted medieval town of Faraone is actually part of the uninspiring town of Sant'Egidio alla Vibrata. To get here, head to Faraone Nuova and take the turn-off when you see the sign 'posta'. The abandoned town is located on Via Faraone Antico.

Upon reaching it, you pass through a majestic round-arched entrance **gate**. The ruined town is almost completely hidden by greenery and is set on the shores of a small river. Just behind the gate is the **Church of Santa Maria della Misericordia**. It is a rather strange feeling to look around the desolate and crumbling church with its damaged frescoes and then to peek into houses, long forgotten and mostly destroyed.

SANT'OMERO There isn't much to bring the tourist to the town of Sant'Omero except for some picturesque old streets and one very important church. The **Church of Santa Maria a Vico** is notable for being one of the very few surviving monuments in Abruzzo to have been built during the first millennium AD (the exact or even rough date is unknown). The interior houses some frescoes dating back to the 14th century. Restoration work has been carried out on the church, most notably during the 19th century.

CIVITELLA DEL TRONTO
Winner: Most Beautiful Villages in Italy; population around 5,000

If you only visit one place in the province of Teramo, it should undoubtedly be the stunning town of Civitella del Tronto. It is a small, wall-enclosed gem about 650m above sea level and is famous for its impressive fortress, important from both an architectural and a historical point of view. The town has withstood long sieges, such as those instigated by the French in the 1550s and again during the Risorgimento (Italian unification). It was voted one of the most beautiful villages in Italy in 2012.

Tourist information
🛈 **Town Hall** Corso Mazzini; 📞0861 918321

Where to stay and eat
🏠 **Hotel Fortezza** (27 rooms) Corso Mazzini 26/32; 📞0861 91321; e info@hotelfortezza.it; www.hotelfortezza.it. On a street off the main piazza not far from the Zunica is Hotel Fortezza. Its rooms are simple & comfortable, though the highlight is its restaurant. If it weren't for the walls completely lined with bottles of wine, the arched structure would appear much as it would have been 500 years ago. The menu is a mix of pastas & meat dishes; try the chicken breast with lemon & the creamy *tiramisù* for dessert. **$$$**

🏠 **Hotel Zunica** (17 rooms) Piazza Filippi Pepe 14; 📞0861 91319; e tremonelle@hotelzunica. it; www.hotelzunica.it. This is the hotel of choice in town. On the main piazza, it occupies an impressive building characterised by its typically Italian wooden shutters. The rooms are large, with solid old-fashioned but simple furnishings & very comfortable beds. The views from the rooms are majestic, with the piazza & churches framed by the valley below. The restaurant is prize winning & makes some superb pasta dishes. **$$$**

12

Other practicalities You will find the Farmacia Izzi Gianfranco (📞 *0861 91374*) on Piazza Filippi Pepe, the main square of the town. Largo Pietro Rosati Latinista, the town's second square, has a **post office** and various **banks** with ATMs.

What to see Civitella del Tronto is a very small town with some of the prettiest medieval streets in the region. Before exploring the handful of churches and the impressive fort, you should visit the **Ruetta d'Italia**, which is said to be the narrowest street in all of Italy. A grown man will need to tuck in his shoulders to get down it, and locals are keen to tell stories of tourists who have become stuck.

Churches
Church of Santa Maria dei Lumi This church and the associated religious complex is just outside the town, off the roundabout at the foot of the hill that takes you up to the town. Restoration has been carried out over the centuries (particularly in 1922 and 1960) but the site has been occupied since the 13th century. The cloister is particularly peaceful and its arches, well and belltower are very attractive. The church itself is impressive, with its paintings by local art students dating back to the 17th century.

Church of San Lorenzo Facing the main piazza is the Church of San Lorenzo, whose present form stems from a late 16th-century reconstruction, following damage during the French siege of 1557. The church is mentioned in documents from 1153, and other changes were added during the 18th century. The interior is a lovely pastel blue, with yellows, golds and light green, and is all the more impressive because it is almost completely covered with religious paintings.

Church of San Francesco This 14th-century church has an adjacent convent which was founded at about the same time. As with many other churches around Abruzzo, is was almost entirely transformed during the 18th century and given a Baroque appearance, but the original floorplan and single-nave layout can still be seen.

The Fortress (*www.fortezzacivitella.it*; ⊕ *daily summer 10.00–13.00 & 14.30–18.30; winter 10.00–13.00 & 14.30–17.30; admission adult €4, child €1*) This is without doubt one of the most impressive fortresses in the region. Its angular lines and dominant position on top of a hill are softened only by views across the terracotta rooftops and the rolling countryside below. Building commenced in 1564 and lasted around 12 years. Some restoration has taken place over the years but in general it remains unchanged from its original layout. Its dominance over the surrounding area ended with the struggles over the birth of the modern Italian state in the early 1860s. The fortress was then largely forgotten until 1973 when a restoration programme began that lasted until 1983. It has been open to the public since 1985.

You will need a good two hours to take in the entire fort. The top level of the fortress (arguably its most impressive) is largely in ruins but the views towards the Gran Sasso and of the town below are spectacular. At the top level of the fortress is the Church of San Giacomo, the burial place of Neapolitan soldiers who died during the battle of 1860. Nearby, is a display of arms from the battle and a large open piazza. A plaque here reads 'The hill opposite you marked the border between the Kingdom of the Two Sicilies and the Pontifical State before the Unification of Italy'.

Getting there From the car park in Largo Luigi Vinciguerra at the foot of the town there is a lift (⊕ *daily 10.00–19.30*) which will take you straight up to the fort if you're not inclined to climb up through the narrow lanes of Civitella.

Around Civitella del Tronto

The Abbey of Montesanto (*Abbazia di Montesanto, Via dell'Abazia; admission free*) It is said that the Abbey of Montesanto, a highlight of the area, may have been founded by St Benedict himself in the year AD540, though the current building dates back only to 1064. One of the most impressive Florentine-style Benedictine centres in the region, it was an important complex during the 13th century but eventually closed in 1797. Set on a hilltop, it is easy to see why, centuries ago, a site such as this was chosen to house a religious complex. The drive from the turn-off on the SS81 is lined with pines and, on arriving at the site's entrance immediately after the cemetery, you are met with a curious though appropriately contemplative sign that, translated, says: 'Know thyself: Who are you? Where are you going?' Pencil pines surround the site and, during the warmer months, the smell of oleander permeates the air.

The church here is the **Church of Santa Maria Assunta**, comprehensively restored in 1992 after some reconstruction during the 17th century. The oldest parts of the church date back to around the year 1100. The church has a single nave, but the site has been much transformed over the years and excavations have confirmed that the site once housed an early medieval church of three naves converted around the 13th century into a single-nave structure. The plain, almost austere, interior has a lovely timber ceiling. It is often open to the public and services during summer are at 17.30.

The **Abbey Gardens** are a peaceful haven with great views over the surrounding countryside. The gardens include a seven-stage 'meditation on the suffering of the Holy Mother'. The instructions translate as:

> A meditation of the pains of the Holy Mother of suffrage in seven stations, from the Annunciation to the Ascension. Stop at every station and recite a Hail Mary and a Glory in honour of the Holy Mary; *ora pro nobis*.

Getting there Follow the SS81 out of Civitella del Tronto towards Villa Lempa. Follow the sign to the Abazia di Montesanto, on a road called the Via dell'Abazia.

TORDINO RIVER VALLEY

The main section of the Tordino River cuts from just south of Giulianova all the way to Teramo. Since parts of it are rather industrialised, it is not the prettiest of valleys, though it does feature some interesting towns. The most notable of these is Campli, situated about 10km north of Teramo.

GETTING THERE AND AROUND

By car Part of the Tordino River crosses the SS80, the main road between the coast, the A14 *autostrada* and the interior of the province. The SS81 and 259 will get you to and from the Vibrata River valley.

By bus ARPA's service between Campli and Civitella del Tronto takes about half an hour, though there is only one departure per day (currently at 10.50). Non-direct services (around three per day) take one–two hours. There are also services from Teramo via Campli and through Sant'Omero and Mosciano Sant'Angelo to the coast. The entire journey takes around two hours.

By train There is a railway line from the coastal town of Giulianova to Teramo, which runs between the SS80 and the Tordino River. However, public transport from the stations along the way to other towns in the valley is almost non-existent.

CAMPLI Compared with nearby Civitella del Tronto, Campli is modest in its treasures. The earliest mention of the town is from AD849. Throughout the Middle Ages, it prospered due to its production of woollen cloth and terracotta vases. Today, it is better known for its artistic and architectural heritage.

Tourist information
Campli Local Tourist Board Piazza V Emanuele II; ☎0861 569321

Where to stay and eat
Hotel Scala Santa (13 rooms) Via Europa 6; ☎0861 569532; e info@hotelscalasanta.it; www. hotelscalasanta.it. Hotel Scala Santa is located about 1km east of the old town & is named after Campli's most famous attraction, the Holy Staircase (see page 230). In fact, parts of the exterior do resemble a church & the interior has some rather ill-fitting & extravagant church-like décor. Despite this, it is a comfortable place & the staff are extremely accommodating. The standard rooms are simply furnished, but superior rooms are more elaborate with somewhat questionable décor. Whilst the restaurant looks like a 1980s function hall, it offers good value for money. HB & FB. **$$$**

Other practicalities There is one **bank** in the centre of town, Banca Tercas (*Corso Umberto I 94*), but there is also an ATM at the **post office** (*Via San Salvatore 72;* ☎ *0861 569977*). Two **chemists** are on Corso Umberto 1: Farmacia del Corso (*Corso Umberto I 74;* ☎ *0861 56180*) and Farmacia Marozzi (*Corso Umberto I 60;* ☎ *0861 56112*).

What to see and do
Collegiate Church of Santa Maria in Platea Situated on the main square, this is the town's most important sight. It was once a cathedral, but was given collegiate status (similar in operation to a cathedral but not the seat of a bishop) in the late 14th century. The current façade and doorway were additions from the 18th century though its belfry remains that of the 14th-century church. The interior is particularly beautiful, its 18th-century wooden ceiling, painted by Teodoro Donato, an artist from Chieti, framed by the clean lines of its pillars and arches. There are some notable paintings such as a *Madonna with Child and Saints*, dating from 1577, and the crypt houses some 14th-century frescoes.

Church of San Francesco This church is found next to the National Archaeological Museum of Campli. Go through its intricate and ornate entrance to be met, on the left and right, by some old, charming frescoes dating back to the 14th century. Of the church's other frescoes, the most outstanding one is the incomplete 15th-century *Pietà*, near the choir.

Museo Nazionale Archeologico/National Archaeological Museum (*Piazza S Francesco;* ☎ *0861 569158;* ⊕ *Tue–Sun 09.00–20.00; admission adult €2, child €1*) This museum, inaugurated in 1988, is dedicated to the early history of the area and is housed in the former convent of San Francesco. There are displays of artefacts dug up from the nearly 600 tombs of the nearby necropolis of Campovalano. Excavations begun in 1964 have brought to light various levels of human remains, the earliest dating back to the 14th century BC. The tombs are recreated in the museum, with the finds placed exactly as they were discovered in each tomb. If you want to explore further, ask about possible visits to the climate-controlled storerooms where items that are not on display are housed.

Palazzo Farnese This civic building, opposite the Collegiate Church of Santa Maria in Platea, has some rather pretty triple-lancet windows. Although it has been rebuilt over the years, it remains one of the region's most distinguished *palazzi*.

BELLANTE Located between Campli and Mosciano Sant'Angelo, Bellante is a small, often ignored little town with a charming medieval **turreted gateway** on which many pigeons have made their home. Bellante also has an old belltower belonging to the **Church of Santa Maria**. Rebuilt like so many others during the 18th century, it has some noteworthy paintings and a Baroque stuccoed interior.

MOSCIANO SANT'ANGELO Mosciano rates a mention for its surviving medieval towers, most notably the well-preserved **Marini Tower** of the 15th century. It is also home to a **Museum of National Sciences** (*Museo di Scienze Naturali; Contrada Colle Leone 34;* ✆ *085 806 1499;* ⊕ *Mon, Wed & Fri summer 10.00–14.00; winter 10.00–13.00; admission free*), with a display of fossils and minerals found in the local area. Next door is the privately owned **Planetarium and Astronomical Observatory**, for which booking is essential (*Osservatorio Astronomico Colle Leone;* ✆ *085 806 1499 for booking & prices;* ⊕ *Mon, Wed & Fri 22.00 & 23.00*).

VOMANO RIVER VALLEY

The main section of this river runs from south of the city of Teramo to south of Roseto degli Abruzzi. The valley itself is characterised by winding roads dotted with olive groves. There are a number of medieval towns, though none as striking as any in the northern part of the province. The valley is also particularly known for the existence of one of only two triangular towers in the region of Abruzzo, the Montegualtieri Tower.

GETTING THERE AND AROUND
By car The Vomano River valley crosses the SS150, which connects the A14 and A24 *autostradas*. The SS81 (which stretches all the way from Pescara Province to Teramo Province) and SR559 will also get you to the valley.

By bus Most of the ARPA services through the Vomano Valley tend to go via Val Vomano and Teramo. A direct service between Cellino Attanasio and Teramo takes roughly an hour, and travels through the towns of Cermignano and Val Vomano.

MORRO D'ORO This rather low-key medieval settlement has one highlight, the **Church of Santa Maria di Propezzano**. Legend has it that a church was built here following a sighting of the Virgin Mary in May 715. However, the present structure dates from the 14th century, when the church's layout was 'modernised'. The church looks particularly striking from the outside. Its little arched brick veranda and the façade's rose window give way to a modest interior and a pretty arched cloister.

GUARDIA VOMANO This otherwise uninteresting town is home to the wonderful **Church of San Clemente al Vomano**. The building has existed since the 9th century and was modified in the early 1100s. One of the additions was the impressive ciborium (a holder for the Eucharist) held up by two rather thin marble pillars. There are also some fragments from some 12th-century frescoes. However, perhaps the most interesting feature here is the glass floor, which allows you to look down on the foundations of the Roman temple on which the church was built.

CASTELLALTO AND CASTELBASSO There isn't much to detain you in the town of Castellalto (roughly translated as 'high-castle'). Instead, head to Castelbasso ('low-castle'), which is actually a district of the former. Given that the whole town was a castle in the past, it still has a well-preserved ring of fortifications, even though parts have been absorbed by neighbouring houses. There are three **towers** of note: the Porta Est (East Gate), Porta Sud (South Gate) and the Piazza Portella Watchtower. The exact date of construction of the South Gate is a little unclear, though the East Gate was built in 1467. The church here is the **Parish Church of Apostoli Pietro e Andrea**, with its doorway dated 1338. Inside are a few paintings of note, one being a *Madonna with Child* from 1620.

MONTEGUALTIERI The town of Montegualtieri is famous for its **triangular tower** (closed to the public), of which there are very few in the region of Abruzzo. (There is a similar tower in the town of Bussi in Pescara Province; see page 88.) The tower is built on a rocky spur overlooking a huge swathe of countryside, an ideal defensive position. It dates back to the 14th and 15th centuries, though there is no evidence to suggest why it was built in the triangular form, or what its purpose was. That said, it was certainly built with defence in mind, as it reaches almost 20m in height. It was restored in the 1970s.

CELLINO ATTANASIO If at all possible, travel to Cellino Attanasio via Montegualtieri. The road takes you through some lovely Mediterranean scenery of gently rolling hills covered with olive groves and vineyards.

The main church here is the **Church of Santa Maria La Nova**, with its prominent belltower. It was founded in the 14th century, but underwent substantial rebuilding and restoration in the mid 19th century. While the outside has a striking entrance dating from 1424, the interior is quite plain in style and decoration. There are remnants of 14th-century frescoes on pillars that were part of the original medieval structure of the church and a candle column from the mid 14th century. There is also a 15th-century tabernacle and a Renaissance tomb.

The town also preserves a section of its old **walls**, the Mura di Cinti. The fortifications were erected in the first half of the 15th century, though the turrets that you can see along the top of the wall were added, needlessly, in the 20th century.

CASTEL CASTAGNA Roughly five minutes' drive north of the town of Castel Castagna is the remarkable **Church of Santa Maria di Ronzano**. Founded sometime during the 12th century, it is hard now to see why such a lonely, isolated church on a plain near a river was given such an astonishing interior. Painted in 1181, the well-preserved frescoes adorning the apse are simply outstanding; they depict scenes from the Old and New Testaments, including the *Last Judgement* and the *Annunciation*. These have survived the ravages of time but in 1183, only two years after the church's frescoes had been painted, a fire, whose traces can still be seen, destroyed many of the others. It is extraordinary to think that the church was once covered in them.

GRAN SASSO D'ITALIA NATIONAL PARK AND SURROUNDS

The areas of the Gran Sasso National Park that fall within the boundaries of the Teramo Province are some of its most attractive, albeit most inaccessible, sections. Jagged mountain peaks fall sharply onto plateaux which give way to rolling hills. A few short kilometres from the boundary with the province of L'Aquila is the tallest peak of the national park, the Corno Grande, which rises to over 2,900m above sea level; it is also the highest peak in mainland Italy, outside the alpine ranges of the north. The second-tallest peak in the national park is the Corno Piccolo, at around 2,655m above sea level.

GETTING THERE AND AROUND

By car From within the province of Teramo the SS80 will take you to within kilometres of Pietracamela and Prati di Tivo, while the A24 (exit San Gabriele Colledara) will enable you to reach Isola del Gran Sasso and Castelli. From Pescara Province it is best to take the SS81.

There is virtually no public transport within this area.

SKIING AND HIKING The best skiing and hiking in the Teramo section of the national park is around Pietracamela (see page 232). A section of the hiking trail, the Sentiero Italia (see box, page 234), crosses the Gran Sasso in this area. However, the hiking around here can be very challenging and it is best to seek advice (see page 234). The most popular skiing area is around Prati di Tivo (part of the local authority of Pietracamela). There are around 18km of trails for all levels of ability.

CASTELLI

Winner: Most Beautiful Villages in Italy; population around 1,300

The village of Castelli, constantly voted in Italy's Most Beautiful Villages programme, occupies one of the most dramatic settings in Abruzzo. Located at 497m on a spur at the foot of a mountain, it is surrounded by the thick forests of the national park and the barren, serrated cliffs of Monte Camicia, which soars to a height of just over 2,500m above sea level.

While first mention of the town is in documents dating from the 9th and 10th centuries, it is modern by Abruzzo standards (much of it dating from the 17th–19th centuries). It does, however, have an interesting 17th-century church, and is home to a Ceramics Museum, dedicated to the products of the famed Castelli ceramic works. Unlike some of the other winning settlements of the Most Beautiful Villages in Italy programme, there aren't many sights in Castelli itself, but its charm lies in its picture-perfect views down alleyways framed by mountain peaks and dense woods.

What to see and do

Parish Church of San Giovanni Battista If there is a 'Sistine Chapel' of Castelli ceramics, then this is it. The doorway is dated 1601 and inside is a fine 12th-century wooden Madonna and Child. However, the highlight is the altar front. It was made in 1647 and covered in majolica panels by local artist Francesco Grue.

Museo della Ceramica/Ceramics Museum (*Contrada Convento;* \ *0861 979398;* ⊕ *Tue–Sun 10.00–13.00*) Set in an ex-Franciscan Convent, the museum in Castelli houses a large collection of ceramics (see box, *The majolica tiles of Castelli*, opposite), from majolica tiles to ornate vases, dating from the Middle Ages. There are a huge number of pieces and some of the works are attributed to the greatest of local ceramic artists: Carlo Antonio, the Cappelletti family and Francesco Grue, the artist of the majolica tiles in the Church of San Giovanni Battista.

ISOLA DEL GRAN SASSO D'ITALIA
As its name – Island of the Gran Sasso – suggests, the town was built on an island between the Ruzzi and Mavone rivers. It occupies a great spot among the foothills of the national park. It has some noteworthy buildings, and sections of its original fortifications can still be seen amongst the houses. The two surviving town gates are the **Porta Canapina** and the **Porta del Torrione**.

Follow the signs out of town and you will reach the town's most important religious building, the 12th-century **Church of San Giovanni ad Insulam**. There is nothing particularly remarkable about its interior, but its simple façade and rose and lancet windows are framed by the woods and peaks of the Gran Sasso to create a beautifully tranquil scene.

PIETRACAMELA
Winner: Most Beautiful Villages in Italy; population around 300
The pretty village of Pietracamela, first settled in the 12th century, is located right in the middle of the Gran Sasso National Park, at 1,005m. It's near to Prati di Tivo (officially part of Pietracamela), a popular hub within the park.

The town's buildings and dwellings are spread out over a rocky spur and, miraculously, many of the old buildings have survived the regular earthquakes that hit the region. In fact, the population has decreased dramatically over the last 50 years and although this is true throughout rural Abruzzo, it is particularly so in Pietracamela because many buildings have fundamental structural flaws. While some residents have chosen to rebuild their houses, many have simply sold or abandoned them. In the past, the villagers were known for a woven woollen fabric known as *carfagni*, created to be almost waterproof but now rarely found.

What to see and do Pietracamela is a maze of picturesque 13th- and 14th-century streets and alleys. The **tower** on the village's fortifications has a window dated 1550 and nearby is the **Church of San Leucio** with a notable 18th-century organ and 16th-century holy water stoup. Other churches here include the **Church of San Donato**, with a 16th-century stone doorway, and the 15th-century **Church of San Giovanni**.

Hiking Walks through the nearby mountains are mostly found to the north of the village. These are well signposted and show the average walking times for each destination. Note that the walk from Pietracamela to Prati di Tivo can be arduous and takes around four hours, particularly if you want to stop en route to take in the scenery and wildlife.

For those wishing to cross the Sentiero Italia in this area, Pietracamela is the place to start. For details, see the box on page 234.

Pietracamela Corno Grande Nature Reserve The Riserva Naturale Corno Grande di Pietracamela includes some of the most prominent areas of the national park, such as the Corno Grande, Corno Piccolo, Campo Pericoli (the 'Dangerous Plains') and even the Calderone Glacier, Europe's southernmost glacier (see box, *Calderone Glacier*, page 235). Seek advice before hiking on the peaks of the national park. Either contact the tourist office in Prati di Tivo or the **Italian Alpine Club Abruzzo** (*CAI-Abruzzo; Viale Gran Sasso, 126;* \ *0871 331882;* e *abruzzo@ caiabruzzo.it; www.caiabruzzo.it*).

PRATI DI TIVO Although officially part of Pietracamela, this nearby hamlet is the more popular of the two when it comes to hiking and wintersports, due to its proximity to the park's two tallest peaks.

Tourist information
Pro Loco Contrada Prati di Tivo; \ 0861 959605; appointments m 347 850 3952. The tourist office is able to give the best advice both on skiing in the area, & on hiking some of the more challenging routes.

THE MAJOLICA TILES OF CASTELLI

Due to the large deposits of clay found in the area, Castelli has long been known in Abruzzo and beyond for the production of hand-painted ceramics. They became popular during the 16th century, though pottery has been made here since at least the 12th century, an industry whose origin is ascribed to Benedictine monks (though some historians believe the craft goes as far back as the Etruscans).

There are two different ways of producing the decorated pots. The older form uses a type of liquid clay that was then painted. The more popular type, however, is a majolica, involving a high-gloss glaze. This glaze is not only important from an aesthetic point of view, but has a practical purpose too. As the glaze is setting, the paint is applied to the pot, and is thus absorbed into the glaze for greater protection (it is extremely hard to scratch off). The piece is then wood fired at least two times. This finish appealed to wealthy clients, who preferred this more polished look to the earlier 'dull' work, and appreciated the greater detail that is possible with this method.

Wander into any of the dozens of ceramics stores in Castelli (they line almost every street) and you will notice that most glazes use only five colours: yellow, blue, green, brown and orange. These are known as the *pentacromia*. Traditional, hand-crafted Castelli ceramics will almost always only use these colours, but in recent years, some of the people of Castelli have become a little more adventurous with their colours and designs.

Examples of this work from Castelli can be seen in museums such as the Louvre, the British Museum, New York's Metropolitan Museum of Art and the Hermitage in St Petersburg.

Every year in July and August, Castelli has a street market that displays and sells a wide variety of ceramics. There are bargains to be had and majolica tiles can be bought at excellent prices. However, you can buy ceramics in Castelli all year round. Try, in particular, the excellent work at **Ceramiche Simonetti** (*Villaggio Artigiano 1;* \ *0861 979493;* e *info@ceramichesimonetti. it; www.ceramichesimonetti.it*).

12

Where to stay and eat

Hotel Amorocchi (50 rooms) Piazzale Amorocchi; ✆0861 959603; e info@ hotelamorocchi.it; www.hotelamorocchi.it. Excellent service, ample facilities & straightforward but comfortable rooms is what the Amorocchi has to offer. Apart from a tennis court, fitness centre & equipment hire (such as mountain bikes & access to a ski school), there is also some nightlife, & guided excursions of the area. HB & FB. **$$**

Hotel Miramonti (92 rooms) Centro Congresso; ✆0861 959621; e miramontiweb@ gmail.com; www.hmiramonti.com. Given Prati's weather, it's not surprising that the Miramonti looks more like a Swiss chalet than a typical Mediterranean hotel. Rooms are extremely comfortable & well

looked after, & the hotel has many facilities, including tennis courts, a swimming pool, gym & sauna. Before the start of the ski season, the hotel advertises special deals for FB stays of 5 days or longer; these are excellent value. HB & FB. **$$**

Hotel Prati di Tivo (28 rooms) Contrada Prati di Tivo; ✆0861 959656; e info@ hotelpratiditivo. com; www.hotelpratiditivo.com. The rather dull exterior of this hotel contrasts with the bright-red decoration of parts of its interior (including the rooms & bar). Rooms are of good size & have some beautiful views. The hotel offers a Club Card, currently priced at €12, which entitles you to discounts of 10% across town on things like ski rentals & eating at some restaurants. HB & FB. **$$**

Skiing There are around 18km of pistes at Prati di Tivo and four chairlifts to whisk you to heights of over 2km above sea level. A number of trails begin within view of the Corno Piccolo, the second-tallest peak in the national park. However, these are some of the more challenging runs. You might have an easier time of it over on Colle Abetone (some 1,750m above sea level), where the trails are nowhere near as steep. For more details see www.pratiditivo.it.

Ski passes Prices here are comparable to other parts of Abruzzo. A daily pass will set you back €25 at the weekend, and €21 on a weekday. Half-day discounts apply. A three-day pass will cost you about €49.

RISERVA NATURALE GOLE DEL SALINELLO/SALINELLO GORGES NATURAL RESERVE AND SURROUNDS There are a number of worthwhile sights in this natural reserve, mainly around Monte Foltrone in the north of the province near Civitella del Tronto. It is also excellent for hiking. There is a plethora of wildlife in the gorges, especially birds (including golden eagles, peregrine falcons and three species of crow). As the cliffs are bathed in sunshine for most of the year the area has a rich Mediterranean flora. Flowers include king's spear, with its pretty yellow flowers, giant fennel and the Mediterranean ephedra.

SENTIERO ITALIA

Roughly translated as the 'Italy Path', this hiking trail stretches 6,166km from Trieste in the north all the way down to Sicily, and then continues on Sardinia. A section of it crosses the area around Pietracamela and Prati di Tivo.

Starting from Pietracamela, the path winds through the Pietracamela Corno Grande Nature Reserve to the hamlet of Prati di Tivo. From there, it crosses the Frignano woods, rising to an altitude of over 1,700m above sea level and eventually makes its way to the Corno Grande (at almost 3km above sea level) before descending back to civilisation. Information about the trail is available from the Italian Alpine Club Abruzzo (see page 233). Seek advice before undertaking this hike: it is certainly not for the faint-hearted, the unfit or those who suffer from vertigo.

Europe's southernmost glacier lies in a small north-facing valley at the base of the Corno Grande (2,912m), the highest point of the Gran Sasso massif and the Apennines. Located north of L'Aquila and west of Pescara, the glacier is positioned high in rugged alpine terrain.

A glacier is a block of ice formed by layers of snow that are compacted into ice under their own weight. The weight of the ever-growing layers of ice pushes the glacier on an imperceptibly slow march down the valley. As the lowest parts of the glacier reach warmer altitudes it slowly melts, creating icy-cold streams and leaving a collection of rocky detritus, known as moraines, which it has eroded from the mountainside. Historically conditions in this part of the Gran Sasso massif have been cold enough to ensure almost permanent snow cover for most of the year and a continual renewal of layers of ice. Unfortunately, for decades the glacier has been melting at a rate greater than annual snowfalls can replace. It is estimated that at this rate it is unlikely that it will survive beyond 2020, providing tangible evidence of climate change. Nevertheless, it still remains a stunning sight amongst the highest jagged limestone crags and peaks of Gran Sasso, where the almost total lack of vegetation makes for a moon-like landscape and a reminder of the harshness of this alpine climate.

GETTING THERE Access to the north side of the glacier is via a chairlift at Prati di Tivo near the village of Pietracmela, which takes you up to La Madonnina (2,015m). From there a network of trails leads to Corno Grande. To access the south side of the glacier, drive through the village of Assergi to Fonte Cerreto and use the chairlift up the mountain. From here follow the marked geological trail which leads to the glacier. It is wise to be well informed and prepared before attempting the hike as at this altitude conditions can deteriorate quickly. Ask about conditions on the mountain at Fonte Cerreto before leaving.

Getting there The reserve occupies part of the Gran Sasso National Park, a short drive from the town of Civitella del Tronto (see page 225). The Sant'Angelo Grotto is signposted off the SS81, just east of Ripe.

Where to stay There is no accommodation in the area, so if you're keen to explore, base yourself in the nearby town of Civitella del Tronto (see page 225).

Macchia da Sole While this town itself isn't that attractive, the nearby **Castel Manfrino** is one of the most dramatic ruined castles in Abruzzo, along with Rocca Calascio (see page 123) and Ocre (see page 142). The castle is set high on a hill east of the township of Macchia da Sole, in a dominating position overlooking the valley. It was constructed during the 12th and 13th centuries as a fortified town and changed hands many times throughout the Middle Ages. It eventually fell into a state of disrepair and was ultimately abandoned.

Hiking There are two particularly interesting walks that start from Macchia da Sole. One takes you through the southern end of the gorge, crossing the river and over to the Sant'Angelo Grotto (see box, page 236). It takes around 2½ hours to get

The grotto has long been known for its hermitage but it is also an important archaeological site. It was identified as a possible site for excavation in the 1870s, although digging didn't begin until 1965. This uncovered many artefacts from the Neolithic to the Roman period, as well as tools and utensils from the hermitage itself. Some of the many finds include a medieval stone oven, a 13th-century altar and Bronze Age ceramics.

You must leave your vehicle at the car park, where there is also a picnic area, and a tourist information point that is rarely open. It is a fairly steep but pleasant walk down to the cave, taking around 15 minutes. You can hear the rushing of the nearby Salinello River as well as the sounds of many insects and birds.

to the grotto at a leisurely pace and takes in some beautiful scenery. The vegetation around here can be quite thick so make sure you are appropriately clothed.

The other walk is up to Castel Manfrino, which takes around half an hour in each direction.

Ripe The village of Ripe is another good place from which to explore the Salinello Gorges and the Sant'Angelo Grotto.

Hiking There are a few well-signposted trails just beyond the tourist information centre (*Centro Visite, Via Rotabile (Frazione Ripe);* \ *0861 918376;* ☺ *Sat–Sun 09.30–17.30, Mon–Fri by prior arrangement,* m *328 611 8276*), which can provide a wealth of information on walking in the area. The most popular of these walks are to the grotto (half-hour), Castel Manfrino (2½ hours) and Macchia da Sole (two hours 45 minutes); times are for the walk in each direction.

13

Chieti

Perched on a hill 330m above sea level and minutes from the Adriatic coast is the small city of Chieti, capital of the province of the same name. It is home to approximately 55,000 people and has the look and feel of a small provincial town. The cityscape is dominated by the belltower of the Cathedral of San Giustino, marking the centre of the city's old town, otherwise known as Chieti Alta ('high Chieti'). At the foot of the hill is Chieti Scalo, the modern town, with its railway station, a few shops and some local industry.

Due to its proximity to Pescara (only a 15-minute drive away) – which has more than double the population and just about double of everything else – Chieti has developed a bit of an inferiority complex. The city is almost completely overshadowed by its larger, brasher neighbour and the fierce loyalty its residents have shown Chieti over the decades is slowly waning. However, the people of Chieti would never admit this and the city's sense of inferiority goes hand in hand, paradoxically, with a cultural sense of superiority (see *People*, page 15).

The reality is that Pescara provides a lifeline for Chieti, especially for the city's young. Chieti has little in the way of entertainment, and its residents tend to descend on Pescara *en masse* for nightlife, shopping and of course, the beach.

That said, Chieti escaped World War II unharmed and as such still has many important historical buildings and churches where Pescara has next to none. In terms of attractions, Chieti now has (since the earthquake of 2009 destroyed so much of L'Aquila) more sights of interest than the other province capitals.

HISTORY

Chieti is set on a hill that has been settled since the 4th millennium BC. The city is said to have been founded originally by a tribe of Arcadians, and it later became the principal town for the Marrucini, an Italic tribe that occupied a small area around what is now the modern city. The Marrucini were great fighters and set their town on one of the highest peaks in the vicinity for greater protection. They came into contact with Rome during the Samnite Wars of the 4th century BC and, following their defeat, became allies of the victorious Romans. The settlement, then known as Theate Marrucinorum, was given *municipium* status by the Roman Empire.

Chieti's population at the height of the Roman Empire was greater than it is today but after the fall of Rome the city became involved in the same coastal skirmishes and raids as its neighbours (having been attacked by the Visigoths and then the Franks in the 8th century); its status and power waned until the advent of Norman rule in the Middle Ages. In the 12th century, the city became the capital of Abruzzo Citeriore which, roughly defined, spanned the area from south of the Pescara River to modern Molise.

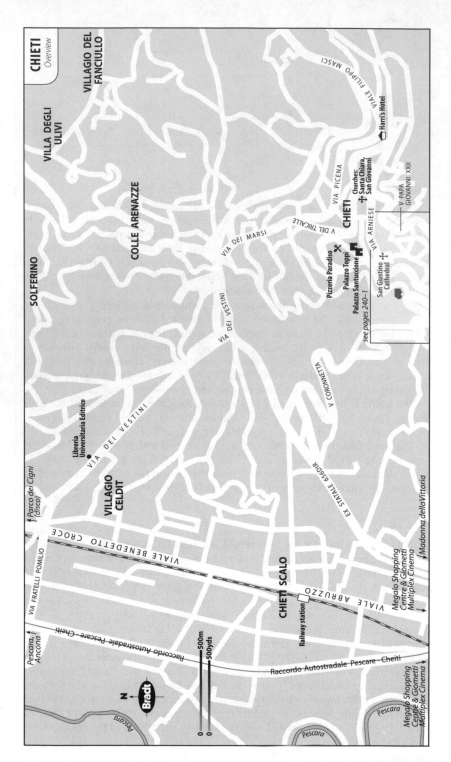

CHIETI
Overview

VILLAGIO DEL
FANCIULLO

VILLA DEGLI
ULIVI

VIALE FILIPPO MASCI

Harri's Hotel

VIA PICENA

Churches:
Santa Chiara,
San Giovanni

CHIETI

V PAPA
GIOVANNI XXII

V DEL TRICALLE

COLLE ARENAZZE

VIA ARNIESE

Pizzeria Paradiso

San Giustino
Cathedral

VIA DEI MARSI

Palazzo Toppi
Palazzo Santucione

see pages 240–1

SOLFERINO

VIA DEI VESTINI

V CORONNETTA

EX STATALE 656DIR

Libreria
Universitaria Editrice

VIA DEI VESTINI

Madonna dellaVittoria

Parco dei Cigni
(disco)

VILLAGIO
CELDIT

VIA FRATELLI POMILIO

VIALE BENEDETTO CROCE

CHIETI SCALO

Megalo Shopping
Centre & Giometti
Multiplex Cinema

Raccordo Autostradale Pescare–Cheiti

VIALE ABRUZZO

Railway station

Pescara,
Ancona

Bradt

N

500m
500yds

0
0

Raccordo Autostradale Pescare–Cheiti

Pescara

Pescara

Pescara

Megalo Shopping
Centre & Giometti
Multiplex Cinema

238

The 17th and 18th centuries brought more hardships for the residents of Chieti, in the form of a serious bout of plague in 1656 and major earthquakes in 1706 and 1713. The latter almost completely destroyed the city and took thousands of lives. These explain why much of the city, especially its churches, was rebuilt in Baroque style.

Chieti was absorbed into the Kingdom of Italy in 1860. During World War II the city was spared the destruction that was meted out on the rest of Abruzzo when it was proclaimed an 'open city', like Rome. This meant that the city was able to take in and look after those displaced by the fighting in surrounding areas. Two decades later, in 1965, the University of Chieti was established and it is now one of the finest and most popular educational institutions in the region. This ensures that Chieti is currently a thriving little city with a large student population.

GETTING THERE

BY CAR Chieti is only a 15-minute drive from Pescara. Depending on where you are in 'greater' Pescara (which includes Montesilvano, Città Sant'Angelo and Francavilla), there are many ways of reaching Chieti. If you're relatively central, take the SS16dir (the Asse Attrezzato) and follow the signs to Chieti. From Montesilvano and Città Sant'Angelo, you are best off taking the A14 *autostrada* a short distance and then the exit for Chieti. From Francavilla, you can take the SS649 to just past Ripa Teatina and then the SS649dir to Chieti.

BY TRAIN Chieti's railway station is in Chieti Scalo, the modern town at the foot of the hill. If you choose to come by train and then wish to go on to Chieti Alta (the old town above), you will need to take a bus for Chieti Alta from outside the station. The train journey from Pescara takes around 15–20 minutes and costs about €1.70.

BY BUS Taking the bus to Chieti is a waste of time. It costs just as much as the train and takes far more time, especially if you get caught up in Pescara's heavy traffic. That said, there are ARPA services from L'Aquila (around 1½ hours, tickets about €7) and Teramo (about one hour, approx €6). Buses from the latter go through the outskirts of Pescara. Most of these services terminate in Chieti Scalo, from where you must then take another bus to the old town.

GETTING AROUND

If you do visit Chieti then chances are you will spend your time in the old town, Chieti Alta. It is very compact and easily seen on foot. There are frequent buses between Chieti Alta and Chieti Scalo's railway station.

TOURIST INFORMATION

i Iat Chieti Head Office Via B Spaventa 47;
☎0871 63640; e presidio.chieti@abruzzoturismo.it

 ## WHERE TO STAY

Because of Chieti's proximity to Pescara and the tendency for visitors to prefer staying near the coast, there are few hotels in the old town.

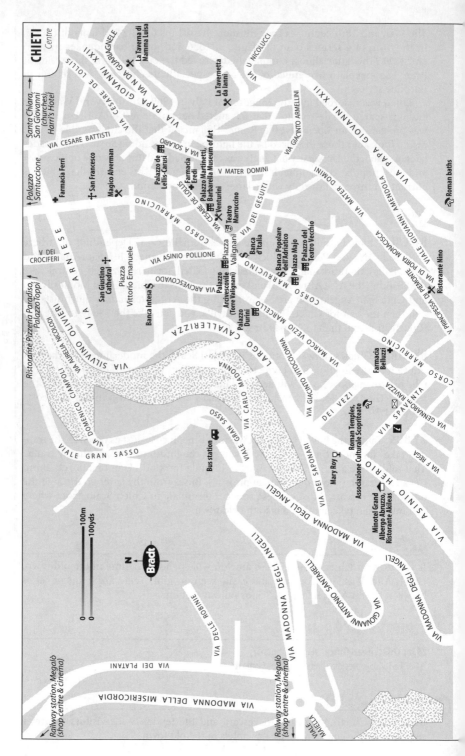

CHIETI
Centre

Santa Chiara, San Giovanni (churches), Harri's Hotel

↑ Palazzo Santuccione

VIA CESARE BATTISTI

Farmacia Ferri
† San Francesco
Magico Alverman ✗

VIA PAPA GIOVANNI XXIII
VIA N DA GUARDIAGNELE
VIA CESARE DE LOLLIS

La Taverna di Mamma Luisa ✗

VIA U NICOLUCCI

La Tavernetta da Ianni ✗

VIA A SOLARIO
VIA A SOLARIO

Palazzo de Lellis-Carusi

Farmacia Fredi

Palazzo Martinetti, Barbarella Museum of Art

V MATER DOMINI

Venturini
Teatro Marrucino ✗

CORSO MARRUCINO

VIA CESARE DE LOLLIS

Piazza Valignani

VIA DEI GESUITI

VIA GIACINTO ARMELLINI

VIA PAPA GIOVANNI XXIII

Roman baths

Ristorante Nino

VIA MATER DOMINI

VIA GIOVANNI AMENDOLA
VIALE GIOVANNI AMENDOLA
VIA DI PORTA MONACSCA

V PRINCIPESSA DI PIEMONTE

V DEI CROCIFERI

VIA ARNIESE

San Giustino Cathedral †

Piazza Vittorio Emanuele

VIA ASINIO POLLIONE

Banca Intesa $

Banca d'Italia
Banca Popolare dell'Adriatico $
Palazzo Majo
Palazzo del Teatro Vecchio

CORSO MARRUCINO

Palazzo Arcivescovile (Torre Valignani)
VIA ARCIVESCOVADO
Palazzo Durini

VIA MARCO VEZIO MARCELLO

Farmacia Belluzzi †

CORSO MARRUCINO

VIA SPAVENTA
VIA GENNARO RAVIZZA

Ristorante Pizzeria Paradiso, Palazzo Toppi ↑

VIA SILVINO OLIVIERI
VIA ARMELLA NICOLODI
VIA DOMENICO CIAMPOLI

VIALE GRAN SASSO

LARGO CAVALLERIZZA

VIA MADONNA
VIALE CARLO SASSO
VIA GRAN SASSO

Bus station

VIA GIAC
VIA MARCO VITOCOLONNA

DEI VEZI

Roman Temples, Associazione Culturale Scopriteate

Mary Roy

VIA DEI SAPONARI

VIA ASINIO HERIO

VIA F REGA

Minotel Grand Albergo Abruzzo, Ristorante Akileas

N Bradt

100m
100yds
0
0

Railway station, Megalò (shop centre & cinema)

VIA DELLE ROBINIE
VIA DEI PLATANI

VIA MADONNA DELLA MISERICORDIA

VIA MADONNA DEGLI ANGELI
VIA GIOVANNI ANTONIO SANTARELLI
VIA MADONNA DEGLI ANGELI

VIA MADONNA DEGLI ANGELI

VIALE MAIELLA

Railway station, Megalò (shop centre & cinema)

VIA DELLE TERME ROMANE

VIA TRIESTE DEL GROSSO

VIA ARISTIDE MATTOLI

VIA DOMENICO CERRITELLI

VIA DEI MARTIRI LANCIANESI

VIALE DELLA LIBERAZIONE

VIA LUIGI COLAZILLI

VALLE AMENDOLA

VIALE DELLA LIBERAZIONE

VIALE EUROPA

VIA FILANDRO QUARANTOTTI

VIA SAN FRANCESCO DI PAOLO

VIA NICOLA NICOLINI

VIA XXIV MAGGIO

VALLE AMENDOLA

VIA UMBERTO RICCI

VIA NICOLA NICOLINI

VIALE DELLA LIBERAZIONE

VIALE IV NOVEMBRE

VIA GUIDO COSTANZI

Gelateria Sigismondi

Piazza Trento & Trieste

VIALE VIALE IV NOVEMBRE

La Civitella

Giardin Pubblici

Vila Comunale National Archaeological Museum

V. CARLO DE TOCCO

VIA SELECCHI

VIA GABRIELE ROSSETTI

VIA GENNARO RAVIZZA

VIA SAN ROCCO

VIA NICOLETTO VERNIA

VIA RAFFAELE PAOLUCCI

Amphitheatre

PIANELL

VIA DEI CELESTINI

VIA GUIDO COSTANZI

VIA UMBERTO RICCI

VIA GIUSEPPE SALVATORE

The Citadel (La Civitella)

VIA GIUSEPPE SALVATORE PIANELL

VIA C. DE CESARIS

VIA SINIBALDO BARONCINI

VIA BERTRANDO DE TURRE

VIALE MAIELLA

Megalo (shop centre & cinema)

Megalo (shop centre & cinema)

241

Harri's Hotel (15 rooms) Via P A Valignani 219; 0871 321555; e chieti@harrishotels.it; www.harrishotels.it. Set on a hill with gorgeous views, Harri's is the only 4-star hotel in Chieti. The owners have been in the business a long time & the hotel runs smoothly with great attention given to the needs of guests. The rooms are unpretentious, with wooden fittings & rather dark tables, chairs & bedspreads. They are quite spacious & many have a balcony with a table & chairs. There is also the added benefit of a roof garden with good views, a sauna & Turkish bathhouse, & a gym, & there's even a shuttle bus that will take you the short distance to the heart of the historic centre. **$$$$**

Minotel Grande Albergo Abruzzo (67 rooms) Via Asinio Herio 20; 0871 41940; e grandealbergo@yahoo.it; www.albergoabruzzo. it. This is a large hotel very close to town & as such is good value for money. The rooms are quite simple though spacious & the staff are welcoming. There isn't much in the way of other amenities though there is a good, cheap restaurant (see Ristorante Akileas, below). This hotel has one of the most confusing websites around; you'd do better to email. **$$$**

✕ WHERE TO EAT

✕ **La Taverna di Mamma Luisa** Via Nicola da Guardiagrele 16; 0871 270271; ⊕ Tue–Sun. It may not look like much from the outside, but the Mamma Luisa is a pleasant surprise: small & intimate, with a touch of traditional mixed with a splash of modern décor. The speciality here is meat of all shapes & sizes, cooked in all manner of ways. Book in advance as the restaurant is often full, particularly on Sat nights. **$$$**

✕ **La Tavernetta da Ianni** Via Papa Giovanni XXIII 2; 0871 346242; ⊕ Tue–Sun. A small family-run establishment, the Tavernetta da Ianni makes no attempt to woo you with special décor or chic furnishings; its business is to offer the simplest, tastiest local food around, something which it does successfully. Pasta dishes are to die for; try the gnocchi. **$$$**

✕ **La Civitella** Via San Rocco 4; 0871 403861; ⊕ Tue–Sun. Down at the southern end of town is La Civitella, a restaurant & wine bar with excellent local dishes & a great selection of wines. Try a meat dish such as the lamb, & any of the Montepulciano d'Abruzzo wines. **$$**

✕ **Magico Alverman** Corso Marrucino 27; 0871 348770; ⊕ Tue–Sun. The Magico Alverman, run by owner Tiziana Santoro, is located on the busiest street in the heart of Chieti's old town. The staff are very accommodating & serve up some excellent pizzas & side dishes. Perfect for dinner after a day of sightseeing. **$$**

✕ **Ristorante Akileas** Via Asinio Herio 20; 0871 41940; www.albergoabruzzo.it. The Grande Albergo's restaurant is excellent value for money, offering 'turistic menus' for as little as €13 for a meat-based menu & – a bargain this – €20 for a fish-based one. These include a starter, a main & second course, a side dish & a bottle of water. The food is reasonably good. **$$**

✕ **Ristorante Nino** Via Principessa di Piemonte 7; 0871 63781; ⊕ Tue–Sun. The Nino has a welcoming atmosphere & very friendly staff. It specialises in local cuisine & offers up some of the best pasta dishes in the city, with the simple Napoli sauce being one of the best. **$$**

✕ **Venturini** Via C de Lollis 10; 0872 330663; ⊕ Wed–Mon dinner. Set in a restored 17th-century convent building, Venturini is a popular restaurant with locals. It specialises in regional dishes, though with a few creative extras, tweaking the recipes of some of the pasta & meat dishes. The latter are excellent, particularly the steaks & lamb. **$$**

✕ **Ristorante Pizzeria Paradiso** Via dei Tintori 47; 0871 346286; ⊕ Tue–Sun. Situated near Porta Pescara in the old town, Paradiso is an ideal choice for those on a budget. The food is generally excellent & the pizzas, not surprisingly, are a highlight. Try the cheap but tasty house red wine. **$**

🍨 **Gelateria Sigismondi** Piazza Trento e Trieste 6/8; 0871 63439; ⊕ Tue–Sun. It's good to know that you don't have to go all the way down to Pescara for a decent *gelato*: this *gelateria* is up with the best of them. The fruit flavours are fantastic. **$**

ENTERTAINMENT AND NIGHTLIFE

With the exception of a few pubs and bars (most of which are very average), Chieti's nightlife is almost non-existent. Most people, particularly the young, head to Pescara for everything from drinking and clubbing to seeing a movie (see *Entertainment, nightlife and drinking* in Pescara, page 62).

♀ **The Mary Roy** Via Asinio Herio, 23; m 338 979 0130; www.maryroypub.com; ⊕ evenings until late. Not far from the cathedral of San Giustino in the centre of town is the Mary Roy, Chieti's only 'Scottish' pub. It is perhaps one of the most successful British pubs in Abruzzo & has been open almost 10 years. It is a good place for an evening drink & is popular with a young crowd. There are often live band nights; check the website for details.

☆ **Discoteca Parco dei Cigni** Via Salara, San Giovanni Teatino; ↖085 44461; www.parcodeicigni.com; ⊕ Sat–Sun until late. If you don't fancy going all the way to Pescara, head to Parco dei Cigni, a 10-min drive away from Chieti. People come from miles around for the dance music. Note that it can become rather crowded & that drinks can be quite expensive.

THEATRE AND CINEMA The early 19th-century **Marrucino Theatre** (*Teatro Marrucino; Via C de Lollis 10;* ↖ *0871 61222; www.atamteatro.it;* ⊕ *Mon & Fri 09.00–12.00, Tue–Thu 09.00–12.00 & 15.30–17.30; admission free except during events*), on Largo Valignani, is delightful. It was designed by Eugenio Michitelli and hosts many concerts, musicals, operas and plays throughout the year (check the website for a full calendar of events). Constructed on four levels, the theatre is lavishly decorated in golds and reds, with an intricate ceiling and chandelier.

Chieti's only **cinema** of note, the Cinema Multiplex Giometti (*Centro Commerciale Megalò, Via Tirino;* ↖ *0872 5400389; www.giometticinema.com*) is actually in Megalò (see box, page 68), a shopping centre about a ten-minute drive from the old town centre. Movies in the original English language are very rarely screened.

SHOPPING

Shopping in the city of Chieti is rather disappointing. Aside from everyday goods such as groceries and clothing, with the odd specialist shop, **Corso Marruccino**, the old town's main street, has little to offer visitors. Given that it is only 15 minutes down the road by car, most Chietini make their way to Pescara whenever they are in the mood for a bit of retail therapy.

If you're after books, Chieti has no branch of the famous bookseller La Feltrinelli, but there is a small selection of books in English at the **Libreria Universitaria Editrice** (*Via dei Vestini 116;* ↖ *0871 565680; www.libreriauniversitaria.it*). There are no English-language magazines or newspapers on sale in the city. Perhaps the most noteworthy recent addition to the Chieti shopping scene is the opening of furniture retail giant **Ikea** (*Via Regolizie;* ⊕ *daily 10.00–20.00*) in nearby San Giovanni Teatino.

OTHER PRACTICALITIES

Banks include Banca Intesa (*Piazza Vittorio Emanuele 15*), Banca d'Italia (*Corso Marrucino 81*) and Banca Popolare dell'Adriatico (*Corso Marrucino 102*). The **post office** is at Via B Spaventa 4 (↖ *0871 401775;* ⊕ *Mon–Fri 08.30–12.30, Sat 08.30–12.30*).

The city's **hospital** can be found at Via dei Vestini 31 (✆ *0871 357442*), and there are several **chemists**:

✚ **Farmacia Belluzzi Massimo** Corso Marrucino 190; ✆ 0871 65879
✚ **Farmacia Ferri Giovanni** Via Arniense 152; ✆ 0871 348759
✚ **Farmacia Eredi Albertazzi** Via C De Lollis 22/24; ✆ 0871 330640

WHAT TO SEE AND DO

ROMAN AND PRE-ROMAN SITES

La Civitella/Citadel (*Complesso Archeologico La Civitella; Via G Pianell;* ✆ *0871 63137; museo@lacivitella.it; www.lacivitella.it;* ⊕ *Tue–Sun till late; admission free*) This opened to the public in 2008, and is the oldest remaining part of the pre-Roman settlement of Chieti. It now houses a museum that displays finds from excavations carried out here over the last 50 years. The Citadel displays various layers of the city's history and it is possible to see the remains of the temples of the Marrucini tribe (see page 237) as well as Roman baths, amphitheatres and homes. In August 2008, the catacombs were opened to the public for guided visits only.

There isn't much left of the **amphitheatre**, situated at the southern end of town near the Citadel. It was built in the 1st century AD and traces of its northern walls are visible. Much of the rest has been incorporated into the surrounding buildings.

The **Piazza dei Templi Romani** (Piazza of the Roman Temples) is found along Via Spaventa. It features three Roman *tempietti*, or 'little temples', built over an even older site of worship during the 1st century AD. There are three distinct temples and a fourth one that has been partially incorporated into the post office on the square. The temples were once at the centre of the Roman town of Teate.

Descending the hill on the eastern fringes of the historic centre will bring you to the **Roman baths** complex. They were built in the 2nd century AD and consisted of an atrium and corridor with elaborate mosaics, as well as nine bathing rooms.

MUSEUMS

Museo Archeologico Nazionale d'Abruzzo/National Archaeological Museum of Abruzzo (*Villa Comunale, Via G Costanzi 2;* ✆ *0871 404392; www.archeoabruzzo. beniculturali.it;* ⊕ *Tue–Sun 09.00–20.00; admission adult €4, child €2*) Along with the Citadel, the National Archaeological Museum of Abruzzo is one of the city's top sights. It is also one of the best archaeological museums in the region and certainly the most important. In 1984, it won the coveted European Museum of the Year award. The museum is housed within the Villa Frigeri, more commonly known as the Villa Comunale (Communal Villa), that was the German command post in the city during World War II.

Most people come to the museum to see the *Warrior of Capestrano* (see page 22), one of the most important statues to have been found in Abruzzo. However, the museum houses a wealth of other artefacts spread out over two floors and (currently) six separate sections. These cover funeral cults in pre-Roman Abruzzo, Italic sculptures, the anthropological collection, the Pansa collection and the numismatic collection. The statues, vases, figurines and tools on display outline the history of Abruzzo from prehistoric to Roman times. The finds come from excavations in places such as Alba Fucens, Amiternum and Juvanum (see pages 131, 119 and 262 respectively). Of note (other than the *Warrior of Capestrano*) are funerary stelae from the 5th century BC, a bronze statue of *Hercules at Rest* from the 3rd century BC and the breathtaking statue of *Hercules at a Banquet* from the 1st century BC, unearthed in Alba Fucens.

Museo d'Arte Barbarella/Barbarella Museum of Art (*Palazzo Martinetti, Via C de Lollis 10;* \ *0871 330873;* ⊕ *Tue–Thu 09.00–13.00 & 16.00–19.00, Fri–Sat 09.00–13.00, first Sun of month 09.00–12.00; admission free*) The Museum of Art is perhaps more of an attraction because of the wonderful Palazzo Martinetti, built in the 17th century, than for its collections. However, there are some interesting pieces and the works on display range from the 15th century to the present day. Don't miss the frescoes in the main room; they are the work of the 18th-century painter Giacinto Diano. Free guided tours are available on Tuesdays (17.00–19.00) and Thursdays (10.30–12.30).

CHURCHES Most churches in Chieti are open in the mornings until lunchtime and then from around 16.00 until early evening. Note that restoration is often in progress, so some of the churches below may not be open when you visit.

Cathedral of San Giustino This cathedral on Piazza Vittorio Emanuele II dominates the old town, and its belltower can be seen from miles around. Although it is the biggest church in Chieti, it is one of the least interesting. Don't let the medieval appearance of the exterior fool you: it is almost completely modern, having been totally rebuilt over the last 70 years. The belltower, however, was built during the 14th and 15th centuries though the top was destroyed in the earthquakes of the early 18th century. The Arti-style cap was added in the 20th century.

Most of the interior dates from the late 18th century and there are a few interesting paintings from the same time. Recently, traces of 14th-century frescoes have been discovered in the church's crypt, which is home to the remains of St Justin (after whom the church is named).

Church of San Francesco della Scarpa The cupola, or dome, of San Francesco della Scarpa (located along Corso Marrucino and founded in the 13th century) is as much a feature of Chieti's skyline as the belltower of San Giustino. Major restoration was carried out in the 17th century, which bequeathed the church its current Baroque appearance and cupola. The interior is as charming as it is intricately decorated and contains many paintings from the 17th century as well as a 14th-century rose window.

Church of Santa Chiara Santa Chiara is one of the most charming places of worship in Chieti. It was founded sometime in the middle of the 17th century, although changes have been made since, particularly during the 20th century. The church's interior is noteworthy for its striking stucco work, attributed to artists from the northern region of Lombardy.

Church of San Giovanni Battista This church, a former monastery of the Capuchin monks, is known for its hand-carved 18th-century wooden altars and paintings from the 16th century, attributed to the Veneto School. It was closed at the time of writing.

Church of Sant'Agostino Originally founded in the 14th century, the Church of Sant'Agostino has been battered by earthquakes as well as being destroyed by

a fire in 1562. There are still parts of its 14th-century façade visible on the eastern exterior walls. The interior houses an intricate altarpiece from the 18th century.

CIVIC ARCHITECTURE There are some exceptional *palazzi* in Chieti. Most are privately owned and cannot be visited, though they are certainly worth seeing from the outside. Most of these are located along Corso Marrucino, and include the **Palazzo de Lellis-Carusi**, complete with frescoes on the outside of the building; the charming **Palazzo Toppi**, with a turreted tower; the **Palazzo Martinetti** (see *Museo d'Arte Barbarella*, page 245), the **Palazzo Arcivescovile**; and the striking **Palazzo Majo**, one of the most interesting in the city. It was built by the wealthy Costanzo family in the 16th century, though the impressive staircase and courtyards were added later. It is the only *palazzo* in the city with a Baroque façade that is still a residential building. Other *palazzi* of note include the **Palazzo Durini**, **Palazzo Santuccione** and **Palazzo del Teatro Vecchio**.

PIAZZAS Chieti is dotted with enchanting piazzas. **Piazza Vittorio Emanuele II** will probably be your first port of call in the old town, and is the home of the **Cathedral of San Giustino**. Unfortunately, it also acts as the main old town car park.

Piazza dei Templi Romani, once the centre of Roman Chieti, has some of the best-preserved Roman remains in the city (see page 244). **Piazza Valignani** is lined with some of the most impressive buildings in town: the Teatro Marrucino (see page 243) and the Palazzo Arcivescovile with the striking **Valignani Tower**, the only building in Chieti to retain all of its original medieval structure.

14

Chieti Province

The province of Chieti is the second-largest of the four regions in Abruzzo. Its gently rolling hills meet with some of the most mountainous regions of the Majella National Park and consequently there are many ancient towns that occupy some of the prettiest spots in the region. The province of Chieti proves to be just as eclectic in its offerings as the others: not only is it known for its mountains but also for having some of the best beaches in Abruzzo. Many, such as the beaches at Fossacesia and Vasto, have been awarded blue flags under the Blue Flag Programme (see page 46).

SUGGESTED ITINERARY

Visit Ortona's castle and continue south to Rocca San Giovanni, one of the villages in the Most Beautiful Villages of Italy programme (see page 25). From here, visit the Abbey of San Giovanni in Venere at Fossacesia, a town with some lovely pebble beaches. Then make your way inland to Lanciano and Guardiagrele. Head south to the gorge of Fara San Martino and continue to the Roman ruins of Juvanum. Continue south again and visit the town of Schiavi di Abruzzo, with its famed Italic temples.

CHIETI PROVINCE: THE NORTH

LANCIANO So far the town of Lanciano has taken a bit of a back seat to places such as Chieti and Guardiagrele (see pages 237 and 251 respectively). However, this might be about to change as a huge restoration programme on its churches and other landmarks seeks to put it on the map. Its hilly streets are dotted with some of the most significant medieval buildings in the province and beg to be explored on foot.

Brief chronology

1181 BC   A settlement said to have been established by Solimus, a refugee from Troy.

3rd C BC   After the Samnite Wars, the town becomes the Roman *municipium* of Anxanum.

1st C AD   The Roman soldier who speared Christ is said to have been born in Lanciano.

500–1000   Town raided and sacked numerous times by the Goths and Lombards (the latter in AD571 during which the town is completely destroyed). In the early 7th century it is brought under the Duchy of Teate (Chieti) by the Byzantines.

1060   The Normans make Lanciano an important centre within the Kingdom of Sicily.

14

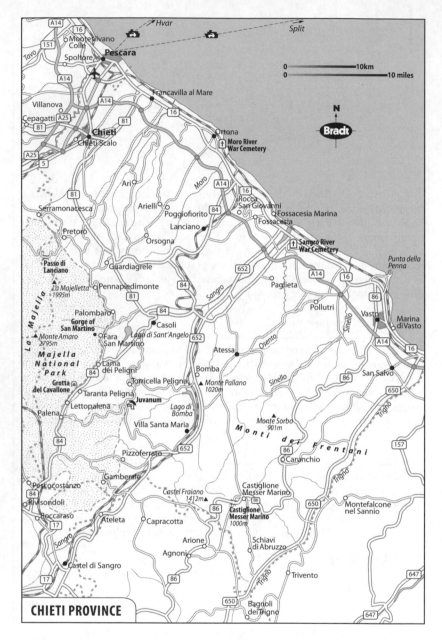

CHIETI PROVINCE

1300s	Lanciano becomes the largest town in Abruzzo, with a population of 6,500. Due to its expanding industries (of wool, silk and ceramics), the town prospers.
1500s	As with most of Abruzzo, the town is brought under Spanish rule.
1860	Lanciano votes to become part of the Kingdom of Italy.
1940s	The town is a centre of resistance against the Germans in central Italy.

Getting there

By car Take the A14 motorway and exit at Lanciano. Follow the signs to Lanciano, which is situated on the SS84. Alternatively, take the SS16 or SS81 and then the turn-off for the SS84.

By train The train between Pescara and Lanciano takes around 45 minutes and costs around €5. From Ortona, the journey takes only 20 minutes. The railway station is located a 20-minute walk west of the town centre.

By bus Because of the short time taken to reach Lanciano by train, it isn't worth taking the bus. However, ARPA do run services from Pescara, Chieti, Ortona and Guardiagrele.

Tourist information

🚹 IAT Lanciano Piazza Plebiscito 51; ✎ 0872 717810; e iat.lanciano@abruzzoturismo.it

🏠 Where to stay

🏠 Hotel Anxanum (42 rooms) Via San Francesco d'Assisi 8; ✎ 0872 43888; e hotelanxanum@tin.it; www.hotelanxanum. com. The Anxanum may seem a run-of-the-mill '60s hotel with little to offer but that is far from the case. Located in the town centre, the hotel has simply decorated rooms with comfortable beds, & is excellent value for money. **$$$**

🏠 Hotel Excelsior (74 rooms) Viale delle Rimembranza 19; ✎ 0872 713013; e info@ hotelexcelsiorlanciano.it; www. hotelexcelsiorlanciano.it. With 10 storeys, this is 1 of the tallest buildings for miles, with fantastic views over the town & surrounding area. It is situated right in the heart of town within minutes of all the attractions. The rooms are unremarkable but clean & comfortable & the hotel has an excellent restaurant (see below). **$$$**

🏠 Agriturismo Angelucci (4 rooms) Via Torre Marino 54; m 3403 415 654; e info@agriturismoangelucci.it; www. agriturismoangelucci.it. With its peach hues and hill views, the Angelucci is a paradise of Mediterranean clichés. It's a small affair, with only 4 rooms, although the highlights here are the setting, the excellent Montepulciano wine & the extra virgin olive oil produced on the premises. Warm, friendly & welcoming. HB & FB. **$$**

🏠 Agriturismo Caniloro (4 rooms) Contrada S Onofrio 134; ✎ 0872 50297; e caniloro@virgilio. it; www.caniloro.it. The rustic charms of the Caniloro's converted barns & farmhouses are a highlight of the area. The accommodation is made up of 3 rooms & 1 apartment, all well appointed & decorated in typical bucolic style. The *agriturismo* produces its own sausages, olive oil, pasta & pizza bread. Don't leave without having tried the *salsicciotto frentano*. HB & FB. **$$**

✕ Where to eat and drink

✕ Excelsior Restaurant Viale delle Rimembranza 19; ✎ 0872 713013; www. hotelexcelsiorlanciano.it. This hotel restaurant rates a special mention. Neither the service nor the quality can be faulted. There are some excellent seafood dishes (try the scampi) & the meat is fresh & tender (the lamb particularly so). The restaurant also has a wine list with over 150 bottles to choose from. **$$**

✕ Stella d'Abruzzo Via F Masciangelo 26; ✎ 0872 729254; e info@stelladabruzzo.it; www.

stelladabruzzo; ⊕ Tue–Sun. The 'Star of Abruzzo' is one of the most popular casual eateries in town, especially with the younger crowd. The pizza menu is quite varied & consists of both 'white' & tomato-based pizzas, & there are also snacks such as *arrosticini*. Try the *focaccia primavera*, with rucola & fresh mozzarella. **$$**

✕ Trattoria Paolucci Via Dalmazia 30; ✎ 0872 710638. Owner Antonietta D'Alonzo runs a tight ship at this simple trattoria. While its decoration might be no-frills, the food has all the elegance &

14

sophistication one could possibly need. The pasta dishes, with their tasty, fresh tomato sauce, are not to be missed. $$
♀ **Circolo Pickwick** Via Piave, 37A; ✆ 0872 49649; ☺ from 18.00. This quirky little bar opened its doors in March 2012, with the aim of mixing good coffee with a dose of culture. The owners offer an eclectic range of entertainment, such as theatre, music & art shows, literary talks & a hearty Sun brunch. Definitely one of the town's highlights.

Other practicalities
The town's **banks** are Banca Caripe (*Corso Trento E Trieste 131*), Banca di Roma (*Corso Trento E Trieste 84*) and Banca Popolare dell'Adriatico (*Corso Trento e Trieste 37/39*). The **post office** is at Via Vittorio Veneto 1 (✆ 0872 721511) and the **hospital** at Via del Mare 1 (✆ 0872 7061). There are also several **chemists**: Farmacia Colalè Rotellini Maria Pia (*Corso Roma 12;* ✆ 0872 712820); Farmacia Sparvieri Rosanna (*Piazza E D'Amico 38;* ✆ 0872 713417); and Farmacia Marciani Anna Maria (*Via Vittorio Veneto 40;* ✆ 0872 712905).

What to see and do
Lanciano has some charming medieval streets and alleys and is an ideal town in which to wander around and lose track of time. It is hard to get lost as it is laid out in a grid-like pattern. The old town is surrounded by an expanse of modern suburbs that are dull and uninteresting compared with the rich historical centre. Unlike many places of this size, the town's main piazza, **Piazza del Plebiscito,** is found at the foot of the old town rather than in the centre. The grid of medieval streets rises to the west and south of the square.

San Francesco Sanctuary of the Eucharistic Miracle
(*Santuario del Miracolo Eucaristico, Corso Roma 1;* ✆ 0872 713189; e info@miracoloeucaristico.eu; www.miracoloeucaristico.eu; ☺ May–Sep, 06.45–12.30 & 15.00–20.00; Sep–May, 06.45–12.30 & 15.00–19.00; admission free) This church and convent house one of the most important relics of the Catholic Church, and it is thus one of the most popular places of religious pilgrimage in all of Abruzzo. The church itself, built on the site of an ancient temple, is rather simple, with marble ceilings and a number of paintings. However, the real attraction lies within the convent, where it is possible to visit the Miracle of the Eucharist and the museum dedicated to it (see box, *The skin of God?*, page 252).

Museo Diocesano/Diocesan Museum
(*Largo dell'Appello 2;* ✆ 0872 712648; ☺ normally Tue & Thu 17.00–20.00, Wed & Fri 09.30–12.30, Sat–Sun 09.30–12.30 & 17.00–20.00; admission €5) This museum was closed at the time of writing for refitting and restoration. It houses a collection of religious artefacts and furniture from the area dating back to medieval times. There are guided tours available in English upon request.

Civico Museo Archeologico di Lanciano/Archaeological Museum
(*Palazzo Stella, Strada Cavour 13;* ✆ 0872 42500; ☺ Mon–Fri 09.00–13.00; admission free) There are many archaeological museums in Abruzzo and it is possible to glaze over at the sight of another one. However, this one contains a number of interesting finds from the Neolithic to the Middle Ages. Of particular note are a bronze helmet uncovered in a nearby necropolis and dated to the 6th century BC and a bust of the goddess Minerva, carved in the 2nd century BC.

Madonna del Ponte Cathedral
The Cathedral of Madonna del Ponte is popular with the old people in the town as Mass is held here a number of times throughout the day. Its imposing façade is on the town's main square, Piazza del Plebiscito. The

interior is largely clad in marble and contains a number of religious paintings by local artists. The Cappella Musicale (*Musical Chapel; coralemadonnadelponte.jimdo.com*) is host to the many local choirs in the area and regularly hosts events (check website for details). The church is actually built over the remains of a Roman bridge.

Church of Santa Maria Maggiore Without doubt the most interesting church in Lanciano is that of Santa Maria Maggiore, with its imposing doorway built in 1317 (to preserve the carvings this is no longer used and you enter around the side). The current church was built in the 13th century on the site of an earlier, 11th-century, church. The interior is flanked by a long series of arches and contains a silver crucifix made in 1422 by Nicola da Guardiagrele.

Medieval town walls and gates Lanciano has some of the best-preserved medieval walls in the region. Built in the 11th century, the most notable section is the **Torre Montanare** on the southern edge of the historic centre; look out for the Aragonese corner tower at the end of Via Spaventa. The town originally had nine entrance points, each with a suitably impressive gate. Of these, the only remaining one is the 11th-century **Porta San Biago**, on the northern edge of town.

GUARDIAGRELE Guardiagrele doesn't actually lie within the Majella National Park but it is the best place from which to explore those sections of the park that fall within the province of Chieti (Caramanico being the equivalent for the province of Pescara). It is situated on a hill to the north of the Laio and Vesola rivers and is surrounded by mountains.

Getting there
By car Guardiagrele is a 30-minute drive from Chieti on the SS81. From Pescara, take the SS16 south towards Francavilla al Mare and turn onto the SS649, which eventually becomes the SS81. Note that if you are coming from the Pescara side of the national park, it is far quicker to make your way down to the SS5 than to go around the park and over the Passo Lanciano.

By bus ARPA services connect Guardiagrele with Pescara and Chieti. The journey to Pescara takes around 1½ hours. Most services travel via Chieti, though there is one a day that travels via Francavilla and up the SS81, bypassing the centre of Chieti. The journey will set you back around €6.

Tourist information
🛈 **Municipal Town Hall** Piazza San Francesco 12; 📞0871 808 6209; ⏱ Tue–Thu 09.00–13.00 & 15.30–18.00, Mon & Fri 09.00–13.00

🏠 Where to stay
🏠 **Hotel Bocca di Valle** (17 rooms) Via Bocca di Valle 66; 📞0872 808002; e info@ hotelboccadivalle.com; www.hotelboccadivalle. com. The Bocca di Valle is a lovely hotel & great value for money. It is situated southwest of the town, a 10-min drive away from the centre, in the suburb of Bocca di Valle. It looks like a residential villa in Tuscany, & the owners take great pride in making their guests comfortable. The rooms are large, bright & airy. The restaurant's food is very good, particularly the meat dishes. HB & FB. **$$$**

🏠 **Bed & Breakfast La Casa di Alba** (1 apt) Via Don Minzoni 2; m 345 307 7035; www. lacasadialba.it. Alba's House is exactly what it claims to be, one of the owner's residences. The B&B is essentially an apartment, with a large living

14

area, spacious bedroom & bathroom & a fully equipped kitchen. One of the highlights, however, is the *laghetto* ('small lake') in the large garden. It is a great place to relax & at only €60 a night including b/fast is excellent value for money. Note that an extra levy of €5pp is charged during peak season. **$$**

🏠 **Casino di Caprafico Azienda Agrituristica** (3 apts) Piane di Caprafico; ☎0871 897492; www.casinodicaprifico.com/eng. A 20-min drive south from the centre of Guardiagrele along the SS81, this farmstay is an excellent place to stay – though you'll need your own

transport. Covering approximately 135ha of lovely countryside, the farm specialises in the production of emmer wheat, a grain akin to spelt. Casino di Caprafico is run by owner Giacomo Santoleri & features a renovated late 18th-century farmhouse, of which parts have been converted into 3 stylish & well-maintained apartments. There are 2 spacious dbls, & a larger apartment that could house 2 couples, all comfortable & tastefully furnished & decorated – & all with views of the peaks of the Majella National Park. They are let by various agencies & it is advisable to book in advance for stays in the summer. **$$**

✖ Where to eat

✖ **Ristorante Bocca di Valle** Via Bocca di Valle 66; ☎0872 808002; www.hotelboccadivalle. com. The restaurant at the Bocca di Valle Hotel is definitely worth a separate mention. This excellent place serves up a menu of dishes typical of the region. Try the *chitarra all'uovo con ragù*, a simple homemade pasta, or the *gnocchi al sugo di papera* (gnocchi with duck sauce). The desserts are in the

same league; order the *tiramisù* if it is available. **$$**

✖ **Ta-pù** Via M della Porta 39; ☎0871 83140; ⏰ Tue–Sat evening. The Ta-pù is popular with locals, particularly for its intimate atmosphere (the restaurant consists of 2 small eating areas), wine list & very good pan-Italian menu. Try any of the meat dishes. **$$**

Other practicalities The town's **banks** are Banca Popolare dell'Adriatico (*Piazza San Francesco 6*), Banca Popolare di Lanciano e Sulmona (*Via Roma 42*) and Banca Toscana (*Largo San Cristoforo 1*). The **post office** is at Via San Francesco 69 (☎*0871 808931;* ⏰ *Mon–Fri 08.00–18.30, Sat 08.00–12.30*).

For **chemists** you'll find Farmacia La Barba Domenico at Via Roma 121 (☎*0871 82226*) and Farmacia Cristini at Via Tripio 134 (☎ *0871 82328*), and the town's **hospital** at Via Anello 6 (☎ *800 324632*).

What to see and do

Cathedral of Santa Maria Maggiore (⏰ daily) The impressive three-level façade of this stunning church, with its sculpture and clock, gives some idea of the historical importance of the town of Guardiagrele. For maximum effect, enter via the portico walkway, complete with charming pillars and arches. The cathedral originally dates from the 12th century, with modifications and restoration taking

---

THE SKIN OF GOD?

The Vatican recognises only a handful of so-called 'miracles', and of these the one housed here in Lanciano, at the San Francesco Sanctuary of the Miracle of the Eucharist, is said to be the most important. During a sermon in the 8th century, it is said that the priest blessed the Host and wine, which consequently transformed themselves into skin and blood. The 'skin', tested and identified as muscle tissue from the heart, is held in a silver monstrance while the five globules of coagulated blood can be seen in a crystal phial, both dating from 1713. The Bishop of Chieti assigned the protection of the miracle to the priests of the convent in 1252.

place over the following centuries. The most significant restoration took place in the 19th century, so the interior is not as old as the façade facing Piazza di Santa Maria Maggiore. There are a number of good works of art to be seen inside. These include a 15th-century fresco by artist Andrea Delitio (signed and dated 1473) and a 14th-century painting known as the *Maria Lactans* that portrays Mary breastfeeding Jesus. Also here is the Cathedral Museum (see below).

Monastery of San Francesco (⊕ daily) This monastery complex was built in the 13th century and is the second most important religious building in the town. The church's main entrance resembles the one on the church of Santa Maria Maggiore in Lanciano (see page 251). The side entrance, which dates from the late 19th century, was actually taken from the Cathedral of Santa Maria Maggiore and rebuilt here. Inside, the complex houses some interesting artefacts, including an intricate gilded statue from the 18th century of St Anthony and his angels. There are also some excellent 16th-century paintings, including an *Annunciation* and *Virgin and Child*. Within the complex is the Archaeological Museum.

Church of San Nicola di Bari (⊕ daily) Found next to the Cathedral of Santa Maria Maggiore, this church's façade dates from the 18th century though the building was erected during the early Middle Ages. There are interesting examples of stuccowork and a few good paintings, including an 18th-century *Virgin with Child*. The only remaining parts of the original façade are the two arches that flank the main entrance.

Capuchin Convent Church (⊕ daily) The outside of this church is largely uninteresting. However, it does contain a beautifully crafted 18th-century high altar made from wood and ivory and decorated with paintings of religious scenes.

Museo del Duomo/Cathedral Museum (*Piazza di Santa Maria Maggiore;* ☏ *0871 82117;* ⊕ *Jun–Sep daily 09.30–12.00 & 16.00–19.00, Oct–May by appointment only; admission €2*) The small three-room Cathedral Museum displays some fine religious items, particularly those from the 17th century. There are statues, busts, ecclesiastical costume and crucifixes by artist Nicola da Guardiagrele (see page 255).

14

Museo Archeologico/Archaeological Museum (*Piazza San Francesco;* \087 800460; ☺ *Jul, 17.00–20.00 Sat & Sun; Aug, 10.00–12.30 & 17.00–20.00 daily; Sep–Jun, by appointment only; admission free*) The small Archaeological Museum of Guardiagrele is found within the Monastery of San Francesco (see above). It was founded in 1999 and has informative displays on the history of the immediate area. Many of the finds in the museum come from the nearby protohistoric Necropolis of Comino, which was in use for over six centuries during the first millennium BC. The museum includes reconstructions of the tombs.

Museo del Costume e delle Tradizioni della Nostra Gente/Museum of Customs and Traditions (*Cloister of Municipal Bldg, Piazza San Francesco;* \0871 808 6209; ☺ *Aug 10.30–13.00 & 17.00–20.00 daily, Sep–Jul by appointment only; admission €2*) This museum began as a project to raise awareness of local society and culture. It is broken up into sections that show local workers, crafts and industries, including seamstresses, cooks and woodworkers. There is also an extensive display of local historical costume as well as recreated domestic rooms.

Skiing Guardiagrele is close to two of Abruzzo's best skiing areas: **La Majelletta** and **Passo Lanciano** (see page 258). Both are located within the Majella National Park and because of the twists and turns in the road are a 30–45-minute drive from the centre of Guardiagrele.

CASOLI A half-hour drive southeast of Guardiagrele is the charming medieval town of Casoli. It is not home to any sights of particular importance, though it is one of the prettiest towns in the area for a stroll through the old streets.

At the highest point of the town is the **Casoli Castle**, a watchtower that is part of an old church, with wonderful views of the peaks of the Majella National Park.

CHIETI PROVINCE: THE SOUTH

ATESSA The rural town of Atessa, set in the hills of the Sangro River valley, is an ideal place to while away a few hours. It has some very picturesque and delightful narrow lanes which make exploring on foot a pleasure. Atessa is best known for the Cathedral of San Leucio (see opposite).

Getting there The town is most easily reached by car. It is on the SS364, reached by exiting the A14 *autostrada* at Casalbordino/Vasto Nord and following the signs. Alternatively take the SS652 from the coast, following the signs to Atessa.

🏠 Where to stay

🏠 **Hotel Select** (11 rooms) Località Piazzano di Atessa 90; \0872 897107; e info@select-hotel.eu; www.select-hotel.eu. Set at the foot of town, the Hotel Select is an ultra-modern hotel – unusual in Abruzzo – & is one of only 2 4-star properties in the area. Its floor-to-ceiling windows, clean lines, trendy pastel colours & funky lobby chairs give it a boutique-hotel feel. The rooms themselves (recently refurbished) are large, modern & extremely comfortable. The bar is a relaxing place for a quiet drink. **$$$$**

🏠 **Hotel L'Anfora** (16 rooms) Contrada Montemarcone 73; \0872 897778; e info@ hotellanfora.com; www.hotellanfora.com. The L'Anfora is located around 4km north of town. Rooms are impeccably clean & sparsely decorated, giving them an airy feel. Common areas are sleek & modern (by Abruzzo standards). The restaurant is excellent. Try the lamb meatballs with tomato base & oregano. **$$$**

🏠 **Hotel La Masseria** (61 rooms) Piazzano di Atessa Via Nazionale 69; \0872 897794;

e info@lamasseria.eu; www.lamasseria.eu. This large, 4-star hotel is more like a country retreat. Whilst not as modern as the Select, it has other attractions, including a large swimming pool &

an excellent restaurant (popular for functions). Clean, bright & airy rooms make for an extremely comfortable stay. It is extremely popular for wedding ceremonies. **$$$**

Where to eat

 ✖ **Il Fondaco dei Domenicani** Via Fontane Vecchie 7; ☏ 0872 853068; www. ilfondacodeidomenicani.it; ⊕ Tue–Sun. This is a beautiful restaurant & definitely the best place to eat in town. The tables are immaculately set out in a bucolic dining room. The menu features a number of traditional dishes such as *maccheroni alla chitarra* (certainly the best pasta dish here). Not to be missed. **$$**

✖ **Perbacco** Via Corso Vittorio Emanuele 95; 0872 851664; ⊕ daily until late. This bar, situated near 1 of the old town gates at its southern end, is set within a restored section of the town's ancient walls. It is popular with locals at weekends & is an excellent spot for a glass of wine or a beer. **$**

Shopping Despite its relatively small size Atessa has some decent shops along the Via del Corso (Via Corso Vittorio Emanuele), which cuts straight through the narrow town. Here, on the town's main street, you will find everything from jewellery and antiques to cosmetics.

Other practicalities There are two **banks** in the town: Banca Popolare di Ancona at Via Piazzano 70, and Banca Caripe at Contrada Piana La Fara 1. For **pharmacies** try Farmacia Falcocchio Giulia at Largo Municipio 9 (☏ 0872 866574) or Farmacia Palombaro Giovanni at Corso Vittorio Emanuele 66 (☏ 0872 866478). The **post office** is at Via Cesare Battisti 21 (☏ 0872 859511).

What to see and do

Cathedral of San Leucio (☏ 0872 853173; ⊕ daily 07.30–12.00 & 16.00–20.00) Aside from Atessa's winding medieval streets this is the town's best-known attraction. The church is mentioned as far back as the 9th century. Legend has it that it is named after St Leucio who defended the town from the fiery wrath of a dragon that inhabited the valley. While the church was founded long before the turn of the first millennium AD, it was rebuilt in the 14th century.

An imposing staircase brings you to the church's amazingly elaborate doorway. Once through, you will see the very grand interior adorned with crystal

---

NICOLA DA GUARDIAGRELE

Nicola da Guardiagrele (1385–1462), actually Nicola Gallucci, was born and died in the town of Guardiagrele. He is responsible for some of the most important religious works of art in Abruzzo. These include the processional cross in Guardiagrele's Cathedral of Santa Maria Maggiore (see page 252), the cross in the church of Santa Maria Maggiore in Lanciano (page 251) and numerous monstrances (ornate structures used to display the holy Host), such as those in Atessa. His Gothic style captured the imagination of many and he travelled as far as Rome and Florence. He worked with Italian artists such as Paolo Romano and Pietro Paolo da Todi. The three collaborated on the 12 silver apostles that were on display in the papal chapel before the sack of Rome in the 16th century.

chandeliers and smothered in gold leaf. As well as the paintings that line the walls, the church also houses a 1m-tall, 14th-century Bible, and an ostensory (monstrance) made in 1418 that is almost as tall and which is the work of Nicola da Guardiagrele (see page 255).

Town gates The town's surviving gates are the **Nuova Porta di San Nicola** (1779) and the 14th-century **Porta di San Michele**. The latter is flanked by two restored 14th-century buildings and leads onto a very picturesque old road.

CARUNCHIO There are few sights as such in the town of Carunchio, but it has in the past been voted one of the Most Beautiful Villages in Italy (see page 25). From a church at its highest point, the houses and medieval buildings seem to tumble down a hillside. For the best views, drive five minutes out of town in any direction.

Carunchio is worth at least half an hour of your time. It is possible to drive around to the top of the town and walk down through its labyrinth of ancient streets and alleys – though keep in mind that any descent has to be followed by an arduous ascent. The church on top of the hill is that of **San Giovanni Battista**. It has a lovely belltower and a fine doorway dating from 1751.

CASTIGLIONE MESSER MARINO Like Carunchio (a 15-minute drive north and east), Castiglione Messer Marino doesn't have any famous landmarks to draw in the crowds. However, it is extremely picturesque, set on the slope of a hill, and is best approached via its southern or eastern entrances for the best views. The town's main church is the **Church of Michele Arcangelo**, founded in the 16th century and containing lovely ceiling paintings from the 18th century.

A 6km drive out of town will bring you to the **Church of the Madonna del Monte**, founded in the 9th century and restored in the 1940s. It is majestically set among the trees on the slopes of Mount La Rocca.

SCHIAVI DI ABRUZZO AND THE ITALIC SANCTUARY While not an unpleasant place by any stretch of the imagination, the real reason to come to Schiavi di Abruzzo is to visit the ancient Italic temples just outside of town. However, just before the northern edge of the town, there is a signpost for the **Passeggiata Panoramica di Monte Pizzuto**. This lovely walk has wonderful views of the valley and looks out onto the town below. It stretches along the ridge for several kilometres, but you only need to walk for about 20 minutes or so to make the most of the views.

The Italic Sanctuary The ruins of Il Tempio Italico (admission free) date back to around the 2nd century BC, even though further excavations carried out in the 1990s continue to bring to light even more ancient treasures.

The most interesting of the two sites is known as the First Temple. All that remains are the limestone steps that would once have been flanked by two large pillars. The site is particularly evocative: a staircase leads to a flat podium backed by mountains and rolling hills.

The other temple, smaller than its neighbour, has been restored and reconstructed, as can be seen from the four pillars by the entrance. While you can't enter the temple itself, it is possible to see the altar inside.

The two temples are surrounded by other ruins uncovered during the excavations, such as a medieval tower to the left. The finds unearthed here are now spread amongst Abruzzo's many archaeological museums. The area is perfect for a Sunday picnic.

Getting there The temples are reached by following the road south out of Schiavi di Abruzzo. When you reach a sharp turn in the road, look for a yellow sign pointing towards the temples. You will have to park your car and take the gravel track down to the site, which is always accessible.

MAJELLA NATIONAL PARK AND SURROUNDS

The province of Chieti spreads into the eastern side of the Majella National Park. Unlike in Pescara Province, there are not many towns here due to the very mountainous terrain. In fact, the national park's tallest peak, Monte Amaro (2,795m above sea level), just sneaks into the province of Chieti. The rest of the mountain marks the border between the provinces of L'Aquila, Pescara and Chieti.

Please be aware that amenities, such as banks and post offices, are scarce in this area, as is accommodation outside the ski resorts.

GETTING THERE
By car The national park occupies the western section of the province of Chieti and is most easily reached by car. From Pescara and Francavilla take the SS81 to Guardiagrele. Two extremely pretty roads run through this area: the SS263 runs parallel to the eastern border of the park, while the SS84 crosses this border.

By bus ARPA services run to Guardiagrele (see page 251). From there, you will need your own transport to explore the heart of the national park.

HIKING AND SKIING There are hundreds of numbered hiking trails in the Majella National Park. In Chieti Province the main trails are labelled from E to H, and have corresponding numbers (for example, E1, G2, and so forth). Pretoro (see below) is an excellent place to hike on the Chieti side, as the trails will bring you to the Passo Lanciano and La Majelletta (see page 258). There are also good trails beginning in the towns of Bocca di Valle (a district of Guardiagrele), Pennapiedimonte and Fara San Martino. For a full map of hiking trails, contact the tourist office in Pretoro (see below) or the Majella National Park headquarters (\ *0864 25701;* e *info@ parcomajella.it).*

The best skiing in the national park is in the area known as Passo Lanciano/La Majelletta (see page 258).

PRETORO The town of Pretoro, on the national park's northwestern fringe, is best known for its skiing. It is only ten minutes by car from the pistes of La Majelletta and Passo Lanciano (see page 258).

⚹ Tourist office Piazza Madonna della Libertà; m 347 796 6526. This tourist office can supply information on skiing in the area. Note that it is not run by the official tourist board but by the local council.

🏠 **Where to stay** As Pretoro is mostly a small ski resort, the accommodation is located in the vicinity of the larger resorts of Passo Lanciano and La Majelletta.

🏠 **Albergo Mamma Rosa** (40 rooms) Via Majelletta 35; \ 0871 896144; e info@ mammarosa.it; www.mammarosa.it. The Mamma Rosa is a good accommodation option right in the thick of the skiing at La Majelletta. It is a large, box-like hotel situated 1,620m above sea level with excellent views of the surrounding national park. The rooms are comfortable if functional,

14

simply furnished & with minimal decoration. The hotel has excellent grounds, a bar, games room & even its own nightclub. There is ski equipment for hire, as well as mountain bikes to hire during the summer. $$$

🏠 **Grand Hotel Panorama** (72 rooms) Via Belladonna, Località Majelletta; ✆0871 896125; e info@grandhotelpanorama.it; www. grandhotelpanorama.it. The best accommodation option in the area is located in Majelletta, about a 20-min drive from the town of Pretoro. The imposing oval structure & small, square windows look like a building from Mussolini's EUR complex in Rome, but the hotel is beautifully set, isolated among the tall peaks of the national park. Brightly decorated with blue carpets & yellow bed throws, the rooms are spacious & well appointed. There is an entertainment area with computer games for kids, as well as a lounge area. During winter, the hotel has top-notch ski equipment for hire as well as providing skiing lessons & passes for La Majelletta & Passo Lanciano. The restaurant serves up some hearty meals, with excellent meat dishes & pasta. HB & FB. $$$

✖ Where to eat

✖ **Mamma Rosa Restaurant** Via Majelletta 35; ✆0871 896144. The Mamma's Rosa's restaurant is well worth a separate entry. It is a simple, no-frills trattoria, furnished with bare wooden tables & chairs. It serves only typical Abruzzese food & the dishes are well presented & very tasty. Try the ricotta ravioli, or the typical *sagne e fagioli* (pasta with beans). The meat dishes are excellent, either the roasted veal or the fantastic liver sausages. This is a great spot to warm your cockles after a day of skiing the slopes. $$

Other practicalities There is only one bank in Pretoro, and it is actually in the **post office** (*Via dei Mulini 3;* ✆ *0871 898420*). There is also a **pharmacy**, Farmacia Masciantonio (*Piazza Madonna della Libertà;* ✆ *0871 898213*), located on the village's main piazza.

What to see and do Pretoro is a pleasant town with some lovely medieval streets perfect for wandering around. The town's most noteworthy church, **San Nicola**, is famous for a lovely 16th-century sculpture of the *Pietà*.

Just outside the town is **Il Grande Faggio** (*Via Fontepalombo 36;* ✆ *0871 898143;* e *info@ilgrandefaggio.it; www.ilgrandefaggio.it;* ⏰ *daily; bookings advised*), an environmental education centre open to the public but which also hosts local school groups. The centre raises awareness of sustainable development and responsible tourism within the national park. It also maintains a **Wolf Sanctuary**, which is a 20-minute climb from the main building.

Hiking Two excellent hiking trails, the E1 and E2, begin from Pretoro at around 500m above sea level and climb steeply to Passo di Lanciano (1,306m) and La Majelletta (1,995m). Note that these cannot be undertaken during winter and spring, when there is too much snow. The best months to embark on these hikes is May to September. Bring plenty of water, and if you intend to reach La Majelletta it is advisable to leave early in the morning.

For more information, contact the Pretoro Tourist Office or the headquarters of the Majella National Park (see *Hiking and skiing*, page 257).

Skiing at La Majelletta and Passo Lanciano The 'little Majella' and the Lanciano Pass, on the border of the provinces of Chieti and Pescara, are popular spots for skiing. While they are two separate areas, in reality they form one large skiing 'complex'. Ski passes start from about €20 per day.

Ski runs There are currently 14 ski runs at **La Majelletta**.

'EASY' (BLUE) RUNS		'MEDIUM' (RED) RUNS		'DIFFICULT' (BLACK) RUNS	
Skiing school	350m	Snow Park	300m	Direttissima	1,300m
Baby	400m	Rifugio	600m	Block Haus	1,500m
Blu 2	600m	Gare 1	800m		
Blu 3	600m	Gare 2	1,200m		
		Sole	1,300m		
		Primavera	1,800m		
		Mamma Rosa	2,000m		
		Lenette	2,500m		

Although the **Lanciano Pass** comprises fewer slopes, they are longer than most of those at La Majelletta:

'EASY' (BLUE) RUNS		'MEDIUM' (RED) RUNS	
Ski school	350m	Terzo	800m
Chiesetta	1,000m	Pistone	1,500m
		Panoramica	2,500m

PENNAPIEDIMONTE This picturesque village, set in a gorge on the eastern edge of the national park, is perfect for a few hours of mooching about. There isn't anything particularly noteworthy in the town except for the **parish church**, built in the 18th century and housing a number of 18th-century paintings by Nicola Ranieri.

Hiking There are three main hiking trails, the G1, G2 and G3, from Pennapiedimonte. The G3 eventually splits into the G4 and G5, which lead to Mount d'Ugni Natural Reserve. Note that these trails are steep and require a lot of climbing. It is best to start early in the morning to give yourself plenty of time.

PALOMBARO Palombaro is another pretty town about a ten-minute drive from Pennapiedimonte. The town is best known for the **Sant'Angelo Grotto**, within which is an 11th-century chapel. Follow the signs from the town for the walking trail which leads to the cave; it takes about two hours.

FARA SAN MARTINO Aside from being a lovely town with bright, sunny streets, Fara San Martino is known for two things: the San Martino Gorge, and its pasta factories.

Where to stay and eat

Hotel del Camerlengo (84 rooms) Località Macchia del Fresco 6; ☎ 0872 980136; e info@camerlengo.it; www.camerlengo.it. The Camerlengo is a rather plain-looking residential-style building with simple though spacious rooms, & there is a pool. The staff are friendly & it is close to the gorge & the pasta factories. **$$$**

Residenza La Piazzetta (7 apts) Via Trento 8; ☎ 0872 980938; e info@residencelapiazzetta.it; www.residencelapiazzetta.it. A favourite with the English & German visitors who come to see the pasta experts elbow-deep in flour. The apartments are small but well-appointed & the surroundings are peaceful. Book well in advance during the warmer months. **$$$**

GORGE OF SAN MARTINO This is one of the most spectacular gorges in Abruzzo, with a long human history as well as a significant natural history. It is signposted just 2km from the foot of Fara San Martino, and is best visited during spring and summer.

At the time of writing, excavations were in hand to uncover an 8th-century abbey not far from the entrance to the gorge, although work stops during the summer so that birds can nest in the gorge. The abbey supposedly contains a cycle of frescoes and was in use up until the 19th century. In times past, the monks who made it their home would charge a levy (always in the form of cheese or bread rather than coins, which were not particularly useful to them) to enter or exit the gorge. The gorge was extremely important for local shepherds and there were about 6,000 sheep here until the 1960s, when other industries (such as the pasta-making) began to take over. By the 1970s there were barely any sheep left and nowadays there is only one active shepherd, Domenico, who is something of a local hero.

The gorge is also an important natural reserve, home to a family of about eight wolves, which live at about 1,600m above sea level. There is also a wide variety of flowers, including the *genziana* whose root is used to make a popular, though illegal, liqueur, and the *scarpetta di venere*, an orchid found only in this gorge.

Furthermore, the gorge provides water to 56 towns in Chieti Province, not to mention the pasta industry in Fara San Martino.

LAMA DEI PELIGNI Lama dei Peligni is one of many towns hugging the slopes of the eastern edge of the national park. As far as towns in the area go, it is quite large and has a few natural attractions worth stopping for.

Where to stay

Casa Albergo Tiroasegno (10 rooms) Via Nazionale Frentana 210; 0872 916004; e info@hotel-tiroasegno.com; www.hotel-tiroasegno.com. The Tiroasegno is a relatively new hotel & is great value for money. The family who own it offer rooms which are modest & simple though spotlessly clean at a fraction of the price of many country stays in the area. Great place to base yourself to explore the surrounding countryside. **$$**

What to see and do

Michele Tenore Majella Botanical Garden (*Via Colle Madonna;* 0872 916010; Jun–Sep, Sat–Sun 10.00–13.00 & 16.00–19.00, Tue & Thu 10.00–13.00; admission €5) Follow the signs out of town towards Colle Madonna and you will reach this well-maintained botanical garden dedicated to the flora of Abruzzo. The gardens were established in 1995 and extend to about 9,000m², housing more than 500 species of plants. Amongst these are some endemic, endangered species, including the pretty *Iris marsica*, the colourful *Adonis vernalis* and the wispy, odd-looking *Centaurea sphaerocephala*. The entrance fee goes towards funding educational programmes and events that keep the gardens solvent. A booklet about the gardens is available at €1.55.

Abruzzo Chamois Reserve (e *info@camosciodabruzzo.it*) You can't actually enter this reserve in the hills just a few minutes west of town. However, you can look into the enclosure and attempt to get a glimpse of the chamois that are penned up here to recover from injury before being released back into the wild. If you approach quietly and have patience you may well get a glimpse of an animal or two. It is a good idea to bring a pair of binoculars.

Hiking The H5 trail goes through the area around Lama dei Peligni. It is possible to walk through the fringes of the national park and back towards Fara San Martino or onwards through the national park as far as Campo di Giove. If you intend to walk the trail between Lama dei Peligni and Fara San Martino, you might want to start from Lama dei Peligni (around 670m above sea level), as it will then take you downhill to Fara San Martino, which is around 380m above sea level. It's a distance of around 7–8km, and will take about three to four hours – or considerably longer in reverse. The walk from Lama dei Peligni to Campo di Giove is around 20km one way, and quite arduous, so you'll need to set aside the entire day.

Around Lama dei Peligni

Grotta del Cavallone (*contact Town Hall, Piazza Umberto I 32, Lama dei Peligni;* ✆ *0872 91221;* ⏱ *daily during summer 09.00–16.00; admission €5*) This cave

14

is also known as Grotta della Figlia di Jorio, because the Abruzzese poet Gabrielle D'Annunzio used it as a setting for his play, *Figlia di Jorio* ('The Daughter of Jorio'). It is found high within the Majella National Park, near the town of Taranta Peligna, and is easily accessible from the main tourist areas on the coast. Situated high in a steep valley on the eastern side of the park, the cave has an impressive view out over the valley and countryside beyond.

The cave itself is about 1km in length and has become quite popular thanks to its ease of access. It was formed over millions of years by the gradual erosion of an enormous layer of limestone. It contains a collection of stalagmites, flowstone and rimstone pools, but most impressive are its caverns, ranging from 10m to 20m wide. Paths have been carefully laid out with a network of bridges, steps and boardwalks, all lit by electric lights.

Getting there A cable car brings visitors up from the SS84 at the base of the valley near Taranta Peligna, some 4km southwest of Lama dei Peligni, in around 20 minutes. It is a good way to get a closer look at the jagged limestone lining the valley sides, which are full of cave openings. From the terminus, there's a marked path leading to the cave itself.

There are also tracks to the grotto in the vicinity of Lama dei Peligni, although these are not recommended for walkers, and some sections are accessible only by 4x4.

PALENA South of Lama dei Peligni along the SS84 is the town of Palena. It suffered extensive damage during World War II as the Gustav Line (see page 14) ran straight through the town. However, the town has managed to retain some of its charm.

Where to stay This area of the province of Chieti sees very little tourism, and as such, accommodation is scarce. However, there is one excellent hotel:

Hotel Terrazzo d'Abruzzo (22 rooms) Via Sant'Antonio Abate 29; 0872 918325; www. terrazzodabruzzo.it. Expect big rooms, good service & superb views of the surrounding area. The owners, the Di Cino family, are at your disposal & will help organise tours of the area. **$$**

What to see The beautiful **Church of the Madonna del Rosario**, founded in the 18th century, has a six-level stone Atri-style belltower that is particularly appealing. Inside you can see a 16th-century wooden statue of the *Madonna and Child*. Another noteworthy building is the **castle**, which has a medieval appearance but has actually been completely rebuilt during the last century.

Not far from the town is the dramatically situated **Sanctuary of the Madonna dell'Altare**, perched on the edge of a cliff at 1,300m above sea level. The small chapel, built over an older structure of the 14th century, is quite plain though its location gives it a special ambience. The church was founded by priests loyal to Pietro Angeleri, who later became Pope Celestine V (see page 110).

THE RUINS OF JUVANUM The Roman ruins of Juvanum are about a 20-minute drive east of Palena, occupying a serene spot on a plateau at almost 1,000m above sea level. Like all other Roman or pre-Roman sites in Abruzzo, there are no opening times or entrance fees.

History The area was settled by the Caraceni, a tribe of Samnites, during the Bronze Age, though it acquired its current name and layout during the Roman era. The town came under Roman rule during the Social Wars and was given the status of *municipium*. The remains of important Roman buildings such as the forum are a testament to its wealth at this time. The location of Juvanum was thought to be particularly healthy: indeed, the name derives from the Latin *iuvare*, which means 'to improve one's health'. It is thought that this is due to the presence of natural springs in and around the town.

During Roman rule, the town expanded, although much of it was damaged during an earthquake in the middle of the 4th century AD. As with most Roman towns in Abruzzo, it was eventually abandoned and pillaged for stone by locals to build homes and shops.

Excavations began in the 1960s and have unearthed numerous finds that are now on display in museums including the National Archaeological Museum of Aburzzo in Chieti (see page 244) and in Rome.

What to see Most of the ruins visible today are from buildings that date from the 3rd–1st centuries BC. The oldest of these includes two hilltop temples from the 3rd century BC. They are located to the southwest of the forum and are said to have been built over even older structures. The well-preserved theatre is found to the south of the forum area and was already in existence when the Romans took over the town after their victory against the Samnite tribes. The remains of the forum, built sometime in the 1st century AD, include the areas where shops and stalls once stood. Juvanum eventually acquired fortified walls in AD325 and it was during the same century that the bath complex was added at the northern end of the town. The remains of a basilica are visible directly to the north of the forum but its date is not known.

COASTAL CHIETI

GETTING THERE
By train Most of the towns on the coast of the province of Chieti are linked by the line that runs from Lecce to Milan. Tickets from Pescara to Ortona cost €2.20 and the journey takes around 20 minutes. From Pescara to Vasto, the journey will take about 45 minutes and set you back around €4.

By car The SS16, otherwise known simply as the Adriatica, runs down the whole of the Abruzzan coast. However, if time is pressing, take the A14 *autostrada*, which runs parallel to the SS16.

FRANCAVILLA AL MARE Though a pleasant little town, Francavilla al Mare is part of a larger urban area consisting of Montesilvano, Pescara, Spoltore and Francavilla al Mare. And, like Montesilvano, it is rather overshadowed by its grand neighbour, Pescara. There isn't anything of historical interest in Francavilla and very little in the way of entertainment (except along the beach on summer nights), so for this you are best off heading for Pescara. However, there are some excellent beaches here, and the town always fares well in the Blue Flag programme.

Tourist information
IAT Francavilla al Mare Piazza Sirena; 085 816649; e iat.francavilla@abruzzoturismo.it

Where to stay
Hotel Claila (9 rooms) Via Nazionale Adriatica 123; 085 491 4494; e info@hotelclaila. com; www.hotelclaila.com. This is one of Francavilla's best places to stay. It is an intimate,

4-star establishment set in a restored 19th-century villa & is more like a wealthy residential mansion than a hotel. Inside, the decoration is impeccable & the rooms spacious & bright. There isn't much in the way of extras (such as a pool), but the level of service & atmosphere make up for that, & the beach is only a minute's walk away. **$$$$**

🏠 **Hotel Guerra** (27 rooms) Viale Alcione 59; 📞085 491 4413; e info@hotelguerra.it; www.hotelguerra.it. With stunning views over the Adriatic, the Guerra is sure to please if you're looking for that perfect balance between beach relaxation & urban buzz. Its rooms have sea views, there's private beach for guests & a restaurant serving local treats. HB & FB. **$$$$**

🏠 **Park Hotel Alcione** (44 rooms) Viale Alcione 59; 📞085 817698; e info@parkhotelalcione.

com; www.parkhotelalcione.com. The Park Hotel Alcione advertises itself as a 'design resort' & the claim is largely borne out; the furniture is hip & modern, the walls painted in funky colours & the rooms large with very comfortable beds. There is also a health & spa centre for guests & a very swanky pool with tiled decking & excellent views. HB & FB. **$$$$**

🏠 **Mare Blu Hotel** (24 rooms) Via Alcione, 159; 📞085 810 032; e info@marebluhotel.it; www.marebluhotel.it. It may not look like much but the Mare Blu is ideally located across the road from the beach. The interior is modern & nicely decorated & the rooms have excellent sea views. The bathrooms are newly renovated & the owners are very welcoming. Good value for money given its location. **$$$**

✗ Where to eat and drink

✗ **Chiavaroli Il Brigantino** Viale Alcione 101; 📞085 810929; ⏰ Tue–Sun. This family-run restaurant has been popular with locals for the last 30 years. It is modern & fresh-looking, with wooden flooring & nicely presented tables, & the service is flawless. It specialises in seafood & is probably one of the best seafood restaurants in the Montesilvano-Pescara-Francavilla area. However, you would be doing yourself a disservice if you didn't leave room for the homemade excellent desserts; try the *tiramisù*. **$$$**

♀ **La Cantinetta** Via Tirino 25; 📞085 691616. La Cantinetta is an excellent wine bar with a wide

variety of the best wines from the area. There is also a good choice of spirits, such as grappa. It is especially popular for pre- & post-dinner drinks. **$$**

✗ **Sheik** Piazza Ionio 1; m 328 977 2592; ⏰ Thu–Sun evenings till late. This is one of the more popular drinking haunts in Francavilla, & people come from Pescara & Montesilvano for a night of drinking & entertainment. It is an 'Arabian Tea Club', traditionally decorated to give it a faux Cairo or Marrakech feel. Large, embroidered cushions line the walls, with low-rise tables & belly dancers thrown into the mix. **$$**

Other practicalities Banks include Banca Intesa (*Piazza Sirena 15*); Banca Popolare dell'Adriatico (*Viale Alcione 139a*) and Banca Toscana (*Via Nazionale Adriatica 177*).

For a **chemist** go to Farmacia Amoroso Paolucci Antonio (*Via Monte Corno 3*; 📞 085 491 0061), Farmacia Russo Rosella (*Via Adriatica 342*; 📞 085 817161) or Farmacia Berardocco Nadia (*Contrada Pretaro 1*; 📞085 454 9649).

The **post office** is at Via Duca degli Abruzzi 1 (📞 085 492 1033).

What to see and do The only reason for coming to Francavilla is to laze around on a pristine beach. However, should you have had too much of the sunshine and crowds, head to the **Michetti Museum** (*Museo Michetti; Piazza San Domenico 1*; 📞*085 491 1161; www.fondazionemichetti.it; admission free;* ⏰ *Mon–Sat 10.00–13.00 & 16.00–19.00*), which displays works by local painter Francesco Paolo Michetti (1851–1929).

ORTONA The town of Ortona, although it is home to one of the largest commercial and industrial ports on the Adriatic, occupies a peaceful spot on a hill overlooking the Adriatic. Because of its strategic position, it was given *municipium* status by the

The Chieti coast is known for its *trabocchi*. Essentially, these are wooden fishing huts jutting out into the sea, connected to the land by wooden ramps. They are built on wooden stilts and have numerous wooden 'arms' for all manner of nets to trap fish.

The earliest examples are actually found on the coast of Puglia in southern Italy and date back to the early 18th century. However, most of Abruzzo's *trabocchi* were built during the 19th century and have been restored over the last 20 years. Generally they are no longer in use. Traditionally there were *traboccanti*, families who made their livelihood from their *trabocchi* and the fish they caught. Today, the term '*trabocchi* coast' refers to the section of the Chieti coast from Francavilla al Mare down to San Salvo, a small town south of the city of Vasto.

Romans and for centuries the town was ransacked by invading armies. However, the damage and suffering inflicted by the besieging Saracen and Venetian armies of the past pales into insignificance when compared with the battles fought in the area during World War II (see *History*, page 14). There's a Commonwealth war cemetery south of the town (see page 269).

Getting there For information on getting to Ortona, see page 263.

From the railway station, which lies on the coast directly east of the town, it is easy to reach the centre of the town on foot. It is not worth waiting for any of the town's buses; their schedules are erratic at best. Exit the station and follow the street to your right, entering the second tunnel on your left. From 1891 to 1943 this tunnel housed a short funicular railway connecting the port area of Ortona to the town centre above. After World War II, steps were built here in order to cut the walking time to and from the station. Take the stairs all the way to a main road and on the other side you will find more steps bringing you to the centre of town. The walk takes about 15 minutes.

Tourist information

🛈 IAT Ortona Piazza della Repubblica 9; ☎085 906 3841; e iat.ortona@abruzzoturismo.it

🏠 Where to stay

🏠 **Hotel Ideale** (24 rooms) Corso Garibaldi 65; ☎085 906 3735; e info@hotel-ideale.it; www.hotel-ideale.it. This 50-year-old 3-star hotel is situated right in the heart of town & occupies a lovely position on a hill overlooking the Adriatic. Staff are extremely friendly, & the owners will go to great lengths to make you feel at home. The rooms are simple though very comfortable, with large beds, very powerful AC & great views. **$$$**

🏠 **Hotel Katia** (34 rooms) Lido Riccio 23; ☎085 919 0411; e info@hotelkatia.com; www. hotelkatia.com. Perfectly situated on a wide stretch of beach, the Katia may look as though it's stuck in a '90s time warp but its rooms are humble but well appointed & it has the added benefit of a private beach for guests. **$$$**

🏠 **Hotel Mara** (106 rooms) Lido Riccio 4; ☎085 919 0428; e info@hotelmara.it; www.hotelmara. it. Hotel Mara, on the coast of Ortona, is situated a few km from the town centre. Opened 40 years ago, the hotel still retains some questionable 1970s décor, though the rooms are bright & airy & offer some great views of either the coast or the hills. The hotel has 2 large swimming pools, though given its position right on the beach, these might seem a little redundant. The American Bar is a nice place to while away the hours over a drink. HB & FB. **$$$**

Where to eat

✕ **Ristorante al Vecchio Teatro** Largo Ripetta, 7; ☏ 085 906 4495; www.alvecchioteatro.com; ☺ Thu–Tue. Though this restaurant is housed in a rather decrepit-looking building, it serves up some of the best seafood dishes for miles around. Try one of the fish-based pasta dishes; they are delicious. $$$

What to see

The Castle This imposing fortification was built in 1452 by King Alfonso of Aragon, reputedly on the foundations of a more ancient fort. Following countless Venetian raids on the city, there were calls to build a fort to protect the town and the local authority of Abruzzo Citeriore footed the bill. The castle originally consisted of five towers and a moat and a very handy inner tower, which could be used to protect the townsfolk in the event of a raid. Like so much of the town and the surrounding area, the castle suffered great damage during World War II, and has undergone extensive rebuilding.

Museo della Battaglia di Ortona/Museum of the Battle of Ortona (*Corso Garibaldi 1;* ☏ *085 906 8207;* ☺ *Mon, Wed & Fri 09.00–13.00, Tue & Thu 09.00– 13.00 & 15.00–18.00; in summer also Sat–Sun 18.00–20.00; admission free*) If you're interested in the history of World War II, then don't miss this museum. It was inaugurated in May 2002, and is dedicated to the Battle of Ortona of December 1943 (see *History*, page 14). The museum, spread over a number of rooms, reconstructs the events leading up to the battle and the fighting itself, giving a rounded picture of its causes, the effects of the battle, and its socio-political ramifications. Pictures show the utter destruction of the city and the personal histories are deeply poignant.

Passeggiata Orientale and Belvedere Tosti This tree-lined promenade hugs the cliff overlooking the Adriatic and is a popular hangout for locals. On a clear day, you can see nearby hill towns and watch the ships coming and going from the port below.

Palazzo Farnese About halfway up the Passeggiata Orientale is this building commissioned by Margaret of Austria in the 16th century. It wasn't completed to its original plan and it now houses the **Archaeological Museum** (*Museo Civico Archeologico;* ☏ *085 906 7233;* ☺ *Mon–Fri 17.00–19.30; admission free*). It contains prehistoric and Roman finds from the nearby area.

ROCCA SAN GIOVANNI
Winner: Most Beautiful Villages in Italy; population around 500

Rocca San Giovanni is a charming little village not far from the coast of the Chieti Province, and engaged in olive oil production. It is first mentioned in documents dating from the 11th century AD. Today, to all intents and purposes, it offers little to occupy your time other than wonderful narrow, sun-drenched lanes. Allow at least an hour or two to simply walk through the village (preferably on a sunny day when the warm pastel colours of the buildings really stand out).

Safari Park (*Contrada Scalzino 27A, Rocca San Giovanni;* ☏ *0872 618012; www. zooabruzzo.it;* ☺ *daily 10.00–19.00; admission adult €12, child €8*) This is the only zoo in Abruzzo, situated about ten minutes' drive from the centre of Rocca San Giovanni, near an exit of the A14 *autostrada*; it is easily found by following the signs. Zoos can be controversial places and you might like to avoid it, yet children will probably find it enjoyable. The Safari Park has numerous separate areas with kangaroos, horses, zebras, camels, emus, swans, penguins, seals, lions, tigers and elephants. There are also plenty of rides, concerts and shows, and frequent themed days; details are available on the website.

FOSSACESIA The town of Fossacesia lies on the SS16, halfway between Ortona and Vasto. It has some splendid Blue Flag beaches, though do note that some of the best beach areas are pebbled so it is best to wear flip-flops or sandals. The town itself is uninteresting apart from the stunning Abbey of San Giovanni in Venere.

Getting there Fossacesia is located along the SS16. From here, follow the signs to the Abbazia di San Giovanni in Venere. Alternatively, take the A14 motorway and exit at Val di Sangro. Follow the signs to Fossacesia and then to the abbey.

 Where to stay and eat

Hotel Levante (23 rooms) Via Adriatica (SS16) 120; 0872 60169; e info@hotellevante.it; www.hotellevante.it. The Levante is located along the coast, not far from the centre of Fossacesia. The owners are eager to please & offer spacious, well-decorated rooms with private beach facilities & an excellent seafood restaurant. **$$$**

Abbey of San Giovanni in Venere (*Viale San Giovanni in Venere, Fossacesia;* 087 260132; e *abbazia@sangiovanninvenere.it; www.sangiovanninvenere.it;* ⊕ *daily Nov–Mar 08.00–18.00; Oct–Apr 07.30–19.30; admission free*) This is one of the most famous and historically significant abbeys in Abruzzo. The current structure was built in 1165 but is said to have been constructed on the site of a Roman temple dedicated to Venus (hence its name, Venere, the Italian for Venus). Its location on a small olive-grove hill 100m from the coast and overlooking the Adriatic makes its situation just as appealing as the building itself.

The entrance into the abbey is through the famous Luna, or moon portal, decorated with some beautiful reliefs. On approach to the abbey, this door appears to be the side entrance but is actually the north-facing main doorway. The nave and its two aisles contain frescoes from the 12th–14th centuries. Some of these are particularly well preserved and vividly coloured, especially those in the crypt.

REMAINS OF AN APOSTLE?

Walking past the rather simple-looking **Church of San Tommaso Apostolo** (085 906 2977; ⊕ *daily 07.00–13.00 & 16.00–20.00*), it's hard to imagine that it is said to contain the remains of one of the original 12 apostles. The bones, belonging to St Thomas, were brought to the town from the Greek island of Xíos in 1258 and are displayed within a glass-fronted altar deep in the church's crypt. The origins of the building are ancient; it was founded on the site of a pagan temple and restored many times during the 12th century, when it was destroyed by both earthquakes and raids by the Normans. Rebuilding took place again during the 17th and 18th centuries. However, the current structure is almost completely the result of rebuilding undertaken after the damage it suffered during World War II.

Il Perdono, the church's 'Forgiveness Fair', is held the first Sunday in May. During this Sunday, a procession makes its way through town and to the church and celebrates the forgiveness of sins through the intervention of St Thomas.

Chieti Province   COASTAL CHIETI

14

The abbey's cloister (⊕ closed at lunchtime) is perhaps even more attractive than the abbey itself. Its landscaped garden, with roses, palm trees and two tall conifers, is framed by charming lancet arches beneath bright, terracotta roof tiles.

VASTO Comparable in size to Montesilvano in the province of Pescara, Vasto is one of the larger cities in the region and a good place to soak up the sunshine and relax. As well as being a good beach resort it is also blessed with historical, architectural and cultural attractions. A wander through the hilltop old town will lead you to a tranquil belvedere with views over the coast below.

History The city's origins are ancient, and folklore has it that Vasto was founded by the Greek hero Diomedes. Archaeological finds from the area date from as far back as the 14th century BC, and the city was later known as Histonium, a coastal town belonging to an Italic tribe called the Frentani. Under Julius Caesar, it became a town of some importance due to its strategic position over the Adriatic coast, although it is not certain if the city ever received the status of a 'colony'. It was, however, a *municipium* and enjoyed a high degree of prosperity under the Roman Empire, acquiring public baths and a theatre. The high quality of the intricate mosaics that have been unearthed demonstrate its former wealth.

Later the city was so devastated by raiding parties that in the 11th century its name changed to Guastaymonis (Il Vasto d'Ammone), or the Waste of Aimone. However, the townspeople were a hardy lot and held on to rebuild and restore the city. Its current layout dates to the 15th century, though it suffered damage during World War II and during a massive landslide in 1956.

After the war the city acquired some industry and promoted itself as a resort. In recent years, it has been the centre of Harvard University's summer programme.

Tourist information
ℹ **IAT Vasto** Piazza del Popolo 18; ✆0873 367312; e iat.vasto@abruzzoturismo.it

⌂ Where to stay
⌂ **Hotel dei Sette** (25 rooms) Via San Michele 66; ✆0873 362819; e hoteldei7@cheapnet. it; www.hoteldei7.it. The exterior of the Sette, located in the historic centre of Vasto, has recently received a much-needed lick of paint & the rooms are modern & well decorated, with immaculate bathrooms. There is also Wi-Fi & apartments with their own cooking facilities. Ask for a room with sea views; it is certainly worth it. **$$$**
⌂ **Hotel Excelsior** (55 rooms) SS16, 266; ✆0873 802222; e info@hotelexcelsiorvasto. com; www.hotelexcelsiorvasto.com. This recently refurbished 4-star property is a very comfortable place to stay. There are several types of rooms, from standard options to large suites. All are spacious & nicely decorated with great attention to detail. There is an excellent bar, a full buffet b/fast & a large outdoor pool area. HB & FB. **$$$**

⌂ **Hotel Monte Carlo** (50 rooms) SS16, 256; ✆0873 801355; e info@hotelmontecarlovasto. it; www.hotelmontecarlovasto.it. The Monte Carlo couldn't compete with the glitzy hotels of its namesake, though it is well situated & offers large if slightly dated rooms. However, it has a very bright & airy feel to it, & each room has a sea view. There is a large pool & private beach facilities. HB & FB. **$$$**
⌂ **Hotel Royal** (38 rooms) Viale Dalmazia 132; ✆0873 801950; e info@hotelroyalvasto.com; www.hotelroyalvasto.com. This beachside hotel offers modern, if slightly cramped, rooms. The hotel also has a large bar & lounge area, as well as private beach facilities for guests. The staff are very welcoming. HB & FB. **$$$**
⌂ **Locanda dei Baroni** (10 rooms) Via San Francesco d'Assisi 68/70; ✆0873 370737; e info@ locandadeibaroni.it; www.locandadeibaroni.it. This small establishment offers rooms redolent of

medieval castle chambers, with 4-poster beds & rustic wooden hues. It has an excellent restaurant, for which it is well known. Try the delicious antipasti made from local produce. **$$$**

🏠 **Hotel Adriatico** (47 rooms) Viale Dalmazia, 138; 📞0873 801431; e info@hotel-adriatico.it; www.hotel-adriatico.it. This whitewashed hotel, which has recently been redecorated, is excellent value for money. It is a funky establishment with modern, clean rooms just seconds from the beach. Though with its large, modern pool, you may just want to while away a few hours in the water with a drink from the bar. The new website often features specials & package deals. **$$**

✘ Where to eat

✘ **Castello Aragona** Via San Michele 105; 📞0873 69885; www.castelloaragona.it; ⊕ Tue–Sun dinner. This is one of the most popular seafood restaurants in town, & with good reason. It has a certain sophistication in decoration, ambience & service, so dress up if you want to eat here. The fish is fresh & tasty & there is an attractive terrace with fantastic views. Try the spaghetti with wild *vongole* or the scrumptious mixed seafood risotto. **$$**

✘ **Cibo Matto** Via Crispi 36; 📞0873 362466; www.cibomatti.it; ⊕ Tue–Sun. As its name ('crazy food') might suggest, this is a funky eatery popular with the town's younger crowd. Whilst the meat dishes are a highlight, particularly the steaks & lamb, the seafood on offer here is also second to none. Dessert includes some of the finest & freshest fruit from the area, so be sure not to miss out. **$$**

✘ **La Taverna** Via Sondrio 3; 📞0873 364165; ⊕ Tue–Sun. This modern tavern sees large crowds at the weekend, so you are advised to book ahead. The food has a typical Abruzzese slant but is largely based on modern Italian cuisine. Pasta dishes are some of the best things here, particularly those that are not tomato-based. **$$**

Other practicalities There are **banks** on practically every street corner in Vasto, and numerous **chemists**. The **hospital** is at Via San Camillo de Lellis 1 (📞 *0873 3081*). The **post office** is at Via Giulio Cesare, 20 (📞 *0873 367294*).

COMMONWEALTH WAR CEMETERIES

Abruzzo contains two noteworthy war cemeteries: the Sangro River War Cemetery and the Moro River War Cemetery. Both are open at all times and there is no entrance fee. Both cemeteries are managed by the Commonwealth War Graves Commission in Rome (*www.cwgc.org*), and honour servicemen who died in World War II.

SANGRO RIVER WAR CEMETERY Just south of Fossacesia are signs leading to this beautiful and peaceful cemetery. From the turn-off, the road leads through some dense woodland before reaching a plateau with stunning views.

The cemetery contains no fewer than 2,617 Commonwealth graves belonging to nationals of the UK, India, New Zealand, South Africa, Australia and Canada (in order of numbers). The cemetery is also one of three war burial sites for Hindus who have been cremated as their beliefs demand.

It is very easy to spend an entire afternoon here, given its tranquil setting and views over the rolling hills. There is a wide expanse of grass for picnics but please do respect the sanctity of the place.

MORO RIVER WAR CEMETERY Just south of Ortona, off the SS16, is the Moro River Canadian War Cemetery. This memorial site is much smaller than the Sangro River cemetery down the road, though it is no less peaceful and thought-provoking. The majority of its 1,615 Commonwealth graves are of Canadian soldiers.

14

$ **Banca Popolare dell'Adriatico** Piazza
Diomede 13
$ **Banca Intesa** Corso Europa 9

Chemists
✚ **Farmacia Pietrocola Filippo** Via Giulio
Cesare 61; ☏ 0873 367192
✚ **Farmacia Domizio Giuseppina** Corso
Garibaldi 74; ☏ 0863 367231

✚ **Farmacia Piccolotti Alberto** Via Cavour 35;
☏ 0873 368546

Doctors
⊞ **Dr Nicola D'Annunzio** Via Giulia 23, ☏ 0873
364334
⊞ **Dr Giovanni Di Nocco** Via San Giovanni da
Capestrano 6, ☏ 0873 365325
⊞ **Studio Medico Gagliardi** Piazza Fiume 10,
☏ 0873 802121

What to see

Museo Archeologico/Archaeological Museum and Palazzo d'Avalos
(*Piazza Lucio Valerio Pudente;* ☏ *0873 367773;* ⊕ *Sep–Jun, Tue–Sun 09.30–12.30 &*
16.30–19.30; Jul–Aug, daily 10.30–12.00 & 18.00–24.00; admission €1.50) Vasto's
Archaeological Museum is housed in the historic Palazzo d'Avalos. The building
dates from the 14th century but was restored in 1427 and again after coastal raids
by the Turks in 1566. The museum occupies five rooms within the building and
contains archaeological finds from the area dating back to prehistoric and Roman
times. Artefacts include large collections of coins, statues and ceramics. It is possible
to view some of the Roman foundations of the original building that stood on the
site. Make sure you explore the charming garden, lined with Roman pillars.

Cattedrale San Giuseppe (⊕ daily) St Joseph's Cathedral is located across
from Palazzo d'Avalos on Piazza Pudente. The original church was founded in the
13th century and would have dominated the skyline for miles around. However, the
current church is a result of 19th-century rebuilding and preserves only the 14th-
century doorway from the original building. The interior is largely modern, though
it houses a 16th-century marble triptych and 19th-century statue of St Joseph.

Church of Santa Maria Maggiore (⊕ daily) The church of Santa Maria
Maggiore is one of the oldest churches in the city and its exact origin is obscure.
However, its current appearance is due to its reconstruction in a Baroque style
during the late 18th century. The interior houses some splendid stuccowork from
the mid 19th century.

Castello Caldora Construction began on this charming castle in 1430, using the
site of an existing structure that probably also had a defensive purpose. It was named
after Giacomo Caldora, a local feudal lord. It has been modified over the centuries
though some traces of the original structure remain, including the ramparts. The
castle is privately owned but it is worth having a walk around the outside.

Roman Vasto Nowhere in Vasto are its historical layers so evident as they are in
Piazza Gabriele Rossetti. The piazza owes its oval shape to being built on the site
of the ancient Roman **amphitheatre**. This was built sometime in the 1st and 2nd
centuries BC and traces, such as its brick foundations, can still be seen at various
places in the piazza, but are most evident as the foundations of the buildings that
now line the square.

Recent excavations have also uncovered a large complex of Roman **baths** on Via
Adriatica. The baths were built during the 2nd century AD and there is a splendid
mosaic of marine life that can be viewed at the site.

Appendix 1

LANGUAGE

PRONUNCIATION With a little practice, Italian is relatively easy to pronounce: as a cardinal rule, words are pronounced cleanly and how they are written. Unlike French or English, every letter (with the exception of silent 'h') is pronounced.

The alphabet The Italian alphabet, a variation on the Latin alphabet, is made up of 21 letters. It excludes the letters j, k, w, x, and y, although as they are considered 'foreign' letters, they are used in a variety of different circumstances for adopted words. They have, too, recently begun to creep into the likes of SMS messages and emails as a lazy substitute. For example, the hard 'ch' sound is often replaced by 'k': so *chi* (who) becomes *ki*. However, this is by no means an official alternative and many Italians frown upon its use.

a	as in **ah**
b	as in **b**ag
c	as in **c**at when preceding a, o, u and h
	as in **ch**eer when preceding e or i
d	as in **d**og, but without aspiration
e	two sounds: as the closed 'e' in p**e**t, or as an open sound as in 'air'
	For example: closed – *mela* (apple); open – *bello* (beautiful)
f	as in **f**un
g	as in **g**o when preceding a, o, u and h
	as in **g**eneral when preceding e or i
h	always silent
i	as in **i**t
l	as in **l**ie
m	as in **m**an
n	as in **n**o
o	two sounds: as the closed 'o' in r**o**se or as the open 'o' in l**o**t
	For example: closed – *con* (with); open – *otto* (eight)
p	as in **p**et
q	as in **q**uick
r	the Italian 'r' is rolled or trilled, with the tongue against the forward palate and gums of the upper teeth
s	before vowels and c, f, p, q, s, t as the 's' in **s**on, and then usually as the 's' in clo**s**ed
t	a hard sound, as in **t**ell but with no aspiration
u	as in r**u**le
v	as in **v**an
z	as in the 'ds' in la**ds** or the 'ts' in lo**ts**

gli	as in the 'lli' in mi**lli**on
gn	as in the 'ny' in ca**ny**on
sc	followed by 'e' or 'i' as the 'sh' in **sh**oot

Stress and accents
A word's natural stress usually falls on the penultimate syllable:

| *Roma* | Rome | *andare* | to go |

However, stress can also occur on the first syllable of a word:

| *pubblico* | public | *mandorla* | almond |

The presence of an accent at the end of a word means that the stress is placed on the last syllable:

| *Papà* | dad (whereas *Papa* means pope) | *caffè* | coffee |

WORDS AND PHRASES
Basics

yes	*sì*	Goodbye	*ciao; arrivederci* (formal)
no	*no*		
Good morning	*buongiorno*	Thank you	*grazie*
Good evening	*buonasera*	You're welcome	*prego*
Hello	*ciao*	Excuse me	*Mi scusi*

Meeting the locals

My name is …	*Mi chiamo …*	Pleased to meet you	*Piacere conoscerti* (informal)
What is your name?	*Come ti chiami?*		*conoscerla* (formal)
I am …	*Sono …*	I don't understand	*Non capisco*
from England	*dall'Inghilterra*	Do you speak English?	*Parla inglese?*
from Australia	*dall'Australia*		
from America	*dall'America*		
How are you?	*Come stai?*		

Useful questions

What does … mean?	*Che significa … ?*	Why?	*Perché?*
Where is …?	*Dov'è …?*	How much does it cost?	*Quanto costa?*
What?	*Cosa?*		
What is it?	*Che cos'è?*	Could you help me?	*Mi potrebbe aiutare?*

Transport/travel

I'd like …	*Vorrei …*	platform	*binario*
a one-way ticket	*un biglietto di solo andata*	plane	*aereo*
		boat	*barca*
a return ticket	*di andata e ritorno*	ferry	*traghetto*
I want to go …	*Voglio andare …*	car	*macchina*
What time does it leave?	*A che ora parte?*	motorbike/moped	*motocicletta/motorino*
		I'd like to hire …	*Vorrei noleggiare …*
The train …	*Il treno…*	a car	*una macchina*
has been delayed	*è in ritardo*	a bicycle	*una bicicletta*
has been cancelled	*è stato cancellato*	ticket office	*biglietteria*

from ... to ...	*da ... a ...*	toilets	*toilette*
railway station	*stazione*	here	*qui*
bus stop	*fermata dell'autobus*	there	*là/lì*
airport	*aeroporto*	bon voyage!	*buon viaggio!*
first class	*prima classe*	north	*nord*
second class	*seconda classe*	south	*sud*
Turn right / left	*Giri a destra/sinistra*	east	*est*
bus	*autobus*	west	*ovest*
train	*treno*		

Private transport

Is this the road to ...?	*È questa la strada per ...?*	Please fill it up	*Il pieno, per favore*
Where is the service station?	*Dov'è il benzinaio?*	diesel	*diesel*
		unleaded petrol	*senza piombo*

Hotel

Where is a good hotel?	*Dov'è un buon hotel?*	a room with bathroom	*una camera con bagno privato*
Do you have any rooms?	*Avete delle camere libere?*	Is breakfast included?	*La colazione è compresa?*
I'd like ...	*Vorrei ...*	key	*chiave*
a single room	*una camera singola*	shower	*doccia*
a double room	*una matrimoniale*	first floor	*primo piano*
a room with two beds	*una camera con due letti*	ground floor	*piano terra*

Eating

restaurant	*ristorante*	Do you accept credit card?	*Accettate carta di credito?*
Do you have a table for ... people?	*Ha un tavolo per ... persone?*	Could you please bring me ...	*Mi potrebbe portare ...*
I am a vegeterian	*Sono vegetariano*	a knife	*un coltello*
Could I see the menu?	*Posso vedere il menù?*	a fork /	*una forchetta*
The bill, please	*Il conto, per favore*	a spoon?	*un cucchiaio*

bread	*pane*	carrots	*carote*
butter	*burro*	garlic	*aglio*
cheese	*formaggio*	onion	*cipolla*
oil	*olio*	peppers	*peperoni*
pepper	*pepe*	potato/potato chips	*patata/ patatine*
salt	*sale*	tomato	*pomodoro*
sugar	*zucchero*	fish	*pesce*
ice cream	*gelato*	mussels	*cozze*
cake	*torta*	salmon	*salmone*
apple	*mela*	tuna	*tonno*
banana	*banana*	steak	*bistecca*
grapes	*l'uva*	chicken	*pollo*
mango	*mango*	pork	*porchetta*
orange	*arancia*	sausage	*salsiccia*
pear	*pera*	lamb	*agnello*

Drinking

Could you bring me a glass of …?	*Mi porta un bicchiere di …?*	bottle	*bottiglia*
still water/	*acqua liscia/*	tea	*thè*
mineral water	*acqua gassata*	milk	*latte*
wine	*vino*	red wine/	*vino rosso/*
beer	*birra*	white wine	*vino bianco*
fruit juice	*succo di frutta*		

Time

What time is it?	*Che ore sono?*	year	*anno*
It is …		today	*oggi*
1 o'clock	*È l'una*	tomorrow	*domani*
2 o'clock	*Sono le due*	yesterday	*ieri*
10 o'clock	*Sono le dieci*	morning	*mattina*
day	*giorno*	afternoon	*pomeriggio*
week	*settimana*	evening	*sera*
month	*mese*	night	*notte*

Days of the week

Monday	*lunedì*	Friday	*venerdì*
Tuesday	*martedì*	Saturday	*sabato*
Wednesday	*mercoledì*	Sunday	*domenica*
Thursday	*giovedì*		

Months

January	*gennaio*	July	*luglio*
February	*febbraio*	August	*agosto*
March	*marzo*	September	*settembre*
April	*aprile*	October	*ottobre*
May	*maggio*	November	*novembre*
June	*giugno*	December	*dicembre*

Numbers

0	*zero*	17	*diciassette*
1	*uno*	18	*diciotto*
2	*due*	19	*diciannove*
3	*tre*	20	*venti*
4	*quattro*	21	*ventuno*
5	*cinque*	30	*trenta*
6	*sei*	40	*quaranta*
7	*sette*	50	*cinquanta*
8	*otto*	60	*sessanta*
9	*nove*	70	*settanta*
10	*dieci*	80	*ottanta*
11	*undici*	90	*novanta*
12	*dodici*	100	*cento*
13	*tredici*	200	*duecento*
14	*quattordici*	1,000	*mille*
15	*quindici*	2,000	*duemila*
16	*sedici*		

Appendix 2

Andrew Burns

GLOSSARY OF FLORA AND FAUNA

FLORA
Flowers and shrubs

Alpine poppy *Papaver alpinum*
Apennine edelweiss *Leontopodium nivale*
Belladonna *Attropa belladonna*
Blue gentian *Gentiana dinarca*
Buttercup *Ranunculus magellensis*
Columbine *Aquilegia ottonis*
Common Turk's cap lily *Lilium martagon*
Cyclamen *Cyclamen repandum*
Dwarf gentian *Gentianella ramose*
Forget-me-not *Myosotis alpine*
Italian bell flower
  Campanula fragilis cavolinii
Knapweed/Fiordaliso delle spiagge
  Centaurea sphaerocephala
Marsican iris *Iris marsica*

Myrtle *Myrtus communis*
Peony *Paeonia officinalis*
Pheasant's eye *Adonis vernalis*
Primrose *Primula vulgaris*
Saxifrage
  Saxifraga marginata, Saxifraga porophylla
Scarpetta di venere *Cypripedium calceolus*
Squill *Scilla autumnalis*
Toothwort *Lathraea clandestine*
Violet *Viola eugeniae*
Woodruff *Galium odoratum*
Yellow gentian *Gentiana lutea*
Yellow-and-black orchid
  Cypripedium calceolus

Trees

Adriatic oak (also Italian or Hungarian oak)
  Quercus frainetto
Alder *Alnus glutinosa*
Aspen (also Trembling poplar)
  Populus tremula
Beech *Fagus sylvatica*
Black hornbeam *Carpinus betulus*
Black pine *Pinus nigra italica*
Black poplar *Populus nigra*
Chestnut *Castanea sativa*
European rowan *Sorbus aucuparia*
Flowering ash *Fraximus ornus*
Hazel *Corylus avellana*
Holly *Ilex aquifolium*

Holly oak *Quercus ilex*
Hornbeam *Carpinus betulus*
Laburnum *Laburnum anagyroides*
Maple *Acer capestre*
Pubescent oak *Quercus pubescens*
Sabine or Prickly juniper
  Juniperus oxycedrus
Swiss mountain pine *Pinus mugo*
Sycamore *Acer pseudoplantanus*
White willow *Salix alba*
Wild apple (also Crab apple) *Malus sylvestris*
Wild cherry *Prunus avium*
Wild pear *Pyrus communis*
Yew *Taxus baccata*

Naturalised trees

Olive *Olea europaea*
Stone pine *Pinus pinea*

Italian pencil pine
  Cupressus sempervirens

FAUNA
Mammals

Apennine chamois
  Rupicapra rupicapra ornata
Apennine wolf *Canis lupus italicus*
Beech marten *Martes foina*
Central European red deer
  Cervus elaphus hippelaphus
Common dormouse
  Muscardinus avellanarius
Common weasel *Mustela nivalis*
Daubenton's bat *Myotis daubentonii*
Eurasian red squirrel *Hysterix cristata*
European badger *Meles meles*
European polecat *Mustela putorius*
European snow vole *Chionomys nivalis*
Fat dormouse *Myoxus glis*

Greater noctule bat *Nyctalus lasiopterus*
Hedgehog *Erinacius europaeus*
Italian red fox *Vulpes vulpes toschii*
Kuhl's pipistrelle *Pipistrellus kuhlii*
Long-fingered bat *Myotis capaccinii*
Lynx *Lynx lynx*
Marsican bear *Ursus arctos marsicanus*
Otter *Lutra lutra*
Pine marten *Martes martes*
Pipistrella bat *Pipistrellus pygmaeus*
Pipistrelle bat *Pipistrellus pipistrellus*
Roe deer *Capreolus capreolus*
Wild boar *Sus scrofa*
Wild cat *Felis silvestris*

Birds

Alpine chough *Pyrrhocorax graculus*
Apennine golden eagle
  Aquila chrysaetos chrysaetos
Common buzzard *Buteo buteo*
Common kestrel *Falco tinnunculus*
Eurasian jay *Garrulus glandarius*
Eurasian kingfisher (also Common
  kingfisher) *Alcedo atthis*
Eurasian sparrowhawk *Accipiter nisus*
Eurasian tawny owl *Tyto alba*
Goshawk *Accipiter gentiles*
Great tit *Parus major*
Green woodpecker *Picus viridis*
Grey heron *Ardea cinerea*

Grey wagtail *Motacilla cinerea*
Hoopoe *Upupa epops*
Little owl *Athena noctua*
Mallard *Anas platyrhinchos*
Northern wheatear *Oenanthe oenanthe*
Peregrine falcon *Falco peregrinus*
Raven *Corvax corvax*
Red-billed chough *Pyrrhocorax pyrrhocorax*
Rock partridge *Alectoris graeca*
White-backed woodpecker
  Dendrocopos leucotos lilfordii
White-winged snow finch
  Montifringilla nivalis
Whiteback woodpecker *Picoides leocotus*

Reptiles

Asp viper *Vipera aspis*
Common European lizard *Lacerta muralis*
Dark green snake *Coluber viridiflavus*
European green lizard *Lacerta viridis*

Grass snake *Natrix natrix*
Orsini's viper *Vipera ursine*
Slow worm *Anguis fragilis*
Smooth snake *Coronella austriaca*

Amphibians

Common toad *Bufo bufo spinosus*
Great crested newt
  Triturus cristatus carnifex
Italian fire salamander
  Salamandra salamandra giglioli

Smooth/common newt
  Triturus vulgaris meridionalis
Spectacled salamander
  Salamandrina terdigitata
Yellow-bellied toad
  Bombina variegata pachypus

Insects

Apollo butterfly *Parnassus apollo*

Longicorn *Rosalia alpine*

Appendix 3

FURTHER INFORMATION

BOOKS While there certainly entire volumes dedicated to Abruzzo, there are mentions in most books that cover the country of Italy, and countless 'promotional' books such as those published by Touring Club Italiano and listed below – although most are only in Italian.

History and literature
Duggan, C *A Concise History of Italy* Cambridge University Press, 1994
Latini, M (ed) *Along the Shepherds' Tracks* Carsa Edizioni, Pescara, 2000
Silone, Ignazio *The Abruzzo Trilogy: Fontamara, Bread & Wine, The Seed Beneath the Snow*, Zoland Books, New Hampshire, USA, 2000

Travel guides
Eremi d'Abruzzo Carsa Edizioni, Pescara, 2000
Guida al Parco Nazionale della Majella Carsa Edizioni, Pescara, 1997
Holidays in Abruzzo Touring Club Italiano, Milan, 2003
Il Parco Nazionale della Majella: Guida ai 38 Paesi Multimedia Edizioni, Pescara, 1997

WEBSITES Listed below is a selection of useful websites to help you research and plan your trip. Those in English as well as Italian are indicated with an asterisk (*).

Transport Italian railway timetables can be found at www.ferroviedellostato.it (*). Bus information is available on the ARPA website (*www.arpaonline.it*), with timetables at http://ro.autobus.it/ro/asp/RicercaOrari.asp?User=arpa. The website for Pescara airport is www.abruzzoairport.it (*).

Background research and planning An excellent general history of Italy can be found at www.lifeinitaly.com/history (*), while www.abruzzoweb.it, www.abruzzoheritage. com, www.initaly.com/regions/abruzzo/abruzzo.htm and www.abruzzo.it (all *) have valuable information for planning your trip.

National and regional parks Many of Abruzzo's major parks have their own website with information in English, including the National Park of Abruzzo (*www.parcoabruzzo. it*), Majella National Park (*www.parcomajella.it*), Gran Sasso National Park (*www. gransassolagapark.it*) and Sirente Velino Regional Park (*www.parcosirentevelino.it*).

News Visit www.tg1.rai.it for national news. Regional news can be accessed at www.tgr. rai.it and www.lacronaca.org, with weather reports at www.meteo.it.

Index